D0203952

Discontents

Paul Hollander

Discontents

Postmodern & Postcommunist

Transaction Publishers
New Brunswick (U.S.A.) and London (U.K.)

Library of Congress Catalog Number: 2001054206
ISBN: 0-7658-0090-X
Printed in the United States of America

Library of Congress Cataloging-in-Publication Data

Hollander, Paul, 1932-
    Discontents : postmodern and postcommunist / Paul Hollander.
        p. cm.
    Includes bibliographical references and index.
    ISBN: 0-7658-0090-X (alk. paper).
        1. Postmodernism—Social aspects. 2. Post-communism. 3. United
    States—Social conditions—1980- I. Title.

HM449 .H65 2001
306—dc21   2001054206

Contents

Part 2: Soviet Communism: Its Fall and Aftermath

Acknowledgements

As on numerous other occasions I would like to thank the Earhart Foundation for its longstanding support of my work. Ieva Zake provided hihgly efficient help in the preparation of the index.

"American Sociology and the Collapse of Communism" first appeared in *Society*, November-December 1992. Reprinted by permission.

"'Imagined Tyranny'? Political Correctness Reconsidered" first appeared in *Academic Questions*, Fall 1994. Reprinted by permission.

"The Attack on Science and Reason," first appeared in *Orbis*, Fall 1994. Copyright © Foreign Policy Research Institute.

"Good Intentions and Unintended Consequences: A Critique of 'Affirmative Action'" first appeared in *Current World Leaders*, April 1996. Current World Leaders is a publication of the International Academy at Santa Barbara. Address inquiries to *info@iasb.org*.

"Reassessing the Adversary Culture" first appeared in *Academic Questions*, April 1996. Reprinted by permission.

"The Durable Significance of the Political Pilgrimages" first appeared in *Society*, July-August 1997. Reprinted by permission.

"Non-Conformist Intellectuals Today" (with Michael Fraser) first appeared in *Academic Questions*, Winter 1997-98. Reprinted by permission.

"Saving Sociology?" first appeared in *Sociological Inquiry* 69:1, pp. 130-147. Copyright © 1999 by the University of Texas Press. All rights reserved.

"Marxism and Western Intellectuals in the Postcommunist Era" first appeared in *Society*, January-February 2000. Reprinted by permission.

"Intellectuals and the War in Kosovo," first appeared in *Partisan Review*, Vol. LXVII, No. 1, 2000 under the title "Thinking about Kosovo in Northampton, Massachusetts and Budapest, Hungary. Reprinted by permission.

"The Mystery of the Transformation of Communist Systems" first appeared in L. Kriesberg and D. Segal, eds., *The Transformation of European Communist Societies*, 1992, with permission from Elsevier Science.

Introduction

This volume continues to wrestle with matters I have been writing about throughout my professional life that began in the early 1960s. It is for the reader to decide if such continuities should be a cause for concern or satisfaction. Concern is warranted when it seems that an author is incapable of liberating himself from confining and possibly dated preoccupations, satisfaction if there is reason to believe that he had chosen to follow some of the important issues of his times which deserve continued attention.

"Intellectuals" have been another recurring topic of my writings; their existence and beliefs are also intimately connected to both modernity (and especially its discontents) and communism. It is they who articulate, analyze, sometimes exaggerate the discontents here referred to. As to their relationship to communist ideals and systems we find among them admirers and critics alike. As a rule the admirers lived outside communist states and the critics within. Often the supporters turned into critics.

These essays, presented in chronological order, can be conveniently grouped around the concepts of postmodernity and communism even if both have somewhat disputed meanings and the latter is more a matter of the past than the present. Much remains to be learned about communist systems, even if few of them survive and their supporting ideology has also been eroded and discredited—though to what extent and how widely remains a matter of debate as some of the writings below also indicate. On the other hand postmodernity, modernity, and especially their discontents can hardly be relegated to the past.

It may be argued that the concept of the "postmodern" has become, in its broader use, a substitute for "modern" although of course the opposite claim has also been made. In the latter view "modern" stands for a unified and universalistic set of values, beliefs and ways of thinking originating in the Enlightenment whereas postmodern is a reaction against such "totalizing" or "essentialist" worldviews and asserts diversity, "deconstruction of all foundations...[and] communicative incommensurability."[1]

As I see it, for the most part, "postmodern" is associated with the more extreme aspects or developments of what used to be called "modern," with a special, new emphasis on localism, particularism, and relativism (moral, political, historical, and aesthetic). For the postmodernist "truth" and perceptions of reality are completely "contextual and "situational." Although the French Enlightenment also opposed and attacked tradition, postmodernists regard the Enlightenment and its values themselves as a tradition, and a particularly pernicious and oppressive one. In the postmodernist view "traditional class politics and faith in progress are being replaced by 'identity politics' and 'new' social movements such as feminism, gay liberation, ecologism, ethnic revivalism, religious neofundamamentalism."[2] Postmodernists attribute an exceptional (and unrealistic) influence to words and language as sources of power and oppression.

Postmodernism is also associated with a wide range of anti-Western positions and especially the rejection of Western rationality, science, belief in reason, and other Enlightenment values. Arnold Toynbee who introduced the concept over a half century ago linked it to "obscure demonic forces, which, if completely unleashed, could overthrow the very structures of Modern Western civilization... suggest[ing] irrationality, anarchy, and threatening indeterminacy..."[3] More recently Daniel Bell associated postmodernism with the far more widely used concept of the counterculture (of the 1960s), a culmination of the modernist "rage against social order," a celebration of the instinctual, impulsive and irrational, a far-reaching attack on middle-class values.[4] Two scientists (in a volume discussed on pp 54-56) write that "postmodernism... embedded and elaborated in the scholarly work of the academic left... is grounded in the assumption that the ideological system sustaining the cultural and material practices of Western European civilization is bankrupt..."[5] (More will be said of postmodernism below.)

The essays in part 1, taken together, illuminate the connections between the discontents the title makes reference to and postmodernity (or modernity). These discontents and the critiques of American society are intertwined. There has also been a longstanding link between the discontents and the misjudgments of communist systems of special interest to me. The idealization of communist systems (which was at the core of the misjudgments) was stimulated by dissatisfaction with Western societies that prompted the search for alternatives.

The dissatisfaction was stimulated not merely by the specific and evident ills of capitalism but by the problems of modernity capitalism brought about, the more elusive frustrations associated with the pursuit of meaning, purpose, and community that modern, free, and pluralistic societies do not readily provide. A discussion of these problems and discontents need not imply an idealization of traditional societies. I certainly do not share "the belief that primitive societies are more harmonious than modern ones, that 'savages' were 'noble,' that life in the past was more idyllic than life today, and that human beings once had a sense of community that had been lost"—a belief "not only reflected in the motion pictures and novels of our popular culture but... deeply engrained in scholarly discourse as well"—wrote Robert Edgerton, the rare anthropologist critical of such views.[6]

My reservations about the familiar critiques of modernity are not based on the belief that contemporary Western societies are flawless, or that the psychological problems of modernity are imaginary. Rather I believe that it remains a destructive illusion that the communist party-states or any version of Marxism-Leninism had or has a solution to these problems.

II

"Postmodern discontents" cover a wide variety of aversions, frustrations, unease and states of mind, including what used to be called alienation before its overuse has come to discourage reference to it. Concerns with "the quality of life" also fall under this heading. According to a survey conducted by the Pew Research Center in the summer of 1999 "misgivings about America today are focused on the moral climate, with people from all walks of life looking sceptically on the ways in which the country has changed both culturally and spiritually."[7] Or as Gertrude Himmelfarb observed, "In poll after poll, even at the height of economic prosperity, a great majority of the American people (as many as two-thirds to three quarters) identify 'moral decay' or 'moral decline' as one of the major problems, often *the* major problem, confronting the country."[8]

The stark question raised by a character in a recent Saul Bellow novel goes to the heart of these concerns: "With what, in this modern democracy, will you meet the demands of your soul?" When Bellow talks about "the human costs of modernity"[9] he refers exactly to the kinds of discontents I have in mind.

What ails people at the present time in Western and especially American society is an inexhaustible subject, all the more since some of these ailments are not entirely novel, but rather more widespread. An extended discussion of these discontents in the United States in last decade of the twentieth century might lead to an obvious question, even objection. How much and what kind of discontent is there to discuss in a society that has experienced over a decade of economic growth, close to full employment, hardly any inflation, falling crime rates, declining teenage pregnancies and other good things? Is there anything to worry about in a country that has become the undisputed superpower of the world and no longer faces another hostile superpower such as the Soviet Union used to be? As one writer saw it, during the last decade of the century "the United States has enjoyed unprecedented economic growth, unrivaled military power and the near-universal vindication of its national creed."[10] The editor of *Foreign Affairs* believed that "The Cold War is won and America dominates the world. From Beijing to Buenos Aires, governments are privatizing state owned companies and dismantling regulations..." Conservatives had much "to cheer about" although they failed to do so.[11]

But unchallenged superpower status is also an invitation to envy, resentment, and hostility as the recent growth of anti-Americanism in many parts of the world indicate. In France a spate of new books reflect "a growing backlash of anti-Americanism... deploring...a society ruled by profit motive" and perceiving the United States as a "dangerous force intent on remaking the world in its own image.... The anti-Americanism today encompasses not a specific policy...but a feeling that globalization has an American face on it..."[12]

The domestic improvements noted above do not necessarily create widespread contentment. Human beings are ingenious enough to be dissatisfied under a wide variety of conditions (as the term "relative deprivation" suggests); economic-material wellbeing is not a guarantor of contentment or serenity. This in fact is the burden of Robert Lane's recent study that examines how rising incomes and standards of living have been paralleled by the decline of happiness and growing depression in the United States and other Western countries.[13] Saul Bellow, without survey data to back him up, explains, "this is cornucopia time, an era of abundance in all civilised nations. Never... have huge populations been better protected from hunger and sickness. And this partial release from the struggle for survival makes people naive. By this I mean that their wishful fantasies are unchecked."[14] Paul Berman was more sympathetic about these fantasies: "I believe that it is possible for modern men and women ... to 'be themselves' to come together, first to fight against the forms of class, sexual and racial oppression that force everyone's identity into rigid molds and keep one's self from unfolding..."[15] He doesn't explain what it means "to be themselves" and what the unfolding self would be like. The unique individuality of every human being Berman entertains was among the taken for granted beliefs of the generation of the 1960s to which he belongs.

The discontents here discussed have many shadings and dimensions ranging from vague, unfocused unease, sense of emptiness to specific social criticism and bitter rage directed at various aspects of the social environment. Once more Saul Bellow put his finger on these matters: "Rage is now brilliantly prestigious.... The rage of rappers and rioters takes as its premise the majority's admission of guilt for past and present injustices, and counts on the admiration of the repressed for the emotional power of the uninhibited and 'justly' angry."[16]

Rage has also been central to feminist sensibilities: "nurturing their anger or practicing it like the piano... anger was absolutely a measure of one's feminist commitment... a sign of one's authenticity, one's radical credentials.... Some feminist writers even speak of 'tending' their anger, of periodically stoking the flames to use it as an energy source for political action."[17]

Politicized rage was very much on display at the Seattle demonstration in November 1999 against the World Trade Organization that has become the symbol of global capitalism or, as lately preferred, "corporate power." In defending the breaking of windows and other property damage (expressions of just rage) and recapitulating perhaps unintentionally the rhetoric of the 1960s, a representative of the current left wrote:

> This system would prefer that people respond to exploitation with complacency and politeness. But what becomes of people who work full time for less than a living wage, without health care, without day care? [it did not seem that many such people attended

the Seattle demonstration, rather, as in the 60s it was students and former students who were the most active and angry—P.H.] What emotion builds up after years of work in dead-end jobs? What happens after you find out you live near a toxic-waste dump?... Rage is a natural and required response...

As the old sixties rhetoric had it, the window smashings in Seattle (like the "trashings" of the sixties) had to be judged against "the larger context of systemic state violence." We were further reminded that "Private property, especially corporate private property, is in itself infinitely more violent than any action taken against it."[18]

It is hard to know how many people share such sentiments at this point in time. Probably only a small minority. But in time of a crisis (political or economic) these angry people could become more prominent political actors and have an impact. Ralph Nader is among the increasingly embittered critics of American society, capitalism and global corporations, leading what an observer called "a destructive crusade"[19] more interested in broad, apocalyptic indictments than in helping consumers in practical matters.

Further light is shed on the discontent here examined by the social scientists Stanley Rothman and Robert Lichter:

> The evidence around us in the culture suggests that many of those in the middle and upper-middle classes have lost the internal gyroscope and external metaphors that gave the lives of previous generations structure and meaning.... They lurch between longings for complete autonomy and the wish to lose themselves in something that will give their lives order—hence the proliferation of cults...[20]

Observations by other thoughtful observers of contemporary American society further help to grasp the nature of these discontents and their connection with freedom and choice. Peter L. Berger wrote, "The clash between the built-in uncertainty of the pluralistic situation and the urge for at least a measure of certainty helps to explain a rather curious phenomenon in contemporary culture—the alternation of relativism and absolutist claims to truth."[21]

Robert Wright addressed the issue from the perspective of evolutionary psychology:

> There is a little bit of the Unabomber in most of us. We may not share his approach to airing a grievance but the grievance itself feels familiar... the serial bomber complains that the modern world, for all its technological marvels, can be an uncomfortable, 'unfulfilling' place to live... there are times when something seems deeply amiss. Whether burdened by an overwhelming flurry of daily commitments or stifled by a sense of social isolation (or, oddly, both); whether mired... in a sense of pointlessness or beset...by unresolved anxiety... whatever the source of stress, we at times get the feeling that modern life isnt what we were designed for.[22]

Wright also noted that "rates of depression have been doubling in some industrial societies roughly every ten years....Suicide is the third most common cause of death among young adults in North America...15 percent of Americans have had a clinical anxiety disorder..." He pointed to social isolation as a preeminent factor in present-day social pathologies and contrasted its prevalence to conditions in hunting-gathering societies which provided intimacy, stability, and "close contact with the same array of several dozen friends and relatives for decades." Whereas in modern society our "affiliative impulses are frustrated... we are designed to seek trusting relationships and to feel frustrated in their absence."[23]

III

Some of the persisting problems of American society have little to do with postmodernity or modernity, although they lend themselves as ammunition to the more comprehensive rejection of society. Foremost among them are race relations and the monumental efforts designed to make amends for the sins of the past. Thomas Sowell summed up the moral and social-political dilemma inherent in these policies as "new injustices among our flesh-and-blood contemporaries for the sake of symbolic expiation, so that the son or daughter of a black doctor or executive can get into an elite college ahead of the son or daughter of a white factory worker or farmer."[24] Notwithstanding such objections preferential treatment is solidly institutionalized although even the majority of faculty members in colleges and universities disapprove of it (both in regard to student admission and faculty employment) as was made clear in a national survey carried out by the Roper Center for Public Opinion Research in 1996.[25]

"Racism" has remained over the last decades a cornerstone of the broader critiques of American society and culture. The recurring, ritualistic charge of racism (as an ineradicable part of American character, history, culture, and society) has become the safest, most conventional, and effortless affirmation of moral virtue—standard topic for sermons, commencement addresses, freshmen orientation programs, assorted academic lectures, presidential disquisitions, innumerable books, newspaper articles, movies, plays and television programs. White guilt and racism is at the center of a new play (acclaimed in two articles in the *New York Times*) the heroine of which (appropriately enough a dean of students) "confesses her own racism in a 20 minute speech... something that few white people would admit to themselves: she is a racist who hates black people."[26]

As a journalist wrote, "a charge of racism, no matter how kneejerk and baseless, will get you into hot water more readily than threatening someone with possible bodily harm."[27] The attitudes and practices associated with racism long ceased to require proof or specification. Numerous social critics (especially whites among them) use it primarily as a stick with which to beat a social system they detest on other, less obvious grounds. Charges of sexual harassment acquired a similar momentum and if the moral opprobrium attached is milder, serious career or workplace consequences can still follow. Daphne Patai, author of a volume examining the "sexual harassment industry," observed, "The power of the charge of sexual harassment is... enormous. It can unleash formidable institutional forces against the alleged harasser, often with a complete absence of due process."[28]

Preoccupation with race and racism is further stimulated by the fact that it is hard to find any major social problem (crime, drug addiction, family disintegration, homelessness, unemployment, AIDS, etc.) that does not have a racial component. It remains conventional wisdom that each of these problems is a product of discrimination, of racism. But, as a critic of Julius Wilson's *When Work Disappears* pointed out "their [black people's] problems were neither entirely caused by the loss of work, nor will they be entirely solved by government action." Moreover

> there is strong evidence that the pathologies began to fester well before the 1970s. Moynihan... raised the flag about the disintegration of the black family in 1965, when most of the jobs... had not yet fled...
>
> In New York, robbery rates remained fairly stable through much of the twentieth century—including the Great Depression, a period of intense joblessness and despair that did not cause any normative changes among blacks or whites. But robbery quintupled from 1962 to 1967... and then doubled again from 1967 to 1972... those were flush, jobful times.[29]

Certain freely expressed beliefs among black Americans are indicative of other problems. Thus "a 1990 New York Times-CBS poll found 10 percent of a sample of black New Yorkers agreeing that the AIDS virus was 'deliberately created in a laboratory to infect black people with an additional 19 percent agreeing that this might be true. Further, as many as 60 percent believed it was true or possibly true that the government was funneling drugs to black communities in a calculated effort to cause harm."[30] In other surveys 35 percent of the black respondents believed that "AIDS was a form of black genocide," 68 percent that "the FBI had been involved in the killing of Martin Luther King." Also widespread were the beliefs that "AIDS was developed by whites to murder blacks," that black patients in hospitals "run a substantial chance of being experimented upon unless they have a black doctor" and others even more bizarre.[31]

It is debatable to what degree, or in what combination such beliefs result from the actual experience of racial discrimination, from an attempt to shift blame to the wider social-political environment for personal failings and problems, or from an exaggerated receptivity to and over-interpretation of cultural messages which encourage and reward a victim mentality among the black population.

Feminism and especially its radical varieties also articulate some of the discontents of postmodernity in its steady and biting critiques of American culture and society. "Patriarchal society" (mistakenly used to describe modern American society) has come to stand for frustrations and discontents which reflect broader and deeper demands of radical individualism, of the endless quest for self-fulfillment, far beyond the freedom from discrimination.

The radical-feminist critiques of American society are perhaps the most sweeping and the richest in anti-intellectual implications; they call into question the most fundamental assumptions and beliefs associated with Western political-social ideals as well as rationality, science, and even the arts. (According to a feminist author Susan McClary "Beethoven's Ninth Symphony unleashes one of the most horrifyingly violent episodes in the history of music... [it] is probably our most compelling articulation in music of the contradictory impulses that have organized patriarchal culture since the Enlightenment."[32])

Of all the critics of American culture and society the radical feminists are the most militantly committed to change language itself, for both symbolic and tactical reasons.

Daphne Patai paraphrased this worldview:

> Our culture...is so infused with patriarchal thinking that it must be torn up root and branch if genuine change is to occur. Everything must go—even the allegedly universal disciplines of logic, mathematics and science, and the intellectual values of objectivity, clarity and precision on which the former depend...

> ... Feminism... bids to be a totalizing scheme resting on a grand theory, one that is all-inclusive as Marxism, as assured of its ability to unmask hidden meanings as Freudian psychology and as fervent in its condemnation of apostates as evangelical fundamentalism. Feminist theory provides a doctrine of original sin: The world's evils originate in male supremacy... it offers a prescription for radical change that is as simple as it is drastic: Reject whatever is tainted with patriarchy and replace it with something embodying gynocentric values.[33]

Although feminism is often associated with "progress" (modernity), there is an aspect of feminism that is reminiscent of old-time puritanism: the fervent warnings against the dangers of heterosexuality.[34] The latter is a more recent development; in its earlier phases feminism championed free sexual expression, including the heterosexual. It is likely that the growing emphasis on victimhood and victimization (rather than liberation) led to feminist puritanism and its demands for censorship of various kinds, to the minute regulation of male-female relationships at work and school and a view of women as always on the verge of victimization, in need of vigilant protection from "sexual harassment" very broadly defined. Like the black demands for non-discrimination mutating into preferential treatment, the feminist agenda for non-discrimination had its own unanticipated results:

> How did we get from clear examples of sexual discrimination in school and workplace to a preoccupation with 'comfort' levels, dirty jokes and passing innuendoes? How did sexual discrimination... and just plain sex get entangled to such an extent that today a bit of overheard banter or a clumsy sexual overture in the office or school is considered as unacceptable and potentially as actionable as... relentless sexual aggression...?

It is likely, as Patai further notes that ."... it is the nature of feminism, as of all other social movements, to propose ever more expansive definitions of the problems over which it seeks to arouse public outrage."[35] Feminists and militant black groups committed to maximising their respective grievances also share the disposition to attribute false consciousness to those members of the putatively victmised group who would not share *their* notions of victimization.

The critiques emanating from the homosexual and lesbian community are also among those based less on material deprivation and social-political discrimination (at least as far as the last quarter century is concerned) than on the more elusive problems of identity and self-realization.

IV

No discussion of the discontents, conflicts, and controversies of American life at the end of the twentieth century society can be complete without reference to four interrelated phenomena: "political correctness," "postmodernism," "identity politics," and "multiculturalism." Each has its roots in the late 1960s and early 1970s and taken together they vindicate the observation that "the once-radical idea of America as a sick society and American government as a corrupt oppressor is now a banality, the informing truism of Hollywood tripe and doctoral theses alike."[36]

These phenomena had a major impact on the cultural climate and especially higher education and the outlook of the cultural elites although they are in various ways contradictory. Thus, on the one hand, political correctness is a widely imposed worldview, is far from relativistic and tolerant. At the same time it is among the politically correct therapeutic imperatives of our times that we must refrain from being "judgmental," let alone "elitist." In turn, multiculturalism praises and celebrates "diversity" and postulates that one culture (worldview, outlook, belief, etc.) is as good as any other (thus it is seemingly relativistic and postmodern)—at the same time it routinely belittles or ridicules Western culture and values. (Feminists dismiss Western culture as the product of "dead white males.)

It would take an unusually daring academic to declare, as the anthropologist George Peter Murdock did in 1965 that "the assertion that all cultures must be accorded equal dignity and respect was 'not only nonsense but sentimental nonsense'...it was an 'absurdity' to assert that cannibalism, slavery, magical therapy and killing the aged should be accorded the same 'dignity'.... as old-age security, scientific medicine and metal artifacts."[37]

The preoccupation with racial and ethnic identity that is the actual essence of multiculturalism has done little to improve race relations. As Elisabeth Lasch-Quinn has written, "The ideal of 'diversity' doesn't merely 'value' differences; it also makes them ineluctable and unbridgeable and final. Such thinking promulgates false new generalizations about people, and an atmosphere of perpetual insults and wounds, rather than a general climate of civility based on equal status..."[38]

The postmodernists deny that there are valid criteria for assessing quality in the arts and question the possibility of telling the difference between high and low culture, but they too shed relativism when it comes to judging Western culture.

Even museums reflect these trends:

> Since the early 1980s art museums have been undergoing an active period of revision, rearranging everything... as part of an attempt to become more egalitarian institutions.... Premised on the notion that our response to art is determined by our race, class and sex, the revisionist museum assumes that we go to it seeking to affirm and to promote the interests of our group identity. Visiting the museum is not an intellectual act but a political one.... To say one painting is better than another, one period of artmaking more successful than another, or one civilization more aesthetically advanced than another has become an act of prejudice... even "classification has come to be seen as an act of domination."[39]

Partisans of identity politics (like those of political correctness) make no pretense of relativism since members of the identity groups derive their sense of identity from pride in group membership (as slogans such as "gay pride," and "black is beautiful" also testify). It is the supposedly unique attributes of their group that is both the source of this pride and of the corresponding contempt for the culture and institutions of the dead (or living) white males of Western ancestry.

Richard Posner suggested a connection between identity politics and postmodernism: "The postmodernist left provides an intellectual framework for 'identity politics.' Having demolished to its satisfaction universal values and criteria, it has cleared the way for the claim that the most important thing about a person is his or her race, ethnicity, sex, sexual orientation and degree of physical or mental disability..."[40] More succinctly Jay Demerath observed that "postmodernism runs interference for political correctness..."[41]

There is also a tension between the postmodernist, multiculturalist vs. identity driven, politically correct intellectual-cultural orientation: "On the one hand it is maintained that one text is as much of a text as another text, but at the same time there is a general claim that some texts are more politically valuable than others."[42] The same goes for political allegiances and beliefs. If there is no solid moral-ethical basis for any particular political position or belief why should Richard Rorty (among others) proclaim his adherence to some sort of old-new leftism?[43] If there is no rational or objective basis for distinguishing one political position or philosophy from another, how to explain the unproblematic attachment to these beliefs which allows him to refer, casually and unhesitatingly to the "ghastly reality of contemporary America"?[44] The answer may be found in his "characteristic inability or unwillingness... to actually engage the issues to which he refers. To engage them would constrain him to adopt a much more tortured and conflicted sense of liberal utopia and the American nation than he wants to project." Further commenting on Rorty's views John Michael (by no means a conservative critic) wrote "This... sounds all very well in theory but what does it mean in practice?"[45]—a question that sums up many currently fashionable intellectual endeavors.

The trends here outlined have been eroding academic-intellectual standards and free expression not only on the campuses but also in the workplace and the mass media. Saul Bellow (once more) rightly summed up the prevailing ethos: "We can't open our mouths without being denounced as racists, misogynists, supremacists, imperialists or fascists."[46]

Higher (as well as lower) education has been the major loser. As one unusually outspoken observer wrote

> Outside the technical fields—the hard sciences, engineering and perhaps few other daunting disciplines—much of what transpires in today's university can be likened to Soviet consumer production at its most bizarre: huge resources are allocated to achieve a most paltry, shoddy result and, when the payoffs deteriorate further, even larger sums are committed and outcomes falsified. Virtually anyone who taught at the college level for twenty-five years or more will confirm that the dumbing down of higher education is not a catchy media invented phrase.

Robert Weissberg who made these observations (himself an academic) also notes that colleges have been transformed to a considerable degree into remedial institutions and standards have been further depressed by the introduction of "ideologically tinged, flattering self-study fields—Black Studies. The African American Experience, Inner City Studies... and many non-remedial classes are *de facto* remedial..." Last but not least there is also the problem of the "social opportunity costs of replacing decent (usually white and Asian) with less competent students."[47] Of late "disability studies" (in the humanities) too made an appearance offering both undergraduate and graduate programs. While of great potential interest it is likely that this too will be a field of "self-study," focused on self-esteem raising for the group concerned.[48]

Even "critical medical theory" has made an appearance incorporating the doctrine that "sickness is a product of power arrangements in society" and the belief that AIDS is "a biological expression of social inequity." One of its representatives proposed "that the goal of public health professionals should be to overthrow the 'competitive meritocracy.'"[49]

By the end of the last century, huge resources had been devoted (on the campuses, in the mass media and certain federal bureaucracies) to denying every one of these observations. Above all preferential treatment has created "a culture of deception." Curtis Crawford wrote: "The pretense that no substantial discrimination by race or sacrifice of quality occurs under affirmative action has spawned decades of evasion, equivocation and duplicity..."[50]

V

I chose a few disparate but revealing domestic events or developments of the last decade of the twentieth century to illustrate the broader trends and problems sketched above. They are the O. J. Simpson trial, President Clinton's affair with the White House intern, the cancellation of the performance of the musical, *West Side Story* in the Amherst, Massachusetts high school, the academic-intellectuals' responses to the exposé of the falsehoods of Rigoberta Manchu, and finally the popularity of Sports Utility Vehicles.

The Simpson and Monica Lewinsky case had several things in common. Both were an obsessive preoccupation of the media and the public for a considerable length of time and reflected the cultural centrality of celebrity status, both shed light on highly patterned social-cultural responses to the violation of major societal values. Both provided new evidence of the moral-cultural relativism: the Clinton affair by the public unconcern with the private morality of the president as reflected in the persistence of his high popularity ratings. It was maintained that "everyone lies about sex" and that 'results' matter more than political character, that determined deceit is outweighed by an accumulation of prosperity." [51] The moral relativism also found expression in the double standards of prominent feminists who excused the president's conduct— precisely the kind they abhorred when engaged in by others—on the grounds of his pro-feminist policies.

The moral relativism in the Simpson case was displayed primarily by the black population and some white radicals. From their point of view it did not matter very much whether or not Simpson was guilty of what he was accused of (murder)—what mattered that as a black man he was a victim of racism. The (largely black) jury too was far less interested in the question of guilt or innocence than in the racism of the Los Angeles Police Department and that of the larger society. These attitudes demonstrated continuity with the axiom that one should never "blame the victim"—the left-liberal conventional wisdom that black Americans are by definition victims, that victimhood is their essential, defining characteristic transcending the specificity of their day to day behavior and particular actions.

A defining moment in the history of political correctness came in the fall of 1999 when the Amherst, Massachusetts high school authorities decided to cancel the scheduled performance of *West Side Story* on the ground that it would offend ethnic minorities (Puerto Ricans primarily) by perpetuating racial stereotypes.[52] While this was a local event, its importance is magnified by the fact that it took place in an academic community where local politics is dominated by highly educated residents. Doubtless the "Peoples Republic of Amherst" (as it is sometimes called) is hardly typical of small towns in America but it is of communities dominated by liberal academics, chronic sufferers of white guilt, and upholders of political correctness in the fullest meaning.

In the prolonged controversy over the banning, I do not recall anybody spelling out precisely what the offensive stereotypes consisted of, or why they offended. It was sufficient to introduce the incantations "racial stereotyping," "racism," and "insensitivity" and the Amherst School authorities caved in (to the small number of students who protested the musical) terrified as they were of being accomplices to an offense no one cares to define anymore.

To evaluate this demonstration of political correctness it may be useful to remind ourselves what racial or any other stereotyping means and how it may apply to *West Side Story*. Stereotyping is generally understood as the groundless attribution of unfavorable characteristics to members of some group, or the distortion and exaggeration of some characteristics they might possess. The assertion that all white people are inherently racist, or all men sexist are such widely used stereotypes.

Much of the current (selective) concern with stereotyping is associated with the preoccupation with self esteem and group identity. On closer inspection it turns out that the same people or groups who are on the warpath against stereotyping are actively engaged in the uninhibited stereotyping of groups *they* dislike—white males, heterosexual housewives, evangelical Christians, opponents of abortion, businessmen, policemen, conservative workers, Southerners, and so on.

Positive stereotyping is an entirely different matter and is closely associated with black studies, women studies, gay studies or, more generally multiculturalism/cultural diversity. Much of what goes under "multiculturalism" is a therapeutic effort at positive stereotyping that seeks to convince some groups of their unique virtues and attributes and assure them that they should have higher self-esteem and are also deserving of social esteem and rewards.

How exactly are Puerto Ricans stereotyped (maligned) in *West Side Story*? The young Puerto Rican males are, in fact, gang members with some propensity to street violence (as were the non-Puerto Rican characters). Were such Puerto Ricans in New York city forty-five years ago non-existent or atypical? Are they today? Is it a racial stereotype to suggest in a musical that such people existed? Is a play or musical (novel or film) obligated even retroactively to present a representative sample or cross section of any group which appear in it? More to the point, are works of art obligated to present positive role models as the old socialist-realist works had in the Soviet Union and other communist states? Some people in Amherst believed that they are. A politically correct musical would portray Puerto Rican nuclear scientists, federal judges, brain surgeons, and altruistic businessmen; among the young, star athletes, valedictorians, peace corps volunteers and other positive role models.

The myth of Rigoberta Menchu and responses to its partial demolition are also reflective of the broader trends here discussed. Although the *New York Times* had covered the controversy, it has been of interest largely to academic intellectuals and their students. Nonetheless the incident is important because it sheds light on the extraordinary receptivity to Menchu's story among Western intellectual elites and because her book has been required reading for tens, possibly hundreds of thousands of college students. The book "became part of a new canon at the intersection of feminism, ethnic studies and literature... regarded... as an authoritative text on the social roots of political violence, indigenous attitudes toward colonialism and debates about ethnicity, class and identity."[53]

The incident is also significant because it illuminates with great clarity postmodern relativism which rejects the idea that the truth of particular events can be clearly established and insists that every witness of or participant in particular events has his or her version of truth—although in this case the truth of a female representative of an oppressed, non-Western minority must be "privileged."

Rigoberta Menchu was, supposedly, a poor Guatemalan peasant woman who suffered greatly during the civil war at the hands of the right-wing military regime and lost several members of her family. Her autobiography entitled *I, Rigoberta Menchu* was first published in Spanish in 1983 and in English in 1984. It became a best-seller and its author an international celebrity and recipient of the Noble Peace Prize in 1992. By 1996 she had received fourteen honorary doctorates among other honors. As the *New York Times* article put it, "Ms. Menchu...tells a wrenching tale of violence, destruction, misery and exploitation as moving and disturbing as a Victor Hugo novel. So powerful was the book's impact that it immediately transformed her into a celebrated and much-sought-after human rights campaigner."[54] The book was also held up as a shining example of the type of reading that is far more compelling and important than the classics of Western literature it often replaced.

Subsequently David Stoll, an American anthropologist working in Guatemala discovered that a good deal of the Menchu story was invented, that many of the tragic events in the life of the author did not take place and her family did not suffer the deprivations described. For example, "in one of the most heartbreaking episodes of the book, Ms. Menchu tells how in 1967 she watched her younger brother Nicolas die of malnutrition while the family was working for slave wages on a coffee plantation....But Nicolas Menchu turns out to be alive and well, the owner of a well kept homestead here."[55] Menchu also claimed to be illiterate whereas she had attended a, by local standards, good boarding school. The book was thus highly and tendentiously inaccurate in many important details.

These revelations had little impact on the admirers of the author and her message. Rather, it was the author of the expose who became subject of criticism and abuse:

> The prestige of *I, Rigoberta Menchu* was so great that when I began to talk about my findings in 1990-1991 some of my colleagues regarded them as sacrilegious. I put myself beyond the pale of decency.... Some colleagues also warned that a white anthro-

pologist did not have the right to undermine a Native American's right to tell her own story... Rigoberta had become an icon, a quasi-sacred figure who could not be questioned without arousing bitter controversy. [56]

The appeals of the book were rooted in the author representing a contemporary personification of the Noble Savage—an authentic, truth-telling, poor, illiterate, victimized third world woman of color. Focusing on her life and sufferings helped to entertain an idealized version of the non-Western world (its virtuous, suffering good people) that could implicitly be contrasted to the guilt and corruptions of the West. Her story confirmed and further stimulated criticism of the United States—held largely responsible for the repressive right-wing government of Guatemala at the time the story took place and the exploitative economic system responsible for the sufferings of Guatemalan peasants.

The incident was reminiscent of the case of Tawana Brawley, the young black girl who falsely accused police officers of raping her in a small town in New York State in 1988. When her story was exposed as a fraud her defenders argued that even if she was not raped *she could have been* and other black women had been. Defenders of Menchu similarly argued that her story, true or not, had a larger significance and factual details did not matter.

Two larger conclusions may be drawn. One is that for those on the left, that is, a substantial portion of academic and other intellectuals, it has remained extremely important to retain fidelity to mythical figures or icons who symbolize a just cause, such as the poor of the Third World. Second and equally important, Menchu's story confirmed by implication the inequity of the United States and its responsibility for poverty and repression in Latin America.

Finally the sports utility vehicles. The reader may wonder what deeper significance can be read into their enormous popularity especially in connection with the discontents of modernity or the problematic aspects of present-day American society? Most obviously their popularity reflects the prosperity of Americans since these vehicles cost significantly more than most regular cars and so does operating them (they are gas guzzlers). But the popularity of SUVs may also be associated with more problematic matters discussed below.

To fully grasp the significance of the phenomenon we must bear in mind that a major shift in consumer behavior has taken place during the 1990s as approximately 40 percent of all cars Americans drive at the present time belong to this category. I believe that three factors explain this trend and none of them is encouraging.

One source of the popularity of SUVs is the sense of security (quite false, as it turns out) their owners allegedly derive from being encased in and control of these large and heavy vehicles with four-wheel drive, seated above drivers of regular cars. These vehicles are supposed to be "rugged," they can go anywhere and are invariably portrayed in the advertisements in some remote, roadless, natural area.[57] Hence the security they offer can also be associated with adventure and adventurousness—flattering fantasies for their largely sedentary, suburban, middle- and upper middle-class owners.

Secondly and more ominously, there is a sense of power, self-assertion (and often aggression) connected with the possession of such a large and heavy vehicle. As one commentator put it, they have been "designed to intimidate other motorists" and look menacing.[58] Not only can they, tank-like, go anywhere, in a collision with regular cars they will crush them.

Thirdly, these vehicles have become a new status symbol, an item of genuine conspicuous consumption: they have far more power, weight, and space than most people need and such excess is the essence of such display. In offering excessive amounts of space and power they resemble stretch limos which, too, are highly impractical and even more wasteful of space and as such also dedicated to display. Both types of vehicles are statements of conspicuous consumption divorced from any discernible need other than ostentation.

SUVs are expensive to buy and operate and their possession is not connected to any genuine need such as living on a dirt road or in a roadless area, or carrying around huge loads. The highly inefficient gasoline consumption, the related air pollution, and the excess space taken by these vehicles is of no concern to their owners.

If this analysis is correct none of the motives for possessing SUVs are appealing or rational; they arise out of insecurity, power hunger, aggression, and status seeking. These attitudes don't speak well of the maturity, sense of security, emotional health or civic consciousness of huge numbers of Americans in the 1990s.

VI

The incidents and developments noted above (except the popularity of SUVs) illustrate the persistence of the critiques of American society during the 1990s many of which are still informed by left-over ideas of Marxism, which "remain preferred explanations of how the world works" among many academic intellectuals.[59] To be sure, these critiques have become less fiery and action oriented in the absence of foreign or domestic crises to which they could be linked. They are also less noticeable because they have become conventional wisdom permeating dominant or mainstream culture and enshrined in cultural institutions.[60]

Meetings of professional organizations such as the American Sociological Association continue to exemplify the taken for granted institutionalization of the spirit of the 1960s. Its most recent, 95th meeting was entitled "'Oppression, Domination and Liberation'... the event promised insights not only into the 'continuing problem of racism' but also into 'other manifestations of social inequality such as class exploitation and oppression on the basis of gender, ethnicity, national origin, sexual preference, disability and age.'" Ralph Nader, although not exactly a card-carrying sociologist, was among the featured speakers and received with great enthusiasm, "his call for action against the ills of American society...thoroughly in the spirit of the occasion."[61]

At a recent conference on globalization sponsored by a variety of foundations and academic institution in New York City and attended by about 500 people the attitudes and beliefs similar to those observed at the ASA meeting surfaced. A participant, John B. Judis, wrote, "much of what I heard suggested the same deep alienation from American society that I fled in 1976" [at a meeting of the California chapters of the New American movement, a socialist organization]. At the New York gathering

Gwendolyn Mink, a tenured professor of politics at the University of California, Santa Cruz and daughter of Hawaii Representative Patsy Mink... declared that "the two-party-system is a sanctuary for middle-class, white-skin privilege." Addressing herself to women in the audience she charged the two-party system with "hounding you into marriage" and "forcing you into relationships with men".... Lawrence Goodwyn, a Duke University historian bemoaned "the stultifying loneliness of American society" and condemned the "authoritarian, male-dominated, white-dominated" political system.... Michael Goldfield of Wayne University... took a swipe at Nader because his "positions on people of color are largely invisible." The key issue in the election, Goldfield said, should be freedom... for Mumia Abu Jamal, the former Black Panther, who on the basis of eyewitness testimony was convicted in 1982 of killing a Philadelphia policeman...

Judis concluded that

> There are today... two American lefts. The reformist, democratic left... [and] the cultural left housed in universities like Duke, and UC Santa Cruz [that] still lives, amnazingly in the bygone world of capitalist pigs, power to the people and Ho, Ho,Ho Chi Minh. And this was their conference. [62]

Multiculturalism, postmodernism, cold war revisionism, anti-anti-communism, nostalgia for the 1960s, dwelling on the historical misdeeds of the United States—each and every one of these trends or schools of thought convey in some fashion that this is an unjust, evil and irrational society, and that Western ideas and institutions that shaped it are correspondingly oppressive or outright evil.

A volume by Eric Foner (*The Story of American Freedom*, 1999), a highly regarded social critic, holder of named chairs in history at both Columbia University and formerly at Oxford is a good illustration of such critiques. As Theodore Draper pointed out the book "might better be described as the story of American unfreedom." A triumph of selective perception and emphasis the book is in effect the history of the oppression of blacks and females (and other minorities). Draper writes,

> the story is largely depressing, a tale of hopeful efforts that failed and of dissident voices that cried out in the wilderness. On most questions he generally cites the views of radical critics....From his account it would be hard to understand why so many millions of immigrants should have come to the United States for more freedom ... Foner is so zealous a partisan of radical sects and opinions that he touches only a portion of American life.[63]

Foner, (like numerous other academic intellectuals) was also determined "to rehabilitate American communism" and he "pays tribute to Communists for enlarging the scope of American freedom."[64]

At the root of these attitudes lies the longstanding, sentimental conviction that "being on the left" means "defending the weak against the strong" as for example Richard Rorty believes.[65] Alas, there is no evidence that in any society where the "left" came to power the principle of defending the weak against the strong came to prevail.

"Being on the left" has become less of a specific prescription for policies than a diffusely sentimental and proud claim on virtue and hope also exemplified by the title William Sloane Coffin (venerable social critic, prominent during the late 1960s) chose for his recent book: *The Heart is a Little to the Left*.[66] In the same spirit Richard Rorty declared that the Left, was the party of perennial hope.[67] Such declarations bring to mind Doris Lessing's observation: "There, as always in great mass movements, reign certain sentimental certitudes that are unchallenged and undiscussed. One is that Socialists [i.e., those on the left] are better than non-Socialists—morally better, that is—in spite the fact that Socialism has created the most monstrous tyrannies..."[68]

Indignation over inequality and assigning responsibility for it remains the unshakable foundation of all critiques of American society. Coffin voiced the traditional left-liberal view that considers social-economic inequality an obvious and avoidable social injustice caused by the moral failure of society, or some groups in it. Crime, poverty, and educational failure, are, in this view, social and not individual failures: "economic coercion is 'violence in slow motion,'" Coffin writes. Further, "crime is a communal failure.... We stress the guilty in order to exonerate the responsible... poverty... is hardly the fault of those Americans willing, even desperate to work" but cannot find jobs. Poverty also explains, in this view, why teenagers get pregnant.[69]

At a conference entitled "Student Achievement in Multicultural School Districts" attended by 140 educators in Massachusetts, "Most panelists agreed that the problems lie with adults—with politicians and administrators who interfere with teaching and with teachers who lack inspiration to spur children to succeed. Inherent racism also plays a large role in student failure, they said.... The basic problem is failing to value each student."[70] Such were the publicly prevailing views of student responsibility and motivation in the late 1990s.

The major premise of the left-liberal conception of inequality is "the presupposition that social groups would be proportionally represented in various activities or institutions, or at various income levels, in the absence of bias and discrimination" although this has never been the case anywhere, any time in history. Thomas Sowell also points out that many groups in no position to discriminate against anyone, or to benefit from discrimination (themselves often the victims of it), have often been over-represented "in high paying occupations, prestigious academic institutions and numerous other desirable sectors of the economy and society."[71]

These highly emotional, taken-for-granted, bedrock beliefs about equality, inequality, and personal responsibility for one's social position (or lack thereof) have been held for the most part by members of various elite groups and among the well educated. A student of social work at Columbia University in New York strikingly personified such beliefs. Having been "struck in the head with a chunk of concrete... she expressed concern for her attacker, speculating that he must have had a troubled childhood."[72]

Such benign views of human misbehavior are in sharp contrast to the vocal demands for harsher punishment for those who commit "hate crimes." Evidently *those* criminals are uninfluenced by social forces, their behavior is freely, willfully chosen and they are fully responsible for their crimes—they *deserve* to be punished. These beliefs are a current example of what I called almost three decades ago "selective determinism."[73] All ideas about the mitigating social influences over individual behavior vanish when it comes to these so-called hate crimes, or certain groups of people. The feminist version of selective social determinism proposes that nothing about men is "socially constructed" because that would "let them off the hook, so men get heavy doses of essentialist attributes," a professor of Women Studies observed.[74]

Andrew Sullivan observed that we live in an era "when group hate emerged as our cardinal social sin." But almost every victim of crime can be considered a victim of some hate crime given the expansive classification of our population as constituted of actual or potential victim groups: women, blacks, Hispanics, lesbians, homosexuals, and the disabled—three quarters of the population who ever become a victim of crime may thus be regarded automatically as a victim of a hate crime, the only exception being healthy, heterosexual white male victims of crime.

Sullivan also asked the logical question, "Why is hate for a group worse than for a person?... the distinction between a crime filled with personal hatred and a crime filled with group hatred is essentially arbitrary."[75]

Although foreign affairs during the 1990s stimulated far less impassioned domestic criticism of the United States as compared to that evoked by Vietnam, Nicaragua, or El Salvador, the economic sanctions against Iraq (imposed in the wake of the Gulf War) and the intervention in Kosovo were seized upon by the most committed critics. The economic sanctions were portrayed as responsible for the deaths of children while the critics resolutely averted their eyes from the refusal of the Iraqi government to use the substantial oil revenues it continued to receive for humanitarian purposes; they also overlooked the continued expenditures on the lavish life-style of Saddam Hussein and his supporting elite which could also have gone a long way to buy medications for children.[76] Many of the old Vietnam-era protestors were now the champions of Iraqi children, including Daniel Berrigan, Helen Caldicott, Noam Chomsky, Ramsey Clark, William Sloane Coffin, David Dellinger, Bishop Thomas Gumbleton, and Howard Zinn. They are joined by celebrities of the world of entertainment such as Ed Asner, Susan Sarandon, Mike Farrell, Robert Altman, Peter Seeger, Richard Dreyfuss, Jeremy Irons, and Richard Gere.[77]

While U.S. participation in the NATO bombing of Kosovo inspired less protest, Noam Chomsky reached the conclusion that it was further irrefutable proof of all the evils he had always associated with this country throughout his professional life. In his view "the real reasons" for the bombing campaign was to stimulate defense spending and solidify American control over Europe.[78]

Given the huge amount of what might be called adversarial messages disseminated by our cultural establishments and educational institutions it remains a question how much cumulative impact they had. American universities and colleges or at least their departments and faculties teaching the humanities and social sciences have become increasingly similar to Latin American universities where there is an "absence of a close relationship between what the students are taught and the real needs of society."[79] To be sure there is no consensus as to what the "real needs of society" are. Those dispensing the messages of political correctness would argue unhesitatingly that what this society really needs is more black and women studies, postmodernism, deconstruction, thus enlightening the younger generations about the evils of white, male, racist patriarchal society and the ills of Western civilization.

Gertrude Himmmelfarb has argued that American society has split into two cultures as the advances of the left-liberal or adversarial beliefs and policies created countervailing tendencies and forces, among them the evangelical movement and the so-called Christian right. She writes that "the cultural divide helps explain the peculiar, almost schizoid nature of our present condition: the evidence of moral disarray on the one hand and a religious-cum-moral revival on the other."[80]

If it is true that the counterculture has become mainstream culture, it remains nonetheless a fact that half or more of the electorate still votes Republican, support traditional Christian values,[81] most of them pay taxes, obey most laws, a sufficient number volunteer for the armed forces, become policemen and prison guards, many work hard for modest wages and abstain from any attempt to overthrow system; nor does the majority of the citizens give any indication of viewing society as hopelessly evil or deformed although I suspect that if called upon few could defend American society against such critiques.

Last but not least the habits of private consumption are by no means effected by the continued of denigration of "mindless consumption," nor do the ritualistic charges of "greed" deter people from trying to maximise their income or launching into a wide variety of business undertakings.

If all this is true ordinary people have shown a great deal resilience to ideas which conflict with their personal experiences.

VII

Several of these essays are relevant to the question of decadence in American society—another topic of long standing interest and one about which it is difficult to reach a firm conclusion.

It is tempting to believe that modernity at some point merges into decadence, that some of the problems and discontents associated with it amount to decadence; postmodernity and decadence are even closer.

Decadence can mean or be associated with a variety of things: the decline of political will of a society or its elites, its inability or unwillingness to defend itself; the fall of civic consciousness or responsibility, the erosion of community, the widespread reluctance or refusal of the citizens to do anything for the "common good"; the decline of work ethic, the refusal to defer gratifications for some long term goal, rampant hedonism, escapism, corruption, crime and especially moral relativism. The decline of participation in public activities, in volunteering, charitable contributions and even "face-to-face sociability," the so-called "civic disengagement" can all be linked to decadence.[82]

Excessive individualism rich in anti-social implications is central to this discussion because it enshrines the supremacy of personal needs and imparts exaggerated notions of uniqueness to individuals. A recent television documentary about a group of upper middle clas teenagers captured this quality vividly. In the words of a reviewer "those teenagers appear to spend every waking minute in frenzied search of their individuality; they're as determined as truffle-hunting pigs to root our their true selves and hold them up for the world to see."[83] This of course is an attitude not limited to the teenagers in question but it is one they learned from the adults around them.

It may be debated endlessly when individualism is "excessive" or how much and what kinds of self-realization, or self-expression is commendable, subversive and atomizing.[84] Celebrities associated with the world of entertainment provide other examples of such individualism and its costs even as some of them seek involvement in public affairs and political causes.

The high divorce rate is perhaps the most obvious example of a socially costly individualism. In our times most marriages seem to break up because people are unwilling to compromise their "personal needs" or "space" or their pursuit of what they consider their "inner essence." Children do not benefit, nor society at large. It may however be argued that the greater marital stability of the past was paid for in greater personal unhappiness.

Decadence may also be associated with the growth of superstitious, irrational beliefs, cults, crazes and the mistrust of science,—again a trend that can be traced to the late 1960s and the counter culture of the period. Indications include the presence on the faculty of Harvard medical school a professor of psychiatry, John Mack, distinguished not only by his firm belief in extraterrestrial creatures but claiming to have among his patients many who consorted with them in various ways.[85] While (as far as we know) there is only one professor at Harvard upholding such beliefs reportedly 93 percent of the American people believe in angels and 49 percent in the government concealing information about UFO-s.[86]

The growing popularity of alternative medicine may also be among the indicators of these trends. One of its major and widely acclaimed practicioner, Andrew Weil M.D. believes that "Sickness is a manifestation of evil in the body... just as health is the manifestation of holyness...In our society...the commonality of religion, magic and medicine is obscured."[87]

Nonetheless American society at the end of the past century sent mixed messages regarding decadence and vitality and widely held personal values. It is possible to cite indicators (some of them noted above) which point to creativity, innovation, flexibility, resilience and idealism in present day American society and culture. One widely publicised study found that the middle classes are still responsible, moderate, tolerant and, for the most part, upholding the traditional middle class values, including work.[88] In times of crisis the patriotic impulses find expression as was the case during the Gulf War in 1991. The United States is still willing and able to engage in various largely altruistic international interventions as in Haiti, Somalia and Kosovo. A spectacular scientific-technological creativity has continued and productivity has kept increasing during the past decade. Most people consume with abandon but they also work hard. In a truly decadent society few people would be willing to pay taxes, to do volunteer work, give to charity, save money, serve in the military or obey the law without the threat of immediate coercive sanction.

Most of the symptoms of decadence, if indeed that is what they are, are to be found in the cultural-moral realm as the cultural-political traditions and foundations of the country remain under attack. Multiculturalism (as generally understod and practised) contributes not merely to lowering educational standards but could have a long term corrosive effect on social-national cohesion as it instructs people to forget that they are Americams first (and therefore owe allegiance to the nation) and members of a racial-ethnic, gender or sexual identity group second. The multicultural indoctrination begins before college. A longitudinal study of Ruben Rumbaut found that in a three year period (1992-1995) there was a substantial decrease (between 9th and 12th grade) in student identification as plain American or hyphenated American and substantial increase in identities based on national origin or ethnicity: "...after three years of American high school these students were more likely to consider themselves Mexicans than Mexican-Americans or Americans." The survey suggested that many newcomers to America "are becoming assimilated into... the world of multiculturalism and groups consciousness." A quantitative content analysis of major history textbooks also found that by the mid-1980s these textbooks were "riddled with multicultural, radical feminist and identity group propaganda." [89] Samuel P. Huntington pointed out that multiculturalism and diversity... deny the existence of a common culture in the United States, denounce assimilation and promote the primacy of racial, ethnic and other subnational cultural identities and groupings... recent immigrants are not subject to the same pressures and inducements as previous immigrants to integrate themselves into American culture. As a result ethnic identities are becoming more meaningful and appear to be increasing in relevance compared with national identity... If multiculturalism prevails and if the consensus on liberal democracy disintegrates, the United States could join the Soviet Union on the ash heap of history.[90]

Huntington probably would agree that these are long-term trends and not irreversible, but for the time being they lend support to the notions of decline or decadence.

Mass culture and its mindless entertainment orientation is another symptom of cultural decline and not because mass entertainments in the past were necessarily superior either aesthetically or morally. It is the massive, intrusive presence of mass (or popular) culture and the penetration of entertainment orientation into realms of life where it does not belong (education, politics, and the arts) that is distinctive of our time. In all probability, this mass culture has the most adverse impact on the poor and uneducated as "the living rooms of even the poorest, most fractured single-parent families are dominated by a single piece of furniture—the color television."[91] Many academic intellectuals are sympathetic toward popular culture because it is non-elitist and often carries the messages of political correctness.

Symptomatic of the mindset of the elites who control the mass media is a recent program on the Cold War on CNN that still exudes the spirit of moral equivalence.[92] Hardly a coincidence that Ted Turner, head of CNN believes that "The United States is the one that doesn't want to get rid of nuclear weapons to save ourselves from the starving masses of the Third World when they come to our doorstep."[93] Why and how Ted Turner has developed such ideas and become a major spokesman of political correctness and American guilt for the ills of the world (third and other) remains to be established. In any event his beliefs mirror the disposition of a large portion of our cultural elites.

At last the results of the November 2000 presidential and congressional elections are also relevant to these reflections as they raise questions about the health of our political system and the meaning of the polarization of the voters the election results reflected. The outcome of these elections had three problematic aspects. One was the very fact of sharp polarization of politial allegiances that might have been at least in part an expression of the cultural polarization of American society noted earlier. Also of some interest is that for the first time in recent decades a far left party (Nader's) participated and provided a home for the most alienated leftist 3 percent of the population who cared to vote. By contrast at the other extreme, Buchanan's party did not emerge as a corresponding symbol of alienation of those on the right, as hardly anyone voted for it. This suggests that those on the extreme or radical right either did not vote or their numbers are much smaller than those of their counterparts on the left.

Secondly, the seemingly endless legal maneuverings the inconclusive results created are a reminder of the excessively legalistic nature of our society. As many commentators pointed out, it is far from clear how desirabile it is that lawyers and judges determine the final outcome of the electoral process. On the other hand some learned commentators thought that the orderly if prolonged legal maneuvering was a civics lesson of sorts, proving once more that political conflict resolution remains non-violent and rule-governed

Thirdly, there is the matter of the governability of the country that has such an evenly divided electorate producing a correspondingly divided senate and congress and a president with little popular mandate (as of this writing in early December 2000 we do not know who that president will be).

VIII

Several pieces in this volume deal with the fall and aftermath of the fall of Soviet communism but none of them reflect the anticipation of that event. I was among many students of Soviet communism who failed to anticipate its collapse although not because I believed (as was more common) that it was successful, either economically or morally. I believed that it would endure because, seemingly, it had perfected methods of control and repression which created a quiescent, passive population of modest expectations and was led by a political elite committed through a combination of self-interest and residual ideological convictions, to its preservation.

It was not easy to predict the fall of Soviet communism, since, as I argued in my recent book,[94] the collapse had much to do with the intangibles of human motivation and decision-making and the inability to anticipate the consequences of these decisions—in the case in point, allowing the public ventilation of grievances (glasnost) which decisively undermined the system.

The collapse of communism (like its origin) is a formidable and thought-provoking subject and disagreements about its character, theoretical inspirations, strength and weaknesses and reasons for its collapse persist. As Michael Scammel put it, "the proper interpretation of communism is very much a live issue."[95] This however is not a view universally embraced; for some authors discussions of communism become quickly and tiresomely associated with the cold war (ancient history) and old battles tediously refought between anti-anti-communists and anti-communists. These old battles concern not merely the nature of communist political systems but also that of communist movements in the West, and especially the United States. These old battles, and the disputes about the character of the American communist movement and party also helps to understand why the euphoria over the demise of the Soviet empire was so short lived.[96]

The fall of Soviet communism made only a modest dent on the revisionist view of Soviet history.[97] While the opening of archives compelled an upward revision of the number of the victims the fundamental disposition toward that system has not changed. Professor J. Arch Getty is probably the best example of the revisionist school of Soviet history having devoted a substantial part of his career to revise downward the number of the victims of the Soviet system and to relatively benign interpretations of the violent domestic policies of that regime. Although he recently upped his estimates he still feels a residual compulsion to mitigate or dissolve the responsibility of that regime—more recently in the name of balance and objectivity. He remains unwilling to entertain the possibility that ideas and ideology, that is, those of Marx and Lenin, had anything to do with Soviet-communist political violence. Professor Getty (and those of his persuasion) is especially disturbed (as shown in his recent review of *The Black Book of Communism*[98] by the moral equation of Nazism and communism the French authors incline to. It seems to escape him that whatever the precise comparative body counts and whatever institutional differences there were between the two systems it is still possible to reach the conclusion that each was unequivocally evil in its own partially distinctive way.

The Nazis carried out their mass murders in a technologically advanced and efficient manner; communist systems carried out mass killings in a more improvised way and without such technology. They did away with people either by shooting them or by creating conditions which assured high mortality rates. As the Russian author Roy Medvedev wrote, "corrective labor camps were calculated not so much to correct as to destroy the prisoners."[99]

Professor Getty also inclines to dispute the idea that there was such a thing as "communist systems" prefering to focus on the differences among communist leaders (and their systems) and overlooks the morally relevant similarities. The latter included the enormous concentration of power, a shared vision of themselves as exceptional historical figures that was combined (paradoxically) with an avowed faith in Marxism-Leninism and a determination to radically change their societies and the behavior of human beings who lived in them. These leaders and their underlings also shared a profound indifference to the desires and goals of these human beings; they treated and mistreated people according to arbitrary social-political criteria that had little to do with actual behavior. It was not only the Khmer Rouge (as Professor Getty writes) that massacred "categories" of people: every communist system categorised people as to their presumed political reliability or unreliability which became the basis of the policies of repression.

As in his other writings Professor Getty seeks to take the moral sting out of Soviet-communist repression by suggesting that it was unplanned, haphazard, "stupid," "incompetent," and ineffective, and not carried out by "a coldly efficient machine." But the system was efficient enough to eliminate its very generously estimated number of designated enemies. The definition and classification of the enemy had many irrational aspects, but once the decision was made to label particular groups or individuals as the enemy they rarely escaped retribution.

It is a telling illustration of the dependence of intellectual judgment on personal sentiment that Professor Getty thinks that there has been an excess of Western writings about Soviet repression, that "Soviet specialists provided us with a full menu of communist atrocities"[100] he writes with evident irritation and distaste. But Solzhenitsyn (whom he mentions as an example of such authors) is hardly a Western "Soviet specialist" and without him and other Soviet (and other communist) exiles and defectors, the Western literature on "the crimes of communism" would be very slight indeed—and even more so if we also excluded Robert Conquest whose conclusions Professor Getty does not find any more palatable than those of the French authors he rebuked.

It is ironic that while so much of Getty's work has carried an obvious and heavy ideological burden he now rebukes the French authors for their own, in the name of a "balance, carefully analyzed history" and greater objectivity.

In a recent volume Getty edited with a Russian author he writes:

> In our study we have not asked the question: What caused the terror? Questions like 'What caused the Thirty Years' War or... the Great Depression?' similarly invite easy answers to answer extremely complex problems. To identify a single main 'cause' would also introduce the notion of inevitability or determinism.... We have posed different queries: What made this all possible? We have provided evidence of numerous factors and elements of the phenomenon, including the tradition of party discipline, corporate mentality and self-interest of the nomenklatura elite, political relations and struggles among numerous groups within the party, elite anxiety and perpceptions of state-society relations, and, last but not least, the 'Stalin factor'... Our study has concentrated on the Bolshevik elite.... In broadest terms, *the story has been about Stalin and the senior elite trying to come to terms with and shape the political and social environment they had inherited... and had shaped by their own policies.* That environment forms the background, the preconditions for terror.[101] [My emphasis]

Several things are noteworthy about the quoted. One is the peculiar, convoluted locution for describing mass murder (see especially italics); the second is a conception of these elites as lacking political will of their own as they cope and "try to come to terms" with conditions they inherited, conditioned as they are by the environment. Thirdly, and most striking is the total, unqualified absence of any reference to ideology in the lengthy enumeration of the "numerous factors." While Getty is now more willing to admit that at least a million rather than a few thousand people were killed (as he had written earlier), he is still reluctant to implicate ideology, the part played by Marxist-Leninist doctrine in the disaster and prefers to avoid passing moral judgement over the atrocities. Nor does he note that if the party elite (and Stalin) were "insecure" (as he asserts) it was an insecurity of their own making that resulted from their own disastrous, ideology driven policies which was bound to undermine whatever legitimacy their rule might have enjoyed earlier.

Getty's continued refusal to give some "causal" significance to ideology and belief is all the more striking because, as Martin Malia pointed out, the crucial factor...in this pseudo-class struggle to defend the 'conquests of socialism' was ideological intoxication.... Yet Getty never looks at the content of doctrine for a key to the Purge. This is all the more amazing since the most striking revelation of the archives is perhaps that all participants... discussed the non-existent 'plot' in the class-struggle terms...even behind closed doors. In truth the Great Terror was a unique case of ideology creating its own political reality.[102]

By removing ideology from his purview Getty is apparently seeking to protect Marxism from disrepute. He may share the disposition of Georg Lukacs who declared that "even if every empirical prediction of Marxism were invalidated, he would still hold Marxism to be true."[103] Similar sentiments lurk behind the relief, Samuel Bowles, a professor of economics expressed upon the collapse of Soviet communism: "The nightmare is over, the dream lives on."[104] In sharp contrast to such beliefs and attitudes, an English author correctly insisted that "It must always be relevant to inquire into the truth or falsehood of a doctrine in whose name people are enjoined to wade through blood to a better future.... Is it not absurd to claim that... what he [Marx]said had no consequences for the millions of people who were murdered by people who used his theories to justify their action?" (Robert Skidelsky: "What's Left of Marx?" *New York Review of Books*, November 16, 2000, p. 26).

Also characteristic of the persistence of the revisionist outlook has been Sheila Fitzpatrik's recent volume[105] which—while not denying the horrors of the Stalin era—sought, simultaneously and somewhat implausibly to put a more cheerful gloss on it by trivializing the sufferings and tragedies. If so many Soviet citizens managed to pursue their daily life unaffected by the terror (as she tells us) could it really have been so dreadful?—is the subliminal message. Or as she put it, "There were fearful things that affected Soviet life and visions that uplifted it [? - P.H.] but *mostly* it was a hard grind, full of shortages and discomfort... Homo Sovieticus was.... above all.. a survivor [my emphasis]." Minus the millions who were not. As a reviewer put it "This would seem a more fitting description of the British home front during World War II than of Russia under Stalin..."[106]

In the responses to the fall of Soviet communism one can also occasionally detect remnants of the old moral equivalence school although it is no longer possible, for obvious reasons, to equate the characteristics and especially, the failings of the United States with those of the Soviet Union. Nonetheless, defunct and bankrupt state socialism can still be equated with surviving capitalism as in the mind of John Le Carré who argued that "though Communism didn't work, capitalism is in much of the world 'a wrecking, terrible force' displacing people and ruining life styles 'with the same recklessness as Communism.'"[107]

In recent years the major issue of contention in the United States has been less the character of defunct Soviet communism than the character of the American communist party and its supporters. For instance, Ellen Schreker "a leading left scholar of McCarthyism" as well as a leading defender of the American Communist movement maintained that "spying [on the part of these communists] wasn't necessarily a categorical evil. American Communists, she says, spied not because they were traitors but because they 'did not subscribe to traditional forms of patriotism.'"[108] It was also Schreker's view that "communism was heterogeneous and creative [while] anti-Communism was... purely malignant. She argued that there was no good kind of anti-Communism—including that espoused in the 1950s by varieties of socialists and liberals."[109] These views and attitudes are not limited to the rarified world of academia: "In the opinion of contemporary Hollywood, Communists in the 1930s and 40s were naive romantics, not traitors."[110]

In the same spirit Ring Lardner, Jr. in a letter to the *New York Times Book Review* averred that "all the Communists I knew were patriotic Americans who thought the idea that all men (and women) are created equal would be more fully expressed under socialism than capitalism."[111] This summed up the romantic view of the American communist movement that was also shown to be seriously flawed by several recent studies based on Soviet archival sources.[112]

Communism, anti-communism, and anti-anti-communism remain a triad intertwined and associated with the spirit of the 1960s which gave rise to anti-anti-communism and the related conviction (held by many American liberals) "that anticommunism of every kind was a blight on our political culture."[113]

The long record of the colorful and breathtaking misjudgments of communist systems on the part of many distinguished and less distinguished Western intellectuals, scholars, journalists, businessmen, and public figures remains significant in the postcommunist era since many of the current disputes can be traced to past misjudgments. To reflect on these disputes and misjudgments does not amount to a reluctance "to let go of anti-Communism" (or communism).[114] No corresponding suggestion has been made that it is time "to let go of Nazism" as its record and nature continues to inspire vast amounts of debate, discussion, and literature that few regard—at least in public—as faintly ridiculous, boring, or obsolete.

The passing of Soviet Communism has given rise to phenomena few anticipated. They include the nostalgia among many East Germans and Russians (among others) for the good old days of stability, socialist "Gemeinschaft," and modest material security.

There is also a new anti-Americanism discernible in Russia and parts of Eastern Europe (discussed on pp. 361-77) that for large parts of the population replaced the reflexive pro-American, pro-Western attitudes which prevailed before the collapse.

The intense ethnic-nationalistic conflicts which followed the fall of the Soviet empire in the former Soviet Union and Yugoslavia were also among the by products of the collapse not widely anticipated. The rise of a criminal mafia in Russia (replacing the political one) was likewise an unpleasant surprise especially given its size and scope.

* * *

The fall of Soviet communism while a great blessing in itself does not herald "the end of history," or the end of serious political conflicts or global harmony. The halting and incomplete Westernization of what used to be the Soviet Bloc is likely to give rise to the kinds of cultural and social psychological problems which prevail in Western societies although before that happens on a substantial scale postcommunist societies will have to grapple with more pressing problems and difficulties.

The discontents which already surfaced in these countries confirm that while political institutions and systems can seriously aggravate and ruin the lives of human beings, they cannot relieve them of the problems and difficulties which arise when the individual confronts the fundamental questions of life (and death) unaided by tradition and unconstrained by political regimentation and physical deprivation.

Notes

1.   *Contemporary Sociology*, January 1996, p.14.
2.   Axel van den Berg: "Liberalism without Reason?" Ibid. p.19.
3.   Matei Calinescu: *Faces of Modernity*, Bloomington: Indiana University Press, 1977, p.135.
4.   Daniel Bell: *The Cultural Contradictions of Capitalism*, New York: Basic Books, 1976, pp. 51-52.
5.   Paul R. Gross and Norman Levitt: *Higher Superstition: The Academic Left and Its Quarrels with Science*, Baltimore, MD: Johns Hopkins University Press, 1994, p. 4.
6.   Robert B. Edgerton: "Traditional Beliefs and Practices—Are Some Better than Others?" in Lawrence E. Harrison and Samuel P. Huntington. eds.: *Culture Matters*, New York: Basic Books, 2000, p.127.
7.   Quoted in Jonathan Chait: "Race to the Bottom," *New Republic*, December 20, 1999, p. 28.
8.   Gertrude Himmelfarb: *One Nation, Two Cultures*, New York: Alfred A. Knopf, 1999, p. 20. For a thoughtful critique of her views see Richard A. Posner: "The Moral Minority," *New York Times Book Review*, December 19, 1999. His main criticism is that she conflates "social phenomena that have different causes" many of which do not reflect moral decay.
9.   "Ravelstein," *New Yorker*, Nov 1, 1999, pp. 101, 99.
10.   Lawrence F. Kaplan: "Fall Guys," *New Republic*, June 26, 2000, p. 23.
11.   Fareed Zakaria: "Whimper on the Right," *New Yorker*, June 5, 2000, p.86.
12.   Suzanne Daley: "Among Old Friends, New Disdain for America" *International Herald Tribune*, April 10, 2000.
13.   Robert E. Lane: *The Loss of Happiness in Market Democracies*, New Haven, CT: Yale University Press, 2000.
14.   Saul Bellow: *Ravelstein*, New York: Viking, 2000, p. 16.
15.   Paul Berman: *Adventures in Marxism*, New York: Verso, 1999, p.167.
16.   Saul Bellow: "Papuans and Zulus," [op-ed], *New York Times*, March 14, 1994.
17.   Daphne Patai: *Professing Feminism*, New York: Basic Books, 1994, pp. 94-95.
18.   Rachel Neumann: "A Place for Rage," *Dissent*, Spring 2000, pp. 90, 91. The last quote (re. private property and violence) was quoted within the article from a communiqué of the ACME collective.
19.   Paul Krugman: "Saints and Profits," [op-ed] *New York Times*, July 23, 2000.
20.   Stanley Rothman and S. Robert Lichter: "Introduction to the Transaction Edition," *Roots of Radicalism*, New Brunswick, NJ: Transaction Publishers 1996, p. xxv.
21.   Peter L. Berger: "Protestantism and the Quest for Certainty," *Christian Century*, Aug 26-Sept 2, 1998, p. 782. I wrote two decades ago, "alongside relativization there may also be observed a determined search for moral absolutes and certainties. It seems as if the moral relativism in the West has given rise to new quests for moral certainties (sometime through revolutionary politics, sometimes religious cults)..." [*Political Pilgrims*, New York: Oxford University Press, 1981, pp. 427-428].
22.   Robert Wright: "The Evolution of Despair," *Time*, August 28, 1995 p.50.
23.   Ibid. pp. 52, 53, 56.
24.   Thomas Sowell: *The Quest for Cosmic Justice*, New York: Free Press, 1999, p. 32. For various assessments of affirmative action see *Society*, July/August 2000 issue entitled "After Affirmative Action?"
25.   The survey results were included in a *Press Release* entitled "NAS Files Brief in University of Michigan Discriminmation Case" of the National Association of Scholars, Princeton, NJ, July 17, 2000.

26.   Chris Jones: "Spotlighting Racism Brings Anxiety as Well as Success" and Maurice Berger: "A Pitiless Mirror Where Audiences See Themselves," *New York Times, Arts and Entertainment*, July 23, 2000 p. 5. Both articles as the play itself were typical in taking for granted the deep seated, ineradicable, and omnipresent character of white racism.

27.   Clyde Haberman: "An Ignorant Cry of Racism Makes All the Knees Jerk," *New York Times*, December 4, 1998 p. A26. The article chronicled the case of the "a well intentioned 3rd grade teacher, who happens to be white, [who] gave her mostly black and Hispanic students a critically praised book about a black girl with kinky hair." The teacher was accused of being "racially insensitive."
      The baseless attribution of racism on a college campus has been given fictional treatment in a recent Philip Roth novel entitled *The Human Stain*, Boston: Houghton Mifflin, 2000).

28.   Daphne Patai: *Heterophobia: Sexual Harassment and the Future of Feminism*, Lanham, MD: Rowman & Littlefield, 1998, p.30.

29.   Joe Klein: "The True Disadvantage," *New Republic*, October 28, 1996, pp. 33, 34.

30.   Timur Kuran: "Seeds of Racial Explosion," *Society*, Sept/Oct 1993, p. 58-59. The article questions the publicly prevailing belief that racism is the root cause of all problems of the black population.

31.   Robert S. Robins and Jerrold M. Post, M.D.: *Political Paranoia: The Psychopolitics of Hatred*, New Haven, CT: Yale University Press, 1977, pp. 63, 62.

32.   Quoted in Patai 1994 cited, p. 150.

33.   Ibid., pp. 116, 183-184.

34.   This puritanism may indeed be connected to what Patai called "heterophobia." (Patai 1988 cited.)

35.   Patai cited 1998, pp. 21, 29.

36.   Michael Kelly: "Banality and evil," *New Republic*, May 5, 1997, p.6.

37.   Edgerton in Harrison and Huntington cited, p.132.

38.   Elisabeth Lasch-Quinn: "Dionysus and Jim Crow," *New Republic*, August 28 & September 4, 2000, p.49.

39.   Lynne Munson: "Revising the Museums," *Academic Questions*, Winter 1999-2000, pp. 53, 55-56.

40.   Richard A. Posner: "The Skin Trade," *New Republic*, October 13, 1997, p.40.

41.   "Postmortemism for Postmodernism?" *Contemporary Sociology*, January, 1996, p. 25.

42.   John R. Searle: "Politics and the Humanities," *Academic Questions*, Fall 1999, pp. 47, 49.

43.   As in his *Achieving Our Country*, Cambridge, MA: Harvard University Press, 1998.

44.   Quoted in David Sidorsky: "Does the Left Still Have the Power to Speak?" *Partisan Review*, No. 1., 2000 p. 125.

45.   John Michael: *Anxious Intellects: Academic Professionals, Public Intellectuals and Enlightenment Values*, Durham, NC: Duke University Press, 2000, pp. 86, 87.

46.   Bellow "Papuas and Zulus" cited.

47.   Robert Weissberg: "Academic Deception for Fun and Profit," *Telos*, Summer, 1998, pp. 145, 147, 148. For a recent major study of such and other problems of higher education see Alan Charles Kors and Harvey A. Silverglate: *The Shadow University*, New York: Free Press, 1998.

48.   Patricia Leigh Brown: "A New Culture Moves on Campus: Viewing Ahab and Barbie Through the Lens of Disability," *New York Times, News of the Week*, August 20, 2000.

49.   Sally L. Satel: "Critical Medical Theory," *Academic Questions*, Spring 2000, pp. 21, 20.

50.   Curtis Crawford: "Weighing the Benefits and Costs of Racial Preference in College Admissions," *Society*, May-June 2000, p.77.

51.   Andrew Sullivan: "Lies That Matter," *New Republic*, September 14 & 21, 1999, pp. 19,20.

52.   "Readers Comment on West Side Story," *Daily Hampshire Gazette*, November 27-28, 1999.

53.   David Stoll: *Rigoberta Menchu: And the Story of All Poor Guatemalans*, Boulder, CO: Westview Press, 1999, p.5, 267.

54.   Larry Rohter: "Noble Winner Accused of Stretching Truth," *New York Times*, December 15, 1988, p.1.

55.   Rohter in *New York Times*, cited p.10.

56.   Stoll, cited p. 216.

57.   A recent exception was an ad for a Mercedes SUV that portrayed it on a superhighway but for a good measure invoked the name of Audubon. It ran as follows: "Autobahn meets Audubon.... There is nothing like the great outdoors. Especially when it's whipping past your window at 147 mph on the autobahn." *New Yorker*, July 24, 2000. On the ethical issues SUVs raise see Marty Rourke: "Highway hulks become an ethical issue" [Los Angeles Times] reprinted in *Daily Hampshire Gazette*, July 28-30, 2000.

58.   Keith Bradsher: "The Latest Fashion: Fear-of-Crime-Design," *New York Times, News of the Week*, July 23, 2000 p. 5.

59.   Dario Fernandez-Morera: *American Academia and the Survival of Marxist Ideas*, Westport, CT: Praeger, 1996, p. 1. The enduring interest in Marxism is also reflected in what have become annual conferences at the Amherst campus of the University of Massachusetts. Over one thousand people were expected to attend the latest of these gatherings. [See "More than 1000 expected to attend Marxism conference" *Campus Chronicle*, September 15, 2000.]

60.   A rather unoriginal observation still valid I made in earlier writings such as *The Survival of the Adversary Culture* (1988), *Decline and Discontent* (1992) and *Anti-Americanism* (1992, 1995). Gertrude Himmelfarb reached the same conclusion in her recent *One Nation, Two Cultures*, cited.

61.   Walter Goodman: "Sociologists to the Barricades: Thinkers Who Would Be Doers See Social Injustice Wherever They Turn," *New York Times*, August 19, 2000.

62.   John B. Judis, "Bad Trip," New Republic, November 13, 2000, p. 46.

63.   Theodore Draper: "Freedom and Its Discontents," *New York Review of Books*, September 23, 1999, pp. 61, 59.

64.   Ibid., p. 60.

65.   Sidorsky, cited ,p. 123

66.   William Sloane Coffin: *The Heart is a Little to the Left: Essays on Public Morality*, Hanover, NH: University Press of New England, 1999.

67.   Sidorsky, cited p. 125.

68.   Doris Lessing: *Prisons We Choose to Live Inside*, New York: Harper & Row, 1987, p. 23.

69.   Coffin, cited pp. 18, 20.

70.   "Forum: If students fail, the system fails," *Daily Hampshire Gazette*, (Northampton, MA) October 20, 1998.

71.   Sowell, cited pp. 35-36. Frederick R. Lynch also noted that "the diversity machine's ideology of proportionalism... has spread from university curricula to news and information services, jury selection, legislative redistricting, mortgage lending, and personnel policies in public and private sector employment." ["The Diversity Machine" *Society*, July-August 1997, p. 33].

72. "Students Face a Violent Reality," *New York Times*, July 30, 2000, p. 21.

73. Paul Hollander: "Sociology, Selective Determinism and the Rise of Expectations," *American Sociologist*, November, 1973.

74. Patai 1994, cited p. 144.

75. Andrew Sullivan: "What is so bad about hate?" *New York Times Magazine*, September 26, 1999, pp. 88,104, 112.

76. Iraq does not allow private relief organizations to operate and turned down "offers of relief from private organizations"; it "will not allow independent experts into the country to assess the living conditions of Iraqis" or UN experts who would seek ways "to improve an oil-for-food program." Even more revealing "Iraq has been exporting medical supplies... [and] sold food from oil-sales program to Syria and Jordan.....At the same time Iraqis are buying large quantities of cigarettes and imported whisky for the use of Mr Hussein's associates..." [Barbara Crosette: "Iraq Wont Let Outside Experts Assess Sanctions' Impact on Lives," *New York Times*, September 12, 2000].
In short there is growing evidence that the sufferings of the people is due to the policies and character of the government of Iraq not the U.S. or the UN sanctions. This is not a possibility the critics of the U.S. would entertain.

77. See, for example, the advertisement (sponsored by the Fellowship of Reconciliation) entitled "Are the Children of Iraq our Enemies?" signed by all those noted above. [*New York Times*, August 6, 2000.]

78. Aryeh Neier: "Inconvenient Facts" (review of Chomsky's *The New Military Humanism: Lessons from Kosovo*, a book Neier called a "dishonest diatribe.") *Dissent*, Spring 2000.

79. Carlos Alberto Montaner: "Culture and the Behavior of Elites in Latin America" in Harrison and Huntington, cited p.63.

80. Himmelfarb, cited p. 117.

81. "58 percent of Americans today say that religion is very important in their lives..." but this compares with 75 percent who considered it very important in 1952; likewise 66 percent at the present time believe that "religion can answer all most of today's problems" 82 percent believed the same in 1957. [Himmelfarb, cited p.96.]

82. This was the topic of the much discussed volume: Robert D. Putnam: *The Collapse and Revival of American Community*, New York: Simon & Schuster, 2000.

83. Nancy Franklin: "Suffer the Children," *New Yorker*, August 21 & 28, 2000, p. 168.

84. See for example Andrew J. Cherlin: "I am OK You're Selfish, *New York Times Magazine*, October 17, 1999.

85. See John Mack: *Abduction: Human Encounter with Aliens*, New York: Charles Scribner's Sons, 1994.

86. Michiko Kakutani: "Reasonable Concerns in an Age of Angels and Aliens," *New York Times*, November 16, 1999.

87. Arnold S. Relman: "Andrew Weil, the boom in alternative medicine and the retreat from science" *New Republic*, December 14, p.32.

88. Alan Wolfe: *One Nation After All*, New York: Viking 1998.

89. John Fonte: "Gramsci's Revenge: Reconstructing American Democracy," *Academic Questions*, Spring 2000, p. 56.

90. Samuel P. Huntington: "The Erosion of American National Interests," *Foreign Affairs*, September-October, 1997, pp. 33, 34, 35.

91. Klein, cited p. 35

92. For a critique of the series see Arnold Beichman, ed.: *CNN's Cold War Documentary: Issues and Controversy*, Stanford, CA: Hoover Institution Press, 2000.

93. Quoted in the *New Yorker*, November 23, 1998 p. 37.

94.   Paul Hollander: *Political Will and Personal Belief: The Decline and Fall of Soviet Communism*, New Haven, CT: Yale University Press, 1999.
95.   Michael Scammel: "The Price of an Idea," *New Republic*, December 20, 1999, p. 33.
96.   See also Edward E. Ericson, Jr.: "Solzhenitsyn, Havel and the Historical Moment" in Robert Conquest and Dusan J. Djordjevich, eds.: *Political and Ideological Confrontations in Twentieth Century Europe*, New York: St. Martin's Press, 1996, p.144.
97.   The major propositions of this revisionism may be summed up as follows: (1) not even under Stalin was the Soviet system totalitarian and the concept is generally useless; (2) the United States and the West bear the major responsibility for the cold war;(3) the number of the victims of the Soviet system under Stalin (and in general) has been greatly exaggerated by Western "cold warriors"; (4) population losses under Stalin had more to do with chaos, conflict among local leaders and the unanticipated consequences of certain policies than with high-level decisions and official ideology; (5) Marxism had little, if anything to do with the characteristics of the Soviet system and its policies.
98.   *Atlantic Monthly*, March 2000.
99.   Roy A. Medvedev: *Let History Judge*, New York: Alfred A. Knopf, 1972, p. 279.
100.   Getty in *Atlantic*, cited.
101.   J. Arch Getty and Oleg V. Naumov: *The Road to Terror*, New Haven, CT: Yale University Press, 1999, pp. 570-571. It should be noted that this is basically a collection of documents with connecting texts provided by the authors.
102.   Martin Malia: "Blood Rites: Must Violence Always be the Midwife of History?" *Book Review, Los Angeles Times*, May 28, 2000 p. 8.
103.   Robert Conquest: *Reflections on a Ravaged Century*, New York: Norton, 2000, p.44.
104.   Quoted in David Horowitz: *The Politics of Bad Faith*, New York: Free Press, 1998, p.28.
105.   Sheila Fitzpatrick: *Everyday Stalinism: Ordinary Life in Extraordinary Times*, New York: Oxford University Press, 2000.
106.   Aileen Kelly: "The Secret Sharer," *New York Review of Books*, March 9, 2000, pp. 33-34.
107.   Quoted in Conquest cited p.47.
108.   Jacob Weisberg: "Cold War Without End," *New York Times Magazine*, November 28, 1999, p.123.
109.   Ibid.
110.   Ibid., p. 157.
111.   "Patriotic Communists" [letter] *New York Times Book Review*, July 18, 1999.
112.   For example: Harvey Klehr et al.: *The Secret World of American Communism*, New Haven, CT: Yale University Press, 1995; Allen Weinstein and Alexander Vassiliev: *The Haunted Wood*, New York: Random House 1999.
113.   Sam Tanenhaus: "The Red Scare," *New York Review of Books*, January 14, 1999, p.44.
114.   Weisberg, cited, p. 122.

Part 1

American Society and the Discontents of Postmodernity

1

Godfather II: The New American Tragedy

Sitting in the movie theatre in downtown Boston, I am surrounded by a largely youthful audience that has respectfully and expectantly gathered to pay homage to the latest American culture hero, the young Godfather. Such unflagging attention to an almost four-hour movie is in itself remarkable, though no more than the degree of vocally expressed identification with its main protagonist. The audience — many student types, the shabbily and well dressed, blacks and whites, young couples, and even families with small children — love every minute of it. They cheer and applaud often at the spectacular displays of brutality and on the occasions when Michael Corleone frustrates his enemies, including the representatives of law and order. As I watch the movie I try to decide what makes it so exceptionally offensive to me and why it is so appealing to others in the audience. (In doing so I note uneasily the "elitism" implied in these questions as I am unwittingly cast into the role of the fastidious culture critic disassociating himself from the popcorn-chewing crowd; I quickly reassure myself by recalling my devotion to popcorn and my capacity to be entertained at times by violent movies.) Irresistibly the movie goads me into sociological reflections on the maladies of our society, something I succeeded in escaping when I saw *Godfather I*. I felt more charitable about it, despite the fact that all that is objectionable in the second installment was present in the first. Moreover, if my memory is correct, in the first *Godfather* there was actually more violence and more luridly displayed. Clearly the issue is not violence per se. Rather it is the skillful exploitation of the prevailing moral confusion and vacuum, through the idealization of something that should not be idealized.

Characteristically the movie begins by presenting Michael Corleone, the sad, careworn, youthful patriarch in an act of display-

3

ing his integrity. He rebuffs a corrupt Nevada senator who demands a payoff in exchange for a new gambling license. The demand is accompanied by ethnic slurs directed at Italian-Americans, and Corleone is thereby also cast into the role of the courageous ethnic underdog confronting the WASP establishment. This episode is followed by a dastardly attempt to assassinate Michael. Machine gun fire bursts through the window into his bedroom just after he gives a tender good-night kiss to his son. A good man's life is endangered by the forces of evil lurking outside in the darkness. The mood is set for the lengthy portrayal of young Corleone's tragic life and personality. We will see him as a lone fighter for justice, a crusader engaged in a nameless campaign designed to redress the balance between the powerless and the powerful, resourcefully battling the corruptions of society. If one did not know that he is a leading gangster it might be inferred from his demeanor that his intense preoccupations are directed at some uplifting scheme designed to improve the fate of mankind. His taciturnity, steady gaze, and serious facial expressions suggest great wisdom, powers of concentration and a contemplative disposition uniquely combined with the will and capacity to act. He has no trouble telling right from wrong and has the courage of his convictions. A young man, wise beyond his years, saddened by the spectacle of human folly, greed and dishonor, devoted to his family, fiercely loyal to his friends—such are the hallmarks of his personality.

There can be no mistake about it: Michael Corleone is intended to be a tragic hero. The tragic aspects of his personality are conveyed in part by his brooding looks and sad expression. Even martyrdom is hinted at—the possibility of being gunned down by rival gangsters. There is also the suggestion of undefined tensions and conflicts raging within him, as well as those which derive from being torn between the demands of his family and his work, between the grim necessity of violence and the imperatives of providing for his clan and devoted followers. It is implied that he resorts to violence without pleasure; either out of self defense (somewhat generously defined, to be sure) or in response to his moral code, perhaps excessively strict but admirable on the whole. Hedonism is alien to him; he is a puritan at heart. Not unlike the proverbial figures of early capitalism propelled by the Protestant Ethic, Michael Corleone keeps adding to his power and wealth in compliance with a mysterious categorical imperative. It is to prove himself, to earn grace, as it were. Never is he portrayed enjoying himself, his wealth, power or family. He is forever preoccupied with the next move, with extending his power, burdened by vast responsibilities. Although sex is remarkably absent, Corleone is the embodiment of potency, of conventional conceptions of virility and masculinity. Moreover, as distinct from the frivolousness and hedonism of the James Bond-type potency fantasies, Corleone has an ingratiating quality of seriousness, and sense of purpose.

The appeal of this movie is inseparable from the figure of Michael Corleone. His rise incorporates many of the traditional elements of the American success story. While the tragic dimensions of his personality are somewhat at odds with the cultural images of success, Corleone, Jr. has much in common with the stereotype of the unhappy rich, propagated for some time by pulp novels and the movies. As with the unhappy rich (who include prominently the celebrities of the entertainment world), his personal relationships suffer from his drive (for power rather than money). As in the case of other personifications of success, achievement does not lead to contentment but to the endless spiral of more of the same. Yet another element in the tragedy of Corleone is the heavy price exacted by his commitment to traditional values which he upholds regardless of the means used and the consequences.

Michael Corleone also fits another venerable Hollywood stereotype, that of the strong, silent, physically attractive, controlled, superbly self-reliant man who occasionally erupts into stormy passion. Women and sex are not particularly important for him; what matters is his "work," his sense of duty, his commitment to higher purposes (never clearly spelled out but constantly hinted at). Michael's appeal as a success symbol is further enhanced by his youthfulness. The enormous power and authority he wields came to him at an early age, and by this unusual combination of youth and power the film makers also paid tribute to the youth cult of our society. There is only one flaw in his conformity to the American success model: he is not exactly a self-made man: he is the second in the dynasty. The movie however obligingly plays up the self-made man motif in the flashbacks to *Godfather I*, the classic self-made man.

Another theme that has special appeal to the younger generations is Corleone's anti-establishment attitudes. He successfully defies the police, the courts, the Senate investigators, and politicians—presented by the makers of the movie as corrupt, impotent fools. (The audience cheered when at the Senate hearings the key witness against him changed his mind but listened in respectful silence to the phony, self-serving statement read by Corleone, defending his moral integrity and patriotism.)

Equally appealing to current sensibilities is Corleone's capacity to live up to his principles, to bridge the gap between theory and practice, talk and action. It is too bad, of course, if in the course of adhering to his principles he must also wipe out his brother (and many others) or beat up and send packing his wife. (She was incapable of making the sacrifices required by the marriage to a man of his responsibilities; she was a sentimental woman unable to grasp the importance of Michael's mission.)

It is not the display of violence per se that makes this movie so offensive. As noted before acts of violence are fewer than in *Godfather I* and they are more carefully rationed, rather than dumped in profusion on the audience. They do remain, nonetheless, important and are preceded by lengthy build-ups. Evidently the producers of the film have learned that too much unadulterated violence, like promiscuous sex, dulls rather than excites the senses. Hence they provide extensive narrative foreplay for each violent episode. What does of course remain offensive is the unthinking, matter-of-fact reliance on violence, the supreme lack of empathy toward the infliction of pain, and the indifference toward the taking of human lives.

What I found most unappealing about the movie was the moral confusion it creates by elevating to the status of tragic hero the ruthless hoodlum and presenting him as a sympathetic character. This is accomplished by diverting attention from the basic facts of life, namely that it is built on, and is devoted to, force, fraud, and brutality. The film does glamorize such a way of life by the personification of the outlaw as wise, thoughtful, good looking, and just and by portraying all his amoral activities as motivated by either self-defense or such laudable principles as loyalty to tradition, family, friends and "business associates."

The current state of American society and culture help to understand the success of *Godfather II*. Its producers have shrewdly capitalized on a variety of prevailing discontents. They succeeded in blending the latter with some of the more timeless appeals of violence, excitement and the genre of the family saga. The movie appeals to American audiences for many reasons. First, it presents a well-ordered (if at times violent) world in which the protagonists have no doubt about right and wrong and are able to punish the bad and reward the good. It is a world pervaded by traditional values which provide meaningful guidance for everyday behavior. Strong family ties prevail, there is no confusion about sex roles, systems of super- and subordination are clear cut, hierarchies well defined. The struggle for survival and success is intense but the resourceful and courageous manage to rise to the top. *Godfather II* symbolizes the successful solution of the problem of powerlessness and anonymity in modern society; he is totally autonomous, his own master, above the law and the maker of his own laws; at once a rugged individualist and part of a group and subculture, heir to a rich ethnic tradition. The audience has no difficulty in wishfully identifying with Michael Corleone: young, handsome, determined, in total control of his life, willing to take risks (which are not imposed but willingly taken on—an important distinction made by Hans Speier, the sociologist). He lives dangerously but avoids the deadening, unrewarding routines of modern existence. What is particularly appealing about his power is the effortless, informal way in which it is exercised. Literally at the flick of his fingers heads roll, fortunes change hands, crimes are obliterated, properties are transferred, territories staked out, politicians become puppets. Successfully challenging the Establishment, firmly anchored in a network of family loyalties and commitments, surrounded by faithful (if somewhat robot-like) retainers, having at his disposal all the wealth anyone can dream of—such is the new tragic hero of popular culture.

Godfather II is not an ordinary romanticized story of gang violence. It is rather an apotheosis of the obsession with power and its ruthless and successful exercise entwined with the nostalgia for strong family ties and a simpler way of life guided by traditional values. The success of the movie is a measure of the frustrations and moral bewilderment that pervades the life of so many Americans today.[1]

Note

1. The movie dealt with in this essay was not the only expression of the romanticization of the Mafia and the associated moral confusion. The book *A Man of Honor: An Autobiography of a Godfather* (1983) by Joseph Bonano and the associated publicity reflected the same attitudes. As a critic wrote "With the gratefully acknowledged

help of the ghost [writer], his editor and lawyer Bonano lies his way through the book in a sentimental yet wily manner... There is nothing there but good feelings and high ideals, nobles motives... *A Man of Honor* is mendacious work of disinformation designed to improve the public image of gangsters... the New York publishers, Simon & Schuster ...acclaim Joe Bonano as one of 'the famous and powerful man in that shadowy and fascinating world (which) represented an expression of the deepest ethnic roots of the Sicilian people...in which loyalty, honor and family ties were paramont.' Bonano thanked Michael Korda of the same publisher "'for recognizing the true me.'" [Stephen Vizinczey: "Honor Mafia Style" in *Truth and Lies in Literature*, London: Hamish Hamilton 1986, pp. 118,120,121.]

2

American Sociology and the
Collapse of Communism

The closing decade of this century, as it coincides with the disintegration of most communist systems, is a good time to reflect on the state of the social sciences in the United States and sociology in particular. These are turbulent times and it is appropriate to ask: What has sociology contributed to their understanding, or to anticipating both the disasters and the unexpected, though welcome, changes?

Since sociology had little to say about communist systems, upon their collapse one is prompted to ask why this was the case and what this indifference suggests about the discipline? Why had so many social scientists missed the opportunity to examine the major and monumental experiment in social engineering that the communist systems had attempted? Why were they not attracted to the possibility of conducting case studies on the connection between social theory (such as Marxism) and political practice? Why were they not anxious to examine the relevance of Western social theories for the experiment? Why had they no appetite for comparing the two outstanding bloodbaths of the century and the conditions that made them possible, the Nazi campaigns of extermination and the mass murders associated with Stalin? And finally, why are they still reluctant to embark on inquiries into the implications of the collapse of these systems for existing theories of society and human nature? (It should be noted here that this lack of interest was not confined to American sociologists.)

To be sure there were some exceptions. John Lewis Gillin, a former president of the American Sociological Society who has been described as "one of the leading authorities on penology in the United States," toured the Soviet Union in the early 1930s and visited some model prisons. He reported on his return: "In accordance with the spirit of the revolution the terms current in capitalistic penology are discarded [in the Soviet Union]. There are no 'crimes.' There is no 'punishment' only measures of social defense."

More recently C. Wright Mills was deeply impressed by the authenticity of the Cuban revolution. He described the descent from the mountains of a handful of guerillas led by Fidel Castro in reverently religious tones. His favorable view of Castro was reassuringly confirmed, during his visit, by Castro's familiarity with his own book, *The Power Elite*. Peter Worsley, an English sociologist writing of Mao's China, was delighted by "the Chinese attempt to transform human values and personal relationships at the level of everyday life, to challenge assumptions that some form of class system is inevitable that the attractiveness of material gratifications must, in the end, reassert itself."

If such are the conclusions reached by some distinguished sociologists, perhaps it has been for the better that not more of them have aspired to exploring and understanding communist societies. I would argue that the long-standing reluctance of American sociology to involve itself with the study of communist systems is a reflection of other problems as well. These problems, characteristic of the discipline as practiced in the United States, include overspecialization, lack of comparative interests, and ignorance of history.

Granted, since American sociology has always shown a resolute indifference toward communist systems their collapse could not be expected to have much impact on either its theories or practices. Anybody seeking greater understanding of communist social systems or institutions would have turned in vain to sociology— Raymond Bauer, Kent Geiger, Mark Field, Alex Inkeles, Barrington Moore, Jr., Walter O'Connor, and the present author are the exceptions. The vast output of American sociologists since the Second World War sheds little light on the nature of these societies.

The language barrier and difficulties of conducting proper empirical inquiries have often been cited as impediments to studying communist societies. While this may be true, it is only part of the explanation. The larger truth is that the vast majority of American sociologists were simply uninterested in communist systems, an attitude that was part of a larger body of indifference toward societies outside the United States and of a corresponding reluctance to undertake comparative studies. A social critical impulse, becoming more intense since the 1960s, strengthened the preoccupation with all things American. Comparing American society to others would have undermined the certainty—a novel form of ethnocentrism—that the United States is a uniquely deformed, exceptionally irrational, corrupt, and unjust society.

Such beliefs could not survive the comparative scrutiny of the specifics of social arrangements elsewhere. They can only thrive as long as little is known about other societies. Comparative studies have the potential to deprive critically inclined social scientists of their belief in the superiority or preferability of social systems that differ from the Western democratic-capitalist variety of which the United States is an example. Should the critic of American society harbor suspicions that the alternatives may not be preferable, he will choose not to look at them too closely, if at all. It is quite likely that many social scientists of vaguely leftist persuasion have been aware for some time that all was not well with the communist utopias but were not anxious to learn more of their defects, of their resounding failures to reach their professed goals.

Only the most incurable optimist would claim that the social sciences, and sociology in particular, have made spectacular progress in the last few decades either in uncovering new explanations of human behavior or theories of social organizations. It would be similarly difficult to assert that they have made much tangible contribution to the alleviation of human misery, or the discernible improvement of social institutions.

There are two general explanations of this state of affairs. One has to do with the inherent limits of the social scientific explanations and predictions of human behavior. No need here to go into much detail. The problem of the multitude of variables shaping human attitudes and actions and the inextricable connections and interactions between environment and heredity is all too familiar. If that were not enough, in the last quarter century a new set of obstacles emerged that hinders and circumscribes the social scientific enterprise in the form of certain values, biases, ideological, political and, of late, even institutional restraints on what the social sciences can explore and reveal. These ideological constraints discourage, and often prohibit outright, any inquiry into certain topics or the drawing of certain conclusions from the research that has been undertaken. They also inhibit the raising of significant questions—the latter an age-old problem in American sociology where professional respectability has often been assured by painstaking, methodologically unassailable studies of relatively trivial and "safe" topics, by "knowing more about less and less."

This state of affairs has arisen not only as a result of the prestige that is accorded to scientific, or putatively scientific, usually meaning quantitative, methodology, but also because many social scientists have mistakenly identified the avoidance of certain topics with an idealistic disposition toward the social world, with a commitment to the improvement of society and social justice. The current, constricted state of the social scientific enterprise is also made acceptable by the fact that rewards continue to flow to work that fails to address certain key issues of social life; much pedestrian research has been institutionalized and one can make a relatively good living out of it at the universities.

Sociology and anthropology have been especially damaged by the political-ideological upheavals and pressures of recent times—more so than economics, political science, or psychology. Perhaps this should be no cause for surprise. Given its uncertain professional-intellectual identity, sociology would be more prone to succumb to outside pressures. After an initial period of optimism that had inspired its founding fathers, sociology has been embroiled in self-doubt and identity crises through much of its existence. Starting with grandiose hopes and aspirations to establish laws of social existence and to parallel the development of the natural sciences, sociology has become a field of inquiry often criticized for belaboring the obvious in barely accessible language, or for involvement with matters of comic triviality.

That such critiques remain valid even today, becomes clear from a brief look at the list of the titles of papers presented at the Eighty-Sixth Annual Meeting of the American Sociological Association in 1991. They include such items as: "Hobbies as marginal leisure: The case of barber shop singing;" "Between gender differences in semantic differential profile of emotion lexicon;" "A psychostructural matrix of individuals' orientation toward action;" "A dialectic interpretation of ethnographic data on post-earthquake recovery;" "Activating gender dynamics in organizational task groups;" and others similarly illuminating. Characteristic of trends in present-day sociology, one paper asked (in its title): "Should and can a white, heterosexual, middle class man teach students about social inequality and oppression?" Marxism remained very much on the agenda as in the papers addressing "Issues and trends in Marxist therapy" and "Marxist considerations of health care."

From its earliest days, sociology in the United States has been intertwined with various idealistic, social engineering impulses. People entered sociology to do good, to use their knowledge for social reform, to improve city life, reduce crime, unemployment, marital instability, and more recently, to launch assaults on racial, ethnic, or gender discrimination and inequality. Also, from its early days, American sociology was resolutely focused on American society to the neglect of all others. Comparative studies were rare, curiosity about other social systems virtually nonexistent.

Anthropology, of course, had a different tradition. For obvious reasons, it could not make American society its major preoccupation. But the social-critical, adversarial strain that surfaced and intensified during the last quarter century also had roots in anthropology although they differed from those of sociology. The social-critical bent in anthropology was nurtured by the sympathetic interest in small, pre-literate societies, which were generally perceived to be morally and culturally superior to large-scale, modern, impersonal, urban-industrial societies, more hospitable to human needs. Most recently, anthropologists would also contrast the environmental destructiveness of modern industrial societies with the absence of such damage on the part of the small, pre-literate ones. That population size has more to do with this difference than an inherent respect for the physical environment is rarely noted. If sociology has been led to an adversarial disposition by a future-oriented search for a better world, anthropology moved to a similar posture by veneration of the past and the sense of loss experienced through modernization. Thus many of those attracted to sociology or anthropology share a sense of discomfort with the society they live in, though for different reasons.

The politicization of sociology in the last quarter century intensified some of the attributes the discipline had from its earlier days. This process had three major sources and took three corresponding expressions: (1) an ethnic-racial consciousness-level raising; (2) feminist-sociology which over the last decade or so has been attracting a growing number of radical feminists who seek to use it for feminist consciousness-level raising and to confirm their notions of victimization and entitlement; (3) versions of neo-Marxism which often combined with feminism and the racial-ethnic preoccupation. All three tendencies were in turn nurtured and bolstered by a profound sense of alienation, a hostility toward dominant American institutions and values as they existed before the 1960s.

In the 1970s and 1980s, attributions and elaborations of racism and sexism became the predominant critique of American society, a new basis for the fundamental rejection of the social system. Increasingly these attitudes came to be treated as givens and in little need of empirical proof. Any denial that one may entertain regarding such attitudes came to be treated as ipso facto proof that one was infected with them. A selective social and cultural determinism, refusal to weigh genetic factors in social explanation, the systematic avoidance of topics that conflict with prevailing left-of-center conventional wisdom, and a growing hostility toward Western cultural values, traditions, and social-economic systems were joined to the three trends.

Attacks on objectivity since the 1960s have also become routine. As the social sciences, and sociology in particular, became the tools of a political struggle and not just instruments of a moderate agenda of social reform, impartiality, or even the effort at impartiality, came to be derided and rejected. The attacks on objectivity have been legitimated since the 1960s by the supposedly lofty and pressing objectives sociology was to pursue: liberation of every kind, social justice, community building, demolishing prejudice and inequality, doing away with exploitation and alienation, raising levels of consciousness, and so on. Given such goals it became easy to dismiss detached data gathering and analysis, or intellectual curiosity for its own sake, as acceptable justification for the sociological enterprise. Theory building too was often dismissed as abstract, academic, and irrelevant to the urgent political tasks of the day. Just as buildings were occupied on the campuses during the 1960s (and since then) under the slogan "no business as usual" so the traditional tasks and concerns of sociology were preempted by the alleged urgency of improving society through radical change. At the same time, and paradoxically so, many academic intellectuals began to turn inward, embracing an ivory tower existence of haughty alienation in the face of political trends outside academia that were far from congenial. One such trend was prolonged Republican control of the American presidency; another was the collapse of communist states and the associated discrediting of Marxism-Leninism wherever the attempt had been made to use its theories as a guide to social engineering or reconstruction.

The gradual institutionalization of the political-ideological constraints that hinder sociology's ability to raise important questions and to give truthful answers is among the most troublesome aspects of academic and intellectual life at the present time. Few today would heed Barrington Moore's advice of over three decades ago:

> The best results emerge from the confrontation of the evidence with a wide variety of ideas, often contradictory ones, acquired in the course of broad reading and some experience of men and affairs. Sometimes the most important discoveries may occur as a consequence of the temporary block produced by an inconvenient fact which forces the investigator to abandon previously accepted explanations.

There is little interest today in inconvenient facts, broad reading, or in abandoning previously accepted explanations. Instead new conventional wisdoms and orthodoxies flourish. For example, while it may be acceptable, indeed fashionable to conduct research on the homeless and on their numbers, when one study found their numbers to be lower than the advocates of the homeless deemed appropriate, the research was attacked and the principal investigator, Peter Rossi, vilified. Likewise, while it has been the moral and professional obligation of all social scientists to support unhesitatingly affirmative action, any attempt at evaluating the actual results of such policies and programs has been carefully avoided; results of these policies appear to be one of the growing number of taboo topics. Policy research, widely practiced during these years, had nothing to say about this matter. Another question that has received no scrutiny is why some minorities, such as Asians (usually included in the protected victim categories), perform extremely well in school and at the university without benefit of role models, while blacks' and Hispanics' greater difficulties are ascribed to a lack of such models.

Few sociologists would venture on an empirical study of the taken-for-granted link between role models, self-esteem, and academic performance, let alone one between self-esteem, collective pride, and academic achievement. The alleged link between group pride and academic achievement remains a major, if unexamined, justification for multicultural studies, a movement that has been sweeping the country since the late 1980s. Such studies have invariably been justified by the argument that, say, learning about the glories of African empires of the past will raise the collective self-esteem of black inner-city teenagers and, in turn, such feelings will translate into improved academic performance.

Few social scientists would wish to become immersed in a close examination of such matters since the findings may call into question the role model/self-esteem theory of learning, new pillars of conventional wisdom in higher education. Sociologists have not been anxious to ask why crime rates increased dramatically during the 1960s and 1970s, at a time when economic and employment opportunities were generally improving. Likewise, only the most intrepid or foolhardy social scientists would attempt to investigate genetic influences on the asymmetrical occupational preferences, aspirations, and attainments of men and women. Besides careful avoidance of such topics, adoption of certain theoretical perspectives and premises also helps to assure political correctness in sociological research. Selective determinism is one theoretical perspective. I was first struck by the phenomenon twenty years ago. Let the reader judge how well my observations made then have stood the test of time:

> Today sociological determinism is generously but selectively applied to excuse, mitigate or condemn different forms of behavior or even the same behavior on the part of different people or groups. There is, for example, an increasing tendency among people of liberal persuasion to view convicted criminals as victims of the system (sometimes even as political prisoners), or extend a measure of sympathy and understanding to those who undertake politically motivated attacks on policemen.
>
> Such acts are seen as reflections of deep frustration with an unresponsive political system that allows little if any choice... social determinism ... becomes suspended when judging the behavior of . groups, such as the military brass, FBI agents, policemen, politicians, corporation executives, Southern "rednecks.". . . In short the bad guys have a choice but the good ones don't... A plausible victim-aggressor scheme needs a device such as selective determinism that relieves some groups of responsibility for their actions but not others.

Since these lines were written, selective determinism has become even more explicit and institutionalized. The major victim groups (those without a choice, and hence without responsibility for their actions and attitudes) include not only ethnic minorities such as blacks, Hispanics, and all women (regardless of their education, occupation, and income), but also homosexuals and lesbians as well as those afflicted with AIDS. Poor whites are not included, nor are orphans, survivors of Nazi or Soviet concentration camps, or other highly patterned traumatic experiences, nor are those suffering from various physical ailments, other than AIDS.

Richard Felson's concept of "blame analysis" further illuminates the phenomenon of selective determinism and its influence on sociological theory and research:

> In blame analysis a theory or explanation is evaluated according to the identity or image it projects for certain groups. Since there is a desire among many sociologists to protect groups who are identified as victims, there is a tendency for theories to be rejected unless they absolve the protected group of any blame. Blame analysis leads one to avoid explanations that posit any causal role for poor people, or groups that are more likely to be poor .... They reject the possibility that discrimination in previous generations can affect the present culture of the group which in turn affects the behavior of group members.... Criminals of lower socioeconomic status are victims of society-the victims of labeling and lack of opportunity, blaming criminal offenders automatically reduces the blame attributed to society-the truly guilty party.... The claim that violence reflects grievances is fine until the victim of aggression is a member of a protected group.... Those who are opposed to homosexuality are called "homophobic." This label implies that those who object to homosexuality have a pathological fear of homosexuals. Now it is the anti-homosexuals, not the homosexuals who have an illness. This suggests that for some sociologists the issue is blame, and not the medical model. They have no objection to the medical model when it is used to stigmatize a group with whom they have a grievance... the central defensive strategy in blame analysis is to focus on external factors and to ignore internal factors in explaining the behavior of the protected groups... [whereas] the offensive strategy in blame analysis is to use internal rather than external variables to explain the behavior of the oppressor.

The latter strategy, needless to say, makes it easier to assign blame. The whole issue of how to define the underdog or victim groups has assumed a new virulence as curricular innovations and reforms—women studies, black, Hispanic, gay, and multicultural studies—seek to address, assist, and energize these groups in their incarnation as victims of society, of an unjust social order. As a recent article noted, in such programs "activist faculty have a ready body of potentially disaffected students—who have been taught to see the world as being divided between oppressors and victims." Thus a professor of Afro-American Studies at the University of Massachusetts at Amherst referred to the May 1992 riots as the beginning of "the liberation of Los Angeles" and described the rioters as "our warriors."

The varieties of selectivity found in the social sciences, especially sociology, include not only selective determinism but selectivity in understanding, empathy, and sensitivity. The new canons of academic rectitude, which have come to permeate the social sciences, demand that the putative victim groups' feelings and perceptions of reality be respected even at the cost of stifling intellectual discourse and the free exchange of ideas. Other groups can be denounced with total impunity; college administrators and regulators of harassment and insensitivity are not concerned with the sensitivity of white males, heterosexuals, WASPs, or conservatives of any color, sex, race, or sexual persuasion.

A new trend in selective determinism also made its appearance in definitions of politically correct violence. This issue was addressed by social psychologist Hans Toch who wrote, "The researcher-advocates are not interested in competing victimization experiences, such as spousal violence that features assaults on husbands by wives [they have their] favorite type of aggressors ... aggressing against the type of victims on whose behalf they wished to mobilize concern." The same applies to discussions of incidents of arson, looting, and indiscriminate violence (such as erupted in Los Angeles in May 1992). Such activities are said to be ways of "sending messages," of expressing frustrations that should be understood and sympathized with by all decent human beings.

While selective victimization along the lines noted remains a major theme and perspective in the social sciences (and in much of public discourse), a counter-trend has appeared that holds the promise of making us all victims entitled to compensation of some kind. The new victims are all those with insufficiently happy childhoods now being offered a chance to enlist in the ranks of already certified victims. It is, in the words of a critic, a movement that "melodramatically refuses to distinguish among levels of suffering or victimization. When a recovery expert suggests that childhood is a holocaust, the implication is that there is no real difference between growing up in an American family and surviving a concentration camp." To be sure this new trend is more prominent in psychology and psychotherapy than in sociology. David Rieff has written about it:

> Imagine a country in which millions of apparently successful people ... have come to believe fervently that they are really lost souls, a country where countless adults allude matter-of-factly to their "inner children" who, they say, lie wounded and in desperate need of relief.... Imagine the celebrities and opinion-makers among these people talking nightly on TV ... about their victimization ... about their addictions and childhood persecutions.
>
> In this country it is taken for granted that no blame for addictions or dependencies can be assigned to those who exhibit them. Terms such as "character," "weakness," and "individual responsibility" are no longer deemed appropriate.
>
> The recovery writers insist that nearly everyone in the United States has been the victim of some instance of child abuse ... Steven Farmer writes in his book *Adult*

Children Of Abusive Parents: "No matter how abuse is defined or what other people think, you are the ultimate judge: If you think you were abused, you were. If you are not sure, you probably were."

By popularizing social and cultural determinism, sociology has contributed to popular acceptance of these schemes of victimization. It is also true, though, that there has been a widespread cultural receptivity toward such determinism and especially its selective varieties, which, paradoxically, combine an increasingly shrill individualism with the claims of victimization, entitlement, and social-cultural responsibility for all personal failures and problems. Sociologists live and work in a society where expectations of personal success, fulfillment, happiness, and self-realization are high and yet in that same society many people seem to believe that the individual is less and less in control of his fate, less and less responsible for his happiness or unhappiness.

The current preoccupations and blinders of American sociology, sampled above, further add to the explanation of why its practitioners have shied away from the study of communist systems including the causes of their collapse. Sociology reflects what might be called a collectivized version of the preoccupation with the self, in this case, with American society, things American and familiar (sociologists, as many of their students, tend to equate the familiar with the relevant and important).

One might also suspect that for my colleagues positioned on the left of the political spectrum the collapse of communism has not necessarily been an altogether welcome development. There are several reasons for this. Perhaps the most important one being that this collapse in some way vindicates the Western, capitalist, and political systems such people dislike. By ending superpower rivalry, the collapse has strengthened the influence of the United States in global affairs—an influence those on the left do not much care for, to say the least. Some are likely to feel that even if the Soviet Union was not an overly attractive social system, at least it supported, economically and militarily, some third world countries they favored: Nicaragua (before the 1990 elections), Cuba, Vietnam, and other seemingly more genuinely socialist or revolutionary states than the Soviet Union itself.

Some American sociologists even mourn the passing of communist systems, believing—despite massive and mounting evidence to the contrary—that these systems took good care of their people. Thus Harriet Gross of the University of Illinois was irritated with all the self-righteous, sanctimonious celebration of the "victory of capitalism over communism" and reminded her readers of the accomplishments of these systems: "These governments ... constructed massive social service delivery systems that eliminated illiteracy, petty street crime, prostitution and a myriad of other social cancers ... Though disadvantaged in consumer gadgetry, their populations are well educated and healthy."

Such sentiments further illuminate American sociologists's unconcern with communist systems. While it is difficult to know how many share Harriet Gross's beliefs, it is safe to say that not many felt strongly critical toward such systems. As far as communist societies were concerned, these scholars were unmotivated by the critical impulses that had prompted them to expose the seamy sides of American life. At the same time, not many could be certain that if they did, in fact, direct their attention to communist societies their researches would demonstrate the inferiority of capitalist systems as compared to the putatively socialist ones. The prudent research strategy dictated avoidance of the topic altogether.

Perhaps even more fundamentally, many American sociologists share with many American intellectuals ambivalent feelings if not outright attraction toward the communist (or state socialist) systems of the past and the few that still survive. This ambivalence most likely rests on their inability to sever the link to the various fantasies about socialism and social justice Marxist socialism had inspired and promised. Richard Rorty's recent remarks may apply here:

> In the wake of the events of 1989 and 1991 it has become clear that American leftist intellectuals stand in need of a new political vocabulary. Visitors from post-revolutionary Eastern and Central Europe are going to stare at us incredulously if we continue to use the word "socialism" when we describe our political goals ... given the suffering they endured under regimes that called themselves Marxist, our Eastern European friends are likely to feel that Marxist rhetoric is no more respectable than Nazi rhetoric .... It is going to take a long period of readjustment for us Western leftist intellectuals to comprehend that the word "socialism" has been drained of force ... many of us are still, alas, on the lookout for a successor to Marxism ... we would be better off assuming ... that the best we can hope for is more of the same experimental, hit-or-miss, two-steps-forward-and-one-step-back reforms that have been taking place in the industrialized societies since the French Revolution.

Residual attraction of Marxism, and the associated attachment to the role of the righteous social critic many social scientists embrace, is not likely to vanish soon. As Irving Louis Horowitz has noted, "It is as if the sins of real men could not be permitted to tarnish the beatification of a disgraced ideology."

Sociology may well recover some of its potential and intellectual thrust, but at least three conditions must be met. First, sociology must regain its freedom to ask any important questions and to report findings that may offend the current politicized canons of propriety; it must be free to defy the reigning orthodoxies of the academic-intellectual community. Second, it must attract a wider range of people than is currently the case, including those who are inspired by genuine curiosity rather than by political-ideological agendas. Third, it must embark on a new course of comparative studies (taking advantage of the new freedom for research in the former communist states), that address some of the old, but still unresolved, important questions of the discipline and the social sciences.

References

Coleman, James. "On the Self-Suppression of Academic Freedom," Academic Questions, Winter 1990/9 1.

Hollander, Paul. "Sociology, Selective Determinism and the Rise Expectations," *American Sociologist*, November 1973.

_____. "Comparative Sociology in the United States and Why There is So Little of It," *Current Perspectives in Social Theory*. 2. JAI Press, 198, 1.

Horowitz, Irving Louis. "The Decomposition of Sociology," *Academic Questions,* Spring 1992.

Moore Jr., Barrington. "Strategy in Social Science," in Political Power and Social Theory. Cambridge, Mass.: Harvard University Press, 1958.

3

"Imagined Tyranny"?
Political Correctness Reconsidered

"How is it that our system of education, instead of merely being useless...is today
manufacturing outcasts and rebels?[1]
—Gustave Le Bon (1841-1931)

"Today political correctness...makes objections to group entitlements indecent."[2]
—Shelby Steele

Political correctness (PC) has emerged during the past decades as the most widespread form of institutionalized intolerance in American higher education—a development for which Herbert Marcuse, among others, deserves some credit, having popularized the idea of "repressive tolerance." PC is a phenomenon at once subtle—when an integral part of the climate of opinion, a taken-for-granted, self-evident rectitude—and crudely heavy-handed, when incorporated into "speech codes" and other regulations. It has been a powerful determinant of the public discourse on the campuses and a potent source of self-censorship, especially among the professorate.

The phenomena PC designates were with us well before the term was introduced and given wide currency. They originated in the 1960s and became pervasive in academic life during the 1970s and 1980s, until, finally, in the early 1990s they were labeled "PC" and began to attract media and public attention.[3] But a new look at PC is warranted for several reasons. The phenomenon has been durable but subject to conflicting interpretations. It had a substantial impact both on the quality of higher education and on the life of the mind in general. Of late, the reality and significance of PC itself have been disputed, despite its widely felt presence. Lastly, PC is no longer confined to its place of incubation, academia, but, as Robert Brustein observed, "spreads its tentacles. . . also into television, radio, journalism, childrearing, even the Academy Awards." Hilton Kramer believes that PC has "succeeded in changing the way books, ideas, and every intellectual and artistic endeavor are discussed and assessed."[4] I will attempt to suggest explanations[5] for the persistence of the phenomena PC has come to designate, a persistence that appears to be compatible with the denials of its very existence or significance.

Several paradoxes surround PC. Of late it has been widely condemned, but such condemnation, more often than not, applies only to its most extreme or lurid manifestations. Many critics of PC are unconcerned with, or actually approve of the beliefs and impulses that are at its core and propel it to the excesses of which they publicly disapprove. Since few in this society are willing to take a public stand against a broadly defined concept of free speech, to the extent that PC indisputably interferes with free expression it is condemned. There are, however, huge disagreements as to *what* constitutes such indisputable interference. And violation of free expression, even when regretfully acknowledged, is often "balanced" against other, allegedly "competing" values, as when student newspapers were destroyed by black students on the campuses of the University of Maryland and the University of Massachusetts at Amherst. At both, administrators responded by lamenting the conflict that the incidents supposedly brought to the fore between the value of free expression on the one hand and the feelings of black students on the other.[6]

While PC has become a form of conventional wisdom, an institutionalized pressure to conform to certain patterns of behavior and public expression, its roots lie in the rebellious, anti-authoritarian beliefs and attitudes of the late 1960s. Beliefs once unorthodox and iconoclastic have been turned into a prescriptive morality, with the eager support of various authorities, including the federal government, Congress, and college administrators. Unexpectedly, the colleges and universities—institutions supposedly dedicated to free thinking, expression, and intellectual debate—have become the most hospitable havens, the strongest bastions, of the orthodoxies and taboos for which PC has come to stand. It is paradoxical that many types of academic discrimination associated with PC are "typically promoted in the name of tolerance, pluralism, and diversity."[7] It is, finally, also paradoxical that, as one commentator put it, "the urge to conform should be so strong in the land of Emerson and Thoreau."[8]

Unfortunately, it has also been the land of demagogues, self-styled prophets, and do-it-yourself religions, a land of luxuriant receptivity to assorted fads and mass hysterias, and a society of sturdy individualists fearful of disapproval by their fellows and yearning to be loved by all.

The term "political correctness" has been the source and subject of considerable confusion. Its use, of course, invites the question "Whose notions of what is politically correct are we talking about?" While it is most often used to refer to left-liberal orthodoxies, there have been attempts to distinguish between "two PCs—the politically and the patriotically correct,"[9] in other words, between the PC of the left and the PC of the right. And, when someone claims to be a critic of PC, we do not always know whether he is critical of the phenomena the concept refers to or of the proposition that such phenomena exist. PC is a somewhat problematic concept also because of its origin in left-wing (Communist Party) jargon and because of the variety of its dimensions. It may be thought of as a climate of opinion, a set of values (and rules seeking to institutionalize and protect them), an outlook, an attitude, a complex of institutional policies, and a particular spirit of conformity, the last being perhaps the most important and consequential.

In any event, it is important to be aware of the two closely related dimensions of PC: the procedural-institutional (embodied in academic policies, such as speech and harassment codes, sensitivity-training programs, preferential treatment of certain minorities, and the like) and the ideological, that is, the beliefs that inspire the policies and shape the climate of opinion. Much of the public discussion has focused on the former, more tangible aspects.

Agreement about the nature or precise definition of PC is further impeded by the disfiguring of language that PC has brought about, in exactly the spirit Orwell identified in his analysis of political propaganda—"as if the altered nomenclature had some indescribable power to abolish the condition by renaming it."[10] PC has spawned a terminology of its own, new and highly imprecise notions (e.g., "heterosexism," "ableism," "lookism") and has altered the meaning of existing words, for example, and most commonly, that of "racism" and "diversity."[11] The growth of imprecise jargon, occasionally combined with religious symbolism, in academic life was observed by Adam Ulam as early as the close of the 1960's:

Of all the forms of addiction, the one to platitudes may yet prove the most insidious...hazy images take the place of concrete objects... When an institution, be it a university or a corporation, is called upon to acknowledge that it is elitist, or racist, or sexist... it is obviously called upon to confess that it is in a state of sin and only after such an admission can penance begin.[12]

Similar assumptions underlie the varieties of sensitivity training—an important devise for administering PC, which calls upon individuals to acknowledge their racism and other similar flaws.

PC has been a product and attribute of what several commentators, including the present one, have called the adversary culture; except for its institutional-policy implications, PC is virtually identical with it. The essence of PC has been "the drive to cast all matters of culture and intellect in political terms."[13] That is to say, the rise and influence of PC is inseparable from what is sometimes called a "tramsformationist" view, one that sees education as a device for bringing about those fundamental changes in American society that began in the late 1960s but remained incomplete. In this view, which is at the root of PC, "Teachers should become 'engaged and transformative intellectuals' as schools are transformed into 'agencies for reconstructing and transforming the dominant status quo culture.'" Or, as a major theorist of PC, Frank Lentricchia, put it, "The professor's task now becomes helping students spot, confront, and work against the political horrors of one's time" (as defined by their PC teachers). As early as 1976, English professor Richard Ohmann recommended that faculty "teach politically with revolution as our end."[14] Remarkably enough, such candid avowals of the political, or politically correct, mission of higher education have been compatible with the continued denials of the existence of PC.

It is important to bear in mind, as the social psychologist Hans Toch pointed out, that "PC is not a coherent system of thought but a disjointed set of verities."[15] Thus, as will become apparent in what follows, PC is compatible both with highly relativistic positions (as in "celebrating diversity," or in the rejection of the idea that there can be objectivity in scholarship) *and* with highly absolutist ones (*e.g.,* when a wide range of attitudes or beliefs is unequivocally condemned and proscribed, or when unhesitating value judgments are made of particular political or economic arrangements or selected cultural beliefs). Thus it would be a grave error to associate PC with an open-minded embrace of "diversity," or *genuine* diversity, since

PC seeks to encourage, and if necessary enforce, uniformity of belief and public expression.

Richard Bernstein, of *The New York Times,* described PC, in one of the early discussions of it, as:

a large body of belief in academia and elsewhere that a cluster of opinions about race, ecology, feminism, culture and foreign policy defines a kind of "correct" attitude toward the problems of the world, a sort of unofficial ideology of the university.[16]

For William Phillips:

it is a loose but useful term denoting a wide movement with many facets. . . essentially a new left configuration. It includes extreme and radical feminist theories, gay and lesbian liberation studies and activities, ideas stemming from the deconstructionists, neo-Marxists, and remnants of old, revolutionary postures.[17]

According to Charles Sykes:

Political correctness turns out to be a form of the larger transformation of society reflected in the ascendancy of psychological over political terminology. What began as the attempt to politicize psychology (and psychologize politics) had led to... the emergence of a new form of therapeutic politics.[18]

Morris Dickstein called it:

a form of groupthink fueled by paranoia and demonology imposed by political or social intimidation. . . [It] is the opposite of pluralism which presupposes that your opponent may actually have something to say and every right to say it. PC's emphasis on victim groups is a calcification of the political sympathies of the sixties into a repressive orthodoxy.... [It] is an attempt to institutionalize virtue, a way of legislating enlightenment.[19]

According to an English commentator, "The phrase refers to attempts. . . to make certain 'sensitive' ideas and words 'off-limits.'"[20] For Glenn Loury, too, PC is "an implicit social convention of restraint on public expression, operating within a given community."[21]

Seymour Martin Lipset regards PC as "the *latest* expression of moralism" in American social history.[22] Russell Baker found the roots of PC's generalized spirit of intolerance deep in American history:

The Puritan character has ever since been willing to put restraints on freedoms when the goal, which in more modern times tends to be moral uplift, requires it. It is the belief in moral uplift that creates the PC doctrine. It aims at nothing less than the perfecting of mankind.

Its goal is to improve the moral nature of the country by ridding the national mind of evil ways of thinking. It assumes that the national mind can be purified by revising the vocabulary with which its thinking is expressed.[23]

While it may well be that there have always been forms of PC associated with different types of politicized morality, the recent variety has been more widespread and consequential than those of the past. Its sources today, unlike former times, include federal as well as state legislation and the judiciary, much of the media, and not just an occasional college president or board of trustees. Especially distinctive and ominous is the fact that it has received the most vigorous support *inside,* not outside, the academic world, whereas even during the heydays of McCarthyism, defenders of the Senator were far more likely to be ostracized by their colleagues than those who were targeted by him.[24] The attempt to intimidate faculties and create campus conformity's from the outside were then quite unsuccessful. By contrast, today many aspects of PC go unchallenged, indeed are supported with docility or alacrity by faculties and college administrations across the country.

While the bulk of PC has to do with (the "correct") ideas regarding race, sex, ethnicity, and sexual orientation, PC also entails beliefs about world history and the world outside the United States. It radiates an unmistakable anti-Western thrust far broader in its sweep than specific critiques of American social institutions and injustices. John Patrick Diggins, among others, noted:

> To be PC was to denounce Western culture from the top down until one found enclaves of third world ethnics in the ghettos of industrial society... The spectacle of PC had no parallel in previous Lefts, whose heroes (Marx, Trotsky, Gramsci) believed in the value of classical education and the future of Western civilization.[25]

These anti-Western themes led to bizarre double standards. Robert Hughes wrote:

> The more politically correct... felt it was wrong to criticize a Muslim country, no matter what it did.... In America, such folk knew it was the height of sexist impropriety to refer to a young female as a "girl" instead of a "woman." In Tehran, however, it was more or less OK for... theocratic bigots to insist on the chador... and to murder novelists as state policy. Oppression is what we do in the West. What they do in the Middle East is "their culture."[26]

PC may descend from its lofty concerns with the historic injustices of Western civilization to seemingly trivial issues of daily life, such as the character of signs on public lavatories, which may perpetuate sexist stereotypes. At the University of California in Santa

Cruz there was prolonged and heated public debate following the discovery (by a "self described feminist") that an image of a "petite, passive woman in a dress" was juxtaposed to "an aggressive, broad shouldered man in pants." We were not informed how it was determined that the male image was "aggressive," and the female's "passive" but demands for its removal were insistent.[27]

While, for the reasons noted above, a somewhat problematic concept, PC has become a clearly identifiable and entrenched presence on campuses and well established in school systems as well.

II

Given the large constituency that shared the premises of PC and had an interest—ideological or material/existential—in its enforcement, it is not surprising that critiques of PC came under attack. Efforts to dismiss or trivialize the phenomenon have been especially widespread in the last two to three years.

The aspect of PC that has most often and most heatedly been denied is its restraint of free expression. The reality of the PC phenomenon, on the other hand, is attested to not only by teachers and students on the campuses, but even by visitors from abroad, people familiar with the totalitarian equivalents of PC, intellectuals from the former Soviet Union. They were reported to "return dismayed by... 'political correctness,' militant feminism, self-conscious egalitarianism, and other manifestations of what they identify with the very intellectual conformity and intolerance that they spent their lives fighting against."[28]

Critics inclined to question the existence of PC have, almost from the beginning, misrepresented it and the phenomena it sought to encompass. A *New York Times* article referred to it as "a grab-bag term used to indict multiculturalism, militant feminism, radical literary theory and everything academic conservatives love to hate."[29] A review, also in the *Times,* portrayed the conflict over PC as one between radicals who wish to broaden the curriculum and traditionalists who do not.[30]

Those denying that there is such a thing as PC usually make two claims. One is that reports of its manifestations are based on unreliable, anecdotal evidence, with which conservatives and rightwingers vastly exaggerate the phenomenon. The other is that the purpose of such exaggerations has been to divert attention from the "real problems" of the campuses and society as a whole. Both arguments tend to be made by people who basically approve of the values and beliefs PC seeks to institutionalize.

Mr. Joel Conarroe, president of the Guggenheim Foundation, wrote:

> The enemies of PC score their points by recycling a handful of supposedly shocking anecdotes about alleged close-mindedness on a few purportedly radicalized campuses.[31]

Mr. Conarroe's difficulty in finding substantial amounts of PC, of the kind he was willing to repudiate, was evidently rooted in his understanding of what PC is. For him, PC means that one is willing "to protest demeaning language or ideas" or feels "compelled to speak out against intolerance." It also means being "politically sensitive." These are all good things, of course, and, if that is all PC amounts to, then, no matter how much there is of it, it need not invite disapproval. On the other hand, Mr. Conarroe sees the use made of PC by reactionaries as "a lethal weapon for silencing anyone whose ideas you don't like." Mr. Conarroe cannot understand why people get "worked up" about these well-meaning attempts to create an "academic etiquette." He presumably feels that, even when a few mistakes are made, they are made by people whose heart is in the right place. He has apparently also convinced himself, thus reversing current patterns of victimization, that it is the upholders of PC who are victimized by the new witch hunters!

Barbara Ehrenreich, another critic of the preoccupation with PC, wrote:

> PC culture. . . is a limited phenomenon. The major problems of American campuses are racial and sexual harassment, alcoholism and the anti-intellectualism of young white Republican males.

Elsewhere she charged that "the American right has put multiculturalism in the place of the international Communist conspiracy as its evil 'all-powerful ideological enemy.'"[32]

Velina Hasu Houston, a feminist writer, in fact detected conspiratorial intent:

> I consider "political correctness" to be a term created by the European American far right in order to maintain its position of power and privilege in this society, a position achieved by a long legacy of racial and sexual oppression.[33]

And in an editorial titled "Time to Retire a Cliché—'Politically Correct'—Shopworn and Blinding," Brent Staples weighed in for *The New York Times:*

In the 1980s, right-wing ideologues stripped the term of irony and began using "political correctness" to describe what they saw as a systematic effort by liberals to crush free and open discourse. But this was an *imagined tyranny*, dreamed up just as right-wing politics reached its apex on campus and in the White House. Nevertheless "politically correct" caught on as a term of derision, aimed at discrediting ideas associated with liberalism. The term is now invoked at every turn: when racial or sexual intolerance is called into question when someone advocates expanding the study of Western culture beyond the classics; when people encounter ideas they don't like.[34]

If indeed "PC" is overused, it is in part because journalists like its snappiness, and because the concerns and criteria of the new political morality are often ill-defined. Dismissing PC as a serious problem (while deploring its occasional excesses) has also been characteristic of many middle-of-the-road, or putatively middle-of-the-road, academics who are apprehensive about being associated with the conservative critics of PC. Gerald Graff began his book on the "culture wars" thus:

If we believe what we have been reading lately, American higher education is in a disastrous state. As pictured in a stream of best sellers, commission reports, polemical articles, and editorials, the academic humanities in particular look like a once-respectable old neighborhood gone bad. The stately old buildings have been defaced with spray paint.., trash litters the ground, and an omnipresent thought police controls the turf. . .enforcing an intolerant code of political correctness on the terrorized inhabitants.[35]

On the basis of such an overdrawn picture Professor Graff succeeds in assuring himself and his readers that the dangers of PC have been greatly overstated. He is among those seeking to carve out a somewhat spurious middle ground, deploring on the one hand the excesses of PC, and, on the other, the "excesses" of those who criticize it.[36]

There are also those who, while definitely not sympathetic to PC, nonetheless feel compelled to balance their critique of it with a critique of the more traditional targets of the liberals. Among them is Robert Hughes.[37] David Bromwich detects "a disparity between the self-contained (mostly left wing) culture of the academy and the static (and rightwing) political culture that dominates America today.[38] But even during the Reagan-Bush years such an alleged dominance of "rightwing political culture" was limited to the presidency.

Dennis Wrong, no friend of PC, claimed that, in writing about and criticizing what in 1988 I called the adversary culture (the source of PC), I was "greatly exaggerating both its prevalence and influence outside a few academic enclaves," that I was "obsessed with the Sixties," and placed "inordinate weight on those years and their surviving echoes." I was "flogging a dead horse." As for the "left domination of major and especially elite universities," he just did not notice any such thing at places like NYU, Columbia, Princeton, Rutgers, and Yale.[39] Although far from a radical, he (and many of his academic colleagues) thought it important to deflate and dismiss the phenomenon, whether we call it adversary culture or PC, presumably to avoid being identified with what he and other liberals see as "the Right," i.e., conservatives who dwell on the topic.

In all probability the phenomenon of PC is also denied because acknowledging it may suggest an obligation to take a stand against it, an obligation that is uncomfortable in the current academic climate. Those publicly objecting to the phenomena associated with PC are often accused of "polarizing the campus," of being unduly polemical. This is another illustration of the extent to which PC has become the new conventional wisdom: any challenge to it is regarded with irritation, or pained surprise, as disturbing the peace. Christina Sommers, a persistent critic of the feminist varieties of PC, was said to have "a reputation as a popular teacher but also as a divisive force [on her campus]. While many colleagues praise her... many also say she seeks to polarize the campus on various issues." In a similar spirit, the American Association of University Professors pointed out that allegations of political correctness came from "an animosity toward equal opportunity and its first effects of modestly increasing the participation of women and racial and cultural minorities on campus." It called for an end to "sloganeering and name-calling" by those making charges of political correctness.[40]

A more subtle (and possibly unintended) questioning of the reality or impact of PC found its way into a "Firing Line" program late last year,[41] which proposed, for the purposes of debate, that "PC is a menace and a bore." The participants failed to clarify how PC could be both a menace and a bore, since what threatens us is hardly ever boring, and a source of boredom in turn is not usually viewed as a serious menace. On this program, too, it was asserted by some of the participants that PC was diverting attention from "the real problems" of America, which were racism, sexism, poverty, AIDS, and the like.

Among the most vocal critics of the idea that PC exists and is a problem has been Stanley Fish. In close spiritual kinship to the late Herbert Marcuse, Fish has been unable to hide his contempt for the free expression of ideas of which he disapproves. Given the sympathy he has for the ideas and policies PC seeks to promote and perpetuate, it is not surprising that he does not find PC objectionable. In his view, discussions of PC come down to "misinformation propagated by rightwing scholars, think tanks and commentators." Not surprisingly, a similar position was taken by the Modern Language Association, itself a pillar of PC.[42]

College administrators have been in the forefront of those inclined to dismiss the phenomenon of PC. In 1991 the American Council on Higher Education conducted a survey of college administrators; they appear to have detected even the vaguest signs of what can be considered political correctness on fewer than 10 percent of college campuses.[43]

The same survey found that only "one in ten colleges and two in doctorate granting institutions experienced controversies" in connection with PC[44]—a finding that in no way corroborates the claim that the phenomenon of PC has been overblown. What it does show is that PC has not been *controversial* on most campuses. The absence of controversy, of course, is among the most powerful indicators of the *success* of PC. Disputes concerning PC come to public attention only in rare and particularly lurid or ludicrous instances and not, as is usually the case, when PC is routinized and passively accepted. It is hardly surprising that college administrators strain to overlook a phenomenon whose existence could be a public embarrassment. More disturbing is the possibility that they may overlook it because they find it so unremarkable, so natural, so much a part of the social-cultural landscape, and indistinguishable from their own view of the world. At the University of Massachusetts at Amherst,

when asked for his impressions on the anti-Political Correctness campaign, Chancellor O'Brien dismissed it as an ill-conceived attempt by the Right to assert itself on college campuses... "it's greatly overstated," he said. "I see it as a part of the conservative backlash. I am not highly sympathetic to it."[45]

It would seem that by the early 1990s the existence of PC was inexorably intertwined with its dismissal and denial.

III

A wide variety of cultural, social, and political factors account for the rise and persistence of PC. We may distinguish between proximate or direct causes on the one hand and, on the other, aspects of

American history, culture, and society that create a susceptibility to it. While Gustave Le Bon may have been wrong about a number of things, his century-old musings (quoted at the beginning) about the links between higher education and social discontent remain suggestive. He could not have foreseen how rapidly past deprivation or disadvantage would be converted into prestige and privilege, that the "outcasts" of the past would some day become governmentally certified victim groups and provided, especially in the academic setting, with institutionalized advantages. The victim groups of the present— a particularly strong presence on college campuses—are in a peculiar position. On the one hand they must continue to assert their victim status, otherwise their claim to special treatment would vanish; on the other, the measures they urge and benefit from are supposed to erase their victimhood. Victimhood and compensatory advantage are thus entwined in a mutually reinforcing yet contradictory embrace. Compensatory measures reduce and ultimately erase victimhood; at that stage, victimization could no longer justify these measures, and thus the influence and privilege of these groups would wane.

The concept Shelby Steele called "a victim focused identity,"[46] originally applied to blacks only, helps to understand not merely why such an identity persists among blacks, but also why it has been eagerly adopted by other groups claiming victimization. Today, successful claim to victimhood in the United States not only assures various forms of preferential treatment institutionalized by the political authorities, it also provides a claim to a higher morality and for special compassion and makes self-righteousness respectable. Steele wrote:

> we allow the mere *claim* (of oppression...) to become a currency of entitlement. This claim does not have to be supported: the child of well-to-do black parents gets preference in college admissions without any evidence of oppression. Group membership alone seals the advantage. These entitlements are a powerful incentive for groups to define their very identity around the claims that justify their advantage.[47]

As the claims of oppression become more difficult to sustain, he argues, the rhetoric of demagogues like Louis Farrakhan becomes especially welcome, since he "distorts and exaggerates the claim of oppression that group entitlements have made the centerpiece of black identity."[48]

The highly interdependent relationship between claims of victimization, a morally enriched sense of identity, and institutionalized compensatory benefits have much to do with the phenomenon of PC, and especially the emotional and political forces driving it. PC is victim-friendly and victim-oriented; the core beliefs and attitudes associated with it are profoundly influenced by ideas and feelings about certain types of victimhood and the ways to remedy them.

It is a major proposition of these reflections that PC, while it transcends race relations, is driven primarily by white guilt toward the black population, that the centerpiece of PC is the "correct" attitude and policies toward oppressed minorities and certified victims—a steadily expanding category, to be sure-among whom blacks occupy a special place. This is so because, for obvious historical reasons, black Americans were and to a large degree remain the most authentic victim group (although those among them holding Ph.D.s and occupying academic positions would hardly seem to qualify). White guilt toward blacks greatly exceeds guilt toward any other type of victim; it has therefore been a powerful source of institutional action and has provided much of the emotional energy and support for the PC edifice. Finally, guilt over the past treatment of blacks has solidified into an essential part of the general critique of American society, integral to the PC outlook; hence those critically disposed, for whatever reason, toward American culture and society will not let go of the race issue.[49]

Arguably the struggle against "racism" has the highest priority on the agenda of PC; none of the other terms of disapprobation connected with other victim groups carries the same weight as "racist." Once affixed, the charge of racism ends all debate and rarely requires substantiation, since so many whites are instinctively, subliminally prepared to accept the accusation; they feel that "these people have been wronged so deeply that nothing we do can really make up for it."[50] In turn these feelings allow "racism" to become the all-purpose explanation of every problem of the minorities:

> Do blacks and Hispanics score poorly on tests? The tests are biased. Having been admitted to schools with substandard test scores and grades, do minorities drop out in disproportionate numbers? The schools don't do enough to celebrate minority culture. Lacking educational credentials, are minorities underrepresented in university teaching and certain professions? Employers are not trying hard enough to recruit them. Having been hired with substandard qualifications, do minorities fail to advance in their jobs? Managers don't "value their differences."[51]

PC often entails a deliberate effort to *deepen* the sense of white guilt, especially among the educated middle classes and campus-based groups. The pursuit of guilt and repentance is the main thrust of most organized consciousness-raising and sensitivity-training activities.

It is an interesting question for the social historian and the historian of ideas how the concepts of victimization and victimhood could have achieved such prominence in a society and what this means for its vitality and coherence.

Next to the feelings noted above, and in combination with them, the most direct cause of the rise and spread of PC has been the presence of a critical mass of people at the colleges and universities, among both faculty members and administrators, who actually believe in the values PC seeks to propagate or institutionalize. They are the "tenured radicals" and earnest administrators, authors of speech codes and harassment manuals, affirmative-action officials, assorted consciousness-raisers, sensitivity-trainers, veterans of the causes of the 1960s, erstwhile activists, protestors, or sympathizers-a mixed group of idealists and opportunists, as more and more people make their living by administering PC. As David Lodge put it,

> disillusioned by the collapse of the utopian dreams of the 1960's and 70's and the electoral triumphs of neoconservative social and economic policies in the 80's, they have turned inward and cultivated their own garden. . .convincing themselves that a radical reform of the curriculum is equivalent to the radical reform of society.[52]

Coincidentally, the pay is good, and jobs are available for a wide variety of politically correct efforts and activities. Relevant here is Barrington Moore's observation that "moral passions without material interests rarely if ever suffice to move large bodies of men and women in a way that leaves a deep mark upon the historical record."[53] In the promotion of PC, moral passions and material interests harmoniously converge. Moreover, these policies are supported by the culture outside the campuses, driven by the larger cultural-political currents here discussed.

Of late, college and university administrators, more than faculties or students, have come to bear a particular responsibility for the reign of PC, since they are in the forefront of enforcing it, with the vocal support of a minority and the timid acquiescence of the majority of the faculties. As Bromwich put it, in many instances "an activist administration has asserted control over curricular reform, as well as over questions of elementary manners that once had been protected by faculty autonomy."[54] The administrators are especially culpable for tolerating and unwittingly promoting violations of free speech-the most egregious result of PC. As Lipset noted,

> the major problem...does not lie in the beliefs and behavior of left-wing teachers or students, but in the weakness of college administrators, who fear notoriety resultant from resistance to activist student protest, particularly when associated with ethnic, racial, and gender issues. Many are reluctant to get into conflicts...to prevent limitations on campus freedom of speech.[55]

Thus it transpired that "those who once tried to lock college presidents out of their offices came to depend on presidents to support their demands."[56]

Many administrators appear to be eager to regulate free speech and expression, through the notorious codes, in order to forestall protest and disruption that creates bad publicity. Doubtless many also believe that they must not allow things to be said in public that might offend victim groups. Administrators have routinized the indulgent treatment of disruption and denial of free speech over the past decades; it is a safe guess that 90 percent of building occupations, class disruptions, interference with invited speakers, and the like, have not resulted in any disciplinary action, even if they have resulted in the setting up of committees. In doing so-or failing to do so-administrators have given tacit encouragement to both censorship and self-censorship.

Adam Ulam offers further clues, rooted in his experiences at Harvard in the late 1960s, for understanding the behavior of administrators, who are less likely to be politically committed ideologues than many professors in departments of English and the Social Sciences. He wrote:

> They were, by their own admission, sinful and old or middle aged and yet claiming to exercise authority over the virtuous youth... This was to become known as the problem of legitimacy...
>
> Before many an administrator and professor now stood the student, stern and unsmiling, demanding an accounting of what *he* has done with this country, with its foreign policy, ...with the environment, ...and what he proposes to expiate his sins. But there was hopefully, a companion image, that of the *kids,* a generation uniquely unspoiled, devoid of the materialist and competitive passion which blighted American society; and instead devoted to innocent merriment and the ideal of brotherhood. With the kids one could have a dialogue, that is if one discarded sinful attributes of authority, experience and the like.[57]

Such attitudes still animate-or, as the case may be, paralyze-administrators, especially when the "kids" or students are "people of color" and therefore in still better moral position to "demand an accounting." The administrative paralysis in face of disruption also has to do with another characteristic of higher education that emerged in the late 1960's, namely,

the unspoken premise of so many today that all of education should be... a form of group therapy... Our whole society seems to have taken to the couch trying to recall the reasons for its trauma... Alienation and identity crisis ride grimly through most of contemporary culture, through literature, theater and cinema.. [58]

Twenty-one years later Alan Wolfe noted,

the management style they [the administrators] understand best is one that speaks in psychological jargon. The position of the university president is no longer, in Max Weber's sense of the term, a calling demanding the sacrifice of self-interest for some higher purpose. It does not require character and rectitude, but the ability to get along with diverse groups.[59]

One may add that in the administrative calculus some groups are far more important (and menacing) than others.

It is also of interest to point out that, while the policies seeking to institutionalize PC have frequently been guided by the desire to maintain peace at almost any cost, the more liberal, permissive, and PC a campus, the more complaints and claims of racism, sexism, heterosexism, homophobia, and other PC grievances there are. As C. Vann Woodward remarked, "the more policies to promote harmony the greater the.., complaint of racial hostility."[60] It may be recalled here that at Smith College, another bastion of PC, a survey commissioned by its president a few years ago found that about 80 percent of those interviewed complained of being subjected to some type of discrimination or insensitivity.[61]

The convergence of the idea of "sensitivity" and PC provides another example of the influence of currents outside academia. Sensitivity used to be thought of as a personal quality, or component of psychotherapy, rather than something political and readily subjected to codes, rules, and regulations. Russell Baker pointed out, "What is odd about the PC people... is their dopey belief that people can be bullied into being kind, good and sensitive to each other."[62] Possibly the growth of the portion of the population undergoing some type of therapy or counseling has contributed to an increasing demand for a reign of sensitivity. More importantly, the concern for sensitivity has its roots in the readiness to grant victim status on more elusive and subjective grounds; typically the claims of "insensitivity" are invoked when no tangible violation of rights or injustices can be established. Lastly, sensitivity to a wide range of offenses, (real or imagined) is also compatible with an expanded conception of individual rights and the belief in individual uniqueness, which are among the reigning notions of our time. The more "unique" the individual, and the more "unique" his or her needs, the easier it is to fail to recognize them adequately and thereby to stray into insensitivity. In turn, these considerations link up with another new mission of education, namely, to improve self-esteem. It has become politically incorrect to suggest that, in the words of John Searle, "it is not the aim of education to make the student feel good about himself or herself."[63] But, above all, concern with "insensitivity" is integral to PC because it allows a broader, less specific conceptualization of victimhood, and a readier receptivity to its claims of restitution.

The prevailing conceptions of victimhood are also connected with yet another broader cultural trend, one much in evidence since the 1960's, namely, the growing belief in the selective social-cultural determination of personal lives.[64] If society, or various social forces and institutions, are mostly responsible for the way our lives turn out, we have reason to demand that society be solicitous toward its victims, the "losers." The merging of what is personal and social is yet another of the legacies of the 1960's, that helps to explain how sensitivity and insensitivity, originally conceived of as highly personal attributes, came to be transformed into social problems, a policy issue that can be encompassed by rules and regulations.[65]

Probably the most insidious legacy of the 1960's, and a gift of radical feminism to PC, has been the claim that "the personal is political" and the attendant demand that the divide between the private and the public realm be demolished. It was this view of life and human relationships that has encouraged and justified the extension of PC to virtually all aspects of life, invading realms generally thought of as private and personal. While an extended refutation of this belief is beyond the scope of this essay, it ought at least be noted that it is empirically incorrect that everything in our lives, especially in our personal lives, revolves around power and domination. Moreover, to the extent that the personal and political do coincide, the overlap ought not be treated as a model of all social and personal relationships. Adam Ulam wrote,

a student of totalitarian society knows that... the extolling of snooping and minding other people's business is proclaimed as the highest form of altruism... [In present-day

American society] there is a disturbing degree of acceptance of the principle that every-thing is everybody's business.

PC has also been a product of cultural trends and currents regarding the mission of higher education. In short PC in large measure rests on the presumption that

in the university you can train people, not in specific skills but in some special wisdom of how society ought to be run.[66]

The new, politically motivated questioning of the usefulness and autonomy of academic intellectual activities is also nurtured by the venerable American tradition of anti-intellectualism, which in turn is congenial with the decline of academic standards that PC brings about or sanctions. Mark Lilla wrote:

What we are experiencing in the name of multiculturalism and PC today is... perfectly consistent with the anti-intellectualism that preceded [them]. The fact that every university today promotes a multicultural education, yet very few demand the real mastery of a single foreign language, is just one more sign that the university is being driven by the same democratic passions that have traditionally hobbled American secondary education.[67]

The egalitarian impulse of American culture, which has greatly intensified since the 1960's and acquired new institutional support, sustains many aspects of PC and its scorn for "elitism." Not only is PC aimed at uplifting certain disadvantaged groups, it also claims, in its multicultural aspirations, that all cultures are equal, that no qualitative judgments can or should be made as between rap music and Beethoven, graffiti and the French Impressionists. (To be sure, on closer examination it turns out that the so-called celebration of diversity rarely includes Western culture.) It is this bizarre egalitarianism that leads to demands and policies aimed at partial demographic "representativeness" in reading lists, that they include (some of the) ethnic groups of the population, sometimes those of different sexual orientation as well. Such "representativeness" leads to the belief and demand that teachers exemplify what they teach, i.e., black studies must be taught by blacks, women's studies by women, and gay studies by homosexuals; presumably only Marxists should teach Marx and only Catholics the thought of Aquinas.[68] It is the new and profoundly anti-intellectual conventional wisdom that membership in a particular group is not only our sole source of identity but also the basis of learning, that we teach what we supposedly are and have learned through personal experience, or certain forms of personal experience. David Bromwich wrote that today:

> a woman starting off a career in literary scholarship has better chances of employment than a man of comparable gifts; but with the widening of opportunity may come a narrowing of the freedom to choose one's subject... The woman may well be expected to teach... a course on "women in literature," or "gender studies" or otherwise conspicuously incorporate a "feminist perspective" in as much of her intellectual work as possible.[69]

The egalitarian impulses of American culture culminated of late in what Aaron Wildavsky called "radical egalitarianism," the insistence on not merely equal opportunity but equal results. In higher education this finds expression in the spread of quotas (whatever they are called) in student admissions and faculty hiring and the demand that not only must certain minorities be admitted to universities in numbers reflecting their ratio to the general population, but they also must graduate accordingly. Tom Hayden's bill to that effect was passed by the California legislature a few years ago but vetoed by the governor. It is an unstated premise of PC that "all necessary abilities are equally distributed among all groups, including the ability to succeed in college."[70] If tests or grades show otherwise, they are "culturally biased."

During the 1970's and 1980's the murky tides of deconstructionism and postmodernism have risen and lent support to the relativistic, relativizing dimensions of PC. The associated attacks on objectivity greatly contributed to attempts to transform the curriculum and academic life in general into interest-group politics. Fred Siegel observed,

> ...the norm of objectivity had until the mid-70's served as a regulatory ideal for academic life. Difficult though it was to obtain, it served as a kind of guiding principle. But, concludes Ernest Gellner, "because all knowledge is dubious, being theory-saturated/ethnocentric/paradigm-dominated/interest-linked (please choose your own preferred variant...), the anguish-ridden author... can put forward whatever he pleases." Reality was to be rewritten and reinforced by a new form of coerced consensus.[71]

The feminist agenda makes its own contribution to the peculiar subjectivity that PC fosters:

> Many in women's studies consider personal experience the only real source of truth. Some professors and texts even claim that women have a way of thinking that is different from the abstract rationality of men, one based on context, emotion and intuition. Fully "validating" women, therefore means celebrating subjectivity over objectivity, feelings over facts, instinct over logic.[72]

Notwithstanding such emphases, apparently women's studies are not warmly tolerant; rather, they explicitly promote PC. For example, according to a survey of the Association of American Colleges, 30 percent of students in women's studies courses at Wellesley College "felt uneasy about expressing unpopular opinions," as against 14 percent who felt this way in non-women's studies. A "reluctance to voice alternative opinions" in such programs was found on many campuses. Among many feminists, intolerance, claims of victimhood, and a taken-for-granted PC shade into one another. Jean Bethke Elshtain observed:

> Most teachers of women's studies presume that if you don't see yourself as a victim you are in a state of false consciousness...[73]

While the politically correct, influenced by postmodernism, often claim that the pursuit of truth and objectivity is a delusion, the evident intolerance and proliferation of taboo topics associated with PC suggest that it has come to represent a peculiar combination of moral relativism and moral absolutism.

Finally, there is the possibility of a connection between the rise and entrenchment of PC and the fall of Communist systems and the damage this wreaked on their legitimating ideologies. To the extent that there remain abroad few if any attractive or respectable causes to agitate, motivate, and preoccupy the adversary culture (e.g., U.S. intervention in Nicaragua), or admirable "national liberation" movements (e.g., Marxist-Leninist guerillas in El Salvador), and since the hope that the Soviet Union may return to some form of authentic socialism has also been dashed, domestic matters have taken precedence. The adversarial energies, earlier at least in part occupied by issues abroad, found and focused on new domestic channels of expression and action. Although greatly resisted and debated in the same circles, the fall of Communism also delivered blows to Marxism, which in turn helped the new ideological trinity (race, sex, ethnicity) to become ascendant and enshrined in PC.

IV

What of the impact of PC? How is one to measure it? It is, of course, difficult to do, because many of its consequences are not quantifiable, and because information is often deliberately withheld when it would be embarrassing to particular individuals or institutions. The well-publicized scandals associated with PC are the tip of the iceberg.

As we have pointed out, most damaging and widespread has been the interference with the free flow of ideas and free expression. Besides the convictions of its promoters, PC has also fed on "the timidity of academics who know better and are fearful about expressing their convictions, or whose convictions are frozen by an anxiety not to offend."[74]

The effects of PC have been apparent when politically incorrect speakers are shouted down or their invitations cancelled for fear of disruption. More difficult to measure is an atmosphere in which "unpopular speakers" are no longer invited for fear of displeasing and mobilizing the politically correct mobs on the campuses.

The impact of PC is evident in the number of speech codes enacted and students disciplined for their violation, and in the number of instances when "politically incorrect" teachers stopped, under pressure, teaching courses that did not conform to the expectations and agendas of the PC.

The tangible impact and expression of PC include preferential treatment based on sex, race, (certain types of) ethnicity, and "race norming" in student admissions. Correspondingly PC is responsible for the fact that countless highly qualified white males or Asian-Americans are not being admitted to the colleges of their choice, commensurate with their abilities and qualifications. PC has also been responsible for an unknown but probably large number of highly qualified white males' not being hired, promoted, or given tenure for similar reasons, and for those terminated for violating some canon of PC.[75]

Also associated with PC is the decline of academic standards across the board and grade inflation. PC is behind the multiplication of special-interest-group programs (women's studies, black studies, gay studies, etc.) and curricular changes based on non-intellectual criteria.[76] Among the many costs of PC one may also count the politicization of professional associations such as the MLA and the Latin American Studies Association (LASA), as well as the rise of litigation either inspired by PC or in protest of its impact.[77] Also among the costs of PC, though again impossible to estimate, is the enormous amount of time spent and *wasted* on discussing its many aspects and implementation.

PC, as expressed in the behavior and policies of college administrators, has also encouraged lawlessness-one of its infrequently noted consequences. When colleges and universities are responsive to intimidation, disruption, and even physical violence, when politically incorrect speakers are harassed or silenced, when student newspapers are destroyed, when the occupation of academic buildings is risk-free and leads to no disciplinary action, students learn the lesson that rules don't matter. In fact, and largely unknown to the general public, the routine occupation of academic buildings by small groups of activists has continued unabated since the 1960's. Typically a group of minority students occupies a building in response to some real or alleged grievance and ritualistically demands immediate compensatory action, usually in the form of increased benefits-scholarships, space for a cultural center, more role-model faculty members, and so on. College administrators treat these occupations as legitimate forms of protest or "input" into academic policy-making. Almost invariably the demands are met, including amnesty for the disruption.[78]

We are not privileged to know when and under what circumstances the influences and effects of PC will begin to wane. While PC began as an effort to institutionalize the right not to be offended and to realize a wide variety of social ideals it is likely to go down in history as yet another failed attempt to make the world a better place by intolerance, rationalized as liberation and social justice.

Notes

1.   Gustave Le Bon, *The Psychology of Socialism* (Wells, Vt.: Fraser, 1965), 370.
2.   Shelby Steele, "How to Grow Extremists," *The New York Times*, 13 March 1994, Op-ed.
3.   The literature on PC is quite substantial and still growing. Virtually every issue of *Academic Questions* and *Measure* provides information on and analysis of some aspects of it. The following is a small selection of helpful sources: *Debating PC*, ed. Paul Berman (New York: Laurel/Dell, 1992); Alan Bloom, *The Closing of the American Mind* (New York: Simon & Schuster, 1987); David Bromwich, *Politics by Other Means* (New Haven, Conn.: Yale University Press, 1992); *The Imperiled Academy*, ed. Howard Dickman (New Brunswick, NJ: Transaction Books, 1993); Dinesh D'Souza, *Illiberal Education* (New York: Free Press, 1991); Gerald Graff, *Beyond the Culture Wars* (New York: W.W. Norton and Co., 1992); Nat Hentoff, *Free Speech for Me But Not for Thee* (New York: HarperCollins, 1992); Roger Kimball, *Tenured Radicals* (New York: Harper & Row, 1990); Guenter Lewy, *False Consciousness* (New Brunswick, NJ: Transaction Books, 1983); Arthur Schlesinger, Jr., *The Disuniting of America* (New York: W.W. Norton and Co., 1992); Paul Vitz, *Censorship: Evidence of Bias in Our Children's Textbooks* (Ann

Arbor, Mich.: Servant Books, 1986); Adam Ulam, *The Fall of the American University* (New York: Library Press, 1972). See also "The Changing Culture of the University," *Partisan Review*, Special Issue, vol. LVIII, no. 2 (1991); and "The Politics of Political Correctness," Partisan Review, Special Issue, vol. LX, no. 4 (1993). See also Harvey Mansfield, Jr., "Political Correctness and the Suicide of the Intellect," *Heritage Lecture* No. 337, 1 October 1991, and Stephen Schwartz, "Who Invented Political Correctness?", *Heterodoxy*, May-June 1994.

4.   Brustein, "Dumbocracy in America," 533, and Kramer, "Confronting the Monolith," 569, *Partisan Review* LX-4. A splendid example of PC's invading art came from London, where a teacher in a primary school would not let her students see the ballet *Romeo and Juliet* "because it was, in her words, 'a blatantly heterosexual love story.'" John Darnton, "Political Correctness: A Quirk the British Can Do Without," *The New York Times*, 13 March 1994, sec. 4, 4. Nor are American schools safe: "School Cancels 'Peter Pan' as Insulting to Indians," *The New York Times*, 8 March 1994, B6. The school in question was in Southampton, L.I.

5.   I have on various occasions written of the same phenomenon without using the term "PC." See *Soviet and American Society: A Comparison* (New York: Oxford University Press, 1973), 163-185; *The Survival of the Adversary Culture* (New Brunswick, NJ: Transaction Books, 1988); *Anti-Americanism: Critiques at Home and Abroad 1965-1990* (New York: Oxford University Press, 1992), esp. chs. 1 through 4, 6, and 10; *Decline and Discontent* (New Brunswick: Transaction Books, 1992), esp. Introduction and chs. 8 through 11 and 14; and "Political Correctness Is Alive and Well on Campuses Near You," *Washington Times*, 28 December 1993, A19.

6.   "Bundles of the University of Maryland campus newspaper disappeared from a student center, a library and other school buildings and were replaced by a leaflet that read: 'Due to its racist nature, *The Diamondback* will not be available today' 'This is a valid form of protest' said Lamont Clark, an officer of the Black Student Union... " "On Campus," *The New York Times*, 3 November 1993, B15.

7.   George M. Marsden, quoted in Peter Steinfels, "Universities Biased against Religion, Scholar Says," *The New York Times*, 26 November 1993, A22.

8.   David Lehman, "Reign of Intolerance," *Partisan Review* LX-4, 601.

9.   Robert Hughes, *The Culture of Complaint* (New York: Oxford University Press, 1993), 83.

10.   Steven Marcus, "Soft Totalitarianism," *Partisan Review* LX-4, 633.

11.   "Terms like sexism, racism and homophobia have bloated beyond all recognition," an observer concluded after immersing herself in Women's Studies programs. Karen Lehrman, "Off Course," *Mother Jones* (September-October 1993), 66.

12.   *The Fall of the American University*, op. cit. n.3, 194, 208.

13.   David Lehman, op. cit. n.8, 598.

14.   Lentricchia and Ohmann, quoted by Jerry L. Martin, "The University as Agent...," in Dickman, op. cit. n.3, 203-204.

15.   Hans Toch, "Politically Correct Approaches to Violence and Aggression," *Criminal Justice Research Bulletin*, Criminal Justice Center, Huntsville TX, vol. 7, no. 5, 1992.

16.   Richard Bernstein, "The Rising Hegemony of the Politically Correct," *The New York Times, The Week in Review*, 28 October 1990, 1.

17.   Phillips, "Against Political Correctness: Eleven Points," *Partisan Review* LX-4, 671.

18.   Charles Sykes, "The Ideology of Sensitivity," *Imprimis* (Hillsdale College), July 1992, 1.

19.   Dickstein, "Correcting PC," *Partisan Review* LX-4, 543-44.
20.   Barbara Amiel, "Campus Newspeak," *Sunday Times*, 16 June 1991.
21.   Loury, "Self-Censorship," Partisan Review LX-4, 609.
22.   Lipset, "The Sources of Political Correctness on American Campuses," in Dickman, op. cit. n.3, 71, emphasis added.
23.   Russell Baker, "With Malice Galore," *The New York Times*, 14 December 1993, A25.
24.   Lipset in Dickman, op. cit. n.3, 76.
25.   John Diggins, *The Rise and Fall of the American Left* (New York: W.W. Norton and Co., 1992), 297.
26.   Quoted in Geoffrey Wheatcroft, "The Friends of Salman Rushdie," *The Atlantic Monthly*, March 1994, 29.
27.   "Bathroom Sign Crusade," *City on the Hill* (student newspaper), Santa Cruz, 22 April 1993.
28.   Serge Schmeman, "Military Rivalry Cools; Culturally, It Heats Up," *The New York Times*, 29 July 1991, A1 and A6
29.   Anthony DePalma, "In Campus Debate, On New Orthodoxy, A Counter Offensive," *The New York Times*, 25 September 1991.
30.   Michiko Kakutani, "Can Politically Correct Ever Be Incorrect?", review of Berman, op. cit. n.3, *The New York Times*, 4 February 1992, C15.
31.   Joel Conarroe, "How I'm PC," *The New York Times*, 12July 1991, Op-ed; see also Heather Mac Donald, "D'Souza's Critics: PC Fights Back," *Academic Questions*, Summer 1992, 9.
32.   Quoted in Eugene Goodheart, "PC or Not PC," *Partisan Review* LX-4, 552, and Kakutani, op. cit. n.30.
33.   Quoted in Lehman, op. cit. n.8, 599.
34.   Staples, "Time to Retire a Cliché...", *The New York Times*, 5 December 1993, Editorial Notebook, sec.4, 20, emphasis added.
35.   Op. cit. n.3, 3.
36.   Carol Iannone, "PC With a Human Face," *Commentary*, vol. 95, no. 9, (June 1993), 44.
37.   Op. cit. n.9.
38.   Op. cit. n.3, ix.
39.   Dennis Wrong, review of Paul Hollander, *The Survival of the Adversary Culture* (op. cit. n.5) in *Contemporary Sociology*, September 1989; correspondence regarding that review in *Contemporary Sociology*, July 1990.
40.   "Philosophy Professor Portrays Her Feminist Colleagues as Out of Touch and 'Hostile to the Family,'" *The Chronicle of Higher Education*, 15 January 1992; "Few Colleges Have Had 'Political Correctness' Controversies, Study Finds," *The Voice* (University of Massachusetts, Amherst), September 1991.
41.   13 December 1993 "Firing Line" debate on the Public Broadcasting System.
42.   "Literature Professors Say 'PC' Claims Are Exaggerated," *Washington Post*, reprinted in *Daily Hampshire Gazette*, January 4-5, 1992, 31.
43.   DePalma, op. cit. n.29.
44.   *The Voice*, op. cit. n.40.
45.   "An Interview with Chancellor O'Brien," ibid.
46.   *The Content of Our Character* (New York: St. Martin's Press, 1990).
47.   Shelby Steele, op. cit. n.2.
48.   Ibid.
49.   "Among those agitated about the racial problems of this country, there are undoubtedly persons whose main concern is the most expeditious removal of the remaining

forms of discrimination; but for others this is a very pleasing demonstration of the inherent wickedness of society, a hair-shirt not to be discarded whatever the improvement." Adam Ulam, op. cit. n.3, 210.

50.   Whites seem to accept their guilt about racism so readily that the concept can open the door for indoctrination and ideological bullying. Even the white civil rights workers who risked their lives in the 1960's in the South were compelled by leaders of the movement to participate in sessions in which they were accused of and obliged to confess their racism. See Martin Lakin, "Sensitivity Training, Diversity Awareness, and Intergroup Conflicts on University Campuses..." *Academic Questions* (Summer 1994), 83-84.

51.   Heather Mac Donald, "The Diversity Principle," *Partisan Review* LX-4, 622.

52.   David Lodge review of David Bromwich, op. cit. n.3, *The New York Times Book Review*, 4 October 1992, 7.

53.   Barrington Moore, Jr., *Reflections on the Causes of Human Misery* (Boston: Beacon Press, 1970), 3.

54.   Bromwich, op. cit. n.3, 27.

55.   In Dickman, op. cit. n.22, 86.

56.   Alan Wolfe, "The New Class Comes Home," *Partisan Review* LX-4, 729.

57.   Op. cit. n.3, 101, 122.

58.   Ibid., 104-105.

59.   Wolfe, op. cit. n.56, 735.

60.   C. Vann Woodward, "Freedom and the Universities," *New York Review of Books*, 18 July 1991, 35; Arthur Schlesinger, Jr., has reached a similar conclusion regarding the consequences of a related form of PC, the sanctioning of self-segregation. He writes, "it is sad, though instructive, that the administrations especially disposed to encourage racial and ethnic enclaves are the ones experiencing the most racial tension..." op. cit. n.3, 114.

61.   For specifics, see Hollander, *Anti-Americanism* [n.5}, 210-214.

62.   Russell Baker, "Supreme and PC Court," *The New York Times*, 3 August 1991, Op-ed, 19.

63.   Searle, "Is There a Crisis in American Higher Education?" *Partisan Review* LX-4, 709.

64.   For a detailed discussion of "selective determinism," see Hollander, *The Many Faces of Socialism* (New Brunswick, NJ: Transaction Books, 1983), 241-251.

65.   Again, Adam Ulam, writing almost a quarter century ago, noted that "the teachers might suggest and the students might believe that most of one's personal problems were the fault of society and, if so, political and social activism could be used as a form of group therapy. [Op. cit. n.3, 78.] More recently an inquiry into women's studies found that they "implicitly downplay individual merit and focus on the systemic forces that are undermining everything women do." Lehrman, op. cit. n.11, 50.

66.   Op. cit. n.3, 179, 50, 189.

67.   Lilla, "Only Disconnect...," *Partisan Review* LX-4, 606-07.

68.   On this topic, see John Searle, op. cit. n.63, especially p. 700.

69.   Bromwich, op. cit. n.3, 21.

70.   John H. Bunzel, "The University's Pseudo-Egalitarianism," *Wall Street Journal*, 12 July 1991, 30.

71.   Siegel, "Anti-Rationalism," *Partisan Review* LX-4, 727.

72.   Lehrman, op. cit. n.11, 48.

73.   Ibid., 64; on feminist consciousness raising in the classroom see also Hollander, *Anti-Americanism* [n.5], 179-180.

74. Goodheart, op. cit. n.32, 551.
75. Among recent and notable cases was that of Edward Hoagland at Bennington College, dismissed on the grounds of the most spurious accusation of homophobia. Edward Hoagland, "Fear and Learning in Vermont," *The New York Times*, 15 June 1991, Op-ed, 23.
76. The addition of great non-Western works to the curriculum does not amount to the triumph of PC, but the removal of great Western works to make room for dubious ideological tracts must be counted among such triumphs.
77. On the politics of LASA, see Alfred G. Cuzán, "The Latin American Studies Association vs. the U.S.: The Verdict of History," *Academic Questions*, Summer 1994, 40; for an interesting example of litigation associated with the reign of PC see Fox Butterfield, "Suit Depicts Fight on MIT Faculty," *The New York Times*, 5 May 1992. The plaintiff, Cynthia Griffin Wolf, charged that "she was harassed for putting traditional scholarly standards ahead of the radical political views of her colleagues."
78. For example, as of this writing 80 students of a total student population of 23,000 at the University of Massachusetts at Amherst are occupying the admissions office, "vowing to remain there until Chancellor Davis Scott meets their demands." The cause in this instance was not a minority grievance. The students... entered the building... disrupting workers and demanding that Scott unconditionally support a zero percent increase in tuition and fees... Singing chants, playing songs of revolution and banging the walls, the students interrupted the workers in the admissions office... "This will become a battle of wills," said David Nunez, spokesman for the protestors, "Some people here are still working... If you see someone on the phone or working at a computer, sit down politely and scream. See how annoying that can be" Nunez urged students... ["Students Occupy UMass Office," *Daily Hampshire Gazette*, 11 February 1994.]

One of the administrative workers wrote:

This was not a peaceful protest... Those of us...unable to lock ourselves into protected space faced students who forced us out of our chairs...went through our drawers and our mail... handled our pictures of our children and other personal possessions... took over the phones and restricted our calls... stole and ate our food, coffee and drinks.... Students came to take over a building but... would not rest until they had taken over the people inside as well. ["Admissions Staff Responds to Protestors," *Massachusetts Daily Collegian*, 15 February 1994.]

Notwithstanding the character of the occupation, "UMass officials have no plans to take action against students who were involved" ["UMass Fee Hike Axed," *Daily Hampshire Gazette*, 14 February 1994].

Not only was no action taken against the occupiers-neither the chancellor nor any other official of the university publicly expressed any disapproval.

4

The Attack on Science and Reason

The American role in world affairs has always been in large measure determined by domestic conditions, not just economic and political ones but intellectual and cultural ones, too. That is especially the case in the present post-cold war period; with obvious and direct external threats no longer exerting compelling pressures, domestic factors have become more consequential. Under these conditions, prevailing levels of social cohesion, the cultural climate, the nature of domestic social and political conflicts, the beliefs of American elite groups, the attitude of intellectuals, and the vitality of American society as a whole become especially important in shaping the American role in global affairs both for now and, more important, for the future, when the foreign pressures weighing upon us may be greater.

The two very different books here reviewed provide profound insights into the state of present-day American society and culture. These volumes, Gertrude Himmelfarb's *On Looking into the Abyss* and Paul R. Gross and Norman Levitt's *Higher Superstition,* are indispensable for updating our knowledge and understanding of what goes on in the academic marketplace and how it influences society at large. The authors, Himmelfarb a historian, Gross and Levitt scientists, provide from their different vantage points both information and argument that ought to give pause to all those concerned with the life of the mind generally, and the social role of intellectuals in American society in particular.

Both books ought to be read by members of Congress, the White House staff, high-ranking civil servants, heads of foundations and universities, staffs of think tanks, literate journalists, and other elite groups who exert influence on American social institutions and monitor cultural trends. Unfortunately, even if the books were widely read, it is not clear how many minds would be changed in the pro-

cess, for one of the distressing aspects of present-day cultural-intellectual life in the United States, highlighted by both these volumes,
is that groups of highly intelligent, well-educated people no longer
fruitfully communicate with one another. Hopes of persuasion
through rational argument are greatly diminished; the notion of rationality itself is under attack. The possibilities of dialogue between
groups of different ideological or philosophical persuasion have
become modest; protagonists talk past each other, and points of views
are routinely dismissed not on the basis of their substance but on the
basis of their source. Why has this come to pass?

Few outside the academic world know or care about the ideas and
posturings associated with postmodernism, deconstructionism, or
structuralism, but, despite their abstruseness, such ideas have become entrenched in many branches of academic life. Postmodernism,
in particular, has become, as Gross and Levitt put it, "the unifying
doctrine of the academic left" (p. 72). Accounting for its popularity
they write:

> If we examine the popularity of postmodernism with a view to understanding its appeal
> to the politically discontented, we see that psychological factors are at work echoing
> those that lured previous generations to Marxism-Leninism, As before, what is offered
> is the possibility of becoming an initiate, part of a blessed elect whose mastery of a
> certain style of discourse confers insight unobtainable elsewhere, and authorizes a
> knowing (and often smug) attitude (p. 73).

But so what? It is far from self-evident that the obscure goings-on
in departments of English, "cultural studies," or the social sciences
affect the cohesion or decline of a society. But they probably do.
Although neither of the books under review explicitly raises the idea
of decadence, it is difficult to read them without bumping up against
the concept. Indeed, what these two excellent books do best is to
help us to grasp the connections between the life of the mind and the
cohesion of social institutions. As Gross and Levitt argue: "It is not
without historical precedent that incoherent or simply incomprehensible opinions have had great and pernicious social effect" (p. 15).
One need only recall the impact of "scientific" racism, complete
with phrenological subdisciplines, on European intellectual life from
the mid-nineteenth to the mid-twentieth century to appreciate the
point.

The pernicious social effects of incoherent, barely comprehen-
sible or obscurantist opinions is clearly discernible as they flow from

present-day academic and intellectual life in the United States into society at large. Foremost among the destructive social effects of postmodernism and other adversarial currents (such as radical feminism, Afrocentrism, radical environmentalism, and so forth) has been a growing hostility to science and, more generally, to rational thought and argument. When entire school districts adopt texts produced by manifestly unqualified people, and the "inanities of Afrocentric 'science'...have a free rein in a number of urban, predominantly black school districts," and when "the condescending belief has taken hold that black children can be persuaded to take an interest in science only if they are fed an educational diet of fairy tales" (pp. 247, 208)—under such conditions, the social and educational consequences of certain ideas become distressingly clear.

By attacking science and suggesting that multiculturalist, or Afrocentrist, or feminist versions of "science" are no less (but more) authentic, postmodernist intellectual relativism helps to perpetuate the scientific illiteracy of black students and all students. Even pointing that out is likely to provoke accusations of racism and sexism, which is why this is rarely done in public.

While most discussions of the decline of the United States focus on matters economic or narrowly educational (that is, mastering competence sufficient for jobs in a modern economy), decline and decadence have more elusive aspects that must be understood before one can proceed to tangible issues, such as the imbalance of trade, declining international competitiveness, productivity, and research and development. Decadence has two major dimensions: moral-psychological and functional-instrumental. Thus, if our work force is less educated, less able to meet the demands of present-day technologies, we must start by understanding the ideas and the ethos that contributed to this state of affairs in the first place, and that is communicated to the supposed beneficiaries of higher (and increasingly) lower education as well.

It is the more elusive, moral, psychological, and intellectual aspects of decadence, or decline, that these two books elucidate, including the decline in the clarity of communications painfully apparent in so much of current academic "discourse."

The eclipse of moral certainties and the crusade against reason are at the core of the first aspect of decadence; it is associated with lack of purpose, and a moral relativism unchecked by sustaining and widely shared values or beliefs. Admittedly, such attitudes are often a form of posturing: few people, including postmodernists, are in fact capable of genuine and consistent moral relativism, let alone unlimited benign tolerance, much as they may advocate such a position. More characteristically, we encounter a selective relativism, a peculiar combination of professed moral (or intellectual, or aesthetic) relativism, and an unstated moral absolutism and partisanship that can be inferred from the unskeptical advocacy of positions taken by the putative relativist. As Gross and Levitt point out, "the strange combination of skepticism ad credulity, characterizes the postmodern stance" (p. 180). In turn, Himmelfarb notes, for example, that while many intellectuals in the liberal democracies glory in 'demystifying' their own culture and nation as Eurocentric, xenophobic, sexist, and racist, they fawn on illiberal Third World nations, provided they are sufficiently anti-Western (p. 121). Likewise, while they subject to merciless scrutiny their own Western culture, they cannot bring themselves to critically examine, among other things, the claims of "multiculturalism," especially its Afrocentric variety.

It is significant and paradoxical that the postmodernists who claim to believe that everything is a matter of opinion, are among the fiercest, most virulent, and radical critics of Western culture. They emerged as the heirs of the sixties' rejection of American society, unable or unconcerned to propose a positive vision for replacing the multiple evils of our allegedly racist, sexist, patriarchal, capitalist, homophobic, and Eurocentric culture. Unhappily, "one of the saddest facts of life is that frustration rarely begets wisdom but it frequently ignites irresponsible fantasy" (Gross and Levitt, p. 233).

Gertrude Himmelfarb is among the handful of scholars in the humanities who powerfully confronts and publicly rejects these trends. It is her premise that "there is an intimate, pervasive relationship between what happens in our schools and universities, in the intellectual and artistic communities, and what happens in society and the polity" (p. xii). Her collection of essays addresses both the intellectual and moral aspects of the burgeoning obscurantism and relativism, especially as they appear in the study and teaching of history. She arrestingly sums up the current state of affairs in the humanities and some of the social sciences: "The beasts of modernism have mutated into the beasts of postmodernism-relativism into nihilism, amorality into immorality, irrationality into insanity" (p. 16).

Her collection includes not only illuminating critiques of postmodernist historiography but also examinations of current approaches to the teaching of literature and philosophy, reflections on Karl Marx, Georg Hegel, and John Stuart Mill, and the contemporary political-historical roles and relationships of religion and nationalism. Looking at current trends in history and biography in particular, Professor Himmelfarb observes that the very idea "that there is such a thing as greatness, genius, uniqueness, that people should celebrate and aspire to such qualities, that there are truths that transcend race, gender and class" is under attack (p. 40). The anti-intellectual and amoral thrust of this attitude is quite momentous. Himmelfarb writes:

> Postmodernism is now confronting us with... a relativism so radical, so absolute as to be antithetical to both history and truth. For postmodernists deny not only suprahistorical truth but historical truth, truths relative to particular times and places.(p. 131)
>
> The presumption of postmodernism is that... because there is no absolute, total truth there can be no partial, contingent truths. More important still is the presumption that because it is impossible to attain such truths, it is not only futile but positively baneful to aspire to them (p. 135).

Passing moral judgments even over phenomena such as Nazism or Soviet totalitarianism becomes problematic, if not altogether impermissible, for the postmodernist: "Looking into the most fearsome abysses of modern times, these historians see not beasts but faceless bureaucrats, not corpses but statistics, not willful acts of brutality and murder but the banal routine of everyday life, not gas chambers and gulags but military-industrial-geopolitical complexes" (p. 18).

The embrace of such a far-reaching moral-intellectual relativism has profound consequences for the life of the mind. Ever more professors of literature disdain the study and interpretation of actual literary works, and there are historians who do little research about actual historical events or periods (pp. 140-42). The contempt for facts even finds expression in the progressive abandonment of footnotes, in the lofty indifference to documenting views and opinions, as Himmelfarb shows in "Where Have All the Footnotes Gone?"

In this compact volume, Himmelfarb succeeds in lucidly cataloging and exposing some of the most profound ills and ailments of American society and cultural life as it approaches the end of the century. In doing so, she personifies and reinvigorates the ideal of the responsible intellectual.

It is of great significance, even if not generally realized, that during the past quarter century or so critiques of science have become a major form of social and culture criticism in the United States. While the social criticism of the 1960s focused on particular social institutions, practices, or evils, the more recent varieties seek fundamental change through "a wholesale revision of cultural categories" (Gross and Levitt, p. 3), that is to say, concepts, ideas, words, ways of looking at the world. This orientation also explains the extraordinary efforts made at purging and transforming our vocabulary so that the "correct" usage should reflect "correct" ideas; the obsession with appropriate terminology on the part of radical feminists, Afrocentrists, and other victim groups is a form of intended thought reform.

In the course of the past two decades, the hostility to science has become a common denominator of the adversary culture and its different constituencies. These attitudes had their roots in the social-cultural protest movements of the 1960s, especially in the counter-cultural fulminations against the impersonality and the rational ordering of society and the highly romantic rejection of the routinized, predictable aspects of life. As the representatives of the protest movements of the sixties and adherents of the adversary culture settled down to academic life, the attacks on science emerged as their major shared preoccupation. Gross and Levitt write: Postmodern skepticism rejects the possibility of enduring universal knowledge in any area. It holds that all knowledge is local, or 'situated'...rigidly circumscribed by interests and prejudices...(p. 72).

The traditional Marxist view that what we think of as science is really 'bourgeois' science, a superstructural manifestation of the capitalist order, recurs with predictable regularity, or refurbished as the doctrine of 'cultural constructivism'.

> The radical feminist view [is] that science, like every other intellectual structure in modern society is poisoned and corrupted by ineradicable gender bias. . . multiculturalists view 'Western' science as inherently inaccurate and incomplete by virtue of its failure to incorporate the full range of cultural perspectives...radical environmentalism condemns science as embodying instrumentalism and alienation from direct experience of nature. What enables [these views] to coexist congenially. . . is a shared sense of injury, resentment and indignation against modern science (p. 5).

The authors see a shared resentment as the main source of the attack on science. But while splendidly describing its varied manifestations, they stop short of attempting to locate the deeper sources of this resentment. And while they observe, correctly, that "science becomes an irresistible target for those Western intellectuals whose sense of their own heritage has become an intolerable moral burden" (p. 220), they do not pursue the matter further to ask: What aspects of this heritage have become so burdensome and loathsome and for what reason?

What really ails the academic Left, the ideological survivors of the sixties, and the adversary culture that make up a large portion of American intellectuals here discussed? The resentment against science, I believe, derives from a broader and deeper source: the resentment of modernity itself. When all is said and done, and when we put together both the most articulate as well as the most inarticulate critiques of capitalism, American society, Western culture and civilization, and Eurocentric thought, what stands out is the rejection of the lack of meaning, purpose, and lost sense of community associated with modernity. To be sure, there are also grievances and injuries (real and imagined) peculiar to gender, race, ethnicity, and (decreasingly) class. But the actual experiences of victimization do not come close to accounting for the ferocity and generality of the rejection and critique directed at American culture and society, since the critics themselves are generally privileged, for the most part academic, intellectuals.

The rejection of the pains of modernity is not the only way to explain the alienation of intellectuals that is behind their postmodernist, multiculturalist hostility to science. Critics of Western intellectuals (among them Raymond Aron, Paul Johnson, Lewis Feuer, Eric Hoffer, Christopher Lasch, Arthur Koestler, and Edward Shils, to name only a few) repeatedly suggested that intellectuals turn on their (Western) societies because they do not feel sufficiently appreciated, because these societies, and the American in particular, have failed to satisfy their need for recognition, influence, and even power—or as Richard Pipes put it recently, because of frustrated ambition.

Gross and Levitt themselves ask in their last chapter: how much difference does the hostility to science really make to the state of American culture and society? Is it an indicator of general decadence, or is it much ado about nothing as far as the country as a whole is concerned? As suggested above, the attitudes and beliefs examined by the two books under review are indeed powerful indicators of decadence precisely because they join together its moral-psychological and functional-instrumental aspects. The hostility to science is significant both as symptom of a profound estrangement from Western culture and rationality, and in its consequences. The latter include the rising levels of scientific illiteracy and the diminishing numbers of Americans interested in its pursuit, as indicated in the gradual takeover of departments of the hard (not social!) sciences by students from abroad.The extraordinary and increasingly radical animus against American society and Western culture that finds expression in the hostility toward science is, in the final analysis, a protest against life perceived as both meaningless and unjust. Perhaps the most serious threat the attitudes here discussed represent—and the most profound symptom of the decadence, at once moral and intellectual, they embody—is that, as Gross and Levitt put it, they leave "no ground whatsoever for distinguishing reliable knowledge from superstition" (p. 45). A noteworthy example of the inroads made by the trends here discussed has been the career of John Mack, M.D., professor of psychiatry at Harvard. After years at the "cutting edge" of various New Age and peace movements, Mack has recently taken to writing about claims of massive extraterrestrial kidnappings and copulations, and advocating their veracity.[1] What is so stunning about Mack's new cause is not that he has adopted it, but the astonishing respectability his claims have garnered in the commercial publishing and media world.

If, as Gross and Levitt persuasively argue, "the health of a culture is measured in part by the vigor with which its immune system responds to nonsense" (p. 217), then we are in sad shape. But thanks to Gross and Levitt and Himmelfarb, among many others, mostly unsung, perhaps the tide will start to turn.

Note

1.   John Mack, *Abduction: Human Encounters with Aliens* (New York: Scribners, 1994). See, also, Stephen Rae, "Humans Report Abduction by Aliens! Harvard Psychiatrist Swears It's True!" *The New York Times Magazine,* Mar. 20, 1994.

5

Good Intentions and Unintended Consequences: A Critique of "Affirmative Action"

I

A state-sponsored, institutionalised struggle against prejudice, discrimination and the associated inequalities is a historically novel phenomenon; most societies through much of recorded history took discrimination and inequality for granted. Deprived and mistreated groups of low status—slaves, lower castes, serfs, the poor, the mentally ill, ethnic minorities and other outsiders—inspired little compassion and few efforts to improve their condition. The very idea of the desirability of social and individual equality (or at least equality of opportunity) has been of recent recent Western origin.

The policy of affirmative action and the plethora of laws and regulations passed on its behalf are among the historically rare attempts made by a society to rectify the results of centuries old discrimination. These policies also exemplify the proverbial unforeseen and unintended consequences of social action (Merton 1957).

Affirmative action has become problematic on many grounds. First and foremost because it shifts the emphasis from individual rights, and accomplishments to group rights and entitlements. Secondly, instead of doing away with the evaluation of human beings in terms of questionable racial categories, it has revived and strengthened thinking in precisely such terms ("Those who, with the best of intentions, have emphasized racial categories at the expense of color blindness must bear some responsibility for legitimizing the racially categorizing thinking that results" (Pinkerton 1995). Thirdly, affirmative action rather than improving race relations had further inflamed them both in the country at large and especially in academic settings where it has been most arduously pursued and implemented: "This backlash has developed on campuses that already have all the things that are supposed to cure it—campuses dominated by racial 'representation' or body-count thinking, campuses awash in affirmative action officers, associate deans for minority affairs, ethnic studies faculty and ethnic student organizations, centers, even separate residences." (Sowell 1989) As Lipset put it "Affirmative action... was transformed into a system of racial preference and today... (it) is rapidly polarizing the politics of race in America." (Lipset 1992:53)

If it is true, as is often claimed that racism has increased during the years and decades when the enormous machinery of affirmative action was set into motion, it may well be connected to the very programs which sought to erase it. On the one hand preferential treament met with the resentment of whites, on the other it raised expectations among the black population (as well as other groups) which it failed to satisfy. While it is no easy matter to determine whether or not white American have become more racist or merely irritated by such preferential treatment—it is a striking fact that during the decades which saw the rise and spread of affirmative action black mistrust of American society and political institutions has increased. During this period radical, extremist figures such as Louis Farrakhan became increasingly prominent and accepted in the black community. In all probability affirmative action has also been a major contributor to the growth of antagonism between blacks and Jews (see for example Friedman 1995) although the latter have been in the forefront of the struggle against racism and discrimination in American society.[1] It is not being suggested here that these developments occurred as a direct result of affirmative action, but that they coincided with its rise and entrenchment and may be counted among its unintended and unforesen by-products.

The critical evaluation of affimative action requires confronting the question what is wrong with preferential treatment or even reverse discrimimation, as compensatory measures for the legacy of mistreatment that reaches back three centuries? It should also respond to the frequently heard argument that preferential treatment is an age old practice, as in the "old boy networks," or when preference is given to the children of rich alumni at private univerities, or when members of the same group of immigrants favor one another.

The new preferences, it is often suggested, are seeking to counter-balance these traditional forms of preferences. But neither the old boy network, nor the mutual and spontaneous favors members of the same ethnic group grant to one another are comparable to the policies of affirmative action in their scope or consequences. Affirmative action and the quotas it has bred "touch all aspects of life. According to the Congressional Research Service, the federal government alone has 160 race and gender preference programs" (Roberts 1995; see also Roberts and Stratton 1995).

An analysis of the idea of affirmative action must begin by noting the burden of semantic dishonesty it has come to carry. As such it has also contributed to the corruption of language and public discourse. A critic noted "... one of affirmative action's most corrosive side-effects has been to oblige everyone involved in it to participate in a massive denial of how exactly it works and what its consequences have been" (Puddington 1995:23). More generally speaking the insistent, pious denial of the essential core of affirmative action (i.e. preferential treatment) has been part of the larger process of transforming race and race relations into "a swamp of euphemism, hypocrisy and cant", leading to the observation that "we can no longer truthfully talk about race" (Peretz 1990:42).

Affirmative action was not originally intended to be a pursuit of the statistical representativeness of black people in every organization, institution or hierarchy, let alone of other groups currently protected and promoted by these programs. It was rather supposed to be an energetic effort to overcome past or present discrimination and their aftereffects. In fact it has become reverse discrimination operating with quotas poorly disguised by various semantic devices such "time tables." This is its major criticism and all the others follow from it.

The original goals of affirmative action were (1) legal-institutional support for ending discrimination against the black citizens[2] of the United States; (2) some degree of compensation for the historical wrongs they suffered; (3) bridging the gap between ideals and realities in American society, namely that between the promise and the accomplishment of equal opportunity; (4) reducing social conflict and bringing about improvements in intergroup relations by ending discrimination and offering expanded opportunities for black people and at last (5) the reduction of the waste of human potentials inherent in arbitrary discrimination.

It will be argued below that few of these goals have been realised and to the extent that they have, it has been at considerable and unforeseen cost to society. While there have been substantial improvements in the condition of black Americans over the lack 30 years—in access to higher education, middle class status, political participation and influence—it is difficult to know if these gains resulted from ending discrimination or from the preferential treatment affirmative action entailed. Thomas Sowell, for instance noted that "... a substantial increase in the number of black students completing college—a 64 jump between 1940 and 1947—occurred without preferences or quotas" (Sowell 1989).

Nobody knows exactly how much good affirmative action has done—*as distinct from the removal of discrimination*. This is an important distinction and at the heart of the debate. A sociologist wrote:

> 20 years after the Civil Rights Act of 1964...there has been no systematic inquiry into the efects of affirmative action... neither its costs to the nation's economy, nor its impact on our country's morale. In an age of program evalutation, when most other social experiments are almost studied to death our profession (sociology) has shown a resolute ignorance about an extraordinarily controversial policy.... It is as if affirmative action has assumed the status of a religious article of faith..." (Beer 1987:63; see also Beer 1988)

In the spring of 1995 an attempt was made at the University of Massachusetts Amherst campus to have a public debate on affirmative action with student and faculty participation. This writer was one of two faculty members willing to offer public criticism of affirmative action and this was not the case because the rest of my colleagues wholeheartedly support it. The reluctance to come forward could best be explained by the widespread apprehension of being called "racist"—a predictable outcome any reservation about affirmative action brings forth on the campuses and elsewhere. This state of affairs is in itself an indication of the transformation of a program from a being a tool of social justice into an icon of political correctnes. Such deformation of public discourse has been among the unforeseen by products of affirmative action. Since the fear of being accused of racism has become pervasive (especially among the educated strata of the population) it has become difficult to discuss the problems of the black population unless apriori defined as the sole product of white racism. It took about 30 years for the findings of the Moynihan Report (earlier denounced as racist) (Moynihan 1965) to become publicly accepted and appreciated.

Similar critiques greeted the studies of busing by James Coleman (Coleman 1966).

In the world of mass entertainment the fear of being accused of racism is similarly pervasive. It results, among other things, in rarely showing in television programs black criminals (and especially violent ones) (Lichter, Lichter & Rothman 1992) since the producers have no desire to be charged with propagating "racist stereotypes". This newly established "socialist realism" in American mass entertainment (for its original meaning see Tertz 1960 and Hollander 1966) requires not only to represent the protected groups proportionally (esp. on television) but to portray them favorably. Thus "minorities have a way of turning out to be kinder, more caring, more lovable folks than the majority" (Goodman, 1995). In "totalling up the minuses of affirmative-action TV" Walter Goodman of the *New York Times* also found that "simplification and glorification" prevail.

Similar attempts to achieve representativeness also shape readings lists and requirements in all institutions of education where the selection of authors is often more influenced by the desire to make reading lists "representative" (of minorities and women), than by the more conventional judgements of quality or excellence.

Outside the campuses and mass entertainment the situation is somewhat different. As of the early 1990s cautious criticisms of affirmative action appeared in the press and politicians began to discuss its unwelcome consequences. For example Senator Joseph Lieberman (D) of Connecticut said that "When we have such policies (as affirmative action) we break those ties in civil society that have held us together... You cant defend policies that are based on group preferences as opposed to individual opportunities, which is what America has always been about" (Purdum 1995).

II

Affirmative action has become a program to achieve a proportional representation of the designated minorities in various fields of employment, in colleges, police forces, even on death row (Rothman and Powers 1994) rather than creating *the opportunity* for members of these groups to compete on more equal terms.[3] "Race norming" has become a major tool for achieving these results. As a critic wrote:

It is an open secret among personnel professionals that race-conscious hiring has become the rule... While employers often resort to quotas or other race-conscious hiring procedures to avoid litigation... they must deny such practices publicly to avoid reverse discrimination lawsuits....

One of America's best-kept open secret is that the Employment Service of the Dept. of Labor has unashamedly promulgated quotas. In 1981 the service recommended that state employment agencies adopt a race-conscious way of recomputing test scores... to avoid adverse impact when referrring job applicants to employers.

Under the recommended procedure called race-norming, each candiate's score is reported not in relation to those of all other canddiates, but only in relation to the scores of the applicants of the same racial group. Black are compared only with other blacks, Hispanics only with other Hispanics. (Gottfredson 1990)

The same problem arises when different standards are applied to minorities than to whites or Asians in college admissions. Such practices while widely denied are common; when occasionally revealed and documented they are dismissed as irrelevant or unimportant (i.e. grade point averages or test scores), such tests are then said to be "culturally biased." It has been the tendency to call all tests culturally biased when group differences in performance show up.

The case of the black musician who was exempted from blind auditioning for the Detroit symphony orchestra (due to threats of witholding funding from the orchestra by black members of the city council) is an example of both how far the desire for representativeness can be carried and its implications for standards and quality. (Wilkerson 1989)

Precisely because of the pressure (that sometimes includes loss of federal funds, or disruptive demonstrations on the campuses) to achieve proportional representation, standards or excellence and even competence have become relaxed, sometimes compromised. It is not the case—though widely and vehemently asserted—that affirmative action merely means that when two *equally qualified* candidates for a position are considered, the minority group member (or the woman) will be chosen. In many instances positions (or grants, fellowships, loans etc) are open only to the minorities (or other protected groups) to begin with. When the pressure to increase the ratio of minorities is great, less qualified candidates will be picked because there just arent enough qualified ones available. Examples of such pressures and policies include

... a Defense Department memo (that) specifies: 'in the future special permission will be required for the promotion of all white men without disabilities.' ... job postings for U.S. Forest Service firefighting positions specified that 'only unqualified applicants will be considered' and Federal Aviation Administration... has recently provided its supervisors with guidelines which state: 'the merit promotion process... need not be utilized if it will not promote your diversity roles.' (quoted in Roberts 1995)

The attempt of the California legislature to mandate proportional graduation of minorities from college (Bunzel 1990, Leo 1991) (vetoed by the governor) was another attempt to create equal results, not opportunities. The implication of such a meausre for standards needs little explication.[4]

III

The vast expansion of affirmative action took place through executive orders and court decisions, rather than through the legislative process; as such it incompletely, if at all, reflects the beliefs or the consensus of the majority of the American voters. Opinion polls indicate that the majority of the population is critical of such programs:

> The Gallup organization has polled on preferences five times since March 1977 and has consistently found that more than 80% of respondents favor a strict meritocratic system in employment and university admissions over a system in which "women and members of minorities" are given preference "to make up for past discrimination". On no occasions... has support for preferential treatment exceeded 11% of the general population. (Nieli 1991)

Lipset concluded that "mass opinion remains invariably opposed to preferential treatment for deprived groups." Even "over-two thirds of the blacks rejected preferential treatment.". A majority (56%) "... favored 'ability as determined in test scores'" (Lipset 1992:54).

A recent graduate of two University of California campuses offered this assessment:

> The affirmative action admissions programs (often euphemistically labelled "diversity programs") created tremendous resentment and hostility among students. The clear pereption was that participants obtained admission, notwithstanding comparatively weak academic records, simply because of the color of their skin, received special tutoring and remedial programs, and were held to lower standards of achievement. (Holo 1995)

It might be argued that even if the majority of Americans are insufficiently enlightened or generous to support such programs and principles it is the duty of the more farsighted elites to exercise leadership and promote these programs because it is "the right thing to do." I will argue that not only are these programs unpopular but they are also in many respects unfair and counterproductive, and persist largely because they are energetically championed by those benefiting (including their administrators) and because of the lingering guilt of white elite groups. Intellectuals and, among them social scientists, are especially susceptible to such feelings, critical as they are in general of the social practices and institutions of their society.[5]

IV

At the root of the problems of affirmative action has been the unconditional attribution of victimhood to each and every black individual regardless of income, education, political power and public recognition. This has been a part of the disposition to blame society for all social ills and inequalities and to exempt the individual from all responsibility for his condition, if deemed to be disadvantaged (I discussed this propensity in relation to the idea of "selective determinism"; see Hollander 1983).

As long as an entire group is perceived as helpless victim of society no amount of compensatory measures will be considered adequate for those championing its interests (for a highly relevant discussion of "blame analysis" see Felson 1991).

It is worth recalling here that the concept of affirmative action has been preceded by that of "compensatory opportunity." The latter made an early appearance in "... the Democratic platform of 1976. That was before 'affirmative action ... was fully established as the prefered euphmism for reverse discirmimnation. Such discrimination is now known as a 'race-conscious remedy'" (Will 1995).

The concept of affirmative action and the programs linked to it emerged in order to accelerate the ending of racial discrimination; they reflected the desire of policy-makers and—initially at any rate, a broad popular consensus—to go beyond a colorblind policy. Affirmative action intended not merely to open the doors closed by discrimination, but to *recruit* qualified black citizens to colleges, jobs in government, industry and every workplace, educational or political institution and organization from which they had been barred on account of the color of their skin and the stereotyped negative attributes associated with it.

The assumption was that discrimination and its legacy had to be overcome not merely by opening up various institutions to those who had earlier been excluded (on the highly irrational ground of the color of their skin) but that *special efforts* were to be made to recruit such individuals to all the places which had excluded them earlier regardless of their capabilities and qualifications. It did not seem to occur to the early advocates and designers of affirmative action that these "special efforts" will turn into the pursuit of statistical representativeness. Nonetheless, affirmative action has become a vast complex of programs of preferential treatment, of reverse discrimination seeking to achieve such statistical representation (for a critical examination of preferential programs and policies in a comparative-international context see Sowell 1990).

The transformation of the meaning of affirmative action has been accompanied by a redefinition of the meaning of racism. No longer a disposition that any group may display it is now widely used as if it were the singular attribute of white people, equated with the ability of white powerholders to oppress blacks ("only whites truly can be racist because only they have the power to oppress" (Bunzel 1991: 64)). It may be recalled here that racism originally meant an attitude of irrational hostility against groups of people (or individuals who belong to certain groups) joined together by some discernible attribute (racial or ethnic) and the belief that each individual is wholly determined by such group membership. World history and contemporary politics abound with examples of groups of people of every conceivable color and ethnicity entertaining such attitudes and stereotypes toward one another and carrying them to murderous extremes.

Another development in the transformation of the concept of racism has been its increasingly broad and unspecific use, the conjuring up of "subtle," "unconscious," or "institutional" racism, more and more divorced from specific, tangible or concrete behavioral manifestations, indicators or incidents. Such a promiscuous attribution of racism to groups, individuals and insitutions has not benefited race relations. The mere questioning of preferential treatment is often treated as indisputable evidence of racism, as is any criticism of the performance or qualifications of any member of a protected minority. Russell Baker, the *New York Times* columnist observed, the term "'Racist' now has a punishing power similar to the power 'Communist' in Red-hunting days when a politician calling you 'Communist' expected your boss to fire you immediately" (Baker 1990).

Alongside the changing interpretations of what racism means came a new view of discrimination. Whereas at earlier times it was seen as something intentional and willed, for instance when embodied in discriminatory laws or exclusionary, if more informal social norms, the new meaning of discrimination came to be a statistical underrepresentation or disparity in the work force, or other organizations, and hierarchies. Hence the rise of the "'disparate impact' standard, which defines as discrimination any policy or job requirement that does not produce race and gender proportionality."(Roberts 1995) Increasingly affirmative action has come to be based on the idea that any statistically disparate representation of the designated minorities (in schools, places of employment, various hierarchies etc) is self-evident proof of discrimination. If black college students failed more often than those of other groups racism was responsible, as it was for the high proportion of criminal offenders or drug users among the young, black male population.

The principle of proportionality must lead one to suspect that if few conductors of symphony orchestras are Black or Hispanic it must be the result of willful discrimination; by the same token if few Jewish officers can be found in the U.S. Special Forces or among firefighters (volunteer or professional) this too must be a result of exclusionary policies[6]; likewise the shortage of black astronomers, geologists and mathematicians (among other scientists) must be ascribed to discrimination, subtle or other; and there may also be reason for serious concern with the underrepresentation of Jews and Asian Americans in the ranks of professional boxers, football and basketball players.

At the same time it has yet to be proposed that the statistical overrepresentation of blacks in basketball or boxing results from discrimination against Asians, Jews or other whites, and hence requires urgent remedy, or that the high proportion of Asians in sciences and engineering had been brought about by affirmative action on their behalf. In itself an interesting question how has it been possible for a protected (and presumably deprived) minority such as the Asian Americans to excell in higher education and especially in the sciences and engineering? How are we to account for the preponderance of Indian and Korean grocers in many big cities? As to the preponderance of females in social work and nursing, is that too the result of being barred from, say forestry, farming, or engineering, or could it possibly reflect their greater interest in the careers more typically chosen?

It is not suggested here that statistical disparities cannot result from discrimination, or of the habits and attitudes which remain in place even after discrimination was removed; what is being suggested is that occupational and educational choices and their patterns have many explanations—cultural, historical, social-psychological—and that the disparities cannot be attributed to discrimination as a matter of course, an attribution which has become the basis of current public policy.

V

The original purpose of affirmative action—the attainment, or approximation of social justice, especially on behalf of "the truly disadvantaged" (Wilson 1987)—has been further obscured by the rise of another justification, that of the striving for "diversity." (see for example Sacks and Thiel 1994) It came to be argued that affirmative action is also beneficial because it creates "diversity". The precise benefits or character of such diversity have rarely been spelled out but the implication has been that it is a self-evident good, leading to, or entailing some kind of automatic psychological and cultural enrichment.

The institutionalised pursuit of diversity here refered to hardly if ever, meant the pursuit of the diversity of opinion, religious belief, political conviction, social class or occupational background, not even a that of broad ethnic diversity.

Just as disadvantage has been narrowly defined so has diversity. Diversity is achieved, in the current conventional wisdom, when the groups currently defined as disadvantaged are properly (proportionally) represented in various settings. If diversity had also been pursued for cultural-intellectual reasons, the representation of people of different outlook, political and religious beliefs, and philosophies would also have been sought. This has not been the case. We have yet to hear of a department or college looking for well qualified evangelical Christians, card-carrying Republicans, female anti-abortion activists, articulate neo-conservatives, anti-communists or credentialed survivors of the Holocaust (or other political atrocities). As it is diversity is usually a codeword for a narrow spectrum of beliefs and attitudes and ethnic backgrounds. According to one interpretation

The argument one now hears (in support of diversity) is that people of color have a distinctive voice, a vision of the world, that is not represented in places where vital decisions are being made... In the new rhetoric of affirmative action...the reason to seek out and hire or admit people of color is that...their perspective will be different from the...perspectives of people who are white... The unfortunate logical corollary is that if the perspective a particular person of color can offer is not distinctive...then that person is not speaking in an authentially black voice—an accusation that has become all too common. (Carter 1991)

In practice this has come to mean (especially on the campuses) that it is not enough to be black (or Hispanic or female etc) to qualify for and benefit from affirmative action, you have to be a politically correct black, Hispanic or female, otherwise you are not a "real black" but an Uncle Tom or "Oreo Cookie," not an appropriate role model. There are today highly qualified but politically incorrect (conservative) black scholars, who have serious trouble getting an academic job, or a decent academic job.

The striving for "diversity" coupled as it has been with "multiculturalism" had its own paradoxical and unforeseen result: widening the distance between the groups of the population resulting from the glorification of the cultural assets and essence of the designated minorities. Such glorification has been part of the efforts to raise their self-esteem—another concept that came to play a growing part in race relations and the striving for racial identity. But, as a psychologist wrote: "Self esteem theorists have it backward. Meaningful self-evaluation and positive self-esteem are usually results, not antecedents of accomplishment." (Stevenson 1994)

It may be argued that affirmative action could actually undermine the self-esteem and the sense of achievement of its beneficiaries who can never be certain to what extent their gains were due to their own efforts and excellence or the result of the preferential treatment accorded to them. There is also the possibility, pointed to by Sowell that when the insufficiently qualified beneficiaries of preferential treatment (in colleges) face difficulties they can only "retain their self respect by continually attacking, undermining and trying to discredit the standards they do not meet, scavenging for grievances and issuing a never-ending stream of demands and manifestoes" (Sowell 1989). These words have a familiar ring to anybody who has taught in a college or university over the past quarter century. It is a further paradox that the pursuit of "diversity" came to be associated with residential and social self-segregation, separate cultural centers, programs of study and other attributes of group identity.

The other argument for diversity is linked to the idea of the role model. Diversity is supposed to assure a steady supply of role models whose very presence is assumed to raise the self esteem, motivation, and levels of achievement of members of the group to which they belong. There is however little evidence that we learn better from, or are more inspired by people who belong to the same racial or ethnic group as we do, or are of the same sex. We learn best from, and are inspired by people who are highly qualified, and dedicated, and impress us with their intelligence, integrity and other good qualities—they become role models regardless of their race,gender, ethnicity, religious affiliation or sexual preference.

VI

Another serious critique of affirmative action is that it has not been a tool of social justice or historical compensation for past wrongs because it has not benefited those who need it most, the poor and uneducated, "the truly disadvantaged" among the selected minorities. A *Study of Race Relations at Harvard College* found in the early 1980s that 70% of black undergraduates came from professional or managerial families (Skerry 1981:63). Many of them might have made it to Harvard without affirmative action though certainly not all.

It is also questionable why affirmative action should apply to all foreign born citizens (or non-citizens) of color although neither they nor their ancestors suffered discrimination in the United States.

The prevailing definitions of disadvantage and deprivation are narrow and problematic, they ignore and exclude many forms of disadvantage. Definitions of being privileged are equally dubious when all white males are placed in that category. It takes little reflection to realize that there are poor, uneducated whites and prosperous, well educated blacks and Hispanics who come from intact families, command high incomes, even political power and influence. A critic wrote: "Affirmative action programs... often benefit those who do not deserve benefits (the sons of Jamaican physicians or wealthy Cuban businessmen, for instance) and require that an arbitrarily selected subset of the population pay the cost" (Nieli 1991). There are even more white women in no way underprivileged in terms of social status, income, education or occupational achievement. Neither skin color or not gender are at the present time automatic and infallible indicators or determinants of either privilege or disadvantage. To treat for example a black Ph.D., lawyer or M.D. as a victim flies in the face of all evidence, including the "bidding wars" academic institutions conduct to get such people. The same goes for black, Hispanic etc. students with high test scores, and good grades avidly pursued by elite institutions.

Disadvantage has many faces including colorblind poverty, broken families, addictions, abusive or neglectful parents, being orphaned, physical or mental deficiencies or disabilities, growing up in an economically and culturally deprived neigborhood or region, having suffered political or religious discrimination or persecution— all of them define or contribute to a deprived condition. To be sure there is also a frequent, but far from invariable clustering of several disadvantages among some ethnic groups such as poverty, problematic family background, and ill health.

In a world of scarcities preferential treatment is always accorded at the expense of somebody. There is no convincing moral argument to justify that the present generation of white males (or females) pay the price for the wrongs commited by previous generations, often centuries ago,—especially given all the other problematic aspects of preferential treatment noted above. For such reasons affirmative action is a festering source of new or intensified racial-ethnic, possibly gender conflicts.

The invidious emphasis on racial, ethnic or gender group pride doesnt foster better group relations either. Nor is it likely that improvements in self-esteem follow when members of a particular group immerse themselves in studying themselves, or their past history. As a social scientist wrote "knowing about the travails and triumphs of one's forebears doesnt necessariliy translate into either self esteem or personal accomplishment" (Ravitch 1990:354). At last it is not even clear, though often taken for granted, that minorities and women have lower self esteem. (Powers, Rothman & Rothman 1990).

VII

A final criticism of affirmative action is that it encourages claims of victimization and an unending preoccupation with grievances since these claims are the basis of it. "The victim focused identity" (Steele 1990) has become avidly pursued for both its material and moral rewards by an increasing number of Americans. More and more groups seek a sense of identity, socio-economic and political advantage in their victimhood, past, present or imaginary.

Claims of victimhood will not be easily surrendered as long as they provide both tangible material-economic advantage (e.g. preferential treatment in college admissions, minority fellowships and special consideration in employment etc.)—and preferential moral treatment and solicitousness accorded to officially recognised victim groups. Tens if not hundreds of thousands of people make their living by justifying, monitoring and administering, in various capacities, affirmative action. Many others draw their salaries from ministering to the needs, moral and material, of the beneficiaries; in addition dubious experts and consultants of diversity and intergroup relations flourish (see for example MacDonald 1993). Since an end to grievances and victimhood would eliminate justifications of affirmative action, victimhood cannnot be relinquished —hence the "victim focused identity." Increasingly what matters is not the actual experience of victimization but past victimization or the possibility of victimization. In part for this reasons supporters of affirmative action are not prepared to say when it should come to an end. Affirmative action has become a self perpetuating group entitlement and no group is likely voluntarily relinquish its benefits.

VIII

The costs, unforeseen consequences and by products of afirmative action may be summed up as follows. For society as a whole the cost has included increased racial-ethnic tension, division and conflict, the growth of fragmentation among ethnic groups, the weakening of national unity and overall cultural cohesion (Schlesinger 1990). An erosion of standards (in college admissions, workplace qualifications etc) has been another major result, as has been the narrowing of public discourse and the decline of free expression and simple truth telling. The massive bureaucracies which designed and enforce affirmative action are another burden for society to bear. For the white, and esp., white male population the demotion of the principle of individual merit has been the most disturbing. For the black population the embrace of the "victim focused identity" has planted the seeds of doubt regarding their own accomplishments and weakened its self-confidence and sense of autonomy. It is difficult to divorce victimhood from a sense of weakness and helplessness.

For all these reasons affirmative action as currently defined and institutionalised does not serve well either social justice, genuine diversity or the cause of improved race relations.

Notes

1. Joshua Muravchik wrote: "From Jessie Jackson's 'Hymietown' remarks, to the rantings of Leonard Jeffries of the City University of New York, to finally, Louis Farrakhan, the anti-Semitic virus crept closer and closer to the center of black consciousness. Signposts along the way include the three-day anti-Semitic rampage in 1991 in the Crown Heights section of Brooklyn; the rise in the open expressions of anti-Jewish sentiment in black popular culture, as in the lyrics of 'rap artists'... and the characters drawn by the film-maker Spike Lee; the propagation of the... utterly false notion that Jews played a prominent role in the slave trade; and opinion polls showing anti-Semitism on the rise among blacks—especially young and better educated blacks—even as white anti-Semitism has declined." (Muravchik 1995:27).

2. It is important to keep in mind that affirmative action was originally intended to apply only to the black population of the United States; to the extent that it has been expanded to other ethnic groups, recent immigrants, women, the disabled, and others, the original purposes of these policies became diluted, and their historical justification undermined.
   This article focuses on affirmative action as it was supposed to apply to the black citizens of the United States.
   The flaws of these policies as applied to all women, the disabled and others have been somewhat different. The preferential treatment of Hispanics also raises different questions; most obviously the historical victimization they suffered in the United States was much milder than the comparable black experience. Those of Asian ancestry, the most highly educated and successful subgroup of the population, are far more dubious candidates for victimhood at the present time. Native Americans are yet another group with distinctive experiences of victimization.
   I should also note here in light of changing terminological fashions that I see no reason to change—from what was deemed an acceptable term for decades, namely black or black American—to the recently popular "African-American" that seeks to direct attention to the African component in the black identity.

3. Nobody seriously entertains the achievement of complete equality since a serious effort to attain it would require, for a start, the abolishing of the family that passes on all kinds of advantages and disadvantages, attitudinal as well as material. It would have to be followed by the systemaic abolition of all types of comparative and competitive assesments of individual and group performances in all aspects of life.

4. There is already a certain amount of "affirmative grading" as well on the part of teachers who are worried of being accused of racism if they give a poor grade to minority students, or are prompted by their social conscience not to give a poor grade. While there is ample anecdotal evidence for such practices it is impossible to know how widespread they are. To the extent that they exist they are clearly linked to affirmative action, or to a dubious conception of it.

5. Lipset observed that "The heaviest support for preferential treatment seems to come from the liberal intelligentsia... the five to six percent of the population who have gone to graduate school, plus those who have majored in the liberal arts..." (Lipset 1992:55).

6. The exclusion of Jews from the protected categories is another inconsistency in defining the grounds for and the purposes of affirmative action. To be sure Jews as a group have been in a far better position than blacks throughout American history. On the other hand the historic sufferings of Jews might be considered equal to or outweighing the deprivations of recent Indian, Chinese, Japanese or Fillippino immigrants to the United States. Statistics would also show many occupations and hierachies where Jews have been underrepresented—by choice or disrimination.

References

Baker, Russel (1990) "Dont Mention It', *New York Times*, May 30

Beer, William R.1987. "Resolute Ignorance: Social Science and Affirmative Action" *Society*, May-June

——1988. "Sociology and the Effects of affirmative Action: A Case of Neglect", *American Sociologist*, Fall

Bunzel, John (1990 "Should UC Admissions Set Ethnic and Racial Goals?", *Los Angeles Times*, July 1,

——1991. "Black and White at Stanford", *Public Interest*, reprinted in Stanford CA: Hoover Institution Reprint Series No. 139

Carter, Stephen L.1991. "I Am an Affirmative Action Baby", *New York Times*, August 5

Coleman, James 1966. *Equality of Educational Opportunity*, Washington DC: U.S.Superintendent of Documents

Felson, Richard B.1991. "Blame Analyis: Accounting for the Behavior of Protected Groups", *American Sociologist*, Spring

Friedman, Murray.1995. *The Creation and Collapse of the Black-Jewish Alliance*, New York: Free Press

Goodman, Walter.1995. "Totalling up the Minuses of Affirmative action TV", *New York Times*, April 23

Gottfredson, Linda S. 1990. "Hiring Quotas Exist, but Employers Wont Tell", (correspondence), *New York Times*, August 1

Hollander, Paul. 1966."Models of Behavior in StalinistLiterature", *American Sociological Review*, June

—————— 1983. "Sociology, Selective Determinism and the Rise of Expectations", in *The Many Faces of Socialism*, New Brunswick: Transaction

Holo, Robert E.1995. "California Action to Benefit Minorities" (correspondence), *New York Times*, July 26

Lichter, R., Lichter L. and Rothman S.1992. *Watching America*. New York: Practice Hall.

Lipset,S.M. 1992. "The Politics of Race", *Current*, June

Leo, John 1991. "California's racial arithmetic", *U.S. News & World Report*, June 24

MacDonald, Heather.1993."The Diversity Industry", *New Republic,* July 5

Merton, Robert K. 1957. "Manifest and Latent Functions" in *Social Structure and Social Theory*. Glencoe, IL: Free Press

Moynihan, Daniel Patrick.1965. *The Negro Family: The Case for National Action*, Washingon DC: U.S.Govt.Printing Office

Muravchik, Joshua. 1995. "Facing Up to Black Anti-Semitism", *Commentary*, December

Nieli, Russel.1991."Majority Rejects Race Preference", (correspondence), *New York Times*, July 24

Peretz, Martin.1990. "Washington Diarist", *New Republic*, May 28

Pinkerton, James P.1995. "Affirmative Action is Dead: Lets Move on", *Los Angeles Times*, January 19

Powers, Stephen P., Rothman, David J., and Rothman, Stanley 1990. "The Myth of Low Black Self-Esteem", *World and I*, March

Puddington, Arch. 1995. "Speaking of Race", *Commentary*, December

Purdum, Todd S.1995. "Senator Deals Blow to affirmative action", *New York Times*, September 10

Ravitch, Diane. 1990. "Multicultualism", *American Scholar*, Summer

Roberts, Paul Craig.1995."The Rise of the New Inequality", *Wall Street Journal*, December 6

————and Stratton, Lawrence M.1995. *The New Color Line:How Quotas and Privilege Destroy Democracy*, Washington DC: Regnery *Public Interest*, Summer

Sacks, David O. and Thiel, Peter A.1994. *The Diversity Myth*. San Francisco: The Independent Institute

Schlesinger, Arthur Jr 1992. *Disuniting of America*, New York: Norton

Skerry, Peter.1981. "Race Relations at Harvard", *Commentary*,January

Sowell, Thomas. 1990. *Preferential Policies: An International Perspective*, New York: Morrow

————1989, "The New Racism on Campus", *Fortune* reprinted in Hoover Institution Reprint Series No. 123

Steele, Shelby.1990. *The Content of Our Character*, New York: St.Martin's

Stevenson, Harold W.1994."'Oscars' Made of Tin",*New York Times*,October 11

Tertz, Abraham. 1960. *On Socialist Realism*, New York: Pantheon

Wilkerson, Isabel (1989) "Discordant Notes in Detroit: Music and Affirmative Action", *NY Times*, March 5

Will, George. 1995. "A spoils system with a constituency," *Daily Hampshire Gazette* (Northampton, MA), March

Wilson, William J. 1987 *The Truly Disadvantaged*, Chicago: Chicago University Press.

6

Reassessing the Adversary Culture

"In the main the national prospect looks brighter than it has for a generation."
—Robert Bartley

"That American culture is unraveling and its institutions becoming ever more fragile is so widely accepted that it doesn't require discussion."
—Robert Bork

"Americans have never had more reason to be confident than we have today."
—Linda Chavez

"We now live in a culture that is deeply corrupted- a liberal culture that in the name of unrestricted freedom has brought us to a condition of moral insensibility."
—Hilton Kramer

"Cross national surveys taken in 1990... and in 1992...find that the overwhelming majority of Americans feel positive about their personal future, a higher proportion than in any other industrial country."
—Seymour Martin Lipset

"From Harvard to Hollywood, the intellectual Left has managed to capture and corrupt most of the commanding heights of American culture."
—George Gilder

"America is an astonishingly resilient society and there is good reason to be hopeful."
—Richard Neuhaus

"Our educational institutions transmit relativism, deconstructionism, multiculturalism, victimization and political correctness."
—Chester Finn, Jr.[1]

Is the time ripe, in the middle of the 1990's, for another reassessment of the cultural-political phenomena we call the adversary culture, (or, estrangement, alienation, multiculturalism, the radical left, or middle class radicalism[2]) and their product, political correctness? Are they at last in eclipse? Are past estimates and analyses of these phenomena becoming obsolete?

There is much division of opinion (as also shown above) among those who try to keep track of these matters, well-known public intellectuals, social critics, observers of and participants in the "culture wars." A recent symposium in *Commentary* on "the national project" (addressed to questions of "balkanization," "breakdown," "dissolution of shared moral values") elicited a wide range of opinions. About one-third of the seventy-two participants were basically optimistic, another third largely pessimistic, and the rest displayed mixed attitudes and included those who "alternate between pessimism and optimism on different days of the week."[3] The assessments were roughly balanced between gloom and good cheer, but virtually all commentators made reference to the same problems without attributing to them the same weight. They included family disintegration, racial polarization, crime, welfare dependence, the influence of popular (or mass) culture, the decline of educational standards, the condition of elite groups, and the more intangible cultural/moral decline, especially relativism.

The pessimistic observations are familiar enough. Besides those quoted they included "the trends towards individual irresponsibility, the evisceration of standards and...the dissolution of a common culture" (Robert Kagan) and a "penumbra of disordered, often acutely unhappy lives manifest in the prevalence of alcoholism, medicalized drug dependence, and the mass consumption of illegal narcotic" (Edward N. Luttwak). Arch Puddington correctly observed that while "we find ourselves engaged in many of the same debates and fighting many of the same battles" as in the sixties, the difference is that "those who previously pressed the anti-American case from outside the institutions of power now occupy positions of influence within the government, the universities and other institutions." In a similar vein Terry Teachout wrote that "The ruling class of the 60s has been succeeded by a new class shaped by Vietnam and racked by self-doubt. Multiculturalism. . .is the natural consequence of this self doubt."[4] It is highly probable that if a similar symposium were held on the pages of *The Nation, The Village Voice* or other left-of-center publications, the views expressed would have been far more uniformly gloomy, though for different reasons. This writer himself has a long record of pessimistic observations regarding the same cultural/political phenomena.[5]

When I first wrote of the politicization of the campuses on these pages in 1989, it appeared that the spirit of the sixties was indisputably dominant, although the concept of political correctness (PC) was yet to be introduced.[6] More recently I argued that in spite of the growing chorus of denial and ridicule PC remains a consequential and widespread phenomenon,[7] a far cry from being an "imagined tyranny" as Brent Staples of the *New York Times* called it.[8] In the same article I noted the campaign to deny or trivialize the significance and extent of PC, the claim that PC is vastly exaggerated, its existence based on anecdotal evidence, that it is a rightwing distraction, for the most part. "Teachers for a Democratic Culture"[9] has been spearheading the campaign against what it perceives to be a conservative resurgence on the campuses and, more specifically, against the idea that PC is an undesirable phenomenon of some importance. An entire volume was released last fall (written by an editor of the "Democratic Culture" newsletter) titled *The Myth of Political Correctness.*[10] Most recently Todd Gitlin (a former 1960s radical) wrote about the "demonization" of PC.[11] He admits—as do others of similar persuasion—to occasional "excesses" (in the service of basically good causes) while dismissing the importance of the phenomenon as a whole. Thus, attempts to deflate the concept of PC and its reality continue, undertaken for the most part by those who have only been critical of its "excesses" rather than the values and beliefs which are its foundation.

It is true that anecdotal evidence is insufficient for proving how widespread and consequential PC has been. On the other hand one must not assume, as many writers on the subject have, that the rise of critiques of PC outside academia signal its demise within.

The debate about the pervasiveness of PC on the campuses could be settled by ascertaining the number of schools (1) with speech codes, harassment codes, terminological codes of PC speech; (2) those that provide preferential treatment of designated groups in student admission, financial aid, and faculty recruitment; (3) those that permit self-segregation for the same groups; (4) those with freshman orientation programs redolent with themes of PC and other academic programs permeated with (or predicated on) themes of PC: black studies, women studies, cultural studies, gay studies, etc.; (5) the number of colleges with required courses in third world studies or multiculturalism; (6) the number of those requiring sensitivity or diversity training programs for staff, faculty, or campus police; and (7) ascertaining the political profile and philosophy of commencement speakers on major campuses would further contribute to a better understanding of the inroads made by the left-liberal sensibility.[12]

There are other aspects of the influence PC or of the adversarial mindset that would be far more difficult to establish, such as the number of highly qualified white males *not hired* in faculty positions, or admitted as students, (especially at elite institutions); the self-censorship exercised by people teaching in the social sciences and humanities (or their abandonment of courses likely to give rise to complaints of racism, sexism, etc.). On these matters one can indeed only rely on the plentiful anecdotal evidence.

Let me mention here a new manifestation of the institutionalization of PC in academia sweeping the country, according to the director of housing services at the University of Massachusetts at Amherst. It is the proliferation of "Special Interest Residential Programs." The latter allow not only selected minority groups to indulge in residential self segregation, (a fairly well known and widespread practice), but extend the privilege to lesbians and homosexuals and some other groups who "choose to live with like minded people to create a community."[13] People sharing the same religious beliefs are not given such opportunities (perhaps they might be if supporters of the Nation of Islam demand their own residential community), nor are those who share ethnic backgrounds other than the officially certified minorities.

In the space below I will examine not so much the persistence of PC in academia but the more intangible and probably more important matter of the climate of opinion in society at large that originally brought it into existence.

A discussion of these political trends and cultural phenomena brings two temptations. One is to insist- having invested a fair amount of time and energy in cataloging and analyzing them - that they persist unchanged. Critics of any social-cultural phenomenon have a vested interest in prolonging its existence, not merely because of their attachment to the familiar topic but also because they too need established targets of criticism to gratify their own hostilities and scapegoating impulses.[14] The second temptation is to give in to wishful thinking that blends with the desire to be at one with the prevailing ethos in one's own environment, to be relieved of marginality by joining the left-liberal consensus—in this case the widely held (at least in public) view on campuses that PC and similar phenomena have been exaggerated and are undeserving of critical attention.

Admittedly there remains on my part a certain morbid fascination with the adversarial mentality and subculture and especially their core belief, that this is the most corrupt, repressive, and unjust social system history has ever known, or—another variation—that this society or country has within its power to transform itself into a land of rationally distributed abundance, harmony, and social justice, but perversely refuses to do so and must therefore remain the target of relentless criticism and rejection.

It is of some importance that, although such notions have remained widespread during the last decade, several books appeared and gained varying degrees of critical acclaim and popularity by authors highly critical of the adversarial phenomena here discussed. They include Allan Bloom: *Closing of the American Mind* (1987), Richard Bernstein: *Dictatorship of Virtue* (1994), Alain Finkelkraut: *The Defeat of the Mind* (1995), Paul Gross and Norman Levitt: *Higher Superstition: The Academic Left and Its Quarrels with Science* (1994), William Henry, III: *In Defense of Elitism* (1994), Robert Hughes: *Culture of Complaint* (1993), Dinesh D'Souza: *Illiberal Education* (1991), Thomas Sowell: *Inside American Education* (1993), and Charles Sykes: *A Nation of Victims* (1992).

It was also during approximately the same period that the target of the adversarial worldview has expanded from the American society to the entire Western heritage of ideas, including science. The leftist, radical feminist, Afrocentrist, and postmodernist attacks on science are a part of the broadly anti-Western thrust that has come to characterize the adversarial outlook. The animus against science has been especially strong among radical feminists.[15]

The anti-Western sentiments found their most potent form in multiculturalism, which essentially celebrates all cultures that are non-Western and embraces all critical views of the West.

Multiculturalism gains strength from its affinity both with the chronic and pervasive American preoccupation with identity (group and individual), and with the more tangible difficulties and discontentments of ethnic groups elsewhere. As Thomas Pavel, a professor of French literature, writes: "In the post-communist era the politics of group identity still provides the disaffected of the earth with the most congenial channel in which to express their discontent."[16]

There are many indications outside academia as well that much of the broader culture and its elite institutions remain hospitable to the adversarial currents, including multiculturalism. An exhibit of American science in the Smithsonian Institution "turns out to be a catalogue of environmental horrors, weapons of mass destruction and social injustice... displays of pesticide residue, air pollution, acid rain, ozone holes, radioactive waste, food additives and nuclear bombs."[17] In turn, the new National History Standards for teaching American history have little to say about the accomplishments of American culture and society, omit major historical figures, but offer an overabundance of information about the historical evils and injustices associated with American society.[18] And when the chances of getting a grant from the National Endowment for the Arts are greatly improved if the applicant reflects "AIDS awareness," (as was recently reported by a former special assistant to the chairman of NEA)[19] we can say that PC has found a home in major institutions of American culture.

It is also among the successes of multiculturalism that the Humanities Fellowships for 1996-97 offered by the Rockefeller Foundation require that such research be conducted almost exclusively outside Western cultural areas; most of the approved "residence [i.e., research] sites" being either non-Western study centers or those concerned with women.[20] Of the five books nominated for the 1995 National Book Award in fiction, two deal with Haiti and one with Puerto Rican families.[21] Major foundations continue to lean toward PC, and liberal foundations "continue to award far more money to liberal groups than conservative foundations award to conservative groups."[22]

The welcome Castro received on his October 1995 visit to New York from representatives of the churches is yet another symptom of the lingering strength of the attitudes here sketched. This vocal foreign detractor of the United States (and self-styled radical socialist) still inspires warmth in the bosoms of the social critics.[23] Sandra Levinson, an editor of the adulatory volume *Venceremos Brigade* (1971), is not only the executive director of the Center for Cuban Studies (associated with the City College system of New York) but continues, unembarrassed, to defend Castro's system in the *New York*

Times.[24]   She is but one of the countless number of tenured radicals in our institutions of higher learning.

There are many good reasons for the tenaciousness of PC and the beliefs and policies associated with it. PC is victim-driven, much of it consisting of attitudes and policies that are supposed to benefit the designated victim groups. While these policies were designed to erase victimhood, the victims feel compelled to continue asserting their victimhood; otherwise, their claims to special treatment (moral and material) would cease to have legitimacy. In this way many idealistic, social-justice-seeking impulses have become transformed into old-fashioned interest-group politics, groups fighting for spoils. In the words of Robert Bork, we are stuck in a situation in which "individuals who have never been discriminated against are preferred to individuals who have never discriminated, regardless of their respective achievements."[25]

The constituency with a vital interest in preserving the gains associated with left-liberal policies includes all those spreading or maintaining the beliefs and rules associated with PC and the adversarial outlook. Their numbers include many, if not all those who teach black studies, women's studies, cultural studies, critical legal studies or gay studies, as well as assorted deans and subdeans, affirmative action officers, and other administrators who devise and enforce harassment and speech codes. All of them have a truly vested interest in these policies—without them they would not have their jobs. At the same time they also tend to believe in these policies and the principles underlying them: careerism and idealism form a package difficult to pry apart.

The notion of "diversity" (poorly defined as it is) offers new justifications for preferential treatment on the ground of vague (educational, cultural, psychological, emotional) benefits and in connection with yet another dubious idea, that of role models. The latter promises that an automatic enrichment process will occur as soon as there is an adequate statistical representation of, say, Native Americans in departments of geology or blacks in astronomy. The same goes for admitting students representative of the current notions of diversity notwithstanding the fact that the same institutions that preach the blessings of diversity eagerly support every effort at self-segregation of the designated minorities once they arrive on campus.

The persistence of PC is closely linked to a durable white guilt since much of PC has to do with, or originates in, race relations. It bears repetition that for the most part PC originated in idealistic impulses, in solicitousness toward the underdog, the victim. These sentiments are congenial to American cultural values and traditions. But the attachment to victimhood also feeds on the more diffuse adversarial, radical social-critical impulses that find vindication in the existence of victim groups, and the more the better. New groups of victims continue to be found at a time when one would have thought that all varieties of victimhood have by now been discovered and claimed. "Middle ageism" is new and likely to be a popular category: "Age discrimination at midlife... which affects more groups and classes than anyone has imagined... viciously curtails the American dream and embitters our image of the life course. It is an urgent issue."[26]

An endless vista of victims stretches over the horizon of American society and provides vindication for the radical social critics. It will not be easy to let go of them. Last but not least, preferentially treated victim groups have a vested interest in prolonging their own status, not merely for material-economic reasons, but, just as important, because of the moral high ground they have been invited to occupy and the solicitousness that goes with it. Victimhood, when widely recognized and given the legal stamp of approval, confers a sense of moral distinction and invites sympathy and compassion; Judeo-Christian religious themes also support the notion that suffering ennobles and somehow deepens our humanity.

The attitudes associated with PC and the adversary culture are further nourished by a selective social determinism: racists, sexists, capitalists, rednecks, homophobes, etc., freely chose their detestable beliefs and ways and hence can be held fully responsible. The chosen victims, by contrast, are helpless products of social history or circumstance, as for example violent criminals who belong to the minorities of the inner city, or selected public heroes of the adversary culture. (It was written of the famous Robert Mapplethorpe by his biographer that he was "predatory, exploitative, self destructive and destructive of others" and that he tortured animals at an early age.) A reviewer of this biography explained: "Could it be that 2-year-old Robert was angry? Could it be that in torturing a little animal (turtles) he was reflecting his own feelings of being tortured by family members? What about his father's rigidity, eating disorder and strict Catholicism? What about his older brother's masculinity?

What about the smothering mother who confessed that Robert was her favorite child?"[27] O.J. Simpson also turns out to be a victim in the eyes of those who share the color of his skin, notwithstanding his wealth, celebrity status, and well-established credentials as a wife beater and his highly probable guilt in the double murders. Reportedly, even battered black women cheered the news of his acquittal.

Although such examples could be multiplied at great length, I am not suggesting that *nothing* has changed over the last decade and especially over the last two years. Since the early 1980s counter trends have also appeared, as shown in the election and reelection of Reagan and most recently in the election of a Republican Congress. At the same time, and curiously enough, under the Reagan administration the cultural influences and impact of middle class radicalism (or the adversarial outlook) have not been rolled back, or even seriously contested. In fact, PC emerged and swept the country during the 1980s but only its most extreme or lurid manifestations gained belated negative publicity; much of PC has been unquestioned and unknown to the general public and unchallenged on the campuses until the last couple of years.

At the same time there has been a growing recognition among academics and other professionals that the imposition of PC (especially through speech and harassment codes) exacts a high price in academic freedom and free expression.[28] Thus, at the present time contradictory phenomena proliferate. While numerous court rulings struck down speech codes, most schools still cling to them and some are anxious to develop new, more comprehensive ones.[29]

It is possible at the present time to locate indicators and arguments both in support of the view that the adversarial attitudes and policies remain vigorous *and* that they are withering. At my own campus, the University of Massachusetts at Amherst (regarded by many outsiders as a flagship of left-radicalism and PC, though I think that it is about average for a big Eastern university), the student newspaper, *Daily Collegian* reported a vote by the undergraduate senate "*against* a proposal to make SAT...[tests] optional in the undergraduate admissions process." Those wishing to do away with them argued that they are "biased against students of color... low income students and women."[30] The same student paper allocated almost a full page to the bitter denunciation of Yitzhak Rabin by a radical third world student following his assassination.[31]

Among the recent changes in the climate of opinion it is important to note that, as of the last two years or so, it has become possible to engage in public criticism of "affirmative action" (centerpiece of political correctness) even on the pages of the *New York Times* and the evening network news. Politicians and journalists are no longer terrified (academics still are) of questioning these policies. Meanwhile, Supreme Court rulings made a small dent in some race and sex-based preferences. The University of California trustees voted in 1995 to phase out these policies, but it remains unclear when and how their decision will be implemented, whether or not the trustees' determination will survive the first sit-ins, trashing and occupation of academic or other public buildings, and other likely expressions of displeasure with the new policies.

Whatever the actual quality of the beliefs in PC, and especially affirmative action, the *policies and institutions dispensing it remain in place,* entrenched and institutionalized. There are tens of thousands of people who make their living from legitimating, administering, and maintaining the current levels of PC, including "diversity and sensitivity trainers" and other dubious experts on intergroup relations.[32]

At the same time, whatever their degree of institutionalization, the beliefs and values that have animated the adversary culture and PC have become stale, partly by the sheer force of repetition. How many more times can individuals, groups, or institutions be accused ritualistically of racism, institutional racism, sexism, homophobia, patriarchal attitudes, and so forth? It is likely that these beliefs are held today with less conviction and probably by fewer people. As Andrew Sullivan of *The New Republic* put it as "an ideology affirmative action in 1995 is beginning to resemble Soviet Communism in 1989. Outside the sheltered elites, the majority of people loathe it. The circumstances in which it was dreamed up no longer exist. It is clearly teetering, its legitimacy under mortal threat."[33]

There has also been some disenchantment on the part of the older Left with identity politics and multiculturalism, viewing them as frivolous distractions from the real problems and conflicts of American society, especially economic inequalities and latent class conflicts.

The key question in the survival of the adversary culture (or middle class radicalism) is whether or not and to what degree its adherents succeed in its transmission to the younger generations.[34] There is little doubt that the major figures of this culture belong to an older generation, that those with the strongest commitment to adversarial values, the most embittered, strident, and widely known critics of American society and Western culture are the generation of the 1960's, old, aging, or middle-aged. There is thus a real possibility that the attitudes and beliefs here discussed will wither as a result of generational change.

William Kunstler recently passed away, although younger successors claim his mantle and he remains revered by many.[35] At the memorial gathering "the scene was akin to a reunion of some long-ago class. Mostly gray-haired and stoop-shouldered, their ranks thinned by the years, the alumni of the radical left of a generation ago greeted and embraced each other."[36] The prominent (or once prominent) and now aging social critics and former activists (who are, for the most part, between the ages of sixty and seventy) include the Berrigan brothers, Noam Chomsky,[37] Johnetta Cole, Harvey Cox, Angela Davis, David Dellinger (he is around eighty), E.L. Doctorow, Andrea Dworkin, Barbara Ehrenreich, Stanley Fish, Fredric Jameson, Jonathan Kozol, Norman Mailer, Ralph Nader, Francis Fox Piven, Adrianne Rich, Theodore Roszak, Gore Vidal, and Howard Zinn -to mention a few. Susan Sontag apparently retired from politics. Tom Hayden too is aging and a long way from his fiery days in the SDS. Among the aging and the aged, critics Richard Barnet, Richard Falk, H. Bruce Franklin, Saul Landau, Staughton Lynd, Michael Parenti, Marcus Raskin, and William Sloan Coffin Jr. are increasingly unfamiliar names. The Institute for Policy Studies (for long the think tank of the radical Left) is not much in the news. It is difficult to come up with any prominent radical social critic under 50; Oliver Stone the moviemaker may be one. In addition, some of the better-known social critics of the past toned down their critiques or changed their attitude altogether, among them Paul Berman, Eugene Genovese, Richard Rorty, and Alan Wolfe.

In the wake of the November 1994 elections (which resulted in the Republican Congress) we are at a paradoxical juncture. I think that the heyday of PC and the adversary culture is over; it may well fade away when the generation of the sixties passes from the scene. On the other hand and paradoxically, the new Congress may in some ways contribute to the persistence of the policies and attitudes associated with PC and the adversary culture: people like to feel besieged, to wage an uphill battle claiming to overcome great odds. Those in the front line who spread or administer PC may now feel that they are beleaguered fighters for social justice, an endangered heroic vanguard (or rearguard), a saving remnant destined to preserve idealistic policies. It may be noted here that spokesmen and publications of the Left have been complaining ever since the early 1970s of their own disarray and fragmentation; they also speak of a lack of impact. Fragmentation is one thing, however, and lack of impact another. Even with the perceived collapse and splintering of the New Left of the sixties, most of its values have been taken up by impassioned single-issue groups: radical feminists, black extremists (secular or religious), radical environmentalists, activist homosexuals, multiculturalists, postmodernist academics, and others.

Radical feminism remains, of course, another important source of support for PC and a component of the adversary culture, though in this area too there have been some changes. Just as it has become possible to raise questions in public about preferential treatment, it has become at least semi-legitimate to suggest that there are some differences between men and women that are not "socially constructed." A group of articulate and courageous women has emerged willing to question the verities of radical feminism, which until recently remained unchallenged, especially on the campuses.[38]

While there is room for cautious optimism, it would be unreasonable to believe—for the many reasons noted above- that the left-liberal ethos in our cultural institutions will rapidly and dramatically vanish. There are, nonetheless, some concluding observations that may point in a more optimistic direction. One is that American culture and society has a limited attention span and a great thirst for novelty; much of PC has been with us far too long to attract sympathetic attention and enthusiastic support. The second point has a more indirect bearing on the subject. I was one among many observers and students of communist systems, (especially that of the Soviet Union), who found it difficult to foresee how and when they would vanish; I used to believe that they would remain with us in the foreseeable future. I was of course wrong and very pleased that I was. By the same token I hope to be proven wrong about the persistence of PC—it may collapse sooner than we expect; the final withering away of the adversarial ethos may be closer than one might guess due to circumstances we cannot fully grasp at the present time.

It is possible that we have entered the stage of cultural *glasnost* in American society. The public questioning of the left-liberal articles of faith and the academic status quo under way is likely *slowly* to undermine the already shaky legitimacy of these phenomena—there is, after all, a link between the public expression of critical ideas and social change.

Notes

1. "The National Prospect-A Symposium," *Commentary* (November 1995): 27, 32, 43, 71-72, 78, 61, 89, 52.
2. "Middle class radicalism," an excellent concept, was introduced by the English sociologist Frank Parkin. It never caught on, at least in America. See his *Middle Class Radicalism: The Social Basis of the British Campaign for Nuclear Disarmament* (Manchester, U.K.: Manchester University Press, 1968).
3. Diane Ravitch, *Commentary* (November 1995): 103.
4. *Commentary* (November 1995): 32, 47, 52, 60-61, 68, 71, 72, 79, 101, 109.
5. See Paul Hollander, *Survival of the Adversary Culture (1988), Decline and Discontent* (1992), and *Anti-Americanism* (1992, 1995).
6. Paul Hollander, "From Iconoclasm to New Conventional Wisdom: The Sixties in the Eighties," *Academic Questions* (Fall 1989).
7. "Imagined Tyranny?' Political Correctness Reconsidered," *Academic Questions* (Fall 1994). For a systematic refutation of the major claims of political correctness see Peter Duignan and L.H. Gann, *Political Correctness: A Critique* (Stanford, Calif.: Hoover Essays, Hoover Institution, 1995).
8. Brent Staples, "Time to Retire a Cliche-'Politically Correct'-Shopworn and Blinding," *New York Times,* 5 December 1993, Editorial Notebook, sec. 4, 20.
9. The designation of this group is reminiscent of terms such as "peoples' democracy" "popular front," or "national liberation movements." I am not suggesting that-like the terms noted above- "democratic culture" was communist inspired but that it too has a misleading component, the alleged commitment to the highly imprecise idea of "democratic culture" intended to appeal to the uncommitted. It would of course have been far more accurate for the organization to call itself "teachers for a left-liberal or left-of-center culture."
10. John K. Wilson, *The Myth of Political Correctness: The Conservative Attack on Higher Education* (Durham, N.C.: Duke University Press, 1995).
11. Todd Gitlin, "Demonizing Political Correctness," *Dissent* (Fall 1995).
12. At least one impressionistic survey shows the predominance of left-of-center speakers, many of them Hollywood and media celebrities. See "Leftists Dominate Commencement Exercises," *Libertas* (Summer 1995), 4.
13. L. Loisel, "Like-minded students find place at UMass: Housing includes gay, minority, wellness floor," *Daily Hampshire Gazette* (Northampton, Mass.), 26 September 1995.
14. Dennis Wrong once wrote that " keeping constant tabs on the errors and irrationalities of the left is sweaty, unrewarding work that Hollander for the most part performs with intelligence and insight. But I am not entirely certain... that he overcomes the temptation to magnify the importance of the subject in order to justify his labors." He argued that these labors persisted far beyond the time when the phenomenon deserved sustained attention, *Contemporary Sociology* (September 1989): 724.

15. Radical feminists proposed, among other things, that "the laws of physics were constructed to maintain white male dominance." Robert L. Park, "The Danger of Voodoo Science," *New York Times,* op-ed, 9 July 1995.

16. Thomas Pavel, "The Global Malady," a review of A. Finkelkraut's *The Defeat of the Mind,* in *Commentary* (November 1995): 134.

17. Park, "Voodoo Science." Cited.

18. See "Special Issue: A Critique of the National History Standards," *Continuity,* 19 (Spring 1995); also Lynne Cheney, "The National History (Sub) Standards," *Wall Street Journal,* 23 October 1995.

19. Lynne Munson, "Art by Committee," op-ed, *New York Times,* 21 September 1995.

20. Humanities Fellowship flier for 1996-97.

21. *Daily Hampshire Gazette,* 16 November 1995, 8.

22. See for example David Samuels, "Philanthropical Correctness," *The New Republic* (18 and 25 September 1995); Robert Lerner and Althea Nagai, "Foundation Leaders," *Alternatives in Philanthropy,* a publication of the Capital Research Center, Washington, DC (February 1995): 1. See also Althea Nagai, Robert Lerner, and Stanley Rothman, *The Culture of Philanthropy: Foundations and Public Policy* (Washington: Capital Research Center, 1991).

23. One hundred religious leaders flocked to the UN mission of Cuba to meet him. It was an "overwhelmingly protestant group" that included national and local clergy. See Lizette Alvarez, "Guliani? He Wouldn't Get Castro's Vote," *New York Times,* 26 October 1995. The adversarial attitudes of the clergy were discussed at some length in chapter two: "The Churches: New Voices of Social Protest," in Paul Hollander, *Anti-Americanism* (New York: Oxford University Press, 1992; New Brunswick, NJ: Transaction Books, 1995).

24. Sandra Levinson, letter, *New York Times,* 9 November 1995, A28.

25. Robert Bork: "Hard Truths About the Culture War," *First Things* (June/July 1995).

26. Margaret Morganroth Gulette, "Middle-Ageism in the Postmodern Economy," *Dissent* (Fall 1995): 508.

27. Quoted in Garry Wills, "Robert Mapplethorpe as Victim," *Washington Times,* 17 June 1995.

28. For a recent example of an outburst of faculty protest against such (proposed) codes, see the letters in *Campus Chronicle* (University of Massachusetts, Amherst), 10 November 1995. See also, Harvey Silverglate, "Harvard Law Caves in to the Censors," *Wall Street Journal* 8 January 1996.

29. At UMass, Amherst, my own school, in the fall of 1995 it was proposed that a new comprehensive harassment code be created to include new groups (or categories of offense) based on "citizenship, culture, HIV status, language, parental status, political affiliation or belief and pregnancy status"; the new code also sought to punish those who *invite* speakers who offend those in some of these groups; it proposed as standard of proof the concurrence of a member of the group allegedly offended. (Memorandum circulated at UMass, Amherst, dated 20 September 1995).

30. *Massachusetts Daily Collegian* (Amherst), 16 October 1995, 4, emphasis added.

31. Hussein Ibish, "The Life and Crimes of General Yitzhak Rabin," *Massachusetts Daily Collegian,* 10 November 1995.

32. The 12 November 1995 Sunday *New York Times* carried a special supplement titled "The Diversity Challenge" and proclaimed, no doubt correctly, that "diversity coordinator is a new career."

33. Andrew Sullivan, "Let Affirmative Action Die," op-ed, *New York Times,* 23 July 1995.

34. In my *Anti-Americanism* (1992, 1995) there is contradictory evidence. The students (undergraduates) surveyed in the mid and late 1980s displayed both what might be called highly patriotic attitudes and those which reflected the impact of prolonged exposure to adversarial ideas. See chapter 6, "The Worldview of College Students," 307-29.

35. See Don Terry, "Chicago Journal: Celebrating William Kunstler's Life and Causes," *New York Times,* 6 November 1995.

36. Richard Perez-Pena, "1000 Honor Kunstler, Defender of Their Faith," *New York Times,* 20 November 1995.

37. Chomsky remains deeply attached to his apocalyptic views of a conspiracy of American corporations and their henchmen to dominate the world. He depicts this plot in a recent book, *World Orders, Old and New* (1994). For a critique of a not entirely unsympathetic reviewer see Richard Wolin, "Noam on the Range," *Dissent* (Summer 1995). Similar beliefs are also firmly held-more in regard to matters domestic than foreign- by Jonathan Kozol. See for example Peter Applebome, "Listening to the South Bronx," *New York Times,* 25 October 1995. Quite possibly Kozol's immense bitterness is also nourished by the feeling he confessed to in the article cited, namely "an enormous sense of having failed in life... I feel, in the end, as if everything I've done has been a failure."

38. See for example Daphne Patai and Noretta Koertge, *Professing Feminism, Cautionary Tales from the Strange World of Women's Studies* (New York: Basic Books, 1994); Christina Hoff Sommers, *Who Stole Feminism: How Women Have Betrayed Women* (New York: Simon & Schuster, 1994); Katie Roiphie, *The Morning After: Se; Fear and Feminism on Campus* (Boston: Little, Brown, 1993); and Elizabeth Fox-Genovese, *Feminism without Illusions* (Chapel Hill, N.C.: University of North Carolina Press, 1991).

7

The Durable Significance of the Political Pilgrimages

By the time the Soviet Union fell apart in 1991 few countries remained to inspire a significant volume of political pilgrimages—a topic I first addressed in a book published in 1981. By 1991 the entire Soviet bloc had disappeared; Nicaragua had ceased to be a destination of political tourists in the absence of a leftist government. China since the 1980s has allowed foreign capitalists to penetrate its economy and has encouraged private entrepreneurship and consumption (although the political monopoly of the Party has been retained); similar trends have developed in Vietnam. Given the anticapitalist convictions of those inclined to political tourism, their interest in these countries was bound to decline. The political system of Cuba has remained largely unchanged, though the country has become more impoverished with the disintegration of the Soviet bloc and the vanishing of its steady support; it still inspires a measure of political tourism that will be discussed below.

Cambodia under Pol Pot lost credibility in the 1970s as soon as the Vietnamese Communist regime went to war with it and defeated it. The conflict made acceptable even on the far left the criticism of the Pol Pot regime for the massacres that had earlier been doubted or outright denied. In this context it may be instructive to recall Noam Chomsky's remarks on this matter, remarks that he has never recanted. They remain a monument to the denial of reality and the surrealistic misjudgment of political systems that only a truly and profoundly alienated intellectual is capable of. In their 1978 book *After the Cataclysm...*, Chomsky and Herman argued that refugee accounts of the Pol Pot massacres were to be treated with skepticism and that those giving credence to them wished "to defame the regime." They compared the Cambodian massacres to those in "France after liberation where a minimum of 30-40,000 people were massacred within a few month's with far less motive for revenge." Elsewhere in the same book they wrote that "where evidence [of the massacres] is subject to some independent check it repeatedly and with remarkable consistency turns out to be fabricated."

Chomsky quoted with approval from an account of Richard Dudman, "an experienced foreign correspondent with excellent credentials," who, while admitting that his visit "amounted to a conducted tour" nonetheless had no hesitation to communicate favorable impressions and "did not find the grim picture painted by thousands of refugees who couldn't take the new order." Dudman (quoted by Chomsky) also noted, among the signs of popular satisfaction, that farm workers

> appeared to be reasonably relaxed at the height of the busy harvest season. They sometimes leaned on their hoes like farm workers everywhere. And they often... waved.... There were no signs of government cadres giving orders or armed guards enforcing the working hours, although individuals seemed to know what was expected.

Chomsky thus aided by Dudman reached the conclusion that

> the peasant population probably did not regard "the austere standard of hard manual labor"...as an onerous imposition of the regime.... one might reach the conclusion that much of the population may well have supported the regime, particularly if it is true, as Dudman was informed... that "decisions were taken collectively" in the cooperatives and even the army.

Whatever happened to the actual pilgrimages, it is probably more important to focus on the mind-set that gave rise to them in the first place and that has by no means disappeared, especially in the United States. Regardless of the fact that there are now far fewer countries upon which longings for a better world may be projected, it remains to be better understood why so many Western intellectuals were so irresistibly drawn to repressive and mendacious totalitarian systems and movements and how they succeeded for long periods of time in overlooking or downplaying their morally debilitating flaws and misdeeds.

Daniel Bell too asked: "Why did not the young zealots read and learn about the history of revolutions, and why...did one and does one see the continual 'process of enchantment', the aching need to embrace revolutionary romanticism which recurs time and again?" Malcolm Muggeridge in 1934 had an answer, limited as it was at the time to the Soviet case:

> The answer...is terribly simple... You are indulgent towards the dictatorship of the proletariat because...You are frustrated revolutionaries, and the spectacle of a revolutionary government in actual existence so intoxicates you that you fall on your knees, senses swooning, in awed worship.... The dictatorship of the proletariat is all-powerful and mouths your aspirations; and you, who have for so long had to be content with spinning your ideas into words, see in it the possibility of translating them suddenly into deeds.

More recently Todd Gitlin, himself a former 1960s radical, referred to a similar mentality: "They were so eager to see the future work; they were hungry to believe that somewhere out there, preferably on the dusky side of the globe where people looked exotic, some decency was under construction."

Doris Lessing sheds further light on the attitudes that are crucial to understanding the pilgrimages:

> These attitudes can only come out of some belief, one so deep it is out of sight, that a promise of some kind had been made and betrayed. Perhaps it was the French Revolution? Or the American Revolution which made the pursuit of happiness a right with the implication that... [it] is to be had as easily as taking cakes off a supermarket counter? Millions of people in our times behave as if they have been made a promise...that life must get freer, more honest, more comfortable, always better.

I have not ceased to wonder how so many Western intellectuals could lose the capacity to differentiate, to note important distinctions between various sociopolitical systems, countries, amounts of repression, corruption, social injustice, organized lying, etc. Such an impaired capacity to make pivotal moral and historical distinctions underlies the phenomenon of the political pilgrimage and the attitudes supporting it. This impaired capacity appears to be a major legacy of the 1960s, its rhetoric, its impatient anti-intellectual, antirationalist mind-set, and its radical revolutionary romanticism.

New Destinations

The new post apartheid South Africa might well have become a new destination for political tourism if it had only moved into a more radical or vigorously socialist-revolutionary direction under a more ruthless and intolerant ruling party. This, however, has not happened under the moderate and conciliatory policies Nelson Mandela pursued. Sociopolitical change has been not revolutionary but incremental and reformist, and as such prosaic - nothing to fire the imagination of Westerners yearning for a new attempt at the radical transformation of the human condition. Even those far to the left of

Mandela, as, for instance Joe Slovo, chairman of the South African Communist Party, embraced moderation and engaged in a certain amount of rethinking. Slovo's recent response to the question of how an intelligent man could have spent as much time as he did in Moscow and its satellite capitals without seeing that his surroundings were repressive, hypocritical and corrupt also helps us understand the mentality of the political pilgrim:

> If you've ever been part of an official delegation, you learn less about a country than sitting in the British Museum and reading about it.... You don't meet the people. You don't actually see the conditions.... people said there were gulags and millions of people incarcerated there, and we were assured that there was no such thing. We didn't go to these areas. We didn't have opportunities to actually check.

Even so, Mr. Slovo confesses that he began to have deep doubts about his communist patrons in the 1960s but suppressed them. To speak out against, say, the crushing of dissent in Czechoslovakia would have meant ostracism from the Communist Party: "The choice that you face is that you either continue to be able to make a contribution to the struggle or not."

Although Slovo differed from the typical political pilgrims or tourists by virtue of his lifelong involvement with the Communist movement, he was nevertheless ignorant of the most disturbing aspects of the Communist systems—the camps—and was conveniently predisposed to doubt that they existed.

Iraq and Iran, because of their intransigently anti-Western positions and policies, acquired a certain attraction for those deeply estranged from Western society and comfortable in the presence of its critics. On the other hand, Islamic fundamentalism was hard to swallow for most Americans. Iraq has been a special case as the apparent victim of the West and its technology (in the Gulf War). Saddam Hussein lacks Fidel Castro's charm and charisma, and the socialist rhetoric of his regime was insufficient to overcome those liabilities. Even so, Iraq had its Western champions (such as Ramsey Clark), always ready to feel solidarity with those hostile to the United States.

More significant than the actual number of political tourists to the Middle East has been the attitude of American academic intellectuals specializing in Middle Eastern Studies. It is from their ranks that the champions of present-day Middle Eastern political systems have risen; their sympathies emanate less from travelogues and more from scholarly (or putatively scholarly) studies and papers.

It appears that the popularity of Middle Eastern Studies among the fiercest critics of the United States and the West is comparable to the popularity of Latin American studies among intellectuals similarly disposed. Although it cannot be ruled out that the actual study of these areas contributes to an awareness of U.S. and Western misdeeds, there are also indications that people who gravitate to such area studies already harbor a strong animus toward the United States and the West as a whole. What has been called the "Arabization" of Middle Eastern Studies lends further plausibility to this speculation.

Two recent observers, Norwell Atkine and Daniel Pipes (themselves specialists in the Middle East), noted that "contempt for traditional America permeates much of the scholarly writing on the Middle East. It disproportionally blames the woes of that region on the United States. It conjures up an American 'warrior culture." In a similar spirit, the United States has been held responsible for the ills of Latin America by many Latin Americanists.

Richard Falk (a venerable critic of American society and foreign policy), who apparently shifted to the Middle East from Vietnam and international law, wrote that American society is "shaped by the commercialization of violence [and is] a culture shaped by rising crime, official corruption and pervasive fear." In his opinion it was the inherently aggressive traits of American culture that led to the Gulf War. It is also symptomatic of the attitudes here sketched that one of the rare books written by a native of the region and critical of Hussein's Iraq and its domestic terror (*Cruelty and Silence* by Kana Makiya) was denounced by Eqbal Ahmad, an area specialist and like Falk a lifelong critic of the United States and the West.

Iran developed at least one model prison (or part of a prison), for the benefit of foreign visitors. Behzad Naziri has been both a member of a delegation to whom the prison was shown and subsequently an inmate. On the former occasion the prison warden "explained that Evin was not really a prison but a university to introduce 'deceived' youngsters to the true teachings of Islam. Hundreds of 'inmates' sitting in orderly rows described humane conditions and warm treatment by the guards." Four months later Naziri (who worked for a French press agency) was arrested. "This time, the prison authorities wasted little time introducing me to the unspeakable cruelties behind closed doors. I immediately ran into some familiar faces - those 'prisoners' I had interviewed before. They were prison guards."

Substituting prison employees for inmates for the benefit of foreign visitors too had precedent in the former Soviet Union.

A promising new destination for political tourists has been the state of Chiapas in Mexico since the peasant uprising of 1994. The uprising was quickly put down, but the rebels withdrew to remote and scenic jungles and mountains and a stalemate developed between them and the government. They were led by a highly articulate, voluble, and romantic figure who wore a ski mask and called himself Subcomandante Marcos and excelled in making statements for the media. Once more a revolutionary social movement appeared bringing together downtrodden peasants and "brigades of young radicals" or "Marxist missionaries" from urban areas.

Subcomandante Marcos was the latest incarnation of the revolutionary intellectual who supposedly closed the gap between ideals and actions. His intellectual credentials were displayed by regaling visitors with "labyrinthian discussion of the work of Julio Cortazar, Borges, Garcia Marquez and other notables." The movement, fiercely anticapitalist and anti-American, called itself "The Zapatista Army of National Liberation" (thereby also making use of an older authentic revolutionary hero) and initially attracted much attention both inside and outside Mexico. As one American sympathizer wrote: "The designation of the Zapatistas as the first post-modern Latin guerilla formation has been confirmed by the intellectual greats and near greats.... [Their] armed audacity and poetic vision have won them an international constituency." Though the rebels continued to control some remote areas the movement did not spread, and media interest declined. There have been few reports of well-known foreigners visiting the guerrillas, though they had extended an invitation to Carlos Fuentes and Noam Chomsky, among others.

Oliver Stone, the well-known filmmaker, was one U.S. celebrity who did visit the guerrillas:

> Oliver Stone is skipping tonight's awards ceremony [the Oscars] to meet with leftist guerrillas in southern Mexico.... Stone said he wanted to see the conditions that prompted an Indian uprising two years ago. The rebels, many of them wearing straw hats and black wool ponchos, greeted Stone with a five-piece mariachi band. "I am here because I believe in their struggle" Stone said after meeting with 23 leaders of the Zapatista National Liberation army. "We are coming on a fact-finding mission...to see with our own eyes the situation."

Although U.S. sympathizers allowed that "ours is a time of actually nonexisting socialism" they were nonetheless encouraged "to see a promise of what a democratic revolutionary movement might look like and sounds like."

The Latin American Studies Association (a steady supporter of Castro's Cuba and Sandinista Nicaragua) passed a resolution in support of the Zapatista rebels. On the same occasion, its members voted down a proposal critical of Cuban humans rights violations.

North Korea

North Korea was one of the few Communist countries that, until recently, had inspired little political tourism. Western leftists appeared indifferent toward a country that has preserved intact its Stalinist institutions and policies—a country where, according to one of the rare Western visitors (Anthony Daniels, an English writer), "everything was either forbidden or compulsory." Gus Hall, head of the Communist Party of the United States, was somewhat atypical in recommending North Korea both as a vacation spot and exemplar of socialism in the wake of the collapse of the Soviet Union.

More recently there has been an increase of tourism, apparently connected with events such as the 1996 Sports and Cultural Festival. According to a report published in early 1997 (in the travel section of the *New York Times)* the regimentation of visitors interfered with their appreciation of the political system. The sites shown on one of these tours were typical of all such tours: the Great People's Study Hall, a cement factory, the house where the Great Leader (Kim Il Sung) was born; the Victorious Fatherland Liberation War Museum, the Martyr's Cemetery (where tourists were required to buy flowers with U.S. dollars). At the opening ceremonies of the International Sports and Cultural Festival, "Muhammad Ali was a guest of honor." Not only was the tour hectic and regimented, but the "guides used virtually every exchange with us as an opportunity to vilify America."

North Korean techniques of political hospitality, as reported by the occasional Western visitor, were remarkable even in comparison with the corresponding efforts of other Communist governments. Anthony Daniels was a member of the British delegation attending the Soviet-financed World Festival of Youth and Students, held in Pyongyang in 1989. His group consisted of people who held their own society in great contempt, estranged enough to extend sympathy to virtually any political systems they perceived as being opposed to their own. As on other occasions the predisposition of these English tourists was bolstered by the special treatment they received. For example, their buses had a police escort with sirens and flashing lights on the six-lane highway leading from the airport to the city, which had

> absolutely no traffic in either direction.... The police escort...transformed a group of unimportant young discontents into people of consequence. This form of flattery exactly suited the psychology of at least some of them, convinced as they were that the country from which they had come unjustly failed to recognize...their manifest talents.

Daniels's companions were not disposed to any skepticism toward the displays produced by the official hospitality. As their

> bus passed through the streets of Pyongyang, the pedestrians stood still and waved to us, and the faithful waved back happily, thinking they were expressing international proletarian solidarity. But for those who cared to observe, the waving of the pedestrians had an odd quality.... They waved stiffly, like automata; as soon as the bus passed their upraised arms dropped like stones to their sides and they walked on. This was friendliness by decree.

At a model secondary school—with no students in evidence, with blackboards never written upon and blackboard dusters never used —one of the tourists commented:

> "Only socialism can do this."...he did not ask whether the school, even if real, was typical, though if he were shown anything good in his own country would immediately retort that it was exceptional.... Here critical thought dissolved at the first sight of the marble entrance hall; far from unintelligent he was a true political pilgrim.

A unique feature of the North Korean attempt to impress foreigners was the total absence of mentally retarded or otherwise handicapped people in the capital. As a *New York Times* reporter also observed, "it appears that the Government has exiled disabled people.. .for fear that foreigners might see them and get a bad impression. North Korean officials deny this, saying that disabled people have voluntarily moved to other parts of the country." Daniels reported that "whenever they were asked about the complete absence from Pyongyang of disabled people, our guides replied with ominous decisiveness: 'This problem has been solved.'"

The disposition of these political tourists was most dramatically revealed at the official opening of the festival in a stadium holding 150,000 people, when the Great Leader arrived and was greeted by the highly orchestrated frenzy. Daniels recalled:

To my horror, the people around me [the British and other foreign delegations] joined in this mindless activity.... What were they cheering, what were they celebrating, what emotion, or rather, pseudo-emotion were they feeling?... There was no external compulsion for these people to behave as they did, to abandon their critical faculties, to lose their identity, to be united in a pseudo-mystical communion with a hundred thousand people of whom they knew nothing.... Yet they could not wait to do so; in fact they rejoiced on doing it, and they felt fulfilled afterwards.

These visitors were not offended by the grotesque cult of Kim Il Sung that was in evidence everywhere and by the omnipresent assault of propaganda:

My companions...did not pause to wonder why or how was it that every person in North Korea without exception wore a badge with a portrait of the great leader. If they had considered it at all, they would have said it was simply because of his popularity.

Another more recent visitor, Professor A. James Gregor of the University of California, Berkeley, also noted that citizens of Pyongyang "pin an enameled portrait of the Great Leader.. .to their breast every morning before departing to work."

During his two week visit Daniels paid several visits to the Pyongyang Department Store No 1:

It didn't take long to discover that this was no ordinary department store. It was filled with thousands of people, going up and down the escalator.. .going in and out of the front entrance in a constant stream.. .yet nothing was being bought or sold. I checked this by standing at the entrance for half an hour. The people coming out were carrying no more than the people entering.... In some cases I recognized people coming out as those who had gone in a few minutes before.... And I watched a hardware counter for fifteen minutes. There were perhaps twenty people standing at it; there were two assistants behind the counter, but they paid no attention to the "customers."...I decided to buy something - a fountain pen. I went to the counter where pens were displayed.. .no more for sale than the Eiffel Tower. As I handed over my money, a crowd gathered around, for once showing signs of animation. I knew.. .that I could not be refused: if I were, the game would be given away completely. And so the crowd watched goggle-eyed and disbelieving as this astonishing transaction took place.

In one of its rare dispatches from North Korea, the *New York Times* provided corroboration for Daniels's account of the techniques of hospitality at the same youth festival in 1989 mentioned earlier:

For a year, factory workers have been struggling with special classes in the basics of English, and everything paintable is gleaming under a fresh coat. Farm trucks are washed before they are allowed on the main roads. Koreans on the street scrutinize oncoming cars and wave whenever they see a foreigner go by.... Ordinary people... seem happy to talk to foreigners.... But conversations often sound exceedingly stilted, and it is rare for a minute to pass without a Korean offering praise to the 77-year-old "great leader"... or the 47-year-old "dear leader", the President's son and heir. More than 1000 Mercedes-Benzes have been imported to take guests around.

This dispatch also suggested that some American visitors resembled the British delegation described by Daniels, both in motives and in level of information about North Korea: "I am taking a look at student struggles throughout the world" a student leader from the City College of New York explained. "I want to make contact with people fighting for social and economic justice all over the world."

There are further, occasional glimpses of the attitudes of Western visitors to North Korea, few as their numbers might be. Most striking is their resemblance to the most deluded Western visitors to the Soviet Union in the 1930s or to Mao's China in the 1960s. The case of Reverend John Swomley, a retired United Methodist professor of ethics and founder of the American Committee on Korea, is typical. Apparently moved by his concern with peace, Reverend Swomley visited North Korea in 1994 as the guest of the government in the company of "two Korean Americans... who had been there before and were fluent in the Korean language" (he does not reveal who they were and what, if any, connections these two had with the North Korean authorities). The tour included all the standard sights assumed to impress Western visitors and regarded by Communist states as incontrovertible evidence of the superiority of their system. Reverend Swomley was taken to "three large hospitals," in one of which he was "permitted to watch open heart surgery on a video screen and...the removal of a tumor in the brain." There was more to follow:

In Pyongyang we visited the Children's Palace.... We saw calligraphy and embroidery classes..., we witnessed a most remarkable stage performance... massed children's choirs... large orchestras of children, male and female singers, acrobats and dancers and 13 accordion players in perfect unison, all of them very young children. At the end of the performance, my interpreter...said to me: "Don't let Americans destroy these children."

Next on the tour came Kim Il Sung University, with its fourteen faculties and ten research institutes and a collective farm complete with "day care nursery, hospital, agricultural college, theater...barbers, hairdressers and shops and an experimental research station." In addition

My colleagues and I also visited a huge automated cement factory, workers' apartments, a University of National Economy [and] a small Roman Catholic Church built in 1986 by its members with an interest-free loan from the government [and] a much larger

Protestant church. Afterward we met with the pastor.... He expressed great concern about US troops in South Korea and urged that they be withdrawn.

There was also a meeting with the Anti-Nuclear Peace Committee followed by a banquet in honor of Reverend Swomley. As to

Kim Il Sung whom we did not meet though he sent personal greetings to us...It seems clear... that he was no Stalinist. He seemed friendly to religion, regularly visited farms, factories, schools, and was frequently in touch with ordinary people. I was told that there is no death penalty in North Korea and no liquidation of opponents but there are "re-educational labor camps" which I was unable to see.

Some of those with whom we talked [it is not clear who they were —P. H.]... interpreted him as benevolent....more like a patriarchal father who makes final decisions....

It is apparent that Kim Il Sung was respected, admired, even venerated. From everything I could gather in my limited contacts, the people liked and believed in him.

As has been the case with other visitors of a similar disposition, Reverend Swomley found support for his beliefs not only in what he had seen but also in what he did not:

We saw no tanks, armored vehicles or fortifications [on the way to the demilitarized zone].... Nowhere along that stretch of road did we see any evidence of the million man army which the CIA has reported is there.

By contrast, on the South Korean side he saw the troops and fortifications guarding the border. He was especially indignant about "the huge concrete wall initiated by the US military"; he compared this wall unfavorably to the Berlin Wall, which at least permitted cross-border visits not allowed at the wall in Korea! In contrast to the South Korean militarization of the border area, in the North he saw "unarmed uniformed soldiers helping farmers to plant rice." Moreover

Other public employees expected to assist farmers on Friday with planting and hundreds of them were also walking from Pyongyang three to eight miles to work in the fields. All appeared well nourished or they would have been unable to walk that distance and work all day in the fields.

Reverend Swomley, needless to say, was blissfully unaware of the chronic mismanagement and inefficiency of agriculture in Communist states and the resulting need to supplement the regular labor force with city dwellers; nor could he imagine that such extra work was not entirely voluntary. His sojourn makes clear that the old-style pilgrim, carefully chaperoned, truly duped, and favorably impressed even by a most repressive police state, is not yet extinct.

The 1994 visit of former president Jimmy Carter to North Korea on a self-styled peace and goodwill mission was another astonishing demonstration of the persistence (or revival?) of attitudes leading to political pilgrimages. He too was favorably impressed by the Great Leader and unaware of, or unbothered by, his grotesque cult of personality. According to a press report: "Mr. Carter heaped praise on Kim Il Sung.... 'I found him to be vigorous, intelligent...well informed... and in charge of decisions about his country.'" Carter also succeeded in the course of his short visit to note "the reverence with which [the North Korean people] look upon their leader." Reportedly he also observed that "Pyongyang is full of pep—its shops remind him of the 'Wal-Mart in Americus Georgia' and at night the neon lights remind him of Times Square."

Perhaps stimulated by the Carter visit and hoping that a neglected and much maligned socialist paradise may be found in North Korea, in 1994 "38 prominent US citizens. . .formed a new national organization, The American Committee on Korea." Among its goals were "to inform and arouse the conscience of US citizens about the US occupation of Korea." Members included both Ramsey Clark and William Sloane Coffin, two prominent political pilgrims of earlier times. The occasional visitors to North Korea deserve to be noted not because their perceptions and judgments were widespread but because their exceptionally outlandish character illuminates the outer limits of credulousness, of the will to believe.

Cuba

Of all the pilgrimage sites, Cuba has maintained the most credibility and popularity, although political tourism to Cuba in the 1990s does not approach the 1960s-1970s levels. Nonetheless, latter-day political tourists still believe that something noble and desirable began in Cuba that has been undermined by the intrigues of the United States and the collapse of the Soviet bloc. In their eyes, Castro's Cuba deserves support and sympathy, hence the popularity of challenging the U.S. government embargo and of sending various forms of assistance. Few among the people who are concerned about shortages in Cuba worry about, say, the needy in Bolivia or Honduras or El Salvador because Cuba's benefactors find the political systems of those countries unappealing. Sending medical and other humanitarian supplies to Cuba can be a political statement as well as a humanitarian gesture.

Edward T. Walsh, a former chaplain at North Carolina State University and a member of the Ecumenical Project for International Cooperation as well as the Baptist Peace Fellowship, was "the first American to be approved by Cuba's Ministry of Higher Education and the Cuban Communist Party to teach" at Matanzas University— an approval in which he apparently took great pride. He was among those arguing (in 1996) with great passion against the embargo and holding the United States responsible for most of the ills of present-day Cuban society. His incomprehension of the character of that society and its political system was so profound that when a Cuban student visited him and said "Professor I probably won't be back to see you again... we Cubans must be careful about getting a bad reputation by hanging around with foreigners especially those with U.S. dollars," Walsh explained the student's reticence by "the sensitive situation created by the fact that some Cubans...are able to buy products with U.S. dollars that most Cubans cannot afford," as if the student had been concerned with the disapproval of other Cubans rather than the attention of the authorities, who strongly discourage unauthorized and unsupervised contact with foreigners.

Some of the old admirers of the Castro regime, such as Carol Brightman, still find much to admire in Cuba in the 1990s, including Castro's efforts to devise a "different kind of socialism"; she was also thrilled about getting him to autograph a baseball cap for her fourteen-year-old son. Likewise Benjamin Spock, the venerable critic of American society, found much to admire and nothing to criticize in Cuba as of 1994. Ted Turner, on good terms with Castro at least since his 1982 duck-hunting visit, recently claimed that "the Cuba visit didn't really change my philosophy.... It gave me some tolerance of the Socialist system that I didn't have before. After seeing it face to face, I didn't see anything that made me afraid."

The impressions of an academic delegation to Cuba (sponsored by the left-of-center Institute of Policy Studies in Washington, D.C.) reflected the durability of the favorable stereotypes during the late 1980s. Bettina Horner, a member of the delegation and president of Radcliffe College at the time, was, among other things, greatly impressed by Castro's concern with public health and willingness to give up cigar smoking to set a good example. She (as did the rest of the delegation) took the position that "human rights begin with access to food, literacy and health care," although she also perfunctorily referred to "the lack of political and civil rights... an issue that deeply concerned members of the American delegation." If so, the highly laudatory report failed to reflect it.

If Bettina Horner without expertise in Latin American affairs had some excuse for her views of Cuba under Castro, the consistently pro-Castro utterances and policies of the Latin American Studies Association (LASA) had no such explanation. The LASA, or those who speak in its name, have a long, unbroken record of leftist political partisanship that has endured into the late 1990s. The association, although supposedly ready and willing to criticize human rights or academic freedom violations anywhere in the hemisphere, steadfastly refused to do so regarding Cuba (or Sandinista Nicaragua) while warmly championing cultural relations with the Castro regime.

Even in the 1990s it is safe to say that Susan Eckstein's approach was typical of that of U.S. academics studying Cuba. Though not wholly uncritical of Castro's system in her 1994 book, she credits it with great accomplishments (in health and welfare, in the reduction of rural/urban and class inequities, and in the position of women and dark-skinned citizens) without examining the price paid for them: the totalitarian dictatorship of Castro - if indeed these achievements are what is being claimed. While she makes occasionally somewhat abstract references to repression, the book does not have a single chapter on or sustained discussion of the massive, institutionalized human rights violations, the regimentation of cultural life, or the historically unprecedented exodus of 10 percent of the population, among other unappealing aspects of the system. She treats Castro's reign as a largely successful effort in social engineering aimed at modernization and greater social justice, marred by the cessation of Soviet bloc assistance and the recalcitrance of human nature. She disbelieves that the Committees for the Defense of the Revolution are neighborhood-level informers and prefers to emphasize their more benign activities, such as recycling and voluntary labor. She does not reflect on how labor can be "voluntary" in a police state such as Cuba.

There are further illustrations of continued indifference of many prominent U.S. intellectuals toward political repression in Cuba.

Kate Millett, the well-known feminist author, in 1994 published a book about contemporary political imprisonment around the world without mentioning Cuba. Her political sympathies are further evidenced by the fact that she devotes six out of a total of eleven chapters to the evils of Western colonialism and one-third of a chapter to Mao's China. Also of some interest here that the use of psychiatric methods against political prisoners in Cuba remains virtually unknown in the United States even though documentation exists (as in *The Politics of Psychiatry in Revolutionary Cuba*).

In 1991 Public Television presented what the television critic Walter Goodman called "a portrait of Cuba without the warts" emphasizing "the benefits brought by Cuban Communism, especially schools, hospitals and guaranteed jobs. The claim that everybody can read is given more attention than what one is permitted to read." Those who wrote the script of this program, "like other observers with a soft spot for totalitarians of the left... seem[ed] torn between the evidence of 30 years of political suppression and economic failure and an enduring will to believe."

It's important to note that the favorable American (and Western European) perceptions of the Cuban political system are closely associated with and dependent on Castro's durability and manipulative skills. Moreover, Castro, among the remaining Communist leaders, has been the least willing to compromise his stern anticapitalist principles, which earned him good points among Western intellectuals, who pride themselves on their aversion to capitalism.

Castro's 1995 reception in France by President François Mitterand was probably the high-water mark of the favorable reputation he has enjoyed. Mrs. Mitterand, who has visited Cuba several times and who is an unabashed admirer of Castro, believes that he is "nothing like a dictator" and that his government has accomplished "the summit of what socialism could do." His five-day visit to New York on the fiftieth anniversary of the United Nations further highlighted his continued general immunity from serious criticism. Robert Torricelli, a U.S. Representative from New Jersey, concerned with human rights violations in Cuba, wrote:

> It is hard to know what is more disturbing—the thought of business leaders like David Rockefeller sitting down to a lunch with Fidel Castro or the sight of hundreds of people at the Abyssinian Baptist Church in Harlem cheering the fatigue-wearing Cuban revolutionary....

> Of all things, a civil rights leader, Representative Charles Rangel, who once led the fight for economic sanctions against the apartheid regime in South Africa, put himself on the church dais with a dictator who has jailed more political dissidents than any other leader in this hemisphere.

There was during this visit "tremendous media coverage with not a single tough question asked.... the feel-good gossipy aspect of the Shaw interview [by Bernard Shaw of CNN] was a landmark television disgrace." Castro was "courted by David Rockefeller, Lee Iacocca, Mort Zuckerman, the Council on Foreign Relations, the luxury magazine *Cigar Aficionado,* businessmen hungry for a shot at the Cuban market... and an eager press." On the same occasion Castro also met for two hours with a group of about a hundred mostly Protestant religious leaders, apparently eager to commune with him; one may presume (on the basis of past utterances from the clergy) that they did not come to complain about human rights violations by the Cuban authorities.

Jacobo Timmerman was among the handful of visiting intellectuals who had reservations about the accomplishment of literacy, one of the regime's major claims to legitimacy. He wrote: "If it is true that every Cuban knows how to read and write, it is likewise true that every Cuban has nothing to read and must be very cautious about what he writes." Rather than enjoying the blessings of literacy, Cubans were immersed in an environment saturated with political messages. Timmerman wondered "whether it would not be preferable to be subjected to subliminal pressures so as to be a consumer of a particular toothpaste rather than forcibly plunged into the collective misery described as a happy, victorious society."

It is possible that Cuba on its own, no longer a protégé of the Soviet Union, may be an even more appealing candidate for the role of the victim of the United States—an essential ingredient in the choice of countries upon which the pilgrims bestowed their affection. Mark Falcoff wrote:

> Even now the Castro regime exercises a residual hold on the loyalties of our cultural elite... all of a sudden...many books, policy studies and op-ed pieces are urging us to provide for Cuba. . . a "soft landing." Could it be that a precipitous collapse threatens to reveal the real bases of its power, and in so doing, sweep away the last of the illusions that have nourished the socialist idea in the West?

Anthony Daniels, another of the rare visitors who cast a skeptical eye on Castro's Cuba, while researching the available reading material for the all those literate Cubans, found bookshops filled with pre

—glasnost Soviet propaganda (in Spanish) including a children's book entitled *"Felix significa felix,* [or] Felix Means Happy,—Felix being none other than Felix Dzherzhinsky, the first chief of the Soviet secret police." He too was impressed by the stultifying abundance of political propaganda:

> To compensate for the lack of goods there was a wealth of exhortatory propaganda....
> How I came to hate those little quotations everywhere: *To create is to be victorious* in the post office, where the clerks behind the counter moved resentfully as though struggling through glue; *Men come in two types, those who love and construct and those who hate and destroy,* on the crumbling walls of dilapidated buildings; *Art is life itself art knows nothing of death,* in the entrance to an art gallery so little visited that it had the atmosphere of a morgue.

It is safe to predict that the Cuban political system will retain an American following as long as Castro stays in power and as long as the system maintains its anti-capitalist policies and rhetoric and thereby succeeds in conveying the impression that Cuba is a communitarian society endowed with a sense of purpose and guided by the pursuit of social justice.

Why the Pilgrimages Still Matter

The disintegration of Communist systems between 1989-1991 had only a modest impact on the *attitudes* here discussed other than substantially reducing the number of countries the pilgrims and tourists could visit. On the other hand, the political pilgrimages and tours matter primarily as symptoms of other, more deeply entrenched and durable attitudes. I have labeled these attitudes variously as alienation, estrangement, reflexive rejection, or an adversarial disposition; they appear to survive regardless of the availability of suitable pilgrimage sites, regardless of the unraveling and discreditation of Communist systems in many parts of the world.

Since the late 1970s, the sources of estrangement from and discontent with Western societies has remained fairly stable. If "socialism" is no longer the name given to the longings and impulses associated with political tourism, the fundamental reasons making the idea of socialism attractive are still there, in particular the "quest for community," or, in the words of Friedrich Hayek, "an atavistic longing after the life of the noble savage...the main source of the collectivistic tradition." Peter Berger referred to the same attitudes as "counter-modernizing" impulses.

There would be no political pilgrims and tourists unless groups of people, and especially the intellectuals among them, did not feel to varying degrees a strong aversion to their own society and its culture, that is, to Western culture. This hostility is in the final analysis a product of an unease and discomfort with life in modern, pluralistic societies. One may even define contemporary Western intellectuals as those among the educated and leisured strata who are most unhappy with the experience of living in these modern (secular, pluralistic, wealthy, and technologically advanced) societies and who are capable of routinely articulating such discontent. There are many other people of some education, leisure, and high living standards who share this distaste without qualifying as "intellectuals"—portions of the clergy, many journalists, some politicians, celebrities in entertainment, those among the guilty rich.

Even if the pilgrimages have greatly diminished, the impulses behind them are still with us, as are the enclaves of what I have called the adversary culture, especially in and around colleges and universities. In these settings many of the values, attitudes, and impulses that animated the pilgrims have become institutionalized, entrenched, and even routinized. They are genuine subcultures with their basic, taken-for-granted assumptions.

One enduring conclusion that may be drawn of the phenomena here considered—among them the bizarre misperceptions of particular political systems and the stunningly misplaced idealistic impulses that led to these idealizations and projections—is that intellectuals, and highly educated people in general, are not well protected either by their education or their cognitive intelligence from major errors of judgment. To put it more simply, emotional dispositions are overpowering. It is especially striking to behold these emotional forces in apparent control of highly trained, often otherwise brilliant minds. Perhaps there is something to the cliché that intellectuals suffer from a deficit of common sense, perhaps due to their insulation from certain prosaic, practical realities, or perhaps due to their reflective disposition and readiness to entertain abstraction. To the extent that more and more intellectuals are academically enshrined, this insulation deepens, as academic enclaves provide a sanctuary from many of the experiences, problems and irritations of the world outside. Many of their inhabitants quite self-consciously rejoice in such insulation from the "mainstream" of the population that they hold in some contempt, especially in the United States. These circumstances also help to explain the persisting popularity of versions of Marxism among academic intellectuals in the West and other trends such as postmodernism and deconstructionism. The latter not only represent new heights of cognitive and moral relativism but are conveyed in language and terminology incomprehensible to those outside academia and even to many within. Jeffrey Herf, a social historian, appropriately designated these endeavors as "the counter-Enlightenment project" and pointed out that "the postmodernist blurring between fact and fiction, and its assumption that all knowledge is the product of power, weakens the discipline of history as such." He also recalled that both Nazism and communism "attacked notions of objectivity, common standards and rules of evidence in favor of forms of what have been called identity politics."

Since the 1980s the major expression of discontent with Western culture and societies has found expression in the concepts, ideologies, and educational reforms associated with "multiculturalism" or "cultural diversity," two terms that, in their current usage, are highly inaccurate and misleading. Although multi-culturalism (or cultural diversity) has been championed by different groups (such as blacks, Hispanics, radical feminists, homosexuals, lesbians), what these groups have in common is an intense hostility to Western traditions, social arrangements, values, and systems of thought, including science.

To be a multiculturalist critic of the United States (or other Western societies) it is not necessary to visit other, putatively superior social systems or cultures. Academic enclaves are sufficient for the incubation and propagation of these views and attitudes. Flights into an imaginary and idealized past may replace pointing to existing, superior societies - an approach especially preferred by Afrocentrists, who probably represent the most influential component of the multiculturalist movement and who would find it particularly difficult to single out actually existing African countries that could inspire admiration or emulation. Multiculturalism, though originating and entrenched on the campuses, has also exerted a strong influence over school systems all over the country as well as over a variety of other institutions, from museums to symphony orchestras.

There are other phenomena that are characteristic of the current cultural landscape in the United States that feed into or reflect the adversarial currents noted. The proliferation of accredited or aspiring victims groups over the past decades—each representing further proof of the inequities of the system—has been a much discussed aspect of U.S. society between the 1970s and 1990s. The late Christopher Lasch observed that in such "a cult of the victim...entitlements are based on the display of accumulated injuries inflicted by an uncaring society."

Another trend linked with multiculturalism has been the propagation of self-esteem as a key to group and individual uplift. It has become a cultural maxim that self-esteem must be raised regardless of what the "self" has achieved, while personal and group failure remain to be ascribed to social conditions and structures. There is at last the phenomenon of identity politics, intertwined with both multiculturalism and the battle for self-esteem. Identity politics assumes that some basic characteristic of human beings, such as race, sex, ethnicity, or sexual preference, is the single determinant and source of a person's true identity and all political interests. Christopher Lasch pointed out that "the same benefits misleadingly associated with religion—security, spiritual comfort, dogmatic relief from doubt—are thought to flow from a therapeutic politics of identity."

The so-called revisionist historiography of the Soviet Union is another symptom of the attitudes that led to political pilgrimages. Whereas it is easier to understand why some of the historians who came of age during the 1960s felt uncomfortable with criticism of the Soviet Union for the Cold War or with the concept of totalitarianism, it is more perplexing why some of them felt compelled more recently to reinterpret the purges of the 1930s and the mass murders under Stalin, endeavors reminiscent of the Holocaust revisionism. The eagerness and energy that some of these historians have devoted to their attempts to humanize the Soviet system, even its Stalinist incarnation, may be explained by their unstated commitment to the image of the United States as the most malevolent force in contemporary or past history. Recently, one of them, Robert Thurston, even managed to produce a book (*Life and Terror in Stalin's Russia, 1934-1941*) that seeks to rehabilitate Stalin himself.

Another less conspicuous but not insignificant trend that too reflects some of the attitudes here discussed is found in other fashions in historiography. I am referring to the concern of American historians with what is usually called "history from below" and various forms of "revisionism," which usually seek to show that American history is far fuller of disgraceful episodes than had been thought earlier. This type of history, a form of retroactive social criticism avoids and ignores the conventional elite groups who used to get the lion's share of historical attention and concurrently idealizes the seemingly forgotten masses, the poor, the non-elites. These endeavors also seek to highlight aspects of American or Western history that further justify the critics' aversion to the society to which they so ambivalently belong.

The most general as well as the most durable explanation of the phenomena here discussed is connected to modernity. It hardly needs to be said that I am not referring to cars or computers but, rather, to the most corrosive of all qualities of modernity, which Christopher Lasch captured when he described the United States today as "a society in which nothing is sacred and therefore, nothing is forbidden." Such a society is a fertile ground for confusion, alienation, vague longings, and discontents, which give rise to political pilgrimages and other quests for meaning.

8

Nonconformist Intellectuals Today

The idea for a study of members and supporters of the National Association of Scholars came to us several years ago. In undertaking it we had two interests. One was practical: to acquire basic information that might be helpful for the organization in its recruitment policies and various activities.

There was a stronger and more purely scholarly motivation driven by the long standing interest of one of the authors in intellectuals as an important and peculiar group of people or social type. Hollander had written a fair amount about the animating beliefs and impulses of left-of-center intellectuals.[1] Now he wanted to learn something about intellectuals who did not fit this all-too-familiar mold. There are in the contemporary American academy a good number of those who do not conform to the stereotype of the alienated, left-liberal intellectual, possessed of idiosyncratic definitions of the underdog (or the victim). These nonconformists do not partake in the prevailing guilt about social ills for which they were not responsible. Nor had they been anti-anticommunists or sympathizers with social movements and political systems that sought legitimacy through some doctrine of socialism or by an alleged commitment to egalitarian values (the last of which were the Sandinistas).

Having criticized left-liberal or "politically correct" intellectuals for some time, Hollander became interested in how intellectuals who do not share the disposition of their colleagues on the left-or, more specifically, those willing to criticize publicly the orthodoxies rooted in the 1960s differ from the upholders and popularizers of those orthodoxies. We were also interested in the possibility that a study of intellectuals who support NAS might shed light on some disputed traits of, and generalizations about, intellectuals.

It remains an open question, in light of the limited data at our disposal to what extent or in what respect (if at all) one may generalize about American academic intellectuals of different political persuasions from a sample of NAS members.

Regarding intellectuals as a group prone to left-wing or left-liberal persuasion has a long tradition in the West. Their major historical incarnations include French enlightenment intellectuals, the Russian intelligentsia of the nineteenth-century, supporters of Dreyfus in France, those of Sacco and Vanzetti in the United States, and the Russian Revolution of 1917, the generations of Western political pilgrims to various communist states, the American and Western European generation of activist students and academics of the 1960s. All these groups have been acknowledged to be, and have identified themselves as left of center. They were generally critical of their society, its political institutions, of capitalism, bourgeois values, and more recently of the United States in particular as the most virulent embodiment of everything they deplored.

Of late, a diffuse anti-Western theme has been added to the more conventional left-liberal attributes. At the present time the typical American academic intellectual (in the humanities and social sciences) embraces or at least pays lip service to the doctrines of "multiculturalism" or "cultural diversity," or at any rate fails to criticize the ascendancy of these deeply anti-intellectual and anti-Western ideas.

Intellectuals flatter themselves that they are the conscience of society, fearless, independent thinkers, defiers of authority, fighters for social justice and free expression, capable of transcending personal advantage for the public good, uninterested in power and material gain, and so on. Belief in many of these attributes can be traced to Karl Mannheim who developed a theoretical basis for such a wishful image. For example, he wrote that intellectuals were bound together by a "common educational heritage;" that they were capable of some great "synthesis" because of their "heterogenous social background": that they were predisposed to "the fulfillment of their mission as the predestined advocate of the intellectual interests of the whole." Mannheim further complimented them by claiming that

We owe the possibility of mutual interpenetration and understanding of existing currents of thought to the presence of such a relatively unattached middle stratum which is open to the constant influx of individuals from the most diverse social classes and groups with all possible points of view.

Not bad. On the other hand Mannheim also noted (more plausibly) that "the fanaticism of radicalized intellectuals ... bespeaks a psychic compensation for the lack of a greater integration into a class."[2]

More recently a moderately left-of-center author observed that the essential identity of the intellectual combined "seriousness. cosmopolitanism, rational skepticism toward any and all ideologies and institutions, strong sensitivity to the historical moment and sympathy with avant-garde art and literature."[3] He hastened to add that hardly anybody lived up to these specifications. To be sure there have also been negative stereotypes of intellectuals, especially in the United States as impractical "eggheads." eternal whiners, subversives, parasites, sometimes true-believer fanatics and so on.[4]

We were curious to learn something about intellectuals who have become at the present time the voice of dissent on the campuses, representatives of a new nonconformity and critical questioning in academic life, surrounded not exactly by "the sea of repression," as Chester Finn, perhaps too strongly, put it. but certainly by a sea of political orthodoxies.[5] If indeed a cardinal attribute of intellectuals is a questioning disposition then intellectuals critical of the regnant conventional wisdoms on the campuses are often among the supporters of NAS.

A study of an ideologically deviant minority is always interesting, and especially so when such attitudes are not stimulated by extrinsic rewards (such as favorable publicity) but on the contrary may involve some degree of risk. That NAS members constitute such a nonconformist minority is also suggested by their small number: it is as of this writing approximately 4.000 compared to other academic organizations as the American Association of University Professors, with 42.000 members and professional organization like the Modern Language Association. which has 31.000 members. The latter while officially nonpolitical has in fact, assumed a major role in sanctioning and promoting beliefs associated with political correctness.

We are not suggesting that to engage in the public critique of political correctness and multiculturalism on the American campuses today is something exceptionally heroic, or that it involves huge risks (certainly not for those who are tenured). Nonetheless, the fact remains that most of our colleagues. and especially those agreeing with us in private, have been acting as if taking a stand against the expressions of political correctness did involve great risks, even some sort of moral danger. John Searle rightly noted that "the most offensive trait of American academics as a class is their timidity. In many cases even those who have tenure are unwilling to take controversial stands (I guess for fear of being hated by their colleagues and students)."[6] Probably even more consequential has been the fear of being denounced as racist, sexist, elitist, and so forth. There is a good deal of discrepancy between public repudiation of the NAS and privately expressed support for its goals. The inconsistency probably does not bespeak of cowardice outright. but more likely sympathy for the idealistic appeals to social justice that have done so much to weaken academic and intellectual standards.

As to the more tangible disadvantages of taking a public stand against the still prevailing orthodoxies on the campuses it would require further study (not easy to carry out) to learn how many politically incorrect white males had difficulty getting jobs, promotions or tenure on account of their unorthodox political beliefs, for questioning some tenet of PC, or simply for being white males.[7] There is mostly anecdotal information on such matters. It would be of similar interest to know how many teachers stopped offering courses on sensitive subjects because of the risk of denunciation.

Clearly, though, there are and have been many Western intellectuals who cannot be defined by the leftist attributes sketched above. They include Raymond Aron. Isaiah Berlin. Albert Camus. Arthur Koestler. George Orwell, or, closer to home, Hannah Arendt, Daniel Boorstin. Sidney Hook, Leszek Kolakowski, Czeslaw Milosz, Edward Shils. Christina Hoff Sommers, Thomas Sowell, Shelby Steele. James Q. Wilson—to name a few. The persecuted dissenters in former or existing communist countries also embody the best of what it might mean to be an intellectual.

With the emergence of the so-called neoconservatives in this country in the early 1970s, the balance has somewhat shifted. New voices entered the marketplace of ideas. Making it harder to generalize about the political attitudes of American intellectuals. But, while outspoken neoconservatives may have influenced national politics, they have had little impact on educational institutions, the mass media, and foundations.[9]

In the early 1980s, Seymour Martin Lipset concluded, after a review of relevant studies. that faculties, especially in the social sciences. "have been disproportionately critical of society and more disposed than other strata to support forces that reject the status quo."[10] A survey of the political attitudes of faculties at leading schools of theology 'found even more evidence of left of-center attitudes. with 14 percent of the respondents describing themselves as " very liberal" and 34 percent as "somewhat liberal."[11]

In 1989, a Carnegie Foundation study, *The Condition of the Professoriate,* found that 57 percent of all faculty polled leaned leftward to a greater or lesser degree while only 27 percent were politically inclined in the other direction. These self-rankings were consistent for various institutions and levels of study for age and sex. and throughout all disciplines in the humanities and social sciences.

It should also be noted that, of late academic administrators perhaps even more than faculty have become the most ardent champions of political correctness. They espouse political correctness while they are also fearful of offending the vocal groups on campus who occupy buildings and otherwise wreak havoc. To the best of our knowledge there are no studies revealing the political disposition and values of academic administrators.

Needless to say, mail surveys and questionnaires are imperfect tools for gauging the intangibles and complexities of personal motivation, attitude and belief The research reported below provides only a limited and partly speculative answer to the question: What do the intellectuals associated with NAS (and included in this survey) have in common, and how do they differ from academics not associated with NAS? Obviously. NAS members share an opposition to the prevailing left-liberal orthodoxies and a willingness to take a public stand against them. In these respects they are unlike other academics. The findings cannot tell in what other distinctive ways NAS supporters differ from the rest of academic intellectuals, and especially those to the left of center.

At the same time we have noted that majorities of academic intellectuals share some of the values and concerns of NAS supporters but are reluctant to express such sentiments publicly. This was also suggested by a recent NAS national survey which found that approximately two-thirds surveyed disapproved of the use of race and sex preferences in higher education.[12] Probably a far greater proportion of NAS members feel the same way.

The Sample

Trying to reach every member of NAS would have been expensive, though far from impossible. We opted to seek out those most active in the organization: people who attend national meetings. Questionnaires were distributed at such conferences in 1993 in San Francisco and in 1994 in Cambridge, Massachusetts. Obviously, most of those who responded have in common their attendance at the national meetings and willingness to complete and return the questionnaires (more people attended the meetings than returned the questionnaire). For these reasons they might be regarded as the activist membership, more committed and embodying the concerns that led to the creation of NAS in the first place. Since we were primarily interested in such people (those strongly opposed to the current orthodoxies) the sample was certainly compatible with the goals of the study. In addition. with the help of NAS president Steve Balch an appeal was also made to chairmen of state affiliates to pass questionnaires to their local members (response to these appeals was spotty). Altogether, 252 responses were received. Percentages that fail to add up to one hundred reflect incomplete or incorrectly executed forms.

Basic Data

Sex: Eighty-seven percent of the respondents were male and 13 percent female. Several interpretations of this may be suggested (in addition to the fact that there are more male than female academics in the U.S.). Many women who are on college and university faculties are more likely to be feminist and if so, may perceive NAS as unconcerned with feminist issues: equally plausible is that women faculty sympathetic to NAS feel more constrained by feminist peer pressures than are males by their left-of-center peers, not because it is easier to intimidate women but because there is more pressure on women faculty by other women to present a united front. A female respondent wrote: "I had been a victim of rather drastic ideological discrimination as a female ... who preferred the history of Western ideas as a field" (rather than some variety of women's studies).

Another hypothesis is that more demands are made on the time of women professionals in academia (and elsewhere) hence they have less time to join organizations, including NAS, and attend their meetings.

Marital status and age: Seventy-nine percent of responding NAS supporters were currently married and 65 percent had children. Ages ranged from 27 to 86 with a mean of 54 years old.

Three explanations of the high average age may be offered. (1) The tenure factor: the nontenured are less likely to join NAS since, given the prevailing pressures, known NAS affiliation does not help in many departments and schools to get tenure. (2) It is also possible that the younger academics (many of them of the 60s generation) are in fact more left-of-center and misperceive NAS as an arch conservative organization.[13] (3) An alternative hypothesis: the younger are more apolitical due to career pressures (as distinct from political), more anxious to publish, or are otherwise preoccupied and hence less likely to add to their professional obligations.

Ethnicity (unless otherwise indicated questions were open-ended calling for self-identification): Seventy percent of respondents identified themselves as Western European (Anglo-Saxon. German. and so forth). Jews made up 21 percent. and these probably reflect the social-historical patterns of Jewish migration from Eastern Europe to the United States and into academic occupations. The 3 percent who responded as East European were presumably gentiles. Only 2 percent characterized themselves as Caribbean or Latin American. One percent was of Asian descent.

This is probably a reasonably accurate reflection of the ethnic background of the American professoriate except for the underrepresentation of blacks and Hispanics. Such underrepresentation. while regrettable. is not surprising since most of these academics entered the profession with the help of affirmative action and NAS is perceived as a critic of it. There are also strong peer pressures in these groups to stay within the bounds of political correctness. On the other hand, well-known. high-profile black supporters of NAS may he too busy to attend meetings or complete questionnaires.

Religion: The largest percentage of respondents admitted to no current religious affiliation, and when these combine with agnostics and atheists the total speaks interestingly about what might he a national pattern in adult religious observance. Thirty percent of our sample reported no affiliation while 27 percent said they were Protestant. 18 percent Catholic. 10 percent Jewish. 4 percent conservative Christian and 11 percent agnostic or atheist.

Socioeconomic background: Close to 40 percent of the respondents come from the working class or the lower middle class as defined by fathers' occupation. These backgrounds included farmer, steelworker. construction worker, janitor, postal clerk, rural letter carrier. salesman, candy store owner, policeman, butcher, miner, carpenter. car mechanic, taxi driver, printer, tailor. railway engineer. boilermaker. wood finisher, laborer, as well as civil servant. Executives, bankers, accountants and other businessmen were father to 28 percent of surveyed members. Twenty-two percent of respondents had parents who could be described as professionals. and, of these. engineers predominated. Only 11 percent had fathers who were lawyers, and 4 percent of the entire sample were sons or daughters of physicians. Only 4 percent had fathers who were professors. though 16 percent had mothers who were school teachers. Only 1 percent claimed that the father was a minister or priest: there were no social workers among fathers and only one among mothers.

We considered these findings significant since available research anecdotal evidence, as well as common sense suggests that occupations most heavily invested in the adversarial mindset are dominated by university professors (in humanities and social sciences), ministers, and social workers (and media celebrities): precisely such groups were the least represented in the social background of the respondents. Data from other questions suggest that half of parents may not have had college education and almost certainly the majority had not attended graduate or professional schools.

These findings lead one to conclude that most of our respondents have been socially mobile with almost 90 percent holding either doctorate or other advanced degrees (unlike their parents). Again, it is a sociological truism that self-made men and women are far less likely to be estranged from or hostile to their society than those more directly and effortlessly benefiting from and sharing their parents higher, more privileged social status. Parental attitudes and socioeconomic status influence children in various ways. sometimes direct, sometimes indirect.[14]

Training: Eighty-seven percent of the respondents held advanced degrees mostly Ph.D.s but also M.D.s and J.D.s. Ten percent had masters degrees. and the remaining 3 percent bachelors. Fifty-three percent listed their degree field as humanities or fine arts, 29 percent were in the social sciences, and 10 percent had professional degrees (medical or legal). Only 9 percent were in the natural or physical sciences.

Nineteen percent obtained their degrees at Ivy League schools and 15 percent at one of three major state universities: Berkeley. Michigan. and Wisconsin. Ten percent of degrees were awarded by major private universities including Chicago and Johns Hopkins. 29 percent by other public universities and 21 percent by other private schools. Six percent got their higher degrees abroad.

Field of specialization: Of our respondents, 60 percent were teaching in the humanities and fine arts. 15 percent in the social sciences, 9 percent in the hard sciences, 8 percent in medicine and law. 3 percent in business school, and 2 percent in education. This finding was somewhat counterintuitive since the sciences, engineering, and business attract the smallest number of left leaning faculty. However the preponderance in the humanities may be explained in another way.

There is much evidence to show that it is the departments of English and literature that have been most heavily saturated with the adversarial ethos or political correctness in recent times. The 1989 Carnegie Foundation study revealed that 70 percent of humanities faculty were left-liberal. The intensity of that bias was equaled only among the faculty in the social sciences. John Searle wrote that "radical politics migrated into academic departments of literature" in part because "Marxism in particular and left-wing radicalism in general have been discredited as theories of politics, society and historical change... Having been refuted as theories of society, these views have retreated into departments of literature."[15] What is more difficult to explain is how teachers of literature came to lose interest in literature, or why in the first place they entered a field that did not interest them.

The large portion of our respondents from such fields suggests that they have reacted strongly against these trends, that there was more to react against in these departments than, say, in business or the hard sciences. NAS supporters doubtless represent small minorities in departments of English but one presumes they are particularly anxious to take a stand against what they see as the perversion of the teaching of literature as well as the beliefs associated with political correctness.

At what type of school employed: Ivy league and other elite institutions: 2 percent: major state universities (Wisconsin, Rutgers, etc.):

10 percent: other public institutions: 37 percent: non-elite private colleges: 25 percent: retired: 12 percent: self-employed: 4 percent: institutes or think-tanks: 2 percent.

These findings raise the questions as to the relative under-representation of NAS supporters in high-prestige institutions. We do not know why this would be the case although it has been found in past research that elite schools have more left-of-center faculty and hence provide a less hospitable environment for those not inclined to similar beliefs.[16]

Scholarship: NAS respondents turned out to be a well-published group. In our sample 55 percent were authors of"one or more books": 38 percent "numerous articles;" and only 23 percent were "not widely published" (in all probability this is substantially above national standards or averages).

In response to a question about their major professional interest and activity 56 percent indicated teaching, 53 percent research. Few chose the third option "academic-professional service activities."

Political self identification: Nine attributes were listed, of which respondents could check up to three.

Option	Selected
conservative	49
neoconservative	29
moderate	29
right of center	21
libertarian	20
liberal	19
left of center	6
radical	4
apolitical	3

It may be worth noting here that a substantial portion (25 percent) of the respondents think of themselves as liberal or left-of-center, and libertarians and moderates comprised 49 percent. Libertarians. of course, may lean to left or right, and moderate may mean moderate conservative or liberal. In any event these choices suggest that, with regard to the political beliefs of its members. NAS is a far from monolithic group. Also of interest that numerous respondents in their comments cautioned against the politicization of NAS, a genuine dilemma for an organization that seeks to counteract the politicization of academic life. (One respondent advised: "Continue to steer clear of non-academic political questions.") There was also some concern that those hostile to NAS may have succeeded in portraying it as a conservative or right-wing organization. (One respondent wrote: "I would like to see less talk about our cause being a 'conservative' one in the sense of identfying with Reaganism. etc. Plenty of old fashioned liberals are with NAS too.")

It should also be recalled here that in the course of the past three decades the meaning of concepts such as "liberal" and "conservative" have undergone considerable change. Increasingly "liberal" came to mean left. or left-of-center. On the other hand, "conservative" or "neoconservative" are today associated with positions which in the past used to be thought of as archetypically liberal. These positions include a focus on individual merit rather than group entitlement, colorblind thinking rather than emphasis on group ties as prime determinants of personal identity, and an unconditional commitment to free expression rather than offering elaborate excuses for restrictions on expression (as for instance, speech codes).

Self characterization (up to 4 choices): The question was "which of the following would he an acceptable characterization of yourself." We hoped to shed some further light on the social or psychological type of person who supports NAS (or at any rate, his self-conception).

While making allowances for the tendency of most human beings to characterize themselves in favorable rather than unfavorable ways, the types of self-identification provided are congruent with active participation in NAS: it requires being a nonconformist (36 percent). a social critic *(35* percent). a good citizen (49 percent) being public spirited (39 percent) and a willingness to take risk (23 percent). 'Compromisers," 'teamplayers and "apolitical academics" (21 percent combined total) are bound to be less often found in the ranks of NAS.

Option Percentage	Selected
good citizen	49
public spirited	39
nonconformist	36
social critic	35
workaholic	31
ordinary academic	24
risk taker	23
retiring scholar	12
defier of authority	19
reluctant participant in public affairs	I 9
polemicist	19
leader	19
activist	18
compromiser	10
team player	8
apolitical academic	3

Motives for Joining NAS [open ended]: Responses to these and the following question provide remarkable illustrations of how pervasive and highly patterned the problems in American higher education have become. From Ivy League schools to small Midwestern private colleges and large state institutions of every kind, the impact of political correctness and the decline of standards is strikingly evident from the expressed concerns that brought members to the NAS.

Percent	Motivation for joining
22	PC and politicization of academia
19	to defend Western canon and traditions
10	support for NAS goals
8	affirmative action issues
8	defense of free speech
7	particular campus incident [related to some of the other categories]
4	decline of academic standards
4	opposition to Left
4	opposition to radical feminism
3	in response to NAS publications
2	friends

Specific, experiential reasons for joining NAS sometimes included such events as 'a sit-in in the office of the president" [of the university] and the attendant cave-in to the demands of the occupiers. Another respondent gave this reason: "1 was stunned by a person who was preaching racism under the guise of multiculturalism" and who also happened to be the director of the Center for Studies in Race and Ethnicity at that campus. One of our colleagues was energized to join upon learning that his university introduced a requirement for ethnic studies without having any other requirements. Another memorable reason given for joining was this: "I was struck (with horror) by the parallels between the coercive conformity of PC and the methods of the Christian Church in its inquisition." Probably most of the "responses to this question could go under the tersely stated desire to save academic freedom."

Perceptions of problems in higher education (overlaps with reasons for joining): The largest percentage (32 percent) of members reported the decline of academic standards as the major problem facing American higher education today. Included in this category was the admission of students who are unqualified and unprepared for college. The second largest category (17 percent) noted the politicization of the academy as the major problem. Opposition to multiculturalism and diversity comprised the third category (12 percent). Discriminatory hiring practices, including affirmative action and group entitlements were seen as a major problem in higher education by 7 percent of those surveyed (but they also were often mentioned among the reasons for joining NAS). Other specifics included threats to free speech (4 percent, political correctness (3 percent), egalitarianism (3 percent, feminism (1 percent), emphasis on "self-esteem" (percent) and administrative "selling out" (3 percent). Four percent of the respondents stated that the social problems of American society had also affected the academy, including apathy and lack of morals. Using the university to solve society's problems was seen as a problem for higher education by 3 percent.

As presented here, these listings fail to do justice to the quality of the responses and the perception of the links between the malaise on the campuses and in society at large. For example one respondent succinctly summarized the major problems of American higher education and culture as "the notion that the world is socially constructed." Even more pithily, another nailed it down as the toleration of ignorance. Another respondent memorably summed up his perception of the academy as sacrificing quality on the altar of self-esteem.

Perceptions of NAS: Members were asked how they thought others on their campus perceived the NAS. 32 percent replied that the NAS was perceived with hostility and/or suspicion: 16 percent felt that the NAS was seen with indifference; 12 percent felt that the perception of the NAS was mixed-both negative and positive; 12 percent did not know how NAS was perceived; only 10 percent felt that NAS was generally perceived in a supportive manner: 8 percent thought that their colleagues were unaware of the NAS.

Here of course. the preponderance of negative (32 percent) perceptions over positive (10 percent) is the most notable finding.

Other groups supported: Respondents were asked to list all of the organizations they were involved in other than the NAS. Those listed ranged from professional associations in various academic fields to political organizations (parties), civic groups and recreational groups such as hiking clubs.

The largest category (33 percent) were such professional organizations as the American Sociological Association and the Modern Language Association. Right-of-center groups comprised the second largest category (quite small as a percentage of the total: 14 percent). The Heritage Foundation. the CATO Institute. and the University Centers for Rational Alternatives were among those listed. Membership in the Republican party at the local, state and national level was the third largest category (but still only 7 percent). Membership in various Democratic party groups was the fourth largest category of organizations, with 5 percent of members surveyed indicating that they belonged to local, state or national Democratic organizations. 5 percent of respondents belonged to local civic groups such as Boy Scouting. Rotary Clubs, and the Daughters of the American Revolution. Equal percentages of respondents belonged to arts groups (3 percent), environmental and outing groups such as the Sierra Club or Audobon Society (4 percent), religious groups (3 percent). and unions, specifically the American Association of University Professors (3 percent). Two percent belonged to military clubs and 4 percent to groups not categorized above. 5 percent of respondents left the question blank or did not belong to any other groups. Another 5 percent of members indicated belonging to special issue groups that included Amnesty International. Handgun Control, and Planned Parenthood. Three percent belonged to the American Civil Liberties Union and 1 percent to the National Association for the Advancement of Colored People. One percent belonged to the National Rifle Association and another 1 percent to the National Right to Life movement.

Practical Recommendations: Respondents made numerous worthwhile suggestions how to improve NAS activities or what new activities the association might undertake. Among those most often mentioned was the establishment of a legal foundation or fund to pursue the goals of NAS and to offer legal assistance to those most seriously victimized by political correctness.

Reaching outside the campuses for support was another idea, including an effort to organize high-school teachers and college alumni. Disseminating the messages and activities of NAS on the internet was yet another idea that has to some extent been put into effect. Several respondents urged NAS to seek wider national publicity of the absurdities in academia; many felt that further efforts should he made to increase membership.

Summary

While the supporters of NAS are a widely disparate group the tentative portrait of a typical member suggests that he is predominantly white, male, older-middle aged, socially mobile, well-educated and well-published, and that he teaches in the humanities and social sciences (the two areas under particular PC pressure). He is actively involved in public life and joined NAS in order to protect academic goals and values from attack and to counteract decades of decline in academic standards,

Clearly, in many ways NAS supporters differ from other academics, but there are also areas of congruence. On pages 23 and 27 of the Carnegie report cited above, 62 percent of its much larger national sample considered grade inflation a problem at their institutions and 67 percent believed that there has been a widespread lowering of standards in American higher education. It is likely that an even higher proportion of NAS supporters would endorse these views.

The most suggestive aspect of the current study is the social background of our sample that helps to explain the roots of the predisposition of this group and its willingness to take certain stands and thereby differentiate itself from other academics. Given their upward social and educational mobility, the NAS supporters sampled do not seem to be prone to the type of often embittered, reflexive social criticism that is associated with a more privileged family background and parental occupations that include academics. the clergy, or social service. Neither is the background of the sample conducive to the idiosyncratic identification with particular groups of "underdogs." A higher average age also generally correlates with the positions our respondents embrace.

In the final analysis we cannot explain why some people are more willing to defy the conventional wisdom of their social setting and risk some verbal abuse or the displeasure of their administrative superiors. Our survey only suggests some of the factors that are likely to predispose toward such attitudes. They included taking the academic-intellectual calling seriously (as also expressed in publishing productivity), nonprivileged social backgrounds, and reaction to unusually heavy doses of the prevailing political-educational ortho-doxies. As in all survey research, the intangibles of personal experi-ence. motivation, and will do not lend themselves to revelation in response to a questionnaire.

Notes

1. Paul Hollander, *Political Pilgrims* (New York: Oxford University Press, 1981): *The Survival of the Adversary Culture* (New Brunswick, N.J.: Transaction Books, 1988); *Anti-Americanism: Critiques at Home and Abroad (New* York: Oxford Uni-versity Press. 1992). See also his American Intellectuals: Producers and Consumers and Social Criticism" in A. Gagnon ed., *Intellectuals in Liberal Democracies* (New York: Praeger. 1987); "Alienation and the Adversary Culture. *Society* (May-June 1988): "From Iconoclasm to Conventional Wisdom" *Academic Questions* (Fall 1989): "Imagined Tyranny"? Political Correctness Reconsidered" *AQ,* (Fall 1994); "Reassessing the Adversary Culture." *AQ* (Spring 1996).
2. Karl Mannheim. *Ideology and Utopia* (New York: Harcourt. 1936). 157, 158, 161, 159.
3. Dennis Wrong. "Commentary After Half a Century." *Dissent* (Winter 1977): 106.
4. For a discussion of the anti-intellectual traditions in the United States, Richard Hofstadter's *Anti-Intellectualism in American Life.* (New York: Alfred A. Knopf, 1962) remains the classic text. The unflattering concept of the "true believer" was introduced by Eric Hoffer in *The True Believer* (New York: Harper & Row. 1951).
5. Chester F. Finn. "The Campus: 'Island of Repression in a Sea of Freedom," *Com-mentary (September* 1989). The uproar over Lino Graglia's remarks last September on racial discrepancies in academic performance is the most striking recent illustra-tion of intolerance on campus.
6. John R. Searle: 'Is There a Crisis in American Higher Education" *Bulletin of the American Academy of Arts and Sciences* (January 1993): 45.
7. For a handful of case studies in reverse discrimination inside and outside academe, see Tom McClintock and Steven McCarthy. *Equal opportunity Denied* (Claremont. Ca: Claremont Institute. 1996): Frederick R. Lynch *Invisible Victims: While Males and the Crisis of Affirmative Action.* (New York: Greenwood Press, 1989): also b\ Lynch. *The Diversity Machine: The Drive to Change The White Male Workplace* (New York: Free Press 1997): see also Thomas Sowell. "Affirmative Action: A Worldwide Disaster." *Commentary* (December 1989).
8. For example. one of our colleagues at the University of Massachusetts, Amherst. stopped teaching a course on social problems after black students complained that he overemphasized black criminality.
9. This argument was developed and documented at some length in *Anti-American-ism: Critiques at Home and Abroad.* It should also be noted here that according to some authors there was during the 1970s and early 1980s a tendency "toward greater conservatism" in the academic world, although "the self-identified left was fairly constant over this period" Richard F. Hamilton and Lowell L. Hargens. 'The Politics of the Professors: Self-Identifications. 1969-1984." *Social Forcess* (March 1993): 607].
10. Seymour Martin Lipset. "The Academic Mind at the Top: The Political Behavior and Values of Faculty Elites." *Public Opinion 46* (1982): 144.

11.   Everett C. Ladd and G. Donald Feree Jr.. "What Theologians Believe, Theology Faculty Survey." *This World* (Summer I 982).
12.   *National Faculty Survey Regarding the Use of Gender and Racial Preferences. in Higher Education,* 16 to 18 October 1996. conducted by the Roper Center for Public Opinion Research at the University of Connecticut for the National Association of Scholars.
13.   A bigger sample would certainly help to find out if there is any pattern regarding the politics of different age groups and about the motives for joining NAS on the part of different age groups.
14.   A major study of such matters found a contrasting pattern of such parental influences among Jews and gentiles. The former followed, with some modifications, the worldview of the parents: liberal parents had liberal or radical children. By contrast radical gentiles usually had conservative parents against whom they rebelled. See Stanley Rothman and S. Robert Lichier, *Roots of Radicalism* (New York: Oxford University Press, 1982).

       A recent article (based in part on Paul Lazarsfeld and Wagner Thielens: *The Academic Mind)* also noted the connection between higher socio-economic background and a more liberal worldview: "Liberal professors ... came unusually often from comfortable middle-class origins ... 48 percent [in the study sample I had fathers who were proprietors, managers. officials or members of a profession Some of our liberal professors had broken away from a background in the business community. (Wagner Thielens in "Academic Freedom Symposium" *William Mitchell Law Review* 22, No. 2 [1966]: 443).
15.   Searle. "Is There a Crisis in American Higher Education?" 35.
16.   Lipset. "The Academic Mind at the Top."
17.   In a future study it might be useful to supplement political self identification with more specific indicators of political attitudes, such as positions taken on major issues in the "culture wars" such as abortion, affirmative action, gun control; welfare. etc.: it would also be of great interest to learn if and when changes in political attitudes may have occurred, and how many NAS supporters number among the so-called "liberals mugged by reality."

9

The Pursuit of Identity, Community and Social Justice: The Cult of Victimhood Revisited

Why in recent years have so many Americans come to feel that they have been victimised in one way or another? Why has the victim status been so eagerly sought and so readily granted? Why have words like "abuse," "sexual harassment," "sexism," and "racism" become overused and simultaneously drained of specific meaning and content?

Even people without the familiar ethnic-sexual claims to victimhood have been eager to join the better recognized victims: white, heterosexual, middle class people of both sexes who discovered how their unloving or inattentive parents performed various psychic mutilations on them at an early age disfiguring them for life.

On the campuses and in liberal, high-income communities few would question any charge of racism, sexism, homophobia, elitism, and so forth. In these settings every opportunity is taken to engage in collective self-flagellation such incidents (real or imagined) provide. Scepticism about such charges is treated as self-evident proof of the racism (or sexism etc.) of the sceptic. Moreover the putative victim instantly becomes the object of favorable attention and moral elevation—a circumstance that helps to explain why such incidents are sometimes fabricated or exaggerated.

The most momentous development in the recent social history of victimhood has been that ascertainable disadvantage, (for example, poverty) or evidence of tangible, willed discrimination ceased to play a part in the inclusion in a victim category. A young and healthy black or Hispanic male, coming from a prosperous, middle or upper middle class family is automatically granted victim status qualifying him for preferential treatment in various walks of life. Any and all women, regardless of socio-economic status, education, professional skills and health are eligible for federally mandated preferential treatment.

Much has been written of victimhood in present day American society; we have been called (by Charles Sykes) "a nation of victims." Robert Hughes concluded that "an infantilized culture of complaint" has been created. Lawrence Mead called the pursuit of victimhood "the politics of disadvantage." A writer in the *New York Times Book Review* noted the rise of a "melodramatic refus[al] to distinguish among levels of suffering and victimization." David Rieff observed that this is a country in which celebrities (Joel Best called them "victim celebrities") and opinion-makers fill the airwaves and newsprint with stories of their victimization talking with greater relish about their "addictions and childhood persecutions" than their power and fame. Public bragging about one's fame and wealth is now complemented by memories of victimization. This may be a contemporary version of the raggs to richess story, from the horrors of child abuse to a new serenity brought by success, shared with millions seeking entertainment (and perhaps hope) in the stories of suffering and renewal. People also write books about their illnesses or produce television documentaries about them.

At another level, the often self-appointed spokesmen of ethnic minorities (i.e., Blacks and Hispanics) and those of women insist, in the face of all evidence, that the victimization of these groups continues unabated and justifies continued preferential treatment. For people whose professional or political existence depends on the continued presence of victim groups it is difficult to face the possibility that the time may be near (or has already come) when their advocacy will no longer be required by the condition of those they claim to represent. Shelby Steele wrote: "Victimization... is what justifies preference, so that to receive the benefits of preferential treatment one must... become invested in the view of one's self as a victim."

Well over 80 percent of Americans seem to belong some victim group: all women, that is half of the population; blacks and Hispanics, another 30 percent or so and the disabled, 15-20percent (some of these categories overlap). To be sure not all them think of themselves as victims, regardless of federal classifications and the efforts of their spokesmen and women. On the other hand many of those not legally classified as victims do think of themselves in such terms and are encouraged to do so by therapeutic experts. John Bradshaw, "a leading figure in the recovery movement "estimated that "approximately 96% of the families in this country are dysfunctional to one degre or another."

How did the two processes—the political-institutional and the therapeutic-individual—creating and legitimating victimhood emerge and converge? How did victimhood become a matter of both social justice and individual psychic fulfillment, a preeminent individual and institutional preoccupation in American society during the last decades of the twentith century?

Several aspects of the current American preoccupation are novel. Whereas most societies through history took the ill treatment and disadvantage of some groups for granted, the law makers of this country laudably designated certain groups as victims of society deserving to benefit of a wide range of compensatory measures. (The German Federal Republic is another rare example of a government providing restitution to a victim group, the Jewish victims of the Holocaust or their suriving relatives and India has programs giving proportional representation in various hierarchies to the "untouchables," victims of the caste system.)

Another novel aspect of the current pursuit of victimhood is the great variety of conditions which give rise to it and the rapid expansion of such categories over a short period of time. Putative or genuine victims are no longer embarrassed by their condition, no longer do they seek to conceal their identity, the source of their victimization. Quite to the contrary, "the victim focused identity" (a concept introduced by Shelby Steele) has become extraordinarly popular. As was reported recently in the *New York Times* many of the disabled " ... say that they would reject being cured even if it were possible... 'I would not trade my disability for anything'" one of them declared; another came "to see disabled people as beautiful... Particularly people on respirators... in wheelchairs, people who spasm a lot, people who drool". The co-founder of the Institute on Disability Culture said "We are proud of ourselves as people with disabilities... We claim our disabilities with pride as part of our identity." Such is the disabled people's version of "black is beautiful."

Better known is the identity-boosting separatism of ethnic groups (excluding those of European or Asian origin) and radical feminists.

Lesbians and homosexuals also see themselves as victims of a "heterosexist" society and proudly affirm their sexual orientation, central to their identity. A new group claiming victim status and simultaneously voicing pride in their identity are "transsexuals" or "people with blured sexual identities." Talking about them the director of the International Foundation for Gender Education in Waltham Mass. said: "All of sudden a lot of [these] people feel 'Hey, I am proud.'"

Publicly affirmed victimhood thus becomes a new, or resurrected source of identity. And it is the pursuit of identity and community that is the most striking common denominator of the different types of victimhood. If so, the popularity of victimhood may have something to do with modernity and its discontents. The pursuit of a distinct identity through affirmations of shared victimhood is in some instances undermined by the victims' claim that there is nothing distinctive about their condition; thus homosexuals insist that anybody can catch AIDS just as easily as they, and sometimes the disabled argue that they are barely different from those who are not. The mentally disabled too voice such feelings. At a recent Western Massachusetts Self Advocacy Conference (reported in the *Daily Hampshire Gazette*, of Northampton, MA) one of them said that "people with mental disabilities 'are happy with themselves' and know how to work through their problems just like everyone else..." Another speaker suggested that "'I see everyone as having a disability...'"

Another paradoxical aspect of the current preoccupation with identity through victimhood is that, based as it is on the idea of a shared and immutable victimhood, it is difficult to reconcile with the goal of personal liberation victims embrace. There is a tension between the pursuit of identity, whatever its alleged source, and the values of personal liberation and uniqueness. Leon Wieseltier wrote, "The question, What is your identity? is really the question, Who are you like? Identity, in other words is a euphemism for conformity. It announces a desire to be subsumed, an eagerness to be known primarily by a common characteristic."

While the tangible advantages of legally certified victimhood are considerable, it would be mistaken to ascribe the popularity of the victims status and self-conception primarily to the economic or educational benefits such categorization yields. Other forces and pressures are at work as well, most apparent in the case of the celebrities dwelling on their past victimization. The self-styled victims at the higher end of the socio-economic scale seek compassion rather than compensation, moral rather than economic benefits. Their revelations of a victimised past are made easier by the general decline of privacy in American society, by the blurring of the line between the private and the public.

The moral-psychological gratification associated with victimhood is not limited to the abused celebrities. The moral rewards of recognized victimhood have a broad appeal, as they entail the conferral of solicitousness, compassion and sympathy. Belonging to a group of victims means membership in a sought-after moral community at a time when self-evident sources of morality are hard to find. Again Shelby Steele wrote: "... when we think of ourselves as victims, we are released from responsibility for some difficulty, spared some guilt and accountability. Our innocence is restored because an injustice was done to us. Injustice is what gives the claim of vicitmization its magic..." The combination of victimhood and moral distinction may also be traced to the surviving remnants of Judeo-Christian beliefs which connect virtue and suffering.

Recognized victims do not merely to shift responsilibility for their grievances or misfortune to forces or entities outside themselves but blame them with undisguised relish. When victims point their finger at their victimizers they reaffirm good and evil, the ultimate moral component of the quest for victimhood.

The inclination to blame is irresistible and apparent in a wide range of situations because by doing so victims affirm their innocence. A righteous anger, or outrage is part of the victim identity and feels good; socially sanctioned victimhood gives new license to the ancient pleasure of blaming others for our troubles. Victims and their spokesmen are never in doubt as to who is responsible for the victimhood in question: men oppress women, whites subjugate blacks, heterosexuals persecute homosexuals, the healthy look down upon the sick, middle class parents deform their children, and the patriarchal, racist, sexist, capitalist, white male, heterosexual power-structure oppresses everyone; dead-white-males (DWM) exert their baleful influence from their graves.

Andrew Hacker, the political scientist wrote in the aftermath of the 1992 Los Angeles riots in the *LA Times*:

> At times the conclusion seems all but self evident that white America has no desire for your [the black population's] presence... Can this nation have an unstated strategy for

annihilating your people? How else, you ask yourself, can one explain the incidence of death and debilitation from drugs and disease; the incarceration of a whole generation of your men; the consignement of millions of women and children to half-lives of poverty and dependence?...

... could it be that if white America begins to conclude that you are becoming too much trouble, it will find itself contemplating more lasting solutions?

Clearly what he had in mind was the idea of the "final solution", a term he shied away from using.

Even the biologically afflicted, AIDS victims and their spokesmen find ways to blame specific social-political forces for their predicament. AIDS activist Larry Kramer wrote in his 1989 book:

... the AIDs pandemic is the fault of the white, middle-class, male majority. AIDS is here because the straight world would not grant equal rights to gay people...

AIDs is our holocaust and Reagan is our Hitler. New York city is our Aushwitz...

I have come reluctantly to believe that genocide is occuring: that we are witnessing... the systematic, planned annihilation of some by others with the avowed purpose of eradicating an undesirable portion of the population.

As these remarks suggests belief in group victimization often has a conspiratorial element. It is not enough to locate blame in impersonal social or historical forces, victimization must be part of a highly motivated conspiracy of identifiable human beings. When confronted with the wide range of frustration and dissatisfaction the human condition entails, the choice appears to be between blaming oneself or others.

A recent (1997) case in point were the allegations of a CIA conspirary to distribute drugs in poor black neighborhoods; in this scenario the drug takers and buyers were wholly without responsibility for their habit; it was caused by the CIA and designed to inflict further deprivations on these groups. In 1990 a telephone poll conducted by the *New York Times* and WCBS-TV found that "a quarter of black New Yorkers believed that the Government 'deliberately makes sure that drugs are easily available in poor black neighborhhods in order to harm black people.' Another third of those polled said that might possibly be true."

An interesting variation on the same theme was proposed in 1997 by Kwame Ture (better known as Stokely Carmichael, the radical 60s activist) to a student audience at the University of Massachusetts at Amherst. He informed them that the FBI, following *its* assassination of Martin Luther King and others, "decided to go to germ warfare to get many people." He himself was one of these victims:

"the FBI gave me cancer" he averred, an assertion that was at least partly true since he was visiting this country to seek treatment for it.

The conspiratorial mentality and the denial of accident are linked: believers in conspiracies (like lawyers specialising in malpractice suits) refuse to believe that bad things can happen without ill will, or at least culpable negligence. AIDS is due to the malevolence of white males; the scarcity of women among mathematicians, mining engineers or foresters is the result of discrimination; the rarity of black oboists or Hispanic cellists in major symphony orchestras can only be accounted for by racism; the same goes for the underrepresentation of these minorities in the fields of of geology or entomology. Any such statistical disparity is due to discrimination.

The prevailing idea of "sexual harassment" provides further illustration of how victims are created by novel interpretations of wrongdoing. As reported in the *New Republic* in 1997 "a harassment complaint was filed [at the University of Nebraska at Lincoln] because a graduate student kept on his desk a snapshot of his wife in a bikini; the university ordered the photo removed" on the ground that such a display constituted the harassment of women who might have seen it. "Penn State removed a painting by Goya [presumably a reproduction of] from a classroom after a professor complained that it constituted sexual harassment... In a pamphlet called 'Preventing Sexual Harassment: A Fact Sheet for Employees' the Maryland Commission on Human Relations notes that 'a sexually hostile work environment can be created' by discussing sexual activities, [or] telling off-color jokes...'"

Daphne Patai, a rare academic critic of these trends pointed out that "We are being trained in how to reinterpret interactions according to a presumption of male wrongdoing." Patai also observes another trend, the training in victimhood: "... article after article... makes the point... that people need to learn how to recognize the injury they suffer" (also known as consciousness level raising). James Nolan (in his *The Therapeutic State*) reported that a member of a federal review panel that examined sensitivity training proposals found that "women who did not perceive themselves as harassed were urged to 'recognize their error as victims of internalized sexism'"—an orientation strikingly similar to that of the "recovery" school, the spokesmen of which insist that people who fail to recall the abuses suffered in their childhood must not conclude that they did not occur. Child abuse may mean "invalidating the experience" of children, or "thwarting their spirituality" according to Charles Whitfield, author of the modestly entitled *Codependence: Healing the Human Condition*.

Increasingly rape has been treated as a metaphor for the generalised oppression of women—a proposition substantiated by statements such as that of Catharine McKinnon: "Politically I call it rape whenever a woman has sex and feels violated." Her remark highlights the prominence of subjectivity in the definition of victimhood also apparent in speech codes and "sensitivity training" based as they are on the assumption that whatever members of designated victim groups consider insensitive, offensive or abusive must be so defined and constitutes victimization.

The interpretation of accidents is part of the trends here discussed. Increasingly they are seen as caused by negligence, if not actual ill will: when an adult forewarned by prominent notices climbs a structure that carries a power line and gets an electric shock the electric company is sued (an actual court case in my area). A young man who was crippled after being shot by the police while attempting to rob a 76 year old victim in the [New York] subway was awarded $ 4.3 by the court. An award was also ordered by the court in the famous case of the woman who drank hot coffee while driving and burned herself for which McDonalds was held responsible. Most recently the psychotic killer Wendell Williamson "was awarded $ 500,000 by a North Carolina jury that held his psychiatrist responsible for his crimes." Heavy smokers sue tobacco companies for their lung cancer. The common thread in all these incidents is the refusal to assign responsibility for accidents (or the decline of health) which result from the willed, negligent or mindless behavior of the "victims".

A major source of the widespread cultural susceptibility to claims of victimhood is the belief in the social-cultural determination of personal lives—a curious and unexpected phenomenon in a society as dynamic, individualistic, and non-fatalistic as American society used to be. Evidently huge numbers of Americans have come to believe that they have little control over their lives and few opportunities for making meaningful choices.

Poor academic performance is also becoming seen as a matter over which individual students have no control whatsoever; objections are raised to making higher demands on the more gifted or hard-working students, often to the very idea of a discriminating evaluation of performance. "Tracking" equated with racism or elitism—in fact the separation of students on the basis of their performance, ability and interests—has been abolished in an increasing number of schools.

There is, what might be called a therapeutic-egalitarian component in the pursuit of victimhood especially prominent in our schools and colleges. Since the late 1960s it has become virtually inadmissible (and politically incorrect) to acknowledge that human beings, including the young, differ greatly in ability and motivation, a denial that is linked to the overestimatation of the hidden potential for excellence. Poor academic performance is rarely explained with any reference to the quality of the work or motivation of the students; if they are "people of color" their efforts must have been undermined by "institutional racism" (which has mysteriously spared Asian Americans); if female, by the sexist inattention of teachers; they may also be classified as "learning disabled", or held back by teachers who fail to stimulate or "challenge" them. But if "challenging" goes too far the teacher may be condemned as "elitist".

"Learning disabilities", is the new epidemic of the 1980s and 90s; as a writer in the *New Republic* put it "In prosperous... school districts around the country, exotic new learning disabilities are popping up...". A correspondent to the *New York Times* wrote in 1997:

> The label 'learning disabled' has been pinned on a million children ... because according to the Diagnostic and Statistical Manual [of the American Psychiatric Association] they have 'attention deficit hyperactivity disorder'... they 'fidget', 'cant concentrate', 'stare out of the window', 'daydream' or 'wont wait their turn'. Any of these behaviors can result in a diagnosis of attention deficit disorder.

Outside the schools the recent Federal Disability Act lends itself to becoming a device for limiting personal responsiblity for questionable job performance. As reported in the *New York Times*

> The new rules say employers should be alert to the possibility that traits normally regarded as undesirable—chronic lateness, poor judgement, hostility to co-workers or supervisors—'may be linked to mental impairments.'
>
> Under the guidelines, an employer may have to provide room dividers, partitions or other soundproofing or visual barriers between work spaces' to help employees who have difficulty concentrating because of mental illness. Experts said a person with schizophrenia, for example, may be unusually sensitive to noise and visual distraction....

> If an employee asks for time off because he is 'depressed and stressed' that is enough to put the employer on notice that the worker is requesting a 'reasonable accomodation' the [Federal] agency said.

The guidelines also discourage employers from taking action against mentally impaired employees "whose appearance and demeanor deteriorated because of [their] disability." In a recent (summer 2000) case farmers in Western Massachusetts were warned by federal officials not to ask prospective farm workers about their height or weight as such inquiries could be construed as discriminatory notwithstanding their clear relevance to the work they were considered for.

Several aspects of modernity is in various ways relevant to the phenomena here discussed. One is the awareness, especially among the educated, that social-cultural-historical forces impinge on personal lives and opportunities. By the same token all claims to victimhood call into question individual responsibility for one's problems or problematic behavior, whether socio-economic or intimately personal. The Los Angeles looters and rioters of 1992 were, according to U.S. representative John Conyers "outraged citizens" not criminals; their congressional representative, Maxine Water called them "rebels." Looting was redefined as a necessity to acquire essential food or consumer goods (although the looters seemed to prefer VCRs and other entertainment related items), and a form of expressive behavior that is a response to repression.

The therapeutic perspective is equally deterministic as it does away with individual responsibility without necessarily blaming society or social forces for personal problems or antisocial behavior. It replaces the immoral or unethical with some mental pathology or maladjustment. The therapeutic perspective turns into social criticism when social institutions or policies are blamed for permitting pathologies to develop or persist.

The therapeutic outlook is bolstered by an optimistic view of human nature and science (including social science): nothing or nobody is hopelessly corrupt or evil, all diseases are subject to alleviation or cure, or will be someday. The therapeutic worldview is especially congenial to American culture and society built on high expectations, optimism, belief in the compatibility of all things highly valued, and the virtually limitless potential of all human beings.

Another relevant aspect of modernity is the decline of communal bonds, an all too familiar theme of the theories of mass society, mass culture, alienation, "the lonely crowd", "the quest for community," etc. In a highly mobile, urban, industrial, bureaucratic, innovation-oriented and individualistic society sustaining communal ties are under atack, while short-lived, synthetic, substitute communities multiply. The traditional bases of belonging—stable residential community, shared work, kinship, religion and other unifying beliefs and ways of life—are difficult to maintain; there is a subversive plurality of values and attachments, a subversive freedom of choice leading to the problems of identity formation. Shared victimization becomes a refuge, a new source of identity.

The preoccupation with self-esteem, a major part of the relentless preoccupation with the self, is also associated with the proliferation of victimhood. (James Nolan reports that "By the middle of 1994 some thirty states had enacted a total of 170 statutes that... sought to promote, protect or emhance the self esteem of Americans.") It is widely believed that victimization leads to low self esteem, or sometimes the other way round: those with low self esteem are easier to victimise. Even victmizers may suffer of low self-esteem, which is why they seek and abuse power. Every social ill, according to this theory could be radically alleviated by raising self esteem. Heightened self esteem (in the therapeutic view) need not be associated either with some tangible accomplishment or the approval of "significant others", it can be wholly self generated, a matter of self or therapeutic suggestion.

Affirmations of victimization are further stimulated by the social critical temper: the more victims, the worse the social order; the spectacle of victim groups makes the critics' case stronger. When it is axiomatic that (American) society is the ultimate victimizer, fact and fiction cease to be meaningful distinctions especially for those among the social critics who are of the "postmodernist" disposition: "Patricia Williams [the legal scholar] doesnt think it matters whether Twana Brawley was lying or telling the truth about being the victim of a racist assault... she was the victim of some unspeakable crime. No matter who did it to her—and even if she did it to herself." Stanley Diamond, a professor at the New School in New York wrote of the same incident that "In cultural perspective, if not in fact, it doesnt matter whether the crime occurred or not... What is most remarkable about this faked crime is that traditional victims have re-created themselves as victims..." More recently according to a professor of anthropology at the University of Massachusetts at Amherst "questions about the truthfulness of a black student's claim that she was assaulted should not overshadow the importance of examing racism in more subtle forms...." For the social critic what matters is the idea of victimhood as a tool of delegitimation of the social system.

At last the slogan "the personal is political" (especially popular among radical feminists) has opened the door to the multiplication of victimhood. If true, then there is no end to the personal problems and grievances which can be linked to and blamed on social forces, no end to their transformation into matters demanding political-institutional attention and solution.

Some counter trends must be noted: for certain types of behavior (not considered either criminal or immoral at earlier times) responsibility has greatly increased. This phenomenon was spotted by Charles Krauthammer and Senator Moynihan a few years ago in articles respectively entitled "Defining Deviancy Up..." and "Defining Deviancy Down". Moynihan calls this "the great wave of moral deregulation that began in the mid 1960s" and Krauthammer "a vast social project of moral levelling... the moral deconstruction of middle class morality."

When a quarter century ago I addressed the phenomenon of what I then called "selective determinism" (in an article in the *American Sociologist*, entitled "Sociology, Selective Determinsim and the Rise of Expectations") I did not anticipate how it will blossom during the next two decades with the coming of the proliferation of certified victim groups and the intense competition for inclusion in them.

I was struck, at the time, by contradictory trends both within the sociological and the public discussions of social and political problems. There was one the one hand a spectacular growth of expectations (of various forms of self-realization) and on the other a growing cultural and social scientific insistence on the many ways in which society frustrates and oppresses the individual and especially those in the disadvantaged groups. On the one hand more and more middle class people fantasized about unheard of personal fulfillments while on the other they embraced a debilitating social determinism. Possibly, the social determinism came to be overemphasized when excessive individual expectations and aspirations collided with social realities and structures. More likely, the selective social determinism has come to prevail as an integral part of social criticism.

The gist of selective determinism (or selective moral relativism) as originally discussed is that some groups are held responsible for their actions and even attitudes but not others. The activities of, say, black criminals or white radicals (the latter at the time setting off bombs) was almost wholly determined by social forces over which they had no control, by a repressive society ("they had no choice but..."). A bank robbery commited by members of designated minorities was either a direct response to dire need, or sometimes a commendably willed action, defined as "political crime", a protest against oppression. In neither case did those involved deserve punishment but compassion, if not outright admiration—that was actually lavished on some of them if their activities were accompanied by the appropriate rhetoric, as in the case of the Black Panthers or George Jackson, or Jack Henry Abbot.

On the other side were those who could not count on such understanding and sympathy, who were wholly responsible for their misbehavior, ideas or policies, seemingly unaffected by social forces and circumstances. I wrote in that article: "the military brass, FBI agents, policemen, politicians, corporation executives, Southern 'rednecks' or Northern construction workers" were free of any social restraint or conditioning, their behavior was freely chosen hence could be judged severely. The innocent victims of social forces deserved sympathy and compassion, while those in (apparent) control of their lives, the alleged victimizers did not.

At the present time the same people who hold forth about the futility and viciousness of building more prisons for ordinary criminals demand harsh punishment for perpetrators of "hate crimes." Feminists do not insist that rapists deserve understanding and need therapheutic rehabiliation rather than punitive incarceration. Presumably social forces play no part in shaping the behavior of the perpetrators of hate crimes and rapists that would reduce *their* responsibility.

The victims (and their spokesmen) in present day American society are in a bind. They are indignant over (certain types of) victimization and seek their alleviation by both therapeutic and political-institutional means, yet they cannot let go of it since victimhood is a source of their identity and moral distinction (as well as some material advantage when rewarded by preferential treatment).

It is a peculiarity of the current forms of victimhood that they lend themselves to two diametrically opposed purposes amd impulses. On the one hand, as George Will put it, we have "... the dispersal of responsibility into a fog of 'socio-economic factors factors... [allowing] "the modern mind ...to spare itself... the cold, blank stare of personal evil." But while the therapeutic redefinition of victimhood encourages such a non-judgmental, morally relativistic stance, the politically correct identification of the victimizer provides a new foundation and outlet for judgemental moral passions and condemnation.

Thus the contemporary pursuit and affirmation of victimhood reflects a durable and deep rooted human disposition that has managed to survive modernization and secularization. It is the impulse to see the world as the stage where the forces of good and evil (victims and victimizers) are locked in battle, where virtue resides in the victim and evil in the victimizer, questionable and changeable as their definitions may be. Socially sanctioned victimhood gives new license to the old pleasure of hating other people, to blaming others for our misfortunes and deprivations, especially when such hatred is linked to a good cause, to some notion of liberation.

10

Saving Sociology?

"... the health of a culture is measured in part by the vigor with which its immune system responds to nonsense." (Gross and Levitt 1994: 217)

"A healthy (coherent) organism has the ability to reject invading organisms....Since sociology is incoherent we have a hard time rejecting foreign objects....Consequently we have put up with an appalling amount of bunk (postmodernism, ethnic 'studies', 'feminist methodology', 'humanistic sociology', 'critical sociology', ethnomethdology, 'grounded theory' and the like)..." (Davis 1994:188)

The title of this symposium suggests—notwithstanding the question mark—that sociology needs to be saved, that it is threatened. Some think it is in a state of advanced decomposition (Horowitz 1993). The question is: how serious is the threat the discipline faces and what are its sources?

We may begin by noting that sociologists increasingly fail to ask what is worth knowing and what is not?[1] Instead they plunge headlong into either highly specialized and methodologically sophisticated investigations of matters of moderate significance, or pursue zealously and with an apparently satisfying sense of resentment the political-ideological issues bequeathed to us by the 1960s.

It should be recalled here that this is a discipline that has had chronic identity crises and recurring bouts of soul searching from its earliest days hence the current note of emergency or sense of foreboding is not exactly new. There have always been sociologists who thought the field was threatened or in a crisis, or at least faced intractable problems; there were also always those outside the field who thought it was an altogether dubious enterprize, enshrining vast collections of platitudes in ponderous jargon.

During the second half of the past century expressions of alarm have intensified become more frequent as well as more ritualized (see for example Mills 1959; Gouldner 1970; "What is Wrong with

Sociology" 1994). It is actually possible that the current problems are more serious and different from those of the past for the reasons discussed below.

The strength and depth of the critiques of sociology depend on the expectations its practicioners have made upon it. It may be worthwhile to recall briefly some of these expectations which have been with us for some time and provide a part of the background of the recent disillusionment and questioning this symposium reflects and seeks to capture.

In this country (which has the largest population of sociologists[2]) people have been generally drawn to the discipline for idealistic reasons but without revolutionary impulses. They were largely liberal, (or "men of the left"), and saw in it a tool for social improvement and reform—piecemeal amelioration of social ills (see also Lipset 1994: 199, 209, 212, 214, 218) to be accomplished by better information, deeper understanding, expanding knowledge. Far fewer in number were those who still held the grand dreams of the founding fathers of creating and cultivating a true science of society that would provide all encompassing theories to explain and predict everything human beings do in groups. There were also those who sought more knowledge and better understanding for its own sake, who pursued various questions about social organizations and problems out of sheer curiosity.

Each of these groups had different expectations but shared a belief that it was desirable and possible to study matters social with *some degree* of detachment, impartiality, disinterestedness or objectivity whatever the goals of the research.

Few would dispute that during the past three decades the discipline has been invaded by the militant pursuit of social-political causes, (or, for some the pursuit of social justice) and that the number of sociologists with an agenda of social change and committment to specific causes has multiplied.[3] Both the programs and specific resolutions passed at the annual meetings of ASA over these decades testify to the prevalence of social-political issues preoccupying its members, or at any rate those organizing and attending these meetings. Over the years ASA passed numerous resolutions at its annual meetings which were explicitly political regarding policy issues both domestic and foreign (Simpson & Simpson 1994: 262-263).

Over these three decades the discipline has also become more constricted regarding its research and teaching agenda. Departments recruiting teachers have apparently bottomless needs for those in race and gender studies, ethnicity, perhaps urban studies and crime but hardly for specialists in other fields unless the other specialty, say, stratification, is linked to gender and race. (The narrowness of these specialties becomes still more apparent given the uniformity of theoretical or philosophical orientation permeating them.)

Few sociologists before the late 1960s—whatever their worldview—confused or conflated the discipline with advocacy, social activism or consciousness level raising. If in the late 1950s Barrington Moore felt called upon to caution about the then allegedly dominant aspirations of an excessive and unrealistic ethical neutrality and objectivity (Moore 1958:89-90)—a mere decade later even the possibility of such aspirations came to be dismissed with scorn and incredulity by many sociologists especially of the younger generation.

Indeed much has changed since the late 1960s. In the decades which followed even the striving for some approximation of impartiality has become suspect as not merely unrealistic but also undesirable. Sociology was to become an instrument of political partisanship to be deployed in the political battles of the times to deal mortal blows to the corrupt social order. (Remember "liberation sociology" and "The Insurgent Sociologist"?) The massive waves of social criticism issueing from that period produced a generation fully convinced that American society has been the most evil, hypocritical and corrupt that ever existed. More recently, with the rise of multiculturalism, this belief came to be extended to Western society and its heritage of ideas as a whole, denigrated as singular repositories of repression and injustice. Particularly resilient has been the belief (even in the post-communist era) that capitalism remains the unparallelled evil of our (and all) times and the font of all ills of society—racism, sexism, ethnocentrism, classism, elitism, homophobia, lookism, ableism, imperialism, genocidal impulses, and every negative human trait ever displayed.

It is hard to know how many sociologists subscribe to these beliefs and share these attitudes but one thing is clear: not many have questioned them in public, and few have defied the new orthodoxies and the associated conformity which descended upon the discipline, indeed upon American academic culture as a whole. It has been especially painful and difficult to challenge the new verities as they spread under the banner of the very best intentions, linked to idealistic goals; the critics could confidently expect to be denounced as racist, sexist, elitist, lookist or homophopbic if they had the temerity to express any reservation about the new orthodoxies, sometimes also called political correctness.

Whatever the beliefs of most sociologists vocal and influential minorities set the tone of the discipline and its professional organization,[4] influenced or ran the major journals, dominated hiring policies and curricular trends on individual campuses, advised publishers and wrote the widely used texts.[5] These trends were not peculiar to sociology but were present in the other social sciences and humanities as well.

As Peter Berger saw it American sociologists

> plunged into an ideological delirium, mostly shaped by Marxist and quasi-Marxist assumptions...
>
> The worst consequence of the ideologization of the discipline that took place in the 1960s and 1970s is the persistent belief that objectivity and 'value-freeness' are impossible and that sociologists, understanding this, should expressly operate as advocates.
>
> This stance need not be restricted to the left... In the great methodological disputes... especially in Germany it was thinkers on the right who took this position most forcefully. The antidote to the 'false ideal' of objectivity was 'German science' and the most elegant formulation of advocacy science came from...Dr Goebbels—'Truth is what serves the German people'...[6]
>
> It is a stance that transforms science into propaganda... Feminists and multicultrualists are the leading representatives of this stance in the American social sciences today. (Berger 1992:17)

It is likely that the shaky professional identity of sociology has made it especially vulnerable to the political pressures and cultural trends of the last decades. While many would argue that the impact of these trends has been benign I believe otherwise. As I see it sociology has become politicized, that is, its cognitive and intellectual aspirations taking second place to the determination to transform it into a tool with which to fight various political battles and causes, and promote social agendas. Critics of this position will reflexively counter by claiming that sociology had always been politicised but it used to be in a more subtle or concealed way, whereas now, the political concerns are out in the open, which is all to the good; they would also contend that what the critics of these developments object to is not politicization as such but rather its currrent forms.

It is possible to make reasonably clear distinctions between the recent forms of politicization (or what Irving Louis Horowitz called the extinction of the difference between scholarship and partisanship (Horowitz 1993:17)) and the values and personal or political preferences of the past which also influenced the field and particular researchers. It certainly cannot be denied that as Stephen Cole put it sociologists have always been "influenced by a large number of personal experiences and non-scientific values.... (whereas) those in the hard sciences, such as physicists 'use primarily cognitive criteria' (Cole 1994: 146-147). Nonetheless there remain important differences between attitudes toward subjectivity and objectivity in the periods preceding and following the 1960s. It is one thing to strive, with incomplete success, for a measure of objectivity or impartiality, and quite anothern to plunge with abandon and relish into untrammelled subjectivity and partisanship.

Being critical of these trends need not amount to suggesting that sociologists become apologists of the social order under which they live, or that they cease to be critical intellectuals. Rather, I am suggesting that a reflexive, taken for granted hostility toward the familiar social setting, an unreflective but impassioned social critical impulse, and the nurturing of a sense of grievance, or resentment are not the best motives for undertaking informative and reliable studies of social phenomena[7]; moreover the unexamined belief that one lives in the worst of all possible societies—the familiar demonizing of American society and its Western roots—doesnt stand up to any critical comparative-historical assessment.

The institutionalization and standardization of the critiques and grievances associated with the 1960s went hand in hand with the suspension or atrophy of critical faculties that is supposed to be the most cherished attribute of the social scientist or the genuine intellectual. When it came to causes, movements or political systems favored by these commited sociologists their critical impulses vanished without a trace. Sociologists basking in the self-styled "critical" designation often became blatantly ideological and apologetical, their criticial faculties stunted or confined at the all too predictable and stereoytyped targets.

An important trend closely related to the developments sketched above has been the growing use of a selective social determinism, a topic I first addressed over a quarter century ago (Hollander 1973, reprinted 1983). To be sure a measure of social or cultural determinism is at the heart of to the sociological enterprize[8] but its increasingly ideological use has been a relatively new development. What I wrote in 1973 is by no means obsolete in the late 1990s:

> the popular social determinism of our days is not consistent but selective... it proposes (or implies) that only the behavior of the 'underdogs' is socially determined, that only people...(in) these groups are not in full control of their lives and behavior... or are equally helpless victims of expectations or 'labelling'...
>
> Today, sociological determinism is generously but selectively applied to excuse, mitigate or condemn different forms of behavior, or even the same behavior on the part of different people. There is, for example an increasing tendency among people of liberal persuasion to view convicted criminals as victims of the system...[9] or extend a measure of sympathy... to those who undertake politically motivated bombings or attacks of policemen... A plausible victim-aggressor scheme needs a device such as selective determinism that relieves some groups of responsibility for their actions but not others. It remains an interesting and little studied question as to what (precise) circumstances of life actually deprive people of making a choice, or limit their responsibility, and in what situations...
>
> ... great poverty and little or no education and among among such factors...but they are not the only ones. (Hollander 1983:243-244)

In the post 1960s view of the world bad people (that usually means the rich and those occupying high bureaucratic positions in government, both types, not incidentally, exclusively white males) have all the free will to misbehave (and hence invite merciless moral criticism),[10] while the new groups virtuous victims (women, blacks, hispanics, AIDS sufferers, the homeless, etc.) are subject to inexorable social forces. Their behavior (such as criminal acts, drug abuse, promiscuousness, multiple pregnancies etc) are shaped (determined) by irressistible institutional or situational pressures and social forces. The victims of society have no choice, and negligible if any control over their behavior and lives.[11] A woman chopping off the penis of her allegedly brutal (but unquestionably sleeping) husband thus becomes the victim at one stroke, (so to speak) and hero in the eyes of radical feminists (Llosa 1996: 315-31).

Sociology has been in the forefront of this somewhat idiosyncratic crusade on behalf of certain victim-groups, propagating an outlook that readily grants victim status to a variety of groups as long as their grievances can be explained by currently acceptable politicial criteria and their plight blamed on the social system. At the same time sociology of late has shown considerable indifference to other, more traditional victim groups which are no longer singled out for compassionate attention: the white poor, the old, the vast numbers suffering of illnesses other than AIDS, children of crippled families or institutional upbringing, disabled veterans and others.

It is an interesting and seemingly contradictory aspect of the current politicization of the discipline that concern with social class receded as so many sociologists turned their attention, quite single-mindedly, to race, gender and ethnicity. William Julius Wilson was sharply criticized for daring to emphasize class over race in the late 1970s (Wilson 1978)—it was a serious violation of the emerging doctrines of political correctness. The decline of interest in class can be further traced to the 1960s when Herbert Marcuse and his followers (re)discovered that the workers were not about to embark on a revolution and—by failing to display the proper detestation of capitalist democracies—showed a deplorably low level of political consiousness for which they could not be forgiven.

The proliferation of victim groups in sociological studies and teaching has been stimulated by the intent to indict American society as a whole: the more victims the more deeply flawed the social order.

The ideological preoccupation with victim groups (real and imaginary) inflicts considerable intellectual damage on the discipline by removing from attention a broad range of problems, topics and questions and by imposing a narrow theoretical-conceptual perspective. For example if one approaches crime with the single minded conviction that it is nothing but a predictable response to socio-economic deprivation or racism, many aspects of it will not be examined and understood; if all political phenomena in the United States are seen as determined by who has more money for campaign financing or briberies, a rather narrow view of political conflict and competition will emerge; if it remains the received wisdom (and point of departure of research) that all racial tensions and problems result from white racism this seemingly intractable matter will not be better understood, let alone remedied.

While I do not claim that the political beliefs or value orientation of sociologists before the 1960s had no influence on their research or teaching there is a vast and discernible difference between the influence of these earlier beliefs (manifest usually in the selection of research topics, rather than in their conclusions) and the more recent self-consciously militant, determined propagation of specific political agendas through teaching and research. If Talcott Parsons' personal political beliefs influenced his theories and if these theories in turn helped to prop up the military-industrial complex such connections were rather tenuous; surely the masters of our empire did not rely on sociologists to legitimate their policies and if they had such expectations they were bound to be badly disappointed by the contribution sociologists made to their objectives and policies.

American sociologists have always been predominantly liberal (Lipset and Ladd 1972; Lipset 1982; Carnegie Report 1989; Lipset 1994) though it must be noted at once that "liberal" meant different things before and since the 1960s. They accepted by and large the status quo though with serious reservations, without regarding the entire social system as uniquely and irremediably corrupt and exceptionally repressive, which is what the generation of 60s activists believed, in or outside sociology.

Before I continue outlining the substantial differences between partisanship in the discipline before the 1960s and the post 1960s politicization I should make clear that my sentiments do not originate in an ideal of a value-free sociology, or in devotion to an attempt to imitate the natural sciences, or in hardnosed number crunching untainted by supposedly extraneous beliefs and values. Personal experiences, beliefs and values inevitably infiltrate the work of sociologists (see again Cole 1994) but they need not lead to intellectually debilitating certainties of outlook and conviction, to predetermined conclusions and intolerance of perspectives and findings which are not congruent with the advocates' position.

It may be asked how is it possible to separate the admissible and sometimes salutory influence of idealistic personal beliefs from undesirable levels of ideological fervor? Can one reasonably object to the current politicization without upholding the ideal of a value free sociology? It can be done, as I hope to show below.

There is a difference between a self-consciously and militantly politicized advocacy-discipline and one which allows for the influence of commitments without totally subordinating research (or teaching) to the values which guide or inspire either. Everybody likes to find facts which support one's theories or view of the world and bolster hypotheses which have been conceived in a complex emotional-personal-philosophical matrix. Perhaps it is just a matter of degree what we are talking about yet it has a great bearing on the outcome of the sociological enterprize.

The degree and depth of committments matter as does the presence or absence of a sceptical enough disposition: the greater or more intense these committments the more single minded will be their pursuit and conclusions or findings congruent with them, and the greater the pressure to find support for the researcher's (or teacher's) beliefs, causes, or politics. It is hard to combine a relatively open mind, a general sense of curiosity and inqusitiveness, a may-the-chips-fall-where-they-may attitude with strong political commitments and beliefs. The deeply committed cherish the unity of theory and practice, of belief and action, of research agendas and their findings—such people are not agnostic and scepticism is uncongenial to them. Whereas, as Barrington Moore pointed out some time ago

> The best results emerge from the confrontation of the evidence with a wide variety of ideas, often contradictory ones... Sometimes the most important disoveries may occur as a consequence of the temporary block produced by an inconvenient fact which forces the investigator to abandon previously accepeted explanations(Moore 1958: 141).

More recently Stephen Cole wrote in the same spirit: "...in all sciences the theories that develop counterintuitive or unexpected results are more likely to be judged to be additions to knowledge" (Cole 1994:143).

Not many of the current crop of committed sociologists are anxious to encounter inconvenient facts or counterintuitive findings. Few radical feminists motivated by the conviction that women are routinely victimized, and rape is their common experience, are likely to undertake a study that seeks to assess *the actual number* of rape victims. The ideological commitment to a belief in the unchanging victimization of women is all too discernible behind the effort to inflate the number of rapes by expanding and diluting the concept by notions such as "date rape," "attempted rape" or "rape experience" that may include almost any unwelcome behavior toward women by men. Radical feminists angrily reject findings that show that the popular and widely held estimates of rape have been excessive.[12]

Not many sociologists will risk ridicule and ostracism by undertaking a investigation of the ratio of wife vs. husband battering. Suzanne Steinmetz, author of an article on "The battered husband"[13] and a director of the Family Research Institute at Indiana University at Indianapolis was subjected to much abuse upon finding that plenty of husband battering also goes on[14] (Dunn 1994).

How many social scientists of differing sexual orientation would design a study (and accept its results) that might point to some significant relationship between sexual orientation and the quality of parenting? What if it were reestablished beyond a shadow of a doubt that black male criminality is much higher than white and that such findings are not due to racist crime reporting or police discrimination? How widely known and accepted have been the conclusion of a study that found that toxic dump sites are *not* concentrated in areas populated by blacks and hispanics but in white working class neighborhoods? (Anderton et al. 1994) Why was Peter Rossi vilified for finding fewer homeless than the homeless advocates claimed to be the correct figure?[15] While Rossi doubtless finds homelessness as deplorable as his critics this did not compel him to inflate the number of the homeless—a good example of separating moral impulses from research findings. Or as Neil Gilbert wrote "one may be deeply concerned about the problem of rape and still wish to see a fair and objective analyis of its dimensions" (Gilbert 1998: 362).

This was not the position of Rossi's detractions. Their critique reveals that committed sociologists (as well as non-sociologists) are disposed to subordinate means to ends—a disposition not necessarily beneficial for learning about the world as it is, as distinct from the way we would like it to be. A critic of Rossi, Charles Hoch objected to the fact that his work did not focus on the goal of improving the condition of the poor by learning about the causes of homelessness. Whereas another study Hoch approved of "... did not attempt to count the homeless for conducting such a count was not crucial given his purposes. Establishing the size of the homeless population is not a necessary condition for analyzing the cause of homelesness among the poor" Hoch revealingly wrote (Hoch 1990:22).

The ends and means relationship was also frankly acknowledged by Hoch when he wrote: "liberals were especially weary of research efforts to count the local (Chicago) homeless because they feared that systematic research would find fewer homeless than earlier estimates had produced... They believed that a lower estimate, legitimized by systematic research, would enable local conservatives to successfully claim that the homelessness was only a marginal problem" (Hoch 1990:13).

Seeking to bolster the subordination of means to ends Hoch also proposed that scientific objectivity be supplemented by something he called "practical objectivity (that) seeks to anticipate, account for and respond to relevant sources of bias"(Hoch 1990: 21). By "bias" he didnt mean the predisposition guiding the research he approved of (which sought to help the poor by taking a more generous estimate of their numbers including the homeless) but he had in mind the bias of conservatives eager to use lower counts of the homeless to legitimate policies indifferent toward the fate of the poor, including the homeless poor. Hoch also criticised Rossi for "extend(ing) the scientific notion of objectivity to the contentious realm of the public domain... (and for) create(ing) damaging practical effects in an ongoing effort to define the homeless as a needy and deserving social group." By laudable contrast

> The advocates (of the homeless) understood the objective, scientific count of the homeless (!) but they also understood that determining who would count as a homeless person was a political decision... Hence the crucial importance the Coalition placed on expanding the study to include peopole living in overcrowded conditions and temporary institutional accomodations. (Hoch 1990: 21).

It could not have been made more clear that politically correct research on the homeless had to be guided by the goal of improving their condition (and of the poor in general) rather than merely learning the facts about their numbers.

In his rejoinder Rossi noted that he had made a distinction between "the literal homeless" and the "precariously housed" which presumably included those living in overcrowded conditions; Rossi sought to establish the numbers of the "literal homeless". He also pointed out that the homeless "advocate community is composed largely of persons in the 'homeless industry': shelter managers, operators of programs for homeless persons and the like. The advocates may represent the interests of the homeless, yet the likelihood is that they represent the interests of their organizations more strongly" (Rossi 1991: 78). If so, one may wonder if pure idealism is the only motive behind the efforts to inflate the numbers of the homeless. Rossi concludes:

> The main message I get from Hoch's article is that I should have carefully taken the interests of the advocate community to heart and accomodated my study accordingly. Why this community's interests should be paramount escapes me, especially when considering the politically motivated myth of 20,000 homeless (in Chicago) that they have advanced. I believe researchers should provide information on vital issues regardless of the radical, liberal or conservative myths that are thereby contradicted. Hoch comes perilously close to saying that some myths are sacred... (Rossi 1991; 80)

The critiques of Rossi raise what has become a contentious question: is it legitimate for a sociologist to undertake research without an associated or underlieing idealistic or amelioristic impulse or goal?

Is it acceptable to study the sources of divorce without wishing to find ways to reduce its incidence, or, perhaps (motivated by another ideological impulse) to use the findings to champion alternatives to the nuclear, heterosexual family? Similar questions can be raised about virtually any major topic sociologists address.

Even more troubling is the question,—especially for those strongly committed to particular notions of social justice—what if the findings of a research project (as in the case of the number of the homeless in Chicago) were to be misused in some manner? Is it incumbent on sociologists to design their research with a view to avoid such possibilities? Should they make sure that a study of criminal violence will not find a disproportionate number of black criminals in order to to avoid inflaming racist sentiment and confirming stereotypes?

The intensity of political-philosophical commitments represents a threat to sociology (or any other field) since it creates strong dispositions to reach predetermined conclusions and tends to merge research and teaching with advocacy, lobbying, exhortation and "consciousness level raising".[16] The strong commitments here refered to have a great deal to do not merely with the selection of problems to be investigated but with the openness to findings which may be at odds with these commitments. The strongly commited activists (in or outside sociology) are less interested in the way things are than in finding vindication for their convictions and policies.

It is likely that political beliefs and biases find even more unrestrained expression in the classroom than in publications since the latter provide a tangible record that can be scrutinised and more easily subjected to critical examination and verification. By contrast what is said in the classroom is fleeting and not open to such scrutiny and is unaffected by conventions of scholarly fact finding aimed as it is at a captive audience usually unable or unwilling to challenge the pronouncements of the instructor. The very existence of highly and openly cause-oriented programs such as Black (or African-American), Hispanic and Women's studies (for a critical examination of the latter see Patai and Koertge 1994) symbolizes the institutional politicization of the curriculum including its sociological aspects.

Is is not easy to agree as to *when* exactly the line is crossed from largely open minded, (if not totally disinterested) research or teaching to political advocacy, as one person's exhortation or advocacy is the self-evident truth or commonplace fact of life for others. But an important dividing line may be drawn between those whose *predominant* motivation is to understand the social world and human behavior and those who seek to change them. (I inserted "predominant" because the separation cannot be watertight; few of us can totally banish the idea that our work will make some difference in "the real world" even if the predominant impulse was curiosity or inqusitiveness. Likewise the activist predominantly motivated by the desire to contribute to change is also likely to take some pleasure in contributing to a better understanding of how things really are, as distinct from how one would wish them to be.)

In moderation the two impulses may be compatible but when the activist impulse overwhelms curiosity—which is another way of describing when "politicization" occurs—the discipline and its intellectual substance suffer. This has been the case of late.

It may also be argued (pessimistically) that a better understanding of human behavior and social institutions is essentially incompatible with the activist disposition because better understanding leads to the realization of the limits of benign and purposeful social action and especially their proverbial unintended consequences.[17] It cannot be ruled out that better understanding and greater knowledge may inspire a measure of resignation, a readier acceptance of the status quo or a belief in only modest possibilities of change—thus more information may confirm the kind of scepticism highly uncongenial to the activist.

The prevailing anti-scientific currents represent another threat to sociology.[18] These currents are closely associated with otherwise diverse trends such as postmodernism, radical feminism and Afrocentrism. As two commentators put it "What enables (them) to coexist congenially... is a shared sense of injury, resentment and indignation against modern science." (Gross and Levitt 1994: lxvii). How did this anti-scientific ethos emerge?

The roots of the anti-scientific mood among many academic intellectuals (including sociologists) can also be traced to the late 1960s when science came to be seen as the handmaiden of the military-industrial complex as well as the purest expression of a cerebral Western (white male) rationality that was under attack by the counter-culture of the period. The anti-nuclear movements too made a contribution to the anti-scientific mood of the times as did the radical environmentalists. Still probably the most intense animosity comes from the radical feminists and the postmodernists. Paul R. Gross and Norman Levitt (two white, male scientists) wrote:

> (P)ostmodern scepticism rejects the possibility of enduring universal knowledge in any area. I holds that all knowledge... is rigidly circumscribed by interests and prejudices... The radical feminist view (is) that science like every other intellectual structure in modern society is poisoned and corrupted by ineradicable gender bias... multiculturalists... view 'Western' science as inherently inaccurate and incomplete by virtue of its failure to incorporate the full range of cultural perspectives.... radical enviromentalists condemn science as embodying instrumentalism and alienation from direct experience of nature. (Gross and Levitt 1994: 5, 45)

Further damage has been inflicted on the discipline by the parroting and vulgarization of the idea that everything is "socially constructed"—a notion at first sight unexceptionably sociological but on closer inspection turning out to be a device that serves to accomodate a peculiar combination of relativism *and* very strongly held beliefs. Radical feminists seem the most partial to this idea frequently used to rebuff any notion that one form of sexual conduct or family arrangement may be preferable to another. Here the reader may recall the volume (Berger and Luckman 1966) which argued that we interpret social reality in a variety of socially or culturally conditioned ways; in no ways did it suggest that all such interpretations are equally valid or that there is no autonomous social reality apart from these "constructions". In the the current usage the concept has become inseparable from postmodernism and has been used to demolish all dictinctions—moral, aesthetic, cognitive-intellectual though not politicial. Nonetheless postmodernists, like other mortals, have their political preferences and biases and it doesnt take long to uncover them once the luxuriant verbiage of their writings is penetrated. It is indeed this expedient alternation of relativism and absolutism that is another notable characteristic of the intellectual landscape of our times, including, regrettably, the endeavours of many sociologists.

For the postmodernist it is futile to even try to make distinctions between what is right and wrong, trivial and significant, morally abhorrent or praiseworthy, high or low culture. It is an outlook that cannot provide guidance on how to select one's research topic or evaluate its findings. Postmodernism is mainly used to denigrate high culture or what used to be considered the accomplishments of Western civilization. But, as noted above, postmodernism stops short in its display of relativism when it comes to the favored causes and beliefs of its own adherents which tend to be of the conventional leftist-adversarial or counter-cultural variety.

There is an interesting and neglected aspect of the "social construction of reality" which links it to what Dennis Wrong used to call "the oversocialized image of man" (Wrong 1976). Surely when everything is socially constructed "the presence in man of motivational forces resisting social discipline is denied" as Wrong argued in his critique of the oversocialized conception of man and the overintegrated view of society (Wrong 1976: 38). Moreover, "The insistence of sociologists on the importance of 'social factors' easily leads them to stress the priority of socialized or socializing motives in human behavior... Man is increasingly seen as a 'role-playing' creature, responding eagerly or anxiously to the expectations of other role players..." (Wrong 1976:40,43).

To be sure the radical feminists and postmodernists would stress power and repression rather than expectations as the guide to and source of behavior. Still, both of these "oversocialized" perspectives impoverish our understanding of human and social behavior by positing a conception of human nature that is completely malleable and molded by the social-cultural setting. As Wrong has asked: "What of desire for material and sensual satisfactions? Can we really dispense with the venerable notion of material 'interests' and replace it with... 'social values'? (or for that matter with "social construction of reality"—P.H)

Both the recent advocates of "the social construction of reality" and those who had earlier favored the oversocialized conception of man assumed that human beings can be coerced or socialized into any role, behavior or belief; both points of views ignore or slight the forces which resist socialization.

New approaches to the concept of deviance are part of the trends here discussed. These approaches too are self-evidently politicized, by products of the strong social-critical impulse. Defining deviance up or down—both processes taking place simultaneously—serves to remove the stigmatization of certain types of behavior while it indicts others. Daniel Patrick Moynihan identified the phenomenon as "the great wave of moral deregulation that began in the 1960s" (Moynihan 1993: 30, 21) whereas Charles Krauthammer spoke of "a vast project of moral levelling.... the moral deconstruction of middle class normalcy.... it is not enough for the deviant to be normalized. The normal must be found deviant" (Krauthammer 1993: 20, 22).

The pursuit of a highly political or cause-oriented agenda by sociologists is also undesirable in the long term because it diverts attention from the still unresolved, big and difficult questions of the field which do not lend themselves to activism or social policy. In making this point it is of interest to compare some of the issues two otherwise highly dissimilar thinkers, Barrington Moore and Isaiah Berlin regarded as important for social thinkers to ponder. Moore wrote about examining "the possibility of putting into practice the principles proclaimed... by the French Revolution... the feasibility of creating a rational society under the conditions of industrial advance... the kind of society that would enable man to make the most of his creative capacities" (Moore 1958:113). In turn Berlin wrote of Nineteenth-century social philosophers of different political persuasion who "... believed that problems of both individuals and of societies could be solved if only the forces of intelligence and virtue could be made to prevail... They believed ...that all clearly understood questions could be solved by human beings with the moral and intellectual resources at their disposal" (Berlin 1969: 5).

Dennis Wrong too was among those reminding his colleagues of the truly important and timeless questions of sociology as for instance: "How are men capable of uniting to form enduring societies...? Why and to what degree is change inherent in human societies and what are the sources of change? How is man's animal nature domesticated by society?... How is social order possible?" (Wrong 1976:32-33).

The rise of ideological concerns here discussed has further intensified a long standing weakness of American sociology: a provincialism, a resolute avoidance of issues, problems or developments outside the historical experience and purview of this country, a contented ignorance of the past and of societies abroad. The current politicized problem orientation reaffirms the belief that America is the measure of all things and only the immediate present here and now is worthy of serious attention. This observation has been highlighted by the apparent inability of American sociology to say anything about the collapse of communist systems—surely a monumen-

tal and unexpected historical development of our times. Why had so
many sociologists (and for that matter other social scientists as well)
missed the opportunity to rexamine the colossal experiment in social engineering communist systems had attempted? Why have they
shied away from trying to explain their failure? Why are they reluctant to embark on inquiries into the implications of the collapse of
Soviet communism for existing theories of society and human nature? Why had they no appetite to compare (in order to to better
understand) the outstanding, monumental bloodbaths of this century (indeed of all recorded history), the Holocaust and the mass
murders under Stalin and Mao?

The opening up of what used to be the Soviet Union has eliminated an old excuse for avoding its study—inaccessibility, secre-
tiveness and the difficulty of access to data gathering.

American sociology had next to nothing to say about the disintegration of Soviet communism, neither during its approach nor after
it occurred; it was a development that—not unlike the earlier existence and character of Soviet type societies—almost completely by-
passed the discipline. While the indifference toward and ignorance
of these societies has been a part of the resolute domestic orientation
of the discipline one may suspect that there was an additional element predisposing to the avoidance of the study of the now extinct
communist systems: these failed societies were anti-capitalist and
their spokesmen often expressed the same critiques of capitalism
and American society many American sociologists embraced. Presumably the collapse of these massive experiments in anti-capitalism was neither entirely welcome nor unproblemtic for many American social scientists and intellectuals and most of them met the challenge to explain it by silence.

Attempting to close on a more positive note I cannot improve on
the observations I made a few years ago about conditions to be met if
we were to see significant improvements in the state of the discipline:

First, sociology must regain its freedom to ask any important questions and to report
findings that may offend the current politicized canons of propriety; it must be free to
defy the reigning orthodoxies of the academic-intellectual community. Secondly it must
attract a wider range of people than is currently the case, including those who are
inspired by genuine curiosity rather than by the familiar political-ideological agendas.
Thirdly sociology must embark on a new course of comparative studies ... which will
address some of the old, important but still unresolved questions of the discipline.
(Hollander 1992: 32)

Sociology (or for that matter any other worthwhile intellectul activity) can be "saved" when it succeeds in reconciling the two seemingly irreconcilable orientations which underlie most social scientific endeavours. On the one hand we are, and cannot avoid being, guided by personal experiences and beliefs of a wide variety, many of them idealistic; but on the other hand we must also have more than a dim awareness that these values and beliefs often push toward intolerant advocacy and unquestioned certainties. A vigilant self-reflectiveness helps to achieve a tolerable balance between these orientations and impulses.

Notes

1.   Moore suggested two criteria that should help to decide what is worth knowing: the utilitarian and the aesehtic. He wrote: "The acquisition of knowledge that diminishes human suffering... certainly satisfies the utilitarian criterion..." As to the aesthetic he argued that "its essence is the discovery of order and pattern in the universe or parts of it." (Moore 1998: 6,10)
2.   I have no actual proof (figures) for this assertion but few would dispute it. The number of departments of sociology in itself makes the claim plausible. The large number of sociologists in this country is a good measure of the collective self-consciousness of a society which never quite managed to take for granted its own existence and peculiarities. Similar explanations may be put forward to account for the even greater number of psychotherapists and other psychologists ministering to the discomforts of modern life American style.
3.   On the other hand it is of some significance that "over 30% of sociology's personnel are not in academic life." (Horowitz 1993: 137). It is likely that this 30% do not belong to the politically correct echelons which inhabit academia.
4.   In this context it is an interesting and revealing paradox that while the ASA has become increasingly politicized participation in its many votes has steadily declined from two-thirds of its members voting in 1959 to one third doing so in 1982 (Simpson & Simpson 1994:268).
5.   Social problem texts in particular have given the impression that the problems dealt with are peculiar to American society (or to those of a capitalist character) and that if non-Western societies had similar difficulties the Western ones were responsible for them. (see also Hollander 1992, 1995: 192-203).
6.   The formulation was similar to Lenin's proposition that morality consists of whatever advances the interests of the proletariat. He reserved the right to himself and the leaders of the Party to determine what these interests were and what action served them best.
7.   On the other hand it cannot be denied that high levels of aggresion sometimes energizes the researcher to uncover interesting phenomena, including shocking injustices earlier overlooked. In the long run such vindictive aggression is unlikely to make a lasting contribution to a better understanding of social institutions and human beings.
8.   Barrington Moore provided a convincing rationale for this proposition without succumbing to the extremes of determinism:
       "... it is very difficult to believe seriously that... anything can happen at any time... There is in human affairs an area of freedom, but it is limited. What the limits

are at any point in time... has to be determined.. through empiricial investigation" (Moore 1958: 151).

9.   An interesting reflection of this attitude in the mass media (established by meticulous content analysis) that in popular television shows violent the criminals are rarely black; instead, and in total reversal of real life patterns, most violent crimes in television plays and movies are committed by well off white males (Lichter, Lichter and Rothman 1991:198). Presumably if questioned about this unrealistic pattern producers of these shows would argue that they do not wish to contribute to racist attittudes and stereotypes by presenting black criminals and that statistics showing their preponderance are, in any event, distorted by racist over-reporting.

10.   Marx himself was far from consistent in this matter. While on the one hand he ceaselesly emphasized that people cannot help thinking and behaving the way they do because of their class or social position, (and that it would be futile to try to change their mind as long as these socio-economic determinants were in place) he denounced with relish all those who disagreed with him.

11.   The true determinist—if any such creature could be found—would abstain altogether from praise and blame. As Isaiah Berlin wrote tongue in cheek: "Praise and blame are functions of ignorance; we are what we are, like stones and trees, like bears and beavers and if it is irrational to blame or demand justice from things or animals, climates or soils or wild beasts when they cause us pain, it is no less irrational to blame the no less determined characters or acts of men" (Berlin 1969: 59-60).

12.   One of the most influential and frequently quoted study of rape found that almost three quarters (73%) of the alleged rape victims themselves disbelieved that they had been raped and 42% had "sex afterwards with their supposed assailants" (Gilbert 1998:358).

13.   She was was harassed by phone, had her children threatened and "her colleagues were lobbied to prevent her from getting tenure; bomb threats were sent to a branch of the American Civil Liberties Union that had invited her to give a talk (Dunn 1994:18).

14.   "Straus and Gelles are two of many researchers who have found domestic violence distributed equally between the sexes" (Dunn 1994: 16).

15.   Rossi wrote that he was subject to "torrents of criticism" and "the longest stretch of personal abuse" he experienced since basic training in the army; that he became "persona non grata" and a "non person" among homeless advocates for finding that the number of homeless was significantly smaller than proposed by the advocacy groups. (Rossi 1987: 79) Similar expressions of displeasure await those who question the number of women raped or battered, or who report subtantial improvements in the condition of the black population and especially decline in discrimination.

16.   The latter is a highly quiestionable, truly elitist concept since it presupposes that there is a self appointed elite that knows how the thinking and beliefs of ordinary people can be corrected and has no hesitation to take the necessary steps to accomplish this goal.

17.   References to unintended consequences have become widespread but actual investigations of specific instances—especially at the historical or macro level - are hard to find. It would for instance be difficult to come up with the name of a single American sociologist who has taken a look at the collapse of Soviet communism with such a perspective in mind and with special reference to the propositions and policies associated with Marxism and their unintended results.

18.   This writer is somewhat suprised to find himself in a position of defending the scientific aspirations of sociology since through much of his career he was among those sceptical toward such orientation.

References

Anderton, Douglas, et al. 1994. "Environmental Equity: The Demographics of Dumping." *Demography* 31(2).

Berger, Peter L. 1992. "Sociology: A Disinvitation?" *Society* (Nov.Dec.)

———————— and Thomas Luckman. *The Social Construction of Knowledge*, Garden City NY: Doubleday.

Berlin, Isaiah. 1969. *Four Essays on Liberty*. New York:Oxford University Press.

Carnegie Report. 1989. *The Condition of the Professoriat*. Princeton: Carnegie Foundation

Cole, Stephen. 1944. "Why Sociology Doesnt Make Progress Like the Natural Sciences." *Sociological Forum* (June).

Davis, James A. 1994. "What's Wrong with Sociology?" *Sociological Forum* 9(2).

Dunn, Katherine. 1994. "Truth Abuse." *New Republic* (August 1)

Gilbert, Neil. 1998. "Realities and Mythologies of Rape." *Society* (Jan.-Feb.)

Gouldner, Alvin. 1970. *The Coming Crisis of Western Sociology*. New York: Basic.

Gross, Paul R. and Levitt, Norman. 1994. *Higher Superstition*.
     Baltimore: Johns Hopkins University Press.

Hoch, Charles. 1990. "The Rhetoric of Applied Research" *Journal of Applied Sociology* 7.

Hollander, Paul. 1973. "Sociology, Selective Determinism and the Rise of Expectations." *American Sociologist* 8.

———————— 1983. *The Many Faces of Socialism*. New Brunswick: Transaction.

———————— 1992a. *Anti-Americanism: Critiques at Home and Abroad*. New York: Oxford University Press

———————— 1992b. "Sociology and the Collapse of Communism" *Society*, (Nov.-Dec.)

Horowitz, Irving Louis. 1993. *The Decomposition of Sociology* New York: Oxford University Press

Krauthammer, Charles. 1993. "Defining Deviancy UP" *New Republic* (Nov.22).

Lichter, S. Robert, Lichter S. Linda and Rothman, Stanley. 1991. *Watching America*. New York: Prentice Hall.

Lipset, Seymour Martin and Ladd, Everett. 1972. "The Politics of American Sociologists." *American Journal of Sociology* 78(7).

———————— 1982. "The Academic Mind at the Top." *Public Opinion Quarterly* 46: 146-68.

———————— 1994. "The State of American Sociology." *Sociological Forum* 9(2)

Llosa, Mario Vargas. 1996. "The Penis or Life: The Bobbit Affair" in *Making Waves*. New York: Farrar, Straus & Giroux.

Mills, C. Wright. 1959. *The Sociological Imagination* .New York: Oxford University Press.

Moore, Barrington. 1958. *Political Power and Social Theory*. Cambridge: Harvard University Press.

———————— 1998. "What is Not Worth Knowing" in *Moral Aspects of Economic Growth*. Ithaca: Cornell University Press

Moynihan, Daniel Patrick. 1993. "Defining Deviancy Down." *American Scholar* (Winter).

Patai, Daphne and Koertge, Noretta. 1994. *Professing Feminism*. New York: Basic.

Rossi, Peter. 1987. "No Good Applied Social Research Goes Unpunished." *Society*, (Nov.-Dec.)

———————— 1991. Going Along or Getting It Right," *Journal of Applied Sociology* 8.

Simpson, Ida Harper and Simpson, Richard L. 1994. "The Transformation of the American Sociological Association," *Sociological Forum*, 9(2).

"What Is Wrong with Sociology." 1995. *Sociological Forum.* 9(2)

Wilson, Julius William. 1978. *The Declining Significance of Race.* Chicago: Chicago University Press.

Wrong, Dennis. 1976. "The Oversocialized Conception of Man in Modern Sociology". in *Sceptical Sociology.* New York; Columbia University Press.

11

Marxism and Western Intellectuals in the Postcommunist Era

"Why was it that particular features and peculiarities of Marxism... became the basis for (Soviet Communist) Party ideology? Why was this ideology... seized upon so passionately by the original fanatics?"—Alexander Yakovlev

"Having been refuted as theories of society these views have retreated into departmentrs of literature, where they still ...flourish."—John Searle

Although much has been written about the relationship between Marxism and intellectuals a reexamination of this relationship would benefit from the radically changed circumstances in the aftermath of the unexpected and historic political changes of the late 1980s and early 1990s. The collapse of Soviet communism had an impact on the Western intellectuals' relation to Marxism that remains far from fully explored; it puts pressure on those among them attracted to Marxism to give more thought to the strength and weaknesses of this theory and its relationship to the practices of the political systems which claimed to be guided by it.

The collapse has also drawn attention to the relationship between Marxist theory and the socialist (or "actually existing socialist") political systems *prior* to their collapse since every one of them averred that Marxism inspired their policies and was the foundation of their institutions and legitimacy. Eric Hobsbawm called them "countries officially committed to Marx's ideas."

Few would dispute that a large (if unquantifiable) portion of Western intellectuals was attracted to some version or aspect of Marxism; many still are. It is impossible to say exactly what proportion since there are no opinion surveys addressed to "intellectuals." Even if the majority of Western intellectuals today could not be fairly characterised as Marxist their beliefs were significantly colored by it; they agreed with many of its basic propositions and especially its impassioned critique of capitalism.

Many Western intellectuals during the past three decades did draw a line between the highly militarised, industrial and bureaucratic Soviet Union and the other Marxist, or Marxist-Leninist countries in the third world. They hoped that these systems would come closer to the realization of Marxian ideals although their very existence in non-industrial, third world countries defied the Marxist scheme of social-historical development and progress dependent on a class conscious, industrial working class and developed capitalism.

There was another question routinely overlooked: how faithful to the spirit of Marxism could political systems be which were dominated by leaders surrounded by personality cults as extreme and grotesque as that of Stalin. Each durable third world Marxist-Leninist system was dominated by such figures: Mao, Castro, Ho Chi Minh, Kim Il Sung and Enver Hoxha (the latter presiding over an honorary member of the third world, Albania).

Has the Collapse helped Western intellectuals to reconsider their relationship to Marxism? Or, as some argue, is this the time to solidify their attachment to Marxist theory, no longer tainted by an unseemly association with political systems which were not "truly" Marxist? An American political scientist, Philip Green said in 1989: "For...leftists around the world... a great albatross has been lifted from around our necks... We are finally free to conduct debate (about Socialism) on our own terms." In Germany Jutta Ditfurth a spokesman of the Green party suggested that "there simply is no need to reexamine the validity of socialism as a model... it was not socialism that was defeated in Eastern Europe and the Soviet Union because these systems were never socialist."

Western intellectuals never lived in societies where Marxism was the foundation of the official belief system and the government in power sought to realize its ideals (successfully or not). This circumstance was among the determinants of their attitude toward these ideas. By contrast, intellectuals who lived in "actually existing socialist" countries were indelibly marked by the institutional attempt to realize some of these ideals. One of them, a Russian intellectual, Alexander Tsipko wrote: "Our experience of Marxism differs a great deal from Western experience. We could see Marxism from the inside, something a Western intellectual was unable to do. Upon the slightest contact with life, the theoretical structures of Marxism lose their attractiveness..."

Unlike such Russian intellectuals chastened by witnessing the attempts to put Marxist ideals into practice, Western and especially American academic intellectuals increasingly congregated in rarified subcultures, enclaves of their own, (on and around campuses) even physically removed from the rest of their society. These academic enclaves inhabited by the like-minded have been conducive to the preservation of beliefs and mindsets associated with a reflexively and habitually adversarial worldview supported by Marxism. This insulation from other currents of thought and information helps to explain the persistence of at least some core commitments to Marxism.

Why Western Intellectuals Have Been Attracted to Marxism

The original attraction of Western intellectuals to Marxism had several sources. For some it was a respectable and sophisticated tool of analysis of social and economic structures; for others a theory of historical development highlighting the interdependence of various social phenomena; it was most popular as an instrument of social criticism aimed at capitalist society.

Reverence for Marxism sometimes coexisted with ambivalence about "actually existing socialist systems" and especially the Soviet Union. Nonetheless many Western intellectuals throughout the 1960s, 70s and early 80s inclined to give the benefit of doubt to the Soviet Union: it was certainly not democratic and has not succeeded in providing its citizens with a high standard of living but at least it was not capitalist. Not being capitalist made it morally preferable to the United States and other Western capitalist democracies. Moreover the Soviet Union helped other, supposedly more authentic revolutionary systems in the Third World, such as Cuba, Vietnam and later Nicaragua, and for this too it was given credit. Many Western intellectuals saw the USSR as a counterweight to the predatory capitalism and imperialism of the United States. Many subscribed to the moral equivalence thesis (between the super powers) but in practice were far more critical of the United States than the Soviet Union.

There were also those among American and Western intellectuals who disliked the Soviet system not for its repressive policies but for bringing discredit to the good name of Marxism, for tarnishing the noble ideals of the founding fathers. For them this was the greatest crime of the Soviet system, not the Gulag, not the Purges, the bloody collectivization of agriculture, or the crushing of the uprisings in Eastern Europe.

What is it in the way of life of Western, mostly academic intellectuals that made them susceptible to the appeals of Marxism? Why did this attraction intensify in the late 1960s and persist almost to the very end of the Soviet empire during a period when, increasingly, the record of communist social systems around the world showed that the attempted realization, even partial realization, of Marxist ideas produced horrific unintended results?

The answer may be found in the very concept of the intellectual. What defines the person whom we call an intellectual is neither a particular occupation, nor level of education, nor social role but a mindset, an emotional focus, certain attitudes. Bearing witness to the injusticies of society matters most to many intellectuals; it is the social critic's role that has been the most important source of their sense of identity, self esteem and meaning in life and the social critical passion of Marxism has been an obvious inspiration for the critics of Western capitalist societies.

Intellectuals share a disposition to a measure of discontent and a strongly felt need to find meaning and coherence in life and the society they inhabit but as a rule they do not succeed. Nor do they typically find comfort in traditional religious beliefs; Western intellectuals as a distinctive group evolved from the secular and vigorously anti-religous tradition of the French Enlightenment. I have described intellectuals as

> ... people with a chronically unappeased appetite for meaning, justice and moral truths, constantly on the lookout for plausible belief systems but incapable of finding them, or adhering to them over long periods of time. This quest and its recurring frustration defines much of their outlook and smoldering discontent as they gravitate to... the role of secular moralist.
>
> Contemporary Western intellectuals belong to the educated and leisured strata who display the most unease and discomfort with life in their societies, with the experience of living in modern—that is, secular, pluralistic, wealthy and technologically advanced—societies and they are capable of routinely articulating such discontent. Max Weber's observation goes to the heart of the defining character of intellectuals and their needs, relevant to their residual attachment to Marxism: "The salvation sought by the intellectual is always based on inner need, and hence it is at once more remote from life, more theoretical... than salvation from external distress, the quest for which is characteristic of nonprivileged classes..."

Intellectuals have high expectations. The late Reinhard Bendix defined "intellectuals as those educated people who criticize the world of the possible", and "attempt to achieve the impossible..." It is the predicament of intellectuals that their high expectations are often combined with what Lewis Feuer called "a Hamlet complex: the intellectual often feels that intellect disabled him... deprived him of the capacities for will and action; he wishes to ...have his every word transmuted to action." Marxism promised to close this gap between ideas and actions, theory and practice, a promise that accounts for its durable appeal.

Intellectuals have also been attracted to Marxism because, despite its scientific aspirations it is rooted in strong moral impulses and certainties. The moralistic essence of Marxian socialism was also noted by Durkheim: "Socialism... is entirely oriented toward the future... It concerns itself much less with what is or what was than what ought to be... Socialism is not a science... it is a cry of grief, sometimes of anger, uttered by men who most keenly feel our collective malaise."

Intellectuals, Marxism and the Discontents of Modernity

The intellectuals' aversion to capitalism is to a large extent an aversion to modernity, that is, to the combination of industrialization, urbanization, bureaucratization and secularization. Modernity also means social isolation, loss of a sense of purpose, of community, few taken for granted certainties, and too many unregulated choices.

The critique of capitalism has increasingly shifted from the material-economic (or political) aspects to the spiritual and psychological. Correspondingly the benefits of socialism came to be seen in recent decades as primarily spiritual: sense of purpose, community, lack of alienation, caring, wholeness, etc. In Western capitalist democracies it is no longer poverty and economic exploitation which are the most strongly felt problems but meaninglessness and the loss of social solidarity. Present day conflicts tend to be ethnic (or religious) rather than class based. A variety of social problems (crime, escapism, family disintegration) are connected to the decline of community and of widely and deeply held beliefs. Robert Nisbet observed almost half century ago that "material improvement that is unaccompanied by a sense of personal belonging may actually intensify social dislocation and personal frustation."

Western intellectuals are today anticapitalist mainly because they regard capitalism as a force that undermines authentic social bonds, disinterested personal relations and all the vital, non-rational gratifications of life; they perceive it as a social-economic system that erodes true feeling. Paul Baran and Paul Sweezy, two American Marxists claimed that under capitalism everyone exists "in a jungle in which there is no love and trust, no purpose worth striving for and no ideal worth fighting for."

Since the 1960s Western intellectuals have also been intensely critical of capitalism on account of its association with "consumerism"—something that might not have occurred to Marx since in his times the problem was that most people consumed too little not too much. The animus toward consumption further suggests that hostility toward capitalism is connected to unappeased spiritual hungers. Consumerism is condemned as an escape from the problems of the world or the true self. Herbert Marcuse was in the forefront of those who regarded consumption as a form of false-consciousness, an activity that gives people worthless satisfactions, illusory pleasures preventing them from improving their society and themselves by means of radical social change. Marcuse and his followers have not made clear what "genuine needs" are which deserve to be gratified and those which do not, and who is to decide what they are, or should adjudicate between conflicting needs.

The aversion to specialization entertained by Marx and Engels also struck a responsive cord in Western intellectuals in recent times (especially pronounced in the United States since the 1960s); they too perceived it as a self evident evil, a destroyer of "wholeness" and true individuality.

Marx and his followers believed that under socialism a new, superior sense of community would emerge unencumbered by traditional beliefs and restraints. Intellectuals found Marxism especially appealing (as Peter Berger among others argued) because it promised a combination of social justice, material progress (or modernity) without alienation, without the destruction of social bonds.

It is an interesting and not widely recognized paradox that Western intellectuals, including the Marxists among them, find traditonal societies attractive whereas Marx held these societies in great contempt. Western Intellectuals and artists have pursued and admired the various incarnation of "noble savages" for centuries. Today the places of vacation and recreation favored by Western intellectuals continue to reflect these predilections. "Quaint" fishing or mountain villages are prized wherever they can be found provided they have indoor plumbing, electricity and ample parking.

Intellectuals find traditional societies appealing because they seem to possess a sense of authenticity, community, simplicity, stability, and strongly held beliefs; they are not impersonal or bureaucratic; levels of work satisfaction are believed to be higher, they are not dominated by the cash nexus or profit motive.

The findings of my *Political Pilgrims* made clear that Western intellectuals who admired the second generation communist societies (China, Vietnam, Cuba, Nicaragua) also found their surviving traditional attributes attractive. These countries appeared to succeed in fusing the authenticity of a traditional society with the benefits of applied Marxism; it seemed that the ravages of modernization were checked by socialist communitarianism. For a long time many Western intellectuals believed that whatever else was wrong with state socialist systems they were free of alienation.

Marxism also promised to conquer personal problems: working for the good of society, and being well integrated into a progressive social movement, party, or collectivity would eliminate the notorious abyss between the personal and the social, the private and the public. Marxism in effect suggested that personal problems were epiphenomenal, rooted in a bad social system; once the system is altered personal problems too would wither away. Alexander Yakovlev, the former chief of ideology in the Soviet party apparatus wrote of "Marx's... idea of the possibility of completely eliminating all the global contradictions of human existence and the antithesis between essence and existence, between individual and universal interests, between private and political life, between spiritual and practical life."

Marxism gratified to a considerable degree the religious or meaning-seeking impulses of intellectuals—an important point since intellectuals have often been thought of as irreverent, iconoclastic, free thinking, inclined to debunking and demistifying, anyhting but religious. As it turned out intellectuals have not been comfortable in a world from which, in Weber's words, the gods have retreated.

Yakovlev further explains why ostensibly secular intellectuals approached Marxism in a quasi-religious spirit: "There is no such thing as pure, unadulterated atheism. When people reject one god they inevitably fashion a hero for themselves on earth and erect a new idol. People search for someone to worship and serve. They need truth absolute... They are always... absolutizing something or relativizing something."

The political ideas of Western intellectuals sympathetic to Marxism often rested on abstract, non-empirical beliefs and largely symbolic matters. Many of them, even as they became more critical of communist systems insisted that their "fundamentals", or the system "as a whole", or its "overall direction" were satisfactory. Such beliefs sufficed for long periods of time to silence doubts in face of disturbing empirical phenomena (this was what Arthur Koestler called, "the doctrine of unshaken foundations"). A convenient degree of insulation from the specifics of social-political realities (i.e., living in the West) was helpful for maintaining this stance but it was the capacity for compart-mentalization, the focusing on a handful of abstract notions deeply internalized that best explain these attitudes, and especially the capacity to sharply dissociate ends from means. Even Georg Lukacs, who had lived in "actually existing" socialist societies (the USSR and communist Hungary) was prey to such axiomatic and unexamined beliefs having remarked that "... in my opinion even the worst socialism is better than the best capitalism." In order to believe this Lukacs had to entertain a quasi-religious notion of socialism that took for granted the essential, self-evident ethical superiority of its goals (over capitalism) and resolutely overlooked all empirical facts calling into question his life-long faith. In the end it came down to matters of faith.

The disposition here sketched is similar to that of conventional religous believers who can rationalize the incomprehensible horrors, injustices, and irrationalities of life experienced here and now because of their deeply felt belief that *in its fundamentals* the world is ordered and permeated by divine purpose (even if not fully grasped by ordinary mortals) and that divine dispensation will *eventually* right all wrongs, if not here than in some other world or plane of existence. The unimaginable but hopeful future is of the same importance for the devotee of communist society ("communist" in the Marxist, utopian sense) as the supernatural world is for the religous believer; in communist society all contradictions will be resolved, all conflicts and scarcities, material or affective (emotional) eliminated.

Disputing Theory and Practice

Unlike the collapse of the other major totalitarian system of our century, Nazi Germany, the fall of Soviet communism did not bring with it an unequivocal, worldwide delegitimation of the ideas which originally inspired the system and its founders. Among Western academic intellectuals Marxism continues to enjoy various degrees of respectability and many remain preoccupied with its rehabilitation. For some of them the most important about the collapse of Soviet communism was that it has provided a new opportunity to "recenter... the debate on our own society" by which Bruce Cumings (an American historian) meant putting forward new, hard hitting critiques of American society based on a purer version of Marxism no longer burdened by association with the likes of Erich Honecker. Cumings also argued that East European communists misunderstood Marx and "institutionalized this failed understanding"—another way of proposing that the theory had nothing to do with the practices it had inspired.

Thus in the eyes of many Western beholders the collapse of the Soviet Bloc did not resolve the question of the relationship between Marxist theory and Soviet-communist practice. As Michael Radu pointed out "Many of us, intellectuals... cannot seem to make peace with the truth that an idea so 'nobly motivated' could have produced such unmitigated disaster. Even today, after the dissolution of the Soviet Union... there is a powerful reluctance to connect the horrors of Soviet reality to the errors of the socialist idea."

While there is no consensus among Western intellectuals about the relationship between theory and practice, it was certainly among the proud claims of Soviet communism (and of each communist state) that it succeeded in uniting theory and practice. To say the least an effort was made to realise *some aspects of the theory* and it resulted in a proliferation of unintended consequences. Martin Malia posed the issue with great clarity:

> The problem is this: Since socialism set out to realize the 'noble dream' of human equality and fraternity, how could it have produced such palpably bad results in Soviet practice? One way to solve the problem... is to blame bad results on Russian backwardness, or on the failure of the Western revolution to come to Bolshevism's rescue, or on the heritage of Ivan the Terrible, and by these means to exonerate socialism itself... Another 'solution' is to say that Soviet Communism was not genuine socialism...

Malia has been among the few who argued that "the Soviet experiment turned totalitarian not despite its being socialist but because it was socialist." He also insisted that "... all the basic institutions of the Soviet order, as they had emerged by 1935... were the creations of ideology..."

Isaiah Berlin was also among the few in the West who did not think that a wide gulf yawned between Marx's ideas and the activities of those who much later sought to implement them: "... there was no liberal humanist Marx to be saved from Stalinist consequences; there was only the young Marx, who believed in 'swift blows and putsches' and the other older one who was resigned to a long revolutionary build-up" (Quoted in Michael Ignatieff: *Isaiah Berlin: A Life*, 1998).

Unlike many Western intellectuals those in Eastern Europe are inclined to believe that *there was* a link between the theoretical inspiration and the practical results (as I also found in my research in Eastern Europe reflected in my recent book). As they see it the discrepancy existed not between theoretical postulates and the institutions created to implement them but between the theory and its *promised results*.

It would be hard to dispute that the founders of the Soviet Union were inspired by the central ideas of Marx especially the maximisation of socio-economic equality based on an economy of great productivity and a highly motivated workforce. The vastly improved social order was expected to include harmonious relationships between all groups in society (with the exception of the exploiters and enemies of the new social order who were to be removed swiftly and painlessly) and a new sense of community and trust among the citizens. All historically known forms of human misbehavior (crime, greed, selfishness, lack of compassion, envy etc) were expected to "wither away". The key economic-institutional measure to attain these goals was the abolition of the private ownership of the means of production. As Leszek Kolakowski wrote: "Marx seems to have imagined that once capitalists were done away with the whole world could become a kind of Athenian agora: one had only to forbid private ownership of machines or land and, as if by magic, human beings would cease to be selfish and their interests would coincide in perfect harmony." The key political measure was to be the dictatorship of the proletariat exercised through the Party.

We cannot guess what Marx might have thought of Lenin's substitution of the Bolshevik Party for the dictatorship of the proletariat, and his attempt to pull off the socialist revolution in a largely peasant society. Nonetheless what Lenin and his followers tried to achieve was not so different from what Marx aspired to in a different setting.

Eduard Shevardnadze's observations reflect an insider's understanding of the relationship between theory (or ideology) and practice: "... tanks and machine guns may only be employed as arguments within the appropriate ideological frame... the executioner has always been preceded by the inquisitor, the axe and block (were) foreshadowed by the dogmas of faith."

In the Western discussions about the relationship between Marxist theory and Soviet-communist practice surprisingly little has been said about the doctrine of class struggle, an essential part of Marxism and one perceived as the defining attribute of history. Those who had lived in "actually existing socialist" states did recognize that the belief in class struggle united theory and practice. The theory of the omnipresence and inexorability of class struggle legitimated the generous use of political violence allegedly required to create a social system that will eventually cease to need it.

Yakovlev noted that "Class struggle... in its crude physical form, the final reorganization of the world..." was an "obsession" of the founding fathers: "This belief in the inevitability of the coming communist world served to justify the numerous and senseless vicitms of the class struggle..." Furthermore,

> The idea that one should not fear creating victims in the course of serving the cause of progress...is very characteristic of Marx....
>
> Moral criteria are... 'revoked' by the brutality and directness of class warfare... eveything that corresponded to the interests of revolution and communism was moral. That is the morality with which hostages are executed, the peasantry was destroyed, concentration camps were built and entire peoples were forcibly relocated.
>
> By making the illusory future more important than humanity Marxism gave people carte blanche to use any means... kindness, conscience, love, cooperation, solidarity, justice, freedom, the rule of law—were unfit, useless. They weakened class struggle.

In short, without the certainties ideological beliefs provided the campaigns of political violence and coercion would have been far less ruthless. By the same token as we reach the 1970s and 80s there is a decline of such beliefs and "without the prop of ideology, the Party's will to coerce eroded"—as Malia summed up the conditions leading to glasnost and the final unravelling.

In the end both the unity and disunity of theory and practice contributed to the unravelling of Soviet communism. The disunity was more apparent: the public ownership of the means of production did not end the exploitation of the workers or made the system more productive or humane; the dictatorship of the proletariat was no more democratic than parliamentary systems under capitalism; the Communist Party was not composed of the most selfless representatives of the working classes; the leaders were not devoted to the welfare of the masses; workers did not have reason to believe that they were masters of their lives, owners of the means of production; communist prisons were no more humane than those in capitalist countries, etc.

But there were also connections between Marxist theory and practice. Communist leaders internalized and acted upon the deeply felt conviction that private property and profit-hunger were the ultimate source of all evil. Likewise Marx's contempt for peasants was embraced and put into practice. Marx's hostility toward traditional religious beliefs and practices also became institutionalised. The powerful elitist-paternalistic disposition of Marx found full expression in the character of the ruling party and its relationship to the masses. There was a connection between belief, economic policies and economic failures, (as for instance in the establishment and perpetuation of collective farms), between the political will of the leaders and its ideological roots.

Marxism was far more vulnerable to reconciling ideals and realities than Christianity; the promises of Christianity (and most major religions) are projected into another plane of existence, those of Marxism were to be realized in this world.

The Blindspots of Marxism

The present day relationship between Western intellectuals and Marxist theory is shaped not only by the ambiguous effects of the Collapse noted above, but also by a growing awareness that Marxism neglects fundamental problems of human existence. Roger Gottlieb is among the apparently small number of authors coming out of a Marxist tradition willing to raise the crucial question of the relationshp between the nature of the theory and the practices it had inspired, and why has it been so difficult to realize the ideals. Some of his questions and conclusions are strikingly similar to those of Yakovlev quoted earlier:

(Do)... the roots of Stalinist terror lie in Marxism's fundamental lack of respect for the individual person and for universal human rights? Will Marxism just *have* to sacrifice innocent lives to some mythical higher purpose? Does the absence of principles held without regard to final consequences mean that Marxist morality will always justify means by utopian ends?

Gottlieb also drew attention to the Marxian optimism about human nature, at once one of its attractions and major flaw:

because the Marxist tradition presupposes... that human fulfillment results from the proper arrangement of human relations and consumption, its model ignores a basic dimension of human experience. The problem arises from some unstated and unexamined premises: If we are given enough bread and justice we will be satisfied and not want more. We will no longer be driven by greed, insecurity, envy, boredom or the fear of death... We will accept ourselves and others. Having achieved equality we will not seek superiority... In short, once external misery is ended, internal misery will dwindle.

Yakolev came to perceive the same weakness of Marxism:

... the individual suffers not only from economic inequality but also from spiritual and bodily vulnerability, from fear of death, from the inherent solitude of human beings. The world and life create a multitude of problems... that cannot be fixed by acheiving an equal relationship to the means of production...
... Can you deduce human esssence from the way an individual makes a living?

He came to the conclusion that

Marx... had no interest in the psychological realms of people, who, as he supposed, would soon become altered because of the inevitable changes in human nature that follow the modifications in the nature of social relations.

Western intellectuals have adopted different ways to deal with the collapse of Soviet communism and its implications for Marxist theory. There are those who still harbor a residual warmth toward Marxism on account of their past, often youthful beliefs and commitments. Others embrace a diluted Marxism that can barely be distinguished from liberalism or social democracy; this watered down version affirms every conceivable human right and opposes every abhorrent political or economic practice or personality trait (e.g. greed, selfishness, dishonesty etc).

For many Western intellectuals Maxism continues to offer a comprehensive and intellectually respectable belief system that combines moral passion with apparent scientific rigor and places them on the side of justice, compassion and other high moral values. As such it continues to help them in maintaining their social critical role which is the major source of their sense of identity and self-esteem.

There are also those (among former Marxist intellectuals) who prefer not think about the validity and vitality of Marxism in the context of the collapse of Soviet communism; they have moved to new preoccupations like multiculturalism, identity politics, postmodernism, deconstructionism, or radical feminism. The postmodernists in particular ceased to be Marxist by virtue of their rejection of the legacy of the Enlightenment and Western rationality that was part of the Marxist tradition.

In the final analysis Marxism had two layers of attraction for intellectuals. The first was linked to social justice, the rational reorganization of society, material progress untainted by the profit motive, the meeting of major and obvious human needs. It is the second attraction that has been the deeper and also more problematic and sinister in its potentialities. It is the allure of the seamless community, new meaning and sense of purpose, the promise of a social system which will reconcile all contradictions of social existence and human aspirations and hence can demand unconditional loyalty and the subordinatation of means to ends.

This may be a good time for Western intellectuals to finally detach themselves from the remaining appeals of Marxism and conclude from the historical record that it is not a theory which can be relied upon to build either substantially better societies or to improve the character of human beings.

References

Peter L. Berger: "The Socialist Myth" *Facing Up to Modernity*, New York: Basic Books, 1977.

Roger Gottlieb: Marxism: *1844-1990: Origins, Betrayal, Rebirth* London: Sinclair & Stevenson 1991.

Paul Hollander: "Marxist Societies: The Relationship Between Theory and Practice", *Annual Review of Sociology*, Fall 1982.

——————: *Political Will and Personal Belief: The Decline and Fall of Soviet Communism*, New Haven, Yale UP, 1999.

Leszek Kolakowski: *Main Currents of Marxism*, Vol.III., New York: Oxford University Press, 1978.

Martin Malia: *The Soviet Tragedy*, New York: Free Press, 1994.

Alexander Yakovlev: *The Fate of Marxism in Russia*, New Haven: Yale University Press, 1993.

Andrzei Walicki: *Marxism and the Leap to the Kingdom of Freedom: The Rise and Fall of Communist Utopia* Stanford, CA: Stanford University Press, 1995.

12

Intellectuals and the War in Kosovo

When I began writing this article in late May 1999 it was by no means clear how and when NATO's airwar against Milosevich will come to an end. Susan Sontag wrote at the time that it was "impossible to see how this war will play out. All the options seem improbable, as well as undesirable." The consensus seemed to be that it will end in some sort of a stalemate, or worse, that NATO will not achieve its objectives: the refugees will not return, NATO troops wont enter in substantial numbers the province and Yugoslavia will keep effective control over it. By the time I finished writing in August 1999 it was clear that things turned out quite different.

In the following I will reflect from two vantage points (Northampton and Budapest) on the unanticipated outcome of the air campaign, the American and Hungarian responses to it and the numerous moral and psychological questions it has raised.

The larger issues of the Kosovo conflict include the notorious and chronic inability to predict the outcome and by products of major historical-political events. It had not been anticipated by Western policymakers that the bombing campaign will accelerate and intensify ethnic cleansing; it was not expected that Milosevich will endure over two months of bombardment. But it was also the conventional wisdom among experts and pundits that air strikes by themselves will not compel the Serbs to give in to NATO demands which turned out to be wrong.

Despite its unexpected success many mistakes were made in the way NATO and the U.S. chose to conduct the war. They included the declaration that no ground troops would be used; the initial "pinprick" bombardment; going to exceptional length to avoid NATO casualties at the expense of the Albanian and Serb civilians; it was also an error to withold support from the Kosovo Liberation Army, the only force on the ground that could have effectively interfered with the ethnic cleansing.

Nonetheless in the end the NATO policy prevailed: Milosevich withdrew his forces, NATO troops entered Kosovo and the refugees did return. Unresolved issues remain including the future status of Kosovo as well as the survival of the Milosevich regime; a variety of moral, political and historical questions are also left behind deserving further attention.

* * *

I was intensely preoccupied with the Kosovo conflict from the beginning of the NATO campaign in late March 1999 until its end in June and had little difficulty identifying Milosevich and his regime with political and moral evil. I also found the behavior of huge numbers of "ordinary" Serbs repugnant, their enthusiastic participation in the ethnic cleansing was one of its preconditions. The removal and brutalization of more than a million people required large numbers of willing and eager participants. The scenes of Serbian crowds engulfed in self righteous nationalistic frenzy on the streets of Belgrade were also singularly unappealing ("... people at rock-concert rallies in Belgrade and other cities, dancing in defiance of NATO and in support of the man they call Slobo" as the *New York Times* described it). Those were images of aggressive self assertion joined to maudlin affirmations of collective victimhood. Mark Mazower of Princeton University observed that "Hatred of Albanians is not something invented by Milosevic; it has deep roots in Serbian political culture... Serb nationalism (is) resentful and narcissistic, claiming victimhood for itself and indifferent to the sufferings of the real victims..." Slavenka Draculic argued (in a Hungarian publication which I read while in Budapest in June) that from the Serbian point of view Albanians have long been invisible:

> If they were noted at all it was only as some sort of an abstract entity... rather than fellow citizens endowed with the same rights... (Serbs) seem incapable to identify with the sufferings of people they do not regard as being of equal stature... the sufferings of their fellow citizens does not elicit any human emotion... the prejudices toward Albanians are comparable to those directed in other cultures at Jews, blacks or gypsies.

I resonated to Daniel Goldhagen's analogy between Nazi-German, World War II Japanese and Serb behavior (proposed in a *New*

Republic article in May 1999) although the scale and quality of the three sets of misdeeds were quite different. As Goldhagen observed

> In all three instances, ... the vicious treatment of the victims has been supported by a large majority...that was beholden to an ideology which called for the conquest of Lebensraum... They believed fanatically in the rightness of these actions... In all three instances the crimes... were carried out by ordinary members of the societies... when their governments moved them to do so. In all three instances the majority of the people whose country was committing these enormous crimes deluded themselves into believing that they were the real victims and that any attempt, such as bombing, to halt the... mass murdering was the real crime.

At the same time I disagreed with those who spoke of genocide or Holocaust in Kosovo on the apparent assumption that no moral indignation or compassion can be generated in our times without invoking genocide or the Holocaust. (Philip Gourevitch wrote in the *New Yorker* that "In a time when the invocation of... genocide has become a staple of sermons on tolerance, one only has to say the word 'Holocaust' to set off a shudder of sympathetic moral rightousness...")

The Kosovo war was one of those historical events which compel new reflections over old and unresolved questions of politics and morality. Among them, how groups and individuals decide which forces or actors represent good and evil in historical conflicts? Under what circumstances are certain forms of behavior deemed morally abhorrent, acceptable, praiseworthy, or matters of profound indifference? Why the premediated murder of unarmed civilians is a matter of essential and justifiable self defense for some observers and a ruthless massacre for others? Why socially conscious bystanders such as intellectuals (presumed to be sensitive to all injustice) are sometimes willing to rationalise political violence while on other occasions respond with spectacular outrage and indignation? How do people, and especially those in power, calculate the costs and benefits of political violence and evaluate the proper relationship between the ends and means?

Kosovo certainly provided abundant examples of the readily available human capacity to dehumanize other humans; Serbs and Albanians excelled in regarding one another as unworthy of any humane sentiment or consideration. The victimizers were, for the most part the Serbs but there is reason to believe that the Kosovar Albanians would reciprocate given the opportunity; they began to do so after their return, if on a far smaller scale and far less methodically.

The Kosovo conflict also offered new illustrations of the familiar contemporary tendency to confuse and conflate self defense and aggression. Once more, the obvious aggressors, the Serbs claimed to have been victimised and under attack even before the NATO bombing. Serbs deprived of electricity and gasoline equated their condition with that of the Albanians who were murdered, raped, robbed, evicted and reduced to refugee status.

An aspect of the violence in Kosovo that has received little attention by those seeking to understand and control its manifestations has been the part played by revenge in political conflicts and the relish and clear conscience with which human beings can harm others in its pursuit. Kosovo seems to reaffirm that a durable lust for revenge is deeply rooted in human nature and also suggests that the quality of political conflicts and the personalities of those in charge of them are not unrelated. Former U.S. ambassador Walter Zimmerman observed that Milosevich is "uncommonly ruthless... (he displays) an insensitivity toward suffering and a coldness toward individual humans. He had a tendency to treat people as pawns on a political chessboard... For such a man, the use of force to rid Kosovo of its entire population would have presented no moral dilemma." The question historians and social scientists will and should continue to wrestle with is what types of societies, cultures or historical circumstances allow (as is so often the case) for such flawed human beings to seize and retain power?

Besides the all too familiar motives and aspects of mass violence and brutality there was also something unusual if not unique about the Kosovo conflict. There was no conventionally defined or easily identifiable "national interest" at stake for NATO and the U.S.—indeed many critics of the involvement were opposed to it for precisely that reason. Milosevich and the remains of Yugoslavia did not militarily or politically threaten the U.S. or the countries of NATO; Yugoslavia was not capable of disrupting oil supplies; there were no prospects that any "dominos" might fall. The brutalization of Albanians in Kosovo was regrettable (such was this line of thinking) but there was plenty of inter-ethnic and other brutality around the globe and the U.S. (or NATO) could not be expected to police the whole world; moreover the Balkans was a notorious "hotbed" or "tinderbox" of "ancient ethnic hatreds" the U.S. could not, and should not be expected to prevent from exploding from time to time. If national interest as generally understood offered little explanation for the U.S. and NATO involvement what did? On this point there was a great deal of disagreement among commentators. For the critics of the U.S. at home or abroad the idea that it would get involved in a war thousands of miles away from home on largely moral or humanitarian grounds was implausible or outright preposterous. And yet strangely enough this was a military intervention dominated by moral and humanitarian considerations in which national interest as usually defined played a small part.

*   *   *

The Kosovo crisis produced interesting and unpredictable splits of opinion in this country. Republicans and other Clinton-haters opposed the intervention largely because it was "Clinton's war" but a more old fashioned, reflexive isolationism has also remeerged on the right of the political spectrum. Jack Kemp (as reported in the *New Republic*) called the NATO intervention "an international Waco" while Patrick Buchanan professed to be ashamed of his country on account of the bombing. It was hard to know if principles, or moral principles played any part in this rhetoric. Many of the critics both among politicians and the general public had trouble supporting military involvement in a part of the world they had difficulty finding on the map.

Political affiliation and prior stands taken often did not predict the attitudes toward U.S. involvement. One could find among the critics of NATO intervention such otherwise dissonant political-intellectual figures as Patrick Buchanan, Jimmy Carter, Noam Chomsky, Daniel Ellsberg, Tom Hayden, David Horowitz, Jack Kemp, and Trent Lott. Among the supporters of NATO were many similarly incompatible figures like Saul Bellow, Zbigniev Brzezinski, Geraldine Ferrarro, Tom Harkin, Tony Judt, Jeane Kirkpatrick, William Kristol, Anthony Lewis, David Rieff, Susan Sontag, Elie Wiesel and Leon Wieseltier.

In many critiques of the airwar the memories of Vietnam loomed large. For Tom Hayden the parallels were obvious: "Bombs couldnt bring peace in Vietnam" so why would they in Kosovo? There was the familiar "quagmire" imagery, reference to "a new (U.S.) imperialism" and "America as the world's policeman."

Critics on the Left (besides Hayden) included Noam Chomsky, Ramsey Clark, Jessie Jackson and other descendants and heirs of the 1960s always predisposed to solidarity with the perceived victims of American power—critics of American society who never encountered a group, nation or political movement hostile to the United States they did not feel drawn to. They have been convinced for a long time that a society so immoral and unjust as that of the United States has no business judging the behavior of others, let alone use its military power to impose its will on them. Chomsky (in a *Harper's* article) compared what he regarded as the spurious humanitarian inmvolvement of NATO and U.S. to Japan's invasion of Manchuria, Mussolini's attack on Ethiopia and Hitler's grab of the Sudetenland. He also took the opportunity to criticize the U.S. for not having taken stronger actions against Pol Pot (used as an illustration of the lack of moral credentials of the U.S. in the fight against humans rights violations) although he used to defend Pol Pot's regime while in power and scorned refugeee reports of its atrocities. Chomsky also suggested that a "rational person" would find it difficult to judge more severely "the Iranian record of intervention and terror than that of the United States..."

The NATO air war often stimulated the moral equivalence reponse. For many critics the accidental bombing casualties among the Serbs civilians carried the same moral weight as the thousands of Albanians murdered and hundreds of thousands methodically plundered and expelled from Kosovo. On his return from Belgrade Jessie Jackson evenhandedly noted that "We demonize Milosevich... They demonize President Clinton." To prove that he was above such simplifications he took the hand of Milosevic and invited him to join in a prayer circle.

Marjorie Cohn an antiwar activist in 1969 (currently law professor at Stanford) "attacked the war... as another case of American imperialism saying the United States 'will protect its markets and international influence at the expense of whatever small country happens to get in the way' ending her speech ... with 'Power to the People!'" the *New York Times* reported. James Rule, a sociologist, writing in *Dissent* explained the war in part as reflecting "the need for a credible enemy" for the American military and other elites. He suggested that repression in Kosovo became intolerable to U.S. policymakers only when it "threatened to roil relations among such crucial U.S. allies as Greece and Macedonia."

Other erstwhile critics of U.S. involvement in Vietnam reached different conclusions; for them the differences between the two situations were apparent and significant: defeating the ethnic cleansing was a good cause, fighting the Vietcong was not. The bombing of Yugoslavia was justified by its objectives even if civilians were sometimes hurt. As far as not intervening elsewhere and at other times: "past irresponsibility in the face of genocide... (is not) a warrant and justification for repeating the mistake" Tony Judt argued as did Stanley Hoffman prominent critic of the Vietnam war: "The fact that the U.S. and its allies failed to respond to cases of genocide or ethnic cleansing all over the world... is not a reason for passivity in Kosovo; it is a reason for remorse..."

Susan Sontag was willing to confront the charge that the NATO intervention was "Eurocentric," that higher value was placed on the lives of Europeans than Africans or Asians:

> Yes, to care about the fate of the people in Kosovo is Eurocentric and what is wrong with that? But is not the accusation of Eurocentrism itself just one more vestige of European presumption... of Europe's universalist mission: that every part of the globe has a claim on Europe's attention?
>
> If several African states cared enough about genocide of the Tutsis in Rwanda... to intervene militarily, say, under the leadership of Nelson Mandela, would we have criticised this intitiative as being Afrocentric? Would we have asked what right these states have to intervene in Rwanda when they have done nothing on behalf of the Kurds and the Tibetans?

Jews in particular seemed to have been torn between two conflicting emotions. On the one hand some Jewish critics of the war— and especially those of the older generations—felt supportive of beleaguered Yugoslavia. This attitude rested on the memories of the heroic Serbs partisans of World War II fighting the Nazis and other antisemitic forces, such as the Croat Ustashis. (A recent article in the *New Republic* by Lawrence Kaplan showed that the contributions of the Serb guerillas to the defeat of Nazis in Yugoslavia have been vastly overrated.)

On the other side were Jews who supported NATO because they strongly resonated to the horror of the ethnic cleansing perceived as having kinship with the Holocaust or being a contemporary approximation of it: "Hanging over Mr Wiesel's visit (to refugee camps in Macedonia) was the phrase 'never again'... I've learned something from my experiences...' Mr Wiesel said 'When evil shows its face, you dont wait... You must intervene.'" the *New York Times* reported. Anthony Lewis quoted Vaclav Havel, another supporter of NATO intervention: "Kosovo has no oilfields to be coveted; no member

nation in the (NATO) alliance has any territorial demands on Kosovo...
It is fighting out of concern for the fate of others... because no decent person can stand by and watch the systematic state-directed
murder..." Lewis added: "NATO air attacks have killed Serbian civilians. That is regrettable. But it is a price that has to be paid when a
nation falls in behind a criminal leader. It happened in Germany.
And it has happened again in Serbia."

Both the critics and supporters of the war alleged that the credibility if not survival of NATO was at stake and led to the intervention.
But "credibility" became an issue *after* NATO's involvement. The
compelling reasons for NATO to intervene were the memories of
Bosnia (that is, the failure to prevent the ethnic cleansing and mass
murders there) and the ample television coverage of the ethnic cleansing of Kosovo. It was by no means essential for NATO and the U.S.
to get involved either in Bosnia or Kosovo except for the moral-
psychological pressure exerted by the visual images of brutalised
the Kosovo Albanians and before them Bosnians.

What was there to gain for the U.S. from independence or autonomy for Kosovo? From militarily defeating the Serbs? From spending huge amounts on the military campaign, on assisting the refugees and their resettlement? From stationing more troops in that part
of the world? Could it have been the desire to intimidate Russia that
brought NATO into Kosovo?—as has also been suspected by some,
both in this country and Hungary. Why would NATO seek to intimidate in this manner a thoroughly weakened and demoralised Russia,
dependent on Western handouts? If anything NATO airstrikes stiff-
ened the backbone of Russia, revived its nationalism and hostility
toward the U.S. and the West, not an outcome sought by NATO.
Solzhenitsyn had an explanation reflecting the resurgent, resentful
nationalism in his part of the world: "NATO wants to impose its order on the world. And Yugoslavia is needed as a terrible example.
'We will punish Yugoslavia and the whole world will tremble.' And
that was not all. He also said that he saw no difference in the behavior of NATO and Hitler."

Were the greedy multinational corporations seeking new markets
behind the military action? They were already in a position to market their products in these regions.

Did NATO or the U.S. seek some geopolitical advantage? New
bases? There were already NATO troops in Macedonia and in Bosnia-

Hercegovina and Albania would have welcomed NATO troops without the Kosovo crisis. Hungary is already a NATO member providing military bases; Bulgaria and Romania are anxious to join.

None of these possibilities carries much conviction. In the end, implausible as it might be, one is left with a preponderance of indications that moral-humanitarian considerations best explain the NATO involvement. It appears that both public opinion (or large parts of it) and the political elites in the U.S. and other NATO countries reluctantly and belatedly came to the conclusion that the well documented, large scale and methodical mistreatment of the Kosovar Albanians justified military action even if no such action took place in other parts of the world on corresponding occasions. These idealistic motives were somewhat tainted by a policy, a determination not to risk any NATO lives for the good cause.

* * *

A trip to Hungary in late May while the airwar was still in high gear provided a new vantage point for pondering the conflict and its moral and historical implications. A visit to the new frontline state, a new member of NATO was likely to provide different perspectives and information from what I learned about the war from the *New York Times* and CNN (not that this was the reason for my visit).

The first tangible indication of the conflict came in Paris where the connecting flight to Budapest was delayed because of the heavy use of European airspace by NATO planes. The second indication was the long line of tanker planes (used for aerial refuelling) lined up at Budapest airport.

In Hungary I took every opportunity to discuss Kosovo with the natives who included both intellectuals, some public figures as well as people of no such distinction, including taxi drivers, old friends and members of my family. I also avidly read the press and listened to radio and television news.

Certain parallels in the attitude of Hungarians and Americans on different sides of the issue became immediately apparent. In Hungary too those opposed to the ruling (right of center) government—and I spoke to many such people especially among the intelligentsia—were opposed to the war because it was supported by the government they disliked. In Hungary too the liberals were deeply divided and in unpredictable ways. Agnes Heller the philosopher and former star pupil of Georg Lukacs categorically supported NATO and its airstrikes while Gyorgy Konrad, the well-known writer and prominent dissident during the communist regime objected to them vehemently.

Among the Hungarian critics of NATO, intellectuals or not, one sentiment dominated: a firm disbelief that such a military campaign could have been undertaken on purely or largely humanitarian, or moral grounds. For understandable historical reasons Hungarians, both educated and less educated are inclined to profound cynicism in public-political matters. They were systematically lied to during the forty years of communist rule and the three freely elected governments since 1989 did not inspire much confidence either especially on account of the corruption they tolerated or abetted. Hungarian history as a whole lends little support to positive conceptions of public morality and politics as this small country endured a succession of invaders, occupiers, and betrayals. There were great selfless heroes in Hungarian history but they usually lost. There is a psychology of suspicion among people in a small and weak country toward the big and powerful—the U.S. and NATO in this case. A sceptical moral relativism is an understandable enough response to decades of fradulent official certainties. Julia Langh wrote (in *Nepszabadsag*, the most widely read daily newspaper):

> ... it has become acceptable that the superplanes of the Good Alliance should nightly fly over our heads to smash the Evil Empire and we must rejoice over this. Because at last we are on the side of Virtue. Because it feels so good to believe that this is all there is to it: that we cannot allow genocide to go on here, in the middle of Europe...
>
> Did we appoint ourselves as the best? Are we designing the new world order, deciding between truth and falsehood, Good and Evil? On what grounds?

Another journalist (Gyula Hegyi) asked (in *Magyar Hirlap*, another daily newspaper) why the Serbs have been singled out as the symbol and repository of evil in the world. He theorized that this happened since Serb nationalism collided with the interests of "globalism" (a murky and overused concept in Hungary as in the United States); the Serbs could not have been allowed to challenge with impunity these interests.

The conspiracy theories included the belief that Hungary was tricked: admitted to NATO just a short while before the airstrikes began only to provide bases for the bombardment and possible ground invasion. While a majority did vote for joining NATO in a referendum many were jittery about the specific obligations membership would entail (but, as a pro-interventionist taxi driver said in more colorful language: you should not expect to copulate without risking impregnation). There was also much disbelief that the bombing of the Chinese embassy in Belgrad could have been accidental—an attitude that combined an overestimation of the military power and technology of the United States with the conspiratorial scenario. Many Hungarians voiced the suspicion that the Monica affair motivated President Clinton to push for intervention to divert attention from his problem just as in the well known movie.

Apprehensions were expressed (in print as in conversation) about Hungary becoming as subservient to NATO as it used to be to the Warsaw Pact, a point of view sometimes implying moral equivalence between the two military alliances. During my visit it was reported in the media that a man threatened over the phone airport auhorities in Budapest (where the tanker planes were based) to shoot down one of them with a handheld missile. There was also indignation about the tanker plane that jettisoned its fuel over cultivated fields when it developed engine trouble.

Weapons' testing as the motive for the bombardment also cropped up as well reference to the destruction of copper mines in Yugoslavia in order to be rebuilt profitably by Western companies. A distinguished writer in a personal conversation speculated that the Jewish background of Madeline Albright and Wesley Clark (?) provided the psychological basis for interventionist sentiment on their part as a form of moralistic over-compensation for downplaying their Jewish identity. (A similar view was also expressed by a writer in the *New Republic* as regards Albright.)

Jewishness in Hungary too played a part in the shaping of attitudes toward the war. Jews who disliked the government as right wing and insufficiently concerned with antisemitism had little sympathy for NATO action. Those like Agnes Heller who would associate ethnic cleansing with the Holocaust took the opposite position.

A young historian argued that the most clear cut opposition to the war was to be found at both political extremes. But only the miniscule far-left "Workers Party" actually supported Milosevich.

There was a specific nationalistic component of the Hungarian concerns with the war: the Hungarian minority of some 300,000 in Vojvodina (part of Yugoslavia) that borders on southern Hungary. Many Hungarians felt that the bombs falling on places like Novisad

(Ujvidek in Hungarian) did particular damage to the lives of Hungarians. There was also apprehension that enraged Serb nationalism might turn after Kosovo on the Hungarian minority and repress them further (they too had lost their autonomous status under Milosevich). Future relations with the Serb neighbor was another concern since Hungary as a NATO member assisted in the air campaign.

A lack of warmth toward the Kosovar Albanians was sometimes discernible reflecting an undercurrent of antipathy toward their Moslem religious affiliations and values. Hungarians do not see how the latter can be reconciled with the Western, European values and attitudes they cherish. Serbs are at least Christian, if also viewed with some misgivings on other grounds.

The disputes and deep disagreements among Hungarian intellectuals raised the same puzzling questions as those among their American counterparts. People of comparable integrity, idealism and apparent moral sensibility wildly and often angrily disagreed, their moral compasses pointing in diametrically opposed directions. Once more I was drawn to the question that preoccupied me during much of my professional and personal life: what triggers moral indignation and compassion, why do we respond in viscerally different ways to comparable moral outrages? Why do we rank them differently?

A long and angry article in *Nepszabadsag* (first published in a major German paper) written by Konrad gave every indication that he was more upset by the NATO bombing of Serb civilians and infrastructure than the ethnic cleansing by Serbs, although he strongly condemned the latter as well. As he saw things it was a case of "the big beating up on the small" that is, "the greatest powers of the world conducting airwar against a little Central European country." He wrote that "when the big beats up on the small I dont root for the big..." He was put off by the similarity between militaristic computer games and the impersonal, computerised advanced technology of high level aerial bombardment. He asked why should "the bridges of Ujvidek (Novisad) be destroyed in defense of the Albanians?" He argued that "It is a big mistake to bomb human beings in the name of human rights."

In this as in other similar disputes in Hungary (as in the United States and elsewhere) the direction of moral indignation was predetermined by conflicting perceptions of who was the underdog, or *the morally privileged underdog, the most deserving victim*—and by different perceptions of who threatened whom. The problem has always been that such perceptions can be highly idiosyncratic. The Nazis felt genuinely threatened by the Jews, Stalin by the kulaks, the Hutus by the Tutsis, the Serbs by the Albanians. Whose threat perception is the most authentic? Who are the true victims and the real victimizers?

To put it differently, attitudes in Hungary as in the U.S. were determined by notions and perceptions of "radical evil in the world." Susan Sontag came to subscribe to the existence of such evil and located it in the Milosevich regime. Konrad, as most liberals, probably does not subscribe to belief in the existence of such evil which is why he optimistically believed that the Kosovo conflict could have been solved by non-military measures and policies aimed at "losening up, domesticating (the Yugoslav regime) and red-cross style rescue of human beings" instead of a strategy, (chosen by NATO) of "crushing, punishing and humiliating." Konrad's views were supported by the Academy of Arts of Germany of which he has been president for the last two years.

Peter Nadas another famous novelist (also well known in the West) disagreed with him (in an article published in the weekly, *Elet es Irodalom*). He saw the Serbs as vastly more powerful than the Kosovar Albanians, and he focused on *their* victimhood. He questioned Konrad's pacifism "as one that supports the rights of the stronger rather than that of the weaker just because there is in the world a power yet stronger" that is, NATO. Nadas rejected "moral equivalence," "the placing of an equation mark... between NATO airstrikes and the activities of the death-commando units carrying out their depredations on behalf of the Serb state."

* * *

The Kosovo war, its many victims and incomplete resolution leaves one with mixed feelings. There is ample reason for gloom as one contemplates this latest example of the ease and abandon with which human beings brutalize one another under the guidance of a depraved and mendacious group of leaders who managed to stay in power; there is new evidence how easily tribalistic nationalism becomes murderous. Among those witnessing the conflict from abroad many intellectuals fell prey to notions of moral equivalence. Their attitudes seemed to have been influenced by old, irrelevant images of who their "real" enemies are: technology, capitalism, modernity, the West, the United States, NATO, whoever they designated as the "topdog," the authentic victimizer.

More encouraging that this time more Western intellectuals —including many who in the past reflexively blamed the U.S. first in any conflict—recognized that even the United States can try to do the right thing and that the power of the Western world organized in NATO could and should be used,—halting and blundering as it had been—in a good cause.

13

Acknowledgements: Appearance and Reality in a Ritual of Academic Life

Ever since my days as a graduate student I have been mystified by and fascinated with the acknowledgements found in scholarly volumes and especially those in the social sciences I was most familiar with. I have read hundreds if not thousands of them in the course of my professional life. As is often the case with various social or cultural phenomena, their significance emerges when they are aggregated. That is to say, while acknowledgements read in isolation from one another may not strike the reader as noteworthy or puzzling, when a large number of them are read in succession questions begin to arise.[1] The reader of these tributes need not be a hardened cynic to hesitate in taking them at face value.

I sensed that in this unlikely source I stumbled upon yet another manifestation of the proverbial divergence between appearance and reality—always of interest for social scientists, intellectuals, and all commentators on modern life. While engaging in a bit of "demystification" in the pages which follow, I also wish to register some reservations about the present-day obsession with concealment—central to influential currents of our intellectual-cultural life and "postmodernism" in particular. Eugene Goodheart's comment explains my reservations about demystification: "Why as a matter of principle, should we trust the hidden rather than the evident sense of an intellectual or cultural product?... The habit of ideological suspicion *when it becomes systematic and totalizing* tends to produce insensitivity to 'higher' values, an inclination to associate truth with a cynical view of motive."[2]

*   *   *

Although the number of individuals whose contributions are acknowledged may vary from a handful to scores,[3] the style and substance of these statements of gratitude are remarkably uniform. They all conjure up a world of unsullied devotion to ideas, unsurpassed collegiality, the warmth of intellectual bonding, the glow of supportive family ties, human generosity and kindness at their best, and redeeming authorial modesty—a world of cooperation, goodwill, and selflessness. Authors invariably benefit from the "unstinting" devotion of colleagues and "the unfailing generosity" of spouses, friends, students, and assorted academic officials. The intellectual debts joyously incurred are usually "vast," teachers and advisers make their "wisdom available at every step." With astonishing frequency authors profess to be "unusually fortunate" to have encountered such individuals (who nevertheless seem to abound in academic life if these tributes are to be believed). Many of these writers confess of their difficulties to find the proper words for expressing their boundless gratitude.

If accepted at face value, acknowledgements of this type would compel us to thoroughly revise not merely our conceptions of the nature of scholarly research and writing, of collegiality, the relationship between authors and editors, the typical marital relations of academics, but human nature itself. Hence the point of departure of these reflections is the sheer implausibility of the phenomenon: from everything we know about human nature, American academic life, the norms of collegiality, and the family life of productive academics—the images of human relationships in and outside academia which emerge from acknowledgements invite skepticism.

Acknowledgements are permeated by hyperbole, effusiveness, overstatement, and exaggeration. Nothing short of "extraordinary," "brilliant," "invaluable," "admirable," "profound," "immeasurable" (usually debt owed), "wonderful," "superb," "uncommon" (usually affixed to "dedication"), and "unwavering" (mostly "support") is good enough to convey gratitude. ("Irreverent" too is frequently encountered as high praise.) Vast numbers of "extraordinarily wise" teachers leave their imprint on these books; "immense" amounts are learned from colleagues; criticism is always "judicious" and "penetrating," cheerfully accepted, and put to good use. Never do we come upon an author who does not wholeheartedly embrace criticism. Sometimes the authors in question seek to scale the heights of poetic expression, playfulness, and lyrical style. One author began his acknowledgements as follows:

My friends will recognize this book for what it is: stone soup. Like the down-and-out swindlers of the fable, I boiled up a pot of water, tossed in some pebbles, then invited passersby to add whatever soup makings they could spare. They added plenty. What's more, they performed a miracle: the stones became edible.[4]

Even publishers, (according, for example, to a famous economist), are "uncommonly" patient and kind. He writes: "I have never quite understood why publishers...do not get tired of authors. Probably they do, but those with whom I have been so happily associated conceal it with a rare and kindly skill." In another instance a senior editor of a major publishing house provided "At each, major junction... encouragement and sound advice, exhibiting admirable patience and just the right amount of editorial prodding..." The vice president of yet another publisher "deserves special praise: from prospectus to publication, his unflagging good faith and professional expertise literally kept the project alive. Advising but never constraining, she turned editorial permissiveness into a virtue."

Supporting staff are thanked by a social historian for "persistence, accuracy and cheerfulness through it all"; an editor for "patience, perseverance and encouragement... indispensable for the whole enterprise." A well-known historian was "blessed by the assistance of a large number of... graduate students" who were among "an embarrassingly large group of individuals" he has become indebted to for their help.

The lavish tributes paid to those who allegedly helped the authors are in sharp contrast with the modest role authors appear to assign to themselves in the creation of their work. Their self-conceptions are disarmingly modest, self-effacing, even self-deprecating, sometimes bordering on confessions of incompetence.

It is the central if sometimes implicit proposition of many acknowledgements that the author would have been incapable of writing and improving the book in question without the "immense" and "invaluable" help of a large cohort of dedicated individuals who either read the manuscript, discussed its topic, offered boundless encouragement, or created favorable conditions for research and reflection thereby promoting creativity; spouses in particular make the author's life tranquil, comfortable, and fulfilled.

More matter of factly, authors thank institutions (colleges, foundations, libraries) for leaves of absence, research grants, office space, access to archives, and other source materials. Often there is further reference to the large number of additional people to whom the author is also "indebted" but who must remain anonymous because of the sheer numbers involved.

The praise lavished on particular individuals tends to be elaborate and fulsome. For example, a social psychologist writes,"... I have had the rare good fortune throughout the writing of this book to review its contents with ( )... I cannot easily measure the debt I owe to ( ), but I would like to pay tribute to his extraordinary understanding of human behavior and thank him for many generosities." A political scientist thanks his colleagues "for invaluable advice and criticism" and particular individuals among them "for unfailing optimism," "for wit," "for poetry," "for needed finickiness," "for high design," his wife "for not telling who really wrote the book." There is much rejoicing, as one writer put it, over "have(ing) acquired a wonderful string of intellectual debts."

Editors of a volume of social criticism reveal that "the personal and intellectual debts incurred in the incubation of this collection of essays are immense." There is reference to the "invaluable aid and advice," "enthusiasm," "perceptive insight," "encouragement and bolstering our spirit" of particular individuals. Best of all, "our best critics remain our closest friends"!

Authors almost compulsively credit luck or good fortune for being able to benefit from the advice, guidance, wisdom, skill, patience, knowledge, insight, etc., etc. of their benefactors. It would seem that luck (in finding these extraordinary people) mattered more than their own skill, perseverance, knowledge, or aptitude; evidently they would have been helpless on their own, as in the case of a writer whose mentor's. "... rigorous and demanding guidance...never ceased to make up for my random and uneven academic inclinations." A sociologist thanked one of the readers of his manuscript for "contribut(ing) immeasurably to whatever cogency these pages possess" after noting "the number of intellectual and personal debts that I shall doubtless be unable to repay in full." A famous sociologist expresses gratitude to "for having taken a brash sophomore in hand to make him see the intellectual excitement of studying... systems of social relations." He pays tribute to another benefactor for "helping... escape from... (his) the provincialism of thinking..." Another paternal figure "has no conception of the full extent of my intellectual debt to him" and is likewise thanked profusely. Some authors go still further in diminishing, with seeming relish, their own role in producing their book by claiming that "all scholarship in this field (as probably in most others) is of necessity a collective enterprise."

*   *   *

A favorite theme of the acknowledgements is the domestic disruptions associated with the creative process and the agonies of single-minded absorption in the project shouldered by all those around the author, especially spouses and children. References to "surviving" the ordeal associated with the writing of a book are common. (It seems the unstated message that a book must have some merit if it required such colossal efforts and prolonged disruptions.) A well-known sociologist writes, "My deepest gratitude, as always, is to my wife and children, who, despite busy lives of their own, find the serenity to put up with me." The apologetic attitude also finds expression in a reference to the "many students and colleagues (who) suffered through my attempts to formulate ideas about culture in seminars, colloquia, and informal discussions."

Acknowledgements suggest that producing a scholarly volume is an enormously difficult, demanding, anxiety producing even depriving undertaking that can only succeed if the author is surrounded by a vast number of dedicated individuals and helpers anxious to meet all his or her intellectual, emotional, or practical needs including huge numbers of friends ready for assistance of every kind.

It is hard to find an acknowledgement that does not make clear that the author is married and very happily so. In the rare instance when there is no spousal reference, the parents, sometimes siblings are thanked, sometimes grown children, as for instance those of a social psychologist who "both cheered and challenged" him by "their intellectual presence and love."

Informing the reading public about marital bliss appears to be obligatory on the part of most authors. These marital images may remind the reader of politicians running for office who regularly allude to their exemplary family life and whose wives hover in the back (or fore)ground and testify by their very presence to the rectitude and normalcy of the campaigner. Perhaps both politicians and writers of social science books sense that substantive accomplishments relevant to the office sought—or the scholarly contribution pursued—are by themselves insufficient to garner goodwill, popularity, and favorable reception.

Spouses occupy a central position in these tributes. A well known political scientist confessed to "owe(ing her) a debt that mere words cannot express. This book in every sense is a joint enterprise..." An anthropologist reported having been "helped much by my wife whose unfettered originality is a constant inspiration..." The author of a popular textbook in sociology owed

> the greatest debt of all to my wife.... Her criticisms and suggestions have influenced the manuscript at every stage of its development.... Because of the magnitude of her contribution... I wanted her to agree to coauthorship, but she too modestly refused. I have reluctantly accepted her decision...

Another sociologist (no longer married) described his spouse as his "closest friend and companion...involved in the writing of this book from the beginning. Possessing the wisdom to celebrate life in spite of its tribulations, she has taught me the difference between analytic pessimism and personal pessimism, which... immobilizes the spirit..."

A social historian refers to his wife as

> a constant source of encouragement. Still my best friend and often best critic, she is the intellectual other of this book, my principal source of dialogue about its large structure and small textures... (the children) the joys of my life have treated my project with bemused tolerance, indulging me in many ways...

A psychologist owes his "greatest debt" to his wife "whose sensitivity, intelligence and wise counsel have improved every page of this book." A well-known sociologist writes:

> My wife... listened and criticized patiently throughout...her readiness to master the history (of the chosen topic)... went, in my opinion beyond the call... she dissected with me each sentence and phrase of the manuscript. This was immensely helpful since my editorial imagination had long since been dulled... our first son... obliged by making his appearance just five days before an earlier version of this book was submitted... as a Ph.D. dissertation. His birth added an air of creativity to the event.

There is the wife who "listened to the 8th and 9th draft of a troublesome passage with the same humor and intelligence as she did the first." A well-published sociologist informed the readers that his wife "not only bore with me through the seemingly interminable preparation of this study, not only surveyed its progress with her exceptional combination of perseverance, deftness and high intelligence, but also did a very important part of verifying, counting, tallying and editing." Another dedicated wife "read several drafts of the manuscript even as she worked and watched after our daughters..." A wife is thanked "for her unfailing belief—expressed in endless ways—that what I was doing was significant" another for being "an all important sustaining force over the years..." Yet another wife "not only bore with me through the seemingly interminable preparation of this study, not only surveyed its progress with her exceptional combination of perseverance, deftness and high intelligence but also did a very important part of verifying, counting, tallying and editing."

It remains a mystery why these intellectually stimulating and creatively contributing spouses did not become designated as co-authors.

*   *   *

The following lengthy quote captures virtually all essential attributes of acknowledgements here discussed:

> If any of the arguments and analyses that follow turn out to hold any water this is no doubt to a large extent attributable to the innumerable fellow students, friends, colleagues, and students of my own who were willing to listen to my half-baked ramblings and helped me turn them into something more or less coherent. A complete list would be impossible, but at the very least would include...(twenty names follow). For specific comments and criticism ...without which the book would have been much worse I am indebted to (nine names follow). I am particularly grateful to ...(two names) without whose strong support and encouragement at crucial junctures this book might never have gone to press. But the greatest debt of gratitude by far I owe to(...) who saw the project through from start to finish, and whose characteristic blend of relentless criticism and unfailing support makes him a superb teacher, colleague and friend.... For helping me with the often extraordinarily demanding word-processing, typing, indexing and library work, I thank (five names to follow). I also owe a great deal to (...) for the truly magnificent job of copy editing she did on the unwieldy manuscript. Finally, a debt of a different kind, but probably the greatest of all, I owe to my wife... without whose support of love through years of obsessive work, illness, uprooting moves and frustrations of all kinds, I would *never* have made it to this point.

Did the author truly believe that his ideas were "half-baked"? That without the vast amount of help he received the book would have been incoherent and indigestible?

In the same acknowledgement there are some counterpoints to the self-deprecating themes, allusions to the substance, complexity and burden of the undertaking that required "obsessive" work, resulted in an "unwieldy" manuscript (the creative energies were hard to contain). Even mundane tasks such as typing, indexing, and library work were "extraordinarily demanding." But thanks to the concentrated efforts of all those wonderful human beings—at once supportive and ready to offer "relentless criticism"—the author overcame all obstacles (it is being suggested that there were many).

The widely read author of a study of (certain aspects of) popular culture was even more dependent on the help of generous individuals:

> This book could not have been written without the help of about 200 men and women... who allowed themselves to be questioned by me, giving freely of their time and knowledge. They were unfailingly courteous... It is impossible to thank each of them individually...
>
> In addition a few individuals so far went beyond the call of friendship or duty in permitting me to sharpen my ideas through extended discussion with them that I must single them out for public thanks. The first is my wife... and who was and is far more than a patient spouse... Her perceptive and forthright comments provided a running critique that compelled me... to clarify and condense...

A well-known social psychologist credits "such readability as it (his book) has" to his editor's "sensitivity to style. She also performed with patience and care numerous other chores that go into the making of a book. I am grateful for her serenity and loyalty as well as her competence."

A general impression the diligent reader of acknowledgments carries away with him is the profusion of brilliant, generous and inspiring human beings who inhabit academia in various capacities and are ready to be at the disposal of their intellectually challenged colleagues. They include "numerous colleagues who provided just the right mixture of involved criticism and independence-fostering detachment." There is praise "for the determination... (they) manifested... (and) displayed in the face of endless distractions and obstacles, and the intelligence and perceptiveness they bought to bear on every situation (without which) the project could not have hoped to succeed even remotely as well as it did."

Almost invariably the brilliance of great figures contrasts with the implicit limitations of the humble author:

> As regards this book, my most immediate debt, both intellectual and personal is to... who taught me, by his own example, the meaning of the phrase 'an infinite capacity for taking pains.' His help and advice extended far beyond editorial criticism and prodded me to rethink, revise and rethink again... I drew freely on his knowledge and suggestions... and always marvelled at his generosity of spirit....
>
> To... I owe more than I can express. The impact of his lectures, altogether magical in my memory, grows rather than diminishes with each passing year...

To... a brilliant and provocative presence in the classroom, I owe whatever sensitivity and appreciation I have for the science of social science. (More thanks to more people follow)

The author of a popular introductory text in sociology writes:

In the preparation of this book I benefited tremendously from the help of a number of people... scholars in several fields were kind enough to read part or all of the original manuscript. My only complaint is that they had so many valuable suggestions that the preparation of the book took much longer than I had planned...

I also owe a special debt to... (the sociology editor of the publisher). His skillful assistance and constant support have been invaluable, and his good humor and enthusiasm made our collaboration a pleasure.

A skillful typist is also a tremendous asset and it was my good fortune to have an excellent one...

The acknowledgements further suggest that not only were the authors fortunate to have brilliant, knowledgeable and authoritative people at their disposal at every step of their undertaking but that these people, in addition to their scholarly qualifications and excellence, were also impressive human beings—patient, kind, sensitive, good humored and good natured.

*　　*　　*

The observations made so far were based on acknowledgements written by men. To find out if female authors approach the task differently, I sampled a comparable number of social scientific (largely sociological) books by female scholars published mostly during the 1980s and 1990s. My findings follow.

The author of a study published in the early 1990s displays all the attributes noted earlier. She writes:

I have been blessed with so much support and accumulated so many debts along the way that it is hard to know where to begin... my words are destined to fall short....

I was fortunate to spend a year in academic paradise as a visiting scholar at.... Surrounded by a uniquely inspiring and stimulating group of colleagues and provided with an exceptionally dedicated support staff....

It has been an honor to work with a group of gifted and dedicated editors... (who) supported me with enthusiasm, creativity and intelligence... a masterful editor whose unerring eye helped me shape the book in a new way... (another editor) rescued me from my worst stylistic habits.... Whatever grace and good sense can be found in these pages is in large measure due to... keen insight and ... deft editorial touch....

Special friends and relatives sustained me and kept me sane through this long project.... My parents... my sisters... (...) nourished me intellectually and emotionally remaining treasured friends and supporters.... (...) provided warmth, friendship and sustenance (both psychological and culinary)... (...) was always there with the nurturance, love and good cheer to keep my spirits up.... Immeasurable thanks go to all of these people for making my life not only full, but fun.

It is impossible to find the right words to thank my husband... and my daughter...

From another volume we learn that "No author is ever alone in writing a text and my indebtedness goes beyond the footnotes and bibliography. It is with great pleasure that I begin by thanking my loving husband... for his enthusiastic support and unwavering encouragement over the years I spent writing this book.... His words of encouragement sustained me through the difficult periods..."

The author of a study on childcare could not have written her book without her "committed teachers... who nurtured (her) passion for scholarship..." she was "blessed in being able to study with..." Her teachers "went beyond the bounds of generosity in mentoring (her) on this project..." Like so many others she also had "a superb research assistant." Every member of her family "has been a source of sustenance and support..." She had "many wonderful conversations with (her) lifelong friend..."; (...) "provided emergency lodging and emotional support during a crucial stage..." and "boosted (her) spirits." Another individual is thanked for her "love, support and humor" that "enriched" her life.

Adding a homey touch to her accolades an author expressed "special gratitude" to the owners of her temporary lodgings "who sent me off with a gift of homemade blackberry jam" and to colleagues "who listened thoughtfully over weekly breakfasts to a series of shifting ideas in a continual blizzard of drafts." Her editor "didn't simply read the manuscript, he inhaled it." Another "extraordinary" editor accomplished "ridding the text of remaining cobwebs...sharing brilliant minds and prodigious energy..." Her typist "kept an eagle eye for errors and maintained her good humor... combine(ing) first rate work with acts of kindness and moments of great fun... (her) partner on the long journey, has been more important to my basic feeling about life than I can say."

The "homey touch," that is, the desire to bring into the acknowledgement something ordinary yet colorful (perhaps to provide relief from weightier academic and intellectual matters which follow) is also apparent in an another author's reference to a "close friend" who helped her to "sketch out the structure of the book on a napkin at the Au Bon Pain"—a restaurant in Cambridge or Boston.

A study dealing with particular problems of women "has been a labor of love and sorrow. Along the way I have been blessed with the companionship of many people who... held me with their emotional, intellectual and financial support..." The same author also thanks her mother "for her passion of poetry and art..." her grandmother and sister and a friend "for her generous spirit, irreverence and passion for music and writing." An "extraordinary group of scholars" taught her "about the life of the mind and the power of intellectual thought as a tool of liberation."

The author of a 1996 study exemplifies lyrical effusiveness to an unusual degree:

> (...) offered me the treasure of his ironic humor and his loyal friendship... gave me the courage and strength to make my feminism a part of my sociology; her warmth and support helped to stay course... (...) cared for me in the same deep and honest way he cares for the world... (!) (...) was always available to buy me coffee, listen to my complaints and offer his reassurances... (...) was and is both my harshest critic and one of my most unflagging and generous supporters... to each of these people I am eternally grateful...
>
> (...) agonized with me over each step of the process. She stayed inside my head and constantly nourished my soul... (...) gave me her friendship at a time when I felt lost in an unfamiliar wilderness... offering both comfort and insightful criticism....
>
> My manuscript editor... impressed and overwhelmed me with her amazing attention to detail....
>
> Many thanks are also due to my husband... for all the times he did the dishes and went to the grocery store and folded the laundry and cooked the dinner and watered the plants even though it wasn't his turn....for fixing the leaking roof in my study,.... his own vision and artistry were a constant source of inspiration...from the depth of my heart I smother with kisses, shower with flowers and promise an endless supply of frozen yoghurt desserts to my beloved mother...

From the acknowledgements of a 1988 volume we learn that "it sometimes feels as though my friends and colleagues have dragged me through the project." Moreover, "I would have never completed this work without the constant prodding, critiques and suggestions from ... the best editor I have ever known and a treasured friend and colleague..." Such self-effacing confessions permeate the tributes written by women perhaps even to a greater degree than those of their male colleagues.

Let me briefly list a few further characterizations—intellectual and emotional—of the helpers found in these acknowledgements:

> "I dedicate this book to my mother and father...for their love and patience... and to my sisters...and their families for their friendship and support over the years... ; "I absorbed as much of their (reviewers' of the manuscript) brilliant and erudite feedback as I could manage...I have entered a state of permanent indebtedness to... his cautious praise...kept me optimistic and humble... (...) gifts of skill and wit made the journey from manuscript to book painless."

Elsewhere editors are thanked for their "wisdom, good humor and endurance" and a reader of the manuscript "for his endless wisdom and emotional support" alongside the obligatory reference to "superb" staff and mentors the author was "fortunate to have"; altogether 103 people are thanked and mentioned by name in this volume.

In a 1986 study the author reveals that (...) shared the anxieties and elations of graduate school and first jobs with me and I still rely on them for advice and support. My dance classes and MCI's phone service provided me with much needed outlets during the process of research and writing... (...) helped me find important ideas buried beneath sometimes half-baked thoughts...his belief in me, when I stopped believing in myself, made a difference"; "My special thanks to... who opened their house, their ice cream freezer and Shakespeare and Company to me in a last idyllic summer of writing.... Three final debts to my parents, who laid the foundation for this book by teaching me that life derives its richness from our relationships with others... to my children, who continue to instruct me in these lessons..."; (...) went far beyond providing an organizational home for the project. He challenged me... the researchers... were an exceptional team... brought tremendous gifts of insight and caring to our work... Vital support roles were played by a wide array of talented people...; "...special debts to my literary agent and dear friend... to (...) who read, ripped apart, comforted and challenged... who read everything, put to rights many a clumsy passage... who lived with me and this book from its inception and whose mighty intelligence informs every page."; "Conversations with her have sparked new visions.... To say that her criticisms have been invaluable is an understatement... (...) has been an extraordinary helper with daring and unique ideas... (...) has been ineffably encouraging and enspiriting. She has helped the process of this book in ways that I cannot begin to count... ; "At every stage of our work we have benefited from the expertise, counsel and spirit of others.... Many friends and family members have given us moral support, extending kindness and care to us... replenishing our spirits at critical moments... Our ultimate debt is to the parents and grown children who... made this book possible and our work a pleasure.... Finally we would each like to acknowledge the other as mentor and muse (this book had two authors - P.H.)—a steady source of encouragement, ideas and insights"; "Thanks to my parents who...have been there for me through thick and thin. My brother... the quintessential comrade. My sister has performed every function a sister, friend and editor can perform... Thank you to my friends. For the things that makes sense, thank you to (...)." And so it goes.

It should be fairly clear from such quotes (and other tributes not cited) that there is no *fundamental* differences between the spirit, style, and substance of acknowledgements produced by males and females. But there are some differences. In the tributes produced by women there is far more reference to parents and siblings than in those of men. I was also struck by women mentioning nurturance and love (received) far more frequently than men. It seemed that writing a book was even more anxiety producing for women than for men. Sometimes this was made quite explicit:

> I find that when I try to write I am productive and enjoy the process about 5 percent of the time. The other 95 percent is pretty miserable. I am either producing bad drafts... going down false alleys, worrying that I have nothing new to say... that what I have to say is wrong, or just plain wishing I was doing something else. Something easier. As a result I would never have produced this book without a lot of help. I needed encouragement that it was worth doing... experts to help me get the facts rights, friends to help me decide which drafts to keep...

It testifies to the truth of the statement quoted that its author assembled the largest army of helpers I ran into: an astonishing total of 124 individuals are listed and thanked with various degrees of intensity. That includes parents, a mother-in-law, lots of brothers and sisters, nieces, and nephews and her husband. Regarding the latter she writes: "I could fill several books with all the ways I should acknowledge the contributions of my husband."

It seems that producing the works in question was more fraught with doubt and uncertainty for women, that their need for support and encouragement was even more voracious than the corresponding needs of men.

*   *   *

Acknowledgements with their endless references to the vast amounts of encouragement and support received invite speculations. Why do these authors profess to have such a huge, almost insatiable need for moral support and encouragement? Why this apparent precariousness of authorial motivation? What pressures compel these implausibly modest self-presentations?

Behind the facade of acknowledgements there may be a less inspiring, or at least far more prosaic reality. Academics, and especially those among them who write and publish books, are highly competitive, often abrasively individualistic, and not always affable "team players." Sad to say not all academic marriages are redolent with generosity of spirit, not all academic intellectuals are immersed in marital bliss nor are beneficiaries of stimulating intellectual exchanges with their spouses. Many academics are not especially anxious to devote vast amounts of their time to discussing, reading, or improving the writings of their colleagues. Moreover, and regrettably so, not all foundations are ready to shower us with grants and not all deans anxious to give us leaves to further the creative process; many editors are less than magnificently endowed with the skills needed to improve our manuscripts or interested in the ideas we wish to convey. (Editors, as part of the publishing enterprise are duty bound to focus on the "bottom line" which often means relentless pressure to shorten and simplify manuscripts in deference to market considerations.)

How then may one attempt to account for the tone and quality of acknowledgements and the gap between appearance and reality they so strongly suggest?

Scholarly acknowledgements are a ritual, a form of paying lip service to deeply entrenched conventions. They are social facts in exactly the sense Durkheim used the term: external to the individual, taken for granted, and exerting of strong pressure to conform to their unwritten requirements. They are opportunities for affirming and reaffirming the values of one's profession, marital bonds, collegial ties, and a sense of community within the academic setting. They also represent a facade concealing unstated motives, calculations, and compulsions.

Academic intellectuals, like most ordinary mortals, conform, consciously or not, to many social-cultural expectations, norms, and values. In their acknowledgements they appear to seek to reassure the reader that despite their rigorous, dedicated, and somewhat impersonal scholarly pursuits they did not cease to be normal, regular human beings capable of warmth, affection, feeling, and gratitude, that they are still enmeshed in personal relations, they did not become isolated, humorless workaholics churning out publications to improve their standing in their profession, and get promotions and pay raises.

In other words, acknowledgements intend to show that success and accomplishment have not gone to the head of their author, that he remains a modest person, an ordinary fellow, a team player and good family man or woman, a member of his or her group and community who is not embarrassed to rely on the help of others. In this regard they resemble politicians running for office who regularly allude to their families, neighbors, hobbies, and other matters that make them seem more ordinary and human. A well-known historian dedicates his book to the local "Boys' Soccer Team" which he had "the pleasure of coaching..."—an activity he regards as "a wonderful escape from one's books, files and statistics" and one which happily proves that he is not a "single-minded scholar." Elsewhere an editor of a volume confides in the reader that the book was conceived in the congenial atmosphere of "an intense week of debate interrupted by cutting onions and uncorking bottles." There were all the other nostalgic recollections of sharing ice cream, frozen yoghurt, coffee, hearty meals, and displaying other expressions of reassuring and cheerful ordinariness. In all such references there lurks a recognition of an implicit deference to the surviving anti-intellectual traditions of American life.

As to the tendency to name dropping—the lengthy lists of benefactors, often more distinguished than the author—there is safety in numbers and in associating the work with other individuals, a bolstering of credibility notwithstanding the incantation that none of those mentioned are responsible for the views expressed or conclusions reached. This is not to deny that large-scale data collection does involve large numbers of people who deserve credit for their work.

The extravagant and often lyrical praise of spouses may in part be explained by the character of many academic marriages leading to a compensatory motivation on the part of husbands. Even in more recent times male academics are often married to comparably well-educated women who raise children, take care of the household, do volunteer work or have part-time jobs and make little use of their education or professional qualifications. (This was especially the case during the 1960s and 70s). Such a disparity is often a source of marital tension and spousal frustration, especially since the rise of militant feminism. Husbands whose career often rested on spousal support had reason to feel some guilt or unease under these circumstances. The extravagant praise of wives and their intellectual contribution to the work in question is an attempt to compensate spouses whose professional competence, educational qualifications, and intellectual potential were not fully realized if at all. To be sure, this explanation cannot be extended to the female author's tributes to the men (or women) in their lives.

The implausibly modest and self-effacing tone of so many acknowledgements may be rooted in the deep-seated and durable American cultural and psychological conflict between the values of egalitarianism and achievement. Successful academic intellectuals apparently feel some pressure to play down their accomplishments, or claims to excellence (at any rate, in public statements) and they do so energetically and with apparent conviction on the occasion here discussed. The public display of humility moderates the individualistic, accomplishment-driven motives that lead—in the case of academics—to the writing of books. Producing a scholarly volume is intended not merely to advance knowledge. Only the well-published academic can expect to rise in his profession; he may not "perish" without publishing but access to tenure, higher rank and salary, or more distinguished places of employment is based on publications and the attention they attract. Whatever the intrinsic rewards of research and writing, they cannot be separated from such extrinsic rewards and from the authors' mobility aspirations. Many Americans, and especially academic intellectuals, while intensely driven to succeed are somewhat ambivalent about a high social-professional status and the income that goes with it, about being part of a society in which rewards are unequally distributed. Many highly educated Americans yearn for lesser inequalities, for genuine equality of opportunity, or better yet, equality of condition or reward.

The self-effacing attitudes here noted may also have something to do with an unease about being a full-time intellectual, a bookish, reflective person in a culture that values action, teamwork, and physical strength and nurtures a degree of suspicion of reflection and intellectuals. As Saul Bellow noted, "the main facts of American life are productive. The overwhelming fact is that of a manufacturing and business civilization. Money, production, politics, planning, administration, expertise... these are what absorb mature men."[5]

It is a further possibility that the sociologists' large contribution to the production of these apologetic and self-denigrating acknowledgements has something to do with the uncertain status and accomplishments of their discipline. Sociology is a newcomer to the academic world, its recognition as a legitimate discipline relatively recent. It remains difficult to explain even to well-educated people exactly what sociologists do, or hope to accomplish, whether it is a scientific discipline or not, and how it has contributed to either our welfare or enlightenment.

Sociologists, by virtue of the basic premises of their discipline, are also more aware of the social aspect or implication of any activity, of the links between the strictly individual and the social, hence the insistent linking of their work to the cooperation and advice of their colleagues, friends, or relatives. From the sociological point of view hardly any human activity is without a group connection or influence.

These effusive, self-effacing tributes also reflect the intellectuals' attempt to gain control over an inherently anxiety-producing situation—the writing and publishing of a book. Much is at stake when an academic volume is launched and everything possible has to be done by the author to reassure himself that the effort was worth making and that the book deserves a favorable reception.

Acknowledgements finally provide an opportunity for a personalized, non-intellectual self-presentation, for showing that the author is a decent human being, likeable and well liked, well connected and integrated into his occupational setting, conscious of his familial and collegial obligations, modest, and good natured. In these tributes authors seek to shed some light on the human being behind the academic intellectual and its highly specialized occupational role; they also provide a glimpse at a wishful fantasy of a way of life and relationships academic intellectuals aspire to.

Notes

1.   Although this is an impressionistic account the reader is entitled to know how I chose my sources and examples. The selection process was truly "random" though not in a social scientific sense. First I looked at my own books which accumulated over a period of forty years; subsequently at those of three colleagues each of whom has different professional interests reflected in their respective libraries.

How did I choose the actual volumes from these four collections? How did I decide which ones to take off the shelf?

I disregarded slim volumes (on the assumption that there was in them less to acknowledge) and those published before the 1960s since I did not intend a historical survey. I also avoided considering acknowledgements that were very short, that is, less than a page.

Even after noting such criteria of selection there remained a partial randomness to the actual process of selection. I was less inclined to reach for books which were physically less accessible, that is, on very high or very low shelves. What books placed high or low had in common and what bias their placement and subsequent avoidance (on my part) introduced is hard to say.

All this still leaves open the question of what is the likely ratio of books with short acknowledgements (and lacking in the attributes which inspired this essay) and those longer and effusive? Whatever the ratio there is a huge number of books with the kind of acknowledgements examined below.

2.   Eugene Goodheart: *The Reign of Ideology*, New York: Columbia University Press, 1997, p.18

3.   In a famous study in social psychology 63 individuals were thanked; in a well-known sociological study 67, in another one 103. The number peaked at 124.

4.   All quotes are anonymous since I don't wish to embarrass anybody. I took however note of the source of each quote and on request can supply them to the reader doubtful of their authenticity.

5.   Saul Bellow: "Scepticism and the Depth of Life" in James E. Miller and Paul D. Herring eds.: *The Arts and the Public*, Chicago: Chicago University Press.

Part 2

Soviet Communism: Its Fall and Aftermath

14

The Mystery of the Transformation
of Communist Systems

"Our insufficient scientific knowledge allows us to foresee little or nothing."
—*Wilfredo Pareto*

The collapse of communist systems[1] provided new evidence of the modest powers of prediction of the social sciences including sociology. Because most American sociologists had little interest in such systems to begin with, their inability to predict their demise should not be surprising. In any event they are in good company since virtually nobody-including those more deeply concerned with these systems in their professional capacity-predicted their speedy unravelling and the circumstances under which this would take place. There were those such as Robert Conquest (1990), the eminent student of the Soviet system, who was "on record that the Soviet system was not viable. What took him by surprise was the speed of the collapse." Admittedly these transformations were unusual, since "In the case of the political restructuring of Eastern Europe in 1989, there was no external threat, no military defeat; to a large extent this was an unprecedented case of a privileged class (that is, the Communist nomenklatura) which, responding to internal pressures for economic and administrative reform, consented to a transfer or sharing of power" (Tiryakian 1991, p. 166).

But if one had few reasons to expect sociologists to foresee these historical transformations should not our discipline, its theories and concepts help to understand these developments *at least in retrospect?*

Although a student of Soviet affairs and communist systems, I was among those who were taken by surprise by the events in Eastern Europe and the Soviet Union. I was incapable of imagining that these systems could fundamentally change in my lifetime, publicly discarding the official ideology, reestablishing free expression and political democracy, and seeking to privatize their economies. The following is both a personal and professional attempt to understand why it was so difficult to foresee these momentous developments and why it remains difficult to fully grasp them at the present time.

It should be noted at the outset that the current unraveling of communist systems refers to three processes in three regions. The first and most dramatic has been the collapse of what used to be the Soviet satellites in Eastern Europe and their virtual transformation into pluralistic societies (though of course even within Eastern Europe the process has varied among different countries, far more incomplete in Albania, Bulgaria, and Romania than in Czechoslovakia, East Germany, Hungary, and Poland). The second setting of similarly dramatic changes has of course been the Soviet Union itself which has moved in the same direction as its former satellites but more haltingly and contradictorily, and where the ruling Party continued to coexist uneasily with various other new social and political forces, at any rate until the failure of the coup of August 1991, which dealt an apparently fatal blow to the Party. Third, the unraveling of communist systems has also began in the Third World. In Nicaragua the pro-Soviet, pro-Cuban ruling party lost power through a free election; in Ethiopia the communist regime collapsed losing the long civil war; Angola and Mozambique began to democratize and undo the state control of the economy. Vietnam too has taken some steps to reform its economy and loosen repression through its ruling party retains the monopoly on power (Shenon 1991). Only China, Cuba, and North Korea remain defiantly untouched by the winds of change; though perhaps in China a slow process of political erosion has continued under the surface even after the massacres and repression of June 1989.

There have been at least four reasons for the failure to predict (and fully understand) the collapse of communist systems in the late 1980s. First, it is always difficult, if not impossible, to predict fundamental transformations as distinct from forecasting incremental change extrapolated from the familiar present by predicting a future that will be a modified version of the status quo. Major historical events not predicted or anticipated in this century include the Russian revolution of 1917, World War I, World War II, the rise of Nazism, the Holocaust, the Cold War, the Korean war, the extension of Soviet control over Eastern Europe after World War II, the invention of nuclear weapons, the Vietnam War and its impact on American society, the Western protest movements of the 1960s, the replacement of a taken for granted racism in the United States by the institutionalization of preferential treatment, and the rise of environmental problems and movements.

Second, if the prediction of genuine social change is always difficult, it is far more so when the change takes place in societies that are not well known or understood, where factual information is inadequate or limited. Until recently this was certainly the case of communist systems which generally wrapped themselves in secrecy, discouraged outside investigation or research, and were often also physically inaccessible either for reasons of geography or political controls, or both. Outsiders, whether social scientists or journalists, were hampered and discouraged from "seeing things for themselves" except in the framework of conducted and deliberately deceptive political tours (see Hollander 1981, 1986, 1987). Sometimes it took decades to learn about the specifics (or basics) of major historical events, as for example the human and economic costs of the Soviet campaign to collectivize agriculture, or the manner in which the Purge Trials were prepared and conducted in the Soviet Union and Eastern Europe, or the power struggles associated with the succession of major leaders in various communist states, or the magnitude of the political violence associated with the so-called Cultural Revolution in China. Data were unavailable (or unreliable) for more mundane matters such as public health, income distribution, death, birth, divorce, crime rates, prison populations, industrial or traffic accidents and many others. Often available data went unpublished. "The essential feature of the Soviet order was massive falsification about the economy, the past, about society, about ecology and about international political motives" (Conquest 1990).

It has also been argued that the problem was not the lack of information but the use to which information was put. For example, a Hungarian author wrote: "the failure of Sovietology to anticipate the crisis of the Soviet system was not due to insufficient levels of information but the placement of the processes which had been observed into such deductive contexts which were premised not on the collapse but long range survival of the system" (Kovacs 1991, p. 83).

This orientation excluded envisioning fundamental transformation and instead focused on the problem-solving capabilities of the system, the survival of which was taken for granted. Detente contributed to this frame of mind as Western leaders, scholars, and public opinion favored a stable and predictable Soviet government; thus an element of wishful thinking, born out of the desire for political stability, colored discussions of the Soviet system. Sometimes there was a failure to draw appropriate conclusions even inside communist societies from information that was available. A Hungarian economist, wrote:

> We knew for example that the socialist industry, indeed the socialist mode of production was not good for the environment, still we did not realize ... the degree of destruction it wrought.... We knew how much alcohol abuse there was, about the high rate of suicides, that in general people died younger than they should have. What we did not know was that these processes were so extensive and acute that they endangered the survival of the system itself. Many of our colleagues were well aware that this system is incapable of absorbing innovation, that the gap between the developed West and our world was growing. But we did not realize how huge this gap has become, how many generations behind our computers, antiaircraft missiles, and refrigerators were.... Everybody knew of the necessity to stand in line, that there were problems of quality as well as genuine scarcities, but for a long time we thought that these difficulties will diminish. Then in the 1980s we learned that they did not improve but got worse, in Poland, Romania, the Soviet Union and by now almost everywhere (in the socialist countries). (Laki 1991, pp. 81-82)

The same could be said about the dormant ethnic tensions and conflicts in the Soviet Union. Their existence was widely known (at least among specialists) but nobody was prepared to say when or how they would erupt and contribute to the decay of the Soviet system. Not unlike economic difficulties, the destabilizing potential of ethnic conflict had been present for decades, indeed from the earliest days of the Soviet Union, but the system managed to live with it, to keep it under control.

It is in the changing ability of communist systems to keep things under control that one must look for the key variable for understanding the recent changes. Even in the countries that subsequently underwent these radical transformations the rapid unraveling of these systems was not seriously anticipated despite the daily experience of their weaknesses and vulnerabilities. In spite of their enormous and visible defects-their inefficiency and mendacity-these systems succeeded impressing both their own citizens and publics abroad with their staying power, monolithic facade, and determination to hang on to power. "There were those who believed that dictatorship makes for stability. No unemployment, no strikes, nobody talking back, a calm atmosphere" (Laki 1991, p. 82).

The third impediment to the better understanding and anticipation of change in these systems have been the theories, concepts, and approaches which were developed for their analysis. As it turned out they did not help to predict change, or not along the lines in which it finally took place. The theories of totalitarianism in particular, which had been widely used in the study of these systems (at least up to a point in time) were indeed unhelpful in predicting change as critics of the theory claimed (see for example Cohen 1985). Yet the totalitarian model did help for lengthy periods to understand the nature of these systems and the interdependence of their institutions. The model also helped to grasp the characteristic relationship between political belief and political action, the mentality of the ruling elites, their attitudes toward power (until recently), and the assumptions governing the distinctive policies of coercion and political violence (sometimes called "prophylactic") that used to be peculiar to communist systems (see Friedrich 1954). While among those who found the totalitarian model applicable to most communist systems for much of their existence, I am ready to admit that these theories provided no help in predicting or understanding their unraveling and no clues to grasping their weaknesses.

This is not to say that other theories or approaches were more helpful. A form of liberal, non-Marxist economic determinism that shaped the outlook of many observers and students of Soviet type societies confidently predicted that change and democratization of these systems will someday occur as a byproduct of improved economic efficiency and productivity and the associated higher living standards. The growth of political pluralism and free expression was supposed to rest on greater material wealth, on overcoming "backwardness." Believers in what used to be called the "convergence theory" proposed that under economic pressures and increasingly similar levels of institutional complexity, capitalist and state socialist systems (or the United States and the Soviet Union) will become increasingly and benignly alike. (There were also a few pessimists who expected the least pleasant attributes and problems of these systems to converge.)

As it turned out the dramatic and wholly unforeseen shift to more democratic and less imperialist policies occurred, in the Soviet Union, under the pressure of severe economic problems of crisis propor-

tion, including the sharp decline of productivity, a stubbornly inefficient economy and system of administration, and a stagnant work
ethic. Contrary to prior conventional wisdom, it was not the security
provided by a strong economy and a satisfied population that
prompted the Soviet leaders to loosen their grip on power but their
alarm and insecurity over an increasingly unproductive economy,
technologically backward military establishment, and impoverished
society. It was the chronic malfunctioning of the system that led to the
introduction of greater freedom of expression and association and even
to renouncing the Party's monopoly on power and to the abandonment
of basic tenets of the official ideology. It was the increasingly manifest
bankruptcy of the Soviet-socialist economic policies and institutions
which forced the Politburo to look for salvation, however hesitantly,
in the forces of the market and private enterprise.

To begin with, the Soviet political elite, Gorbachev included, was
not interested in a complete overhaul of Soviet institutions:

> In April 1984, after the swamp of the Brezhnev-Chernenko years, the nomenklatura
> delegated power and the right to reshuffle personnel to a reform-minded leader, charg-
> ing him with carrying out a modernization of the political system, but without changing
> its fundamental structure and maintaining the basic prerogatives of the apparatus. In his
> speech to the All-Union Student Forum in November 1989, Gorbachev acknowledged
> that initially the issue was only that of straightening out certain deformations in the
> social organism. (Bunin 1991, p. 30)

What began as an attempt to reform (rather than transform) the
system subsequently led to unintended changes, to the loss of control and political cohesion, especially as the long suppressed ethnic
rivalries resurfaced.

In Eastern Europe, once the Soviet imperial will was undermined
and the Brezhnev Doctrine[2] publicly repudiated, the changes were a
more or less foregone conclusion. The Eastern European societies
were ready to discard the Soviet-imposed structures when it was
clear that Soviet force will not be used to prevent these transformations as had been the case on earlier occasions (East Germany in
1953, Hungary in 1956, and Czechoslovakia in 1968). This is how
a former Hungarian dissident, currently the mayor of Budapest, described these processes in Hungary (which were also taking place in
other parts of Eastern Europe):

> Change did occur... after the communists realized that they could not control the eco-
> nomic bankruptcy of the policies they had provoked. They realized that the populace

would not continue to tolerate the steady decline of their living standards... They realized that Hungary would soon be unable to meet its debt payments and that the West would not extend new loans. They realized that they could preserve their power only by brute force and dictatorship... that resorting to force would make Hungary's isolation from the rest of Europe permanent.. they also knew that tanks would not cure the nation's economic ills.... Four decades of communist doctrine had not induced the majority of the nation to identify with the Communist cause. (Demszky 1991, pp. 46-47)

Astonishingly enough it emerged-and not only in Hungary and the rest of East Europe but also in the Soviet Union-that seventy or forty (as the case may be) years of political education and indoctrination had little or only a transient impact on generations raised and submerged in the Soviet-communist political culture. Having been blanketed by political slogans, propaganda and education all their lives seemed to have intensified the discontent generated by the system.[3] This too was a largely unexpected revelation of the last few years which most observers and students of communist systems were ill prepared to foresee or interpret even in retrospect. Western scholarship had no adequate theoretical or conceptual tools with which to grasp the depth and distinctive characteristics of the discontents communist systems generated and which in the final analysis provide the best explanation of their demise.

Among the Western and especially American concepts and approaches that proved unhelpful for predicting or even understanding in retrospect the breakdown of communist systems, mention should also be made of the moral equivalence "theory" hugely popular during the past twenty years or so. It postulated not merely that there was little to choose in moral terms between the United States and the Soviet Union but also that their shared shortcomings derived from institutional-structural similarities (for an exposition of the concept and its varied applications, see Barnet 1977). The idea of moral equivalence between the superpowers also proposed that both were equally responsible for the sorry state of the world, and especially the arms race, that both were unjust social-political systems and neither could claim any moral superiority over the other. Many more specific propositions were derived from the theme of moral equivalence: both countries are equally imperialistic; both countries are run by unpopular, amoral, and illegitimate elites (which take advantage of and seek to perpetuate the false consciousness of the masses); both countries pollute the environment and fail to meet the spiritual needs of their citizens, among other things. It should be noted here that the uses of this concept tended to be far from even-handed; more often than not the United States was perceived as more responsible for the problems of the world than the Soviet Union, more bellicose, more uncompromising, more riddled with social injustice, more corrupt, and so forth. The reflections of the British author Jan Morris provide a good example of this asymmetry:

> you are both paranoiac-two ideologically stunted giants... whose preposterous dinosaurian posturings menace the survival of everyone. But the Russians have cause to be paranoiac! ...They are a grand and tragic nation. But you! The most powerful, the most enviable, the richest, the most fortunate nation of the world. You have no excuse for paranoia. (1983)

The moral equivalence approach was especially popular among the Western supporters of the peace movements in the 1980s (and before) who regarded a critical view of the Soviet Union as a source of friction predisposing to conflict and therefore to be avoided at all costs. This outlook denied or seriously obscured differences of all kinds between the super powers, be they historical, cultural, political-institutional, economic. Not surprisingly this approach also made it difficult to discern the differences between the stability and legitimacy of these two systems resting on well defined structural differences.[4]

It is clear in retrospect that the critical view of the Soviet Union and other communist systems was more informative and accurate than the benignly uncritical one which overlooked the distinctive characteristics and vulnerabilities of these systems ultimately leading to their breakdown. To the extent that the moral equivalence school perceived and multiplied alleged similarities between the United States and the Soviet Union, it has also been nourished by the irresistible American disposition to project characteristics of American society upon others. Richard Pipes (1984), the historian of Russia, wrote:

> Nothing is more difficult to convey to an American audience (than the idea)... that Soviet society and its political culture are significantly different from those familiar to Westerners.... Americans feel uncomfortable when told that other people are "different"...because it is a basic premise of American culture.., that people are everywhere the same and only conditions under which they live differ. This belief in the identity of human nature and human interests and the view that conflict is rooted in ignorance, prejudice and misunderstanding is the source of the widespread belief that if the American and Soviet leaders only got together they could solve all the problems dividing their countries. (pp. 278-279)

The Western and especially American approach toward the study of the Soviet system was also plausibly criticized for focusing "on a presumed center consisting of the quantifiables, the economy, the armed forces... .The periphery-geographical, social, cultural, ethnic-was neglected. The imported Western presumptions of economic rationality had left little room for the traditions and values that shape behavior in different cultures." The Western models were criticized as having "left out the passions-the appeal of ethnic loyalty and nationalism, the demands for freedom of religious practice and cultural expression, and the feeling that the regime had simply lost is moral legitimacy" (Connor 1991, pp. 177, 176).

More recently a new effort was made to offer a theoretical scheme for understanding these developments in Eastern Europe (including the Soviet Union) by placing them in a broader, global and chronological context. Tiryakian wrote:

> I would propose that this set of movements (i.e., especially those in the communist countries) be viewed as a Third Wave of post-World War II protest movements directed towards challenging the authority and legitimacy of the modern state... (and) ... a Third Wave of social mobilisation against the modern authoritarian state. The cluster of these movements of democratisation include their manifestation in Chile, South Africa, China (the only negative outcome) and above all, the various movements in what had been during the Cold War viewed as the... "Soviet Bloc." (1991, pp. 167. 168)

Tiryakian designated as the first wave the post-World War II anticolonial movements for independence in the Third World and the second wave the unrest and protests of 1968 occurring mostly in Western countries.

Although at a very high level of generality similarities may be discerned among these three waves of protest movements (as well as others), the differences are far more striking. Indeed each wave had its peculiarities. To begin with the protests in Eastern Europe and other communist states were not directed against "the modern state" (a far too undifferentiated abstraction) but against very specific forms of domination embodied in Marxist-Leninist one-party systems. Moreover the rebels and reformers in communist systems admired the democratic Western states and sought to recreate them in their own countries. By contrast protestors in the West (not unlike the rulers of communist systems) had nothing but contempt for liberalism and bourgeois democracy, imbued as they were with diffuse utopian impulses and with a passionate rejection of life in modern industrial society, as experienced in the West. The Western protest movements of the 1960s became increasingly radical, intolerant and hostile to Western values, including cultural values. They were utopian movements, seeking an elusive blend of individual fulfillment and communal bliss, indifferent to and uncomprehending the problems of real scarcity which understandably enough were matters of concern both to the protest movements in the Third World and to those in communist states. In turn protest movements in the Third World were narrowly focused on national independence and displayed from the beginning an authoritarian streak which reached full fruition with the seizure of power. Virtually none of these postcolonial societies became democratic or promoted broad popular participation in matters public and political, nor were they preoccupied with the dehumanization visited upon human beings by modernity, the material blessings of which they also coveted.

Among the distinctive attributes of communist systems was the capability to generate intense and durable discontent due to the widespread experience and awareness of the gulf between theory and practice, propaganda and reality, political promise and material fulfillment. In every society social ideals diverge from daily practices but communist systems magnify and intensify awareness of this divergence by the flagrant and routinized denials of reality, by the magnitude of their promises and the massiveness of their propaganda campaigns to which they subject their population. Rather than succeeding in indoctrinating or brainwashing their people, these systems implanted historically unparalleled levels of cynicism, dissatisfaction, sense of deprivation and disgust with the powers-to-be. These attitudes may for long periods of time remain invisible, repressed or suppressed as long as the risk of expressing them is unambiguously communicated by the authorities and the instruments of coercion are wielded without hesitation.

The reactions to the theory-practice gap, and the resulting loss of legitimacy of communist systems, cannot be assimilated into a theory of a general legitimation crisis of the modern state entertained by Habermas and endorsed by Tiryakian (1991, p. 169). Submerging the distinctive features of these three waves of protest and placing them into a broad global context do not help to better grasp the character of any one of them and especially those which erupted in the late 1980s in communist states.

Both favorable and antagonistic attitudes toward communist systems gave rise to misconceptions. Neither those favorably inclined nor those hostile toward these systems were in a good position (for different reasons) to envisage their breakdown or radical transformation. However, I am persuaded that on the whole those critical had a better understanding of how these systems functioned, if not of how they disintegrated. While those favorably inclined overlooked or outright denied the loss of legitimacy of these systems, those critical regarded their illegitimacy and unpopularity as inconsequential for their survival.

Although not disposed to confuse the facade of unanimity and spurious mass support with genuine legitimacy and the strength it yields, those critical of communist systems (including this writer) nonetheless greatly overestimated their cohesiveness and staying power. Since they regarded these systems both morally flawed *and* threatening, it was hard to reconcile these notions with the idea of vulnerability and to perceive of the link between the liabilities and defects of these systems and the nascent forces for change. The critics believed that popular dissatisfaction, contained for so long by proven techniques of intimidation, was largely irrelevant for the survival of these systems as long as a committed and privileged elite, and groups subservient to them, remained in control of institutions vital for the preservation of power and as long as the subservient majority internalized its own powerlessness.

In all these assessments threat or risk perception also played a part. To the extent that communist systems were seen as dangerous they could not also be perceived as weak. By the same token, those favorably disposed toward these systems were likely to emphasize some of their weaknesses which made them less threatening in their eyes. Thus a selective threat (or risk) perception also influenced perceptions of the character of communist systems and estimates of their benign transformation (on theories of risk perception, see Wildavsky and Dake 1990).

In other words, the critics, including this author, were well aware of the unpopularity, illegitimacy, repressiveness, material backwardness, economic malfunctioning, administrative inefficiency and general mismanagement prevalent in these countries. They were also keenly aware of the vast gulf between the promises and the accomplishments of these governments but they still believed that they could persist indefinitely despite these shortcomings. This belief was probably reinforced by the lingering influence of the totalitarian model which highlighted the unique organizational and coercive strengths of these systems.

It appeared that these highly unpopular and depriving systems could persist for several reasons. One were the refinements in methods of social control and the resulting high and stable levels of intimidation among the population. Here were polities designed to function without the consent of the governed who were not only regimented by an exceptionally powerful and inventive police state apparatus but also systematically deprived, over time, even of visions of alternatives to the existing regime. Moreover, there was little in the past history of these countries, and especially that of the Soviet Union, which would have provided a basis or model for a democratic or pluralistic reconstruction of society.

The critics, pessimistic about the possibilities of democratic change in communist systems, also concluded that their leading elites succeeded in stabilizing and keeping popular expectations low, especially the expansion of personal and group freedoms. Laki responded to the same question—why was the demise of these systems generally unanticipated—by stating: "On the one hand we underestimated the destablising forces, corroding the system, while on the other we overestimated the stabilising ones which helped the system to survive" (1991, p.81).

This is not to say that even in this perspective communist systems were perceived as completely immune to (milder forms of) change, especially in the East European countries such as Poland and Hungary, but these changes did not portend fundamental alteration in the distribution and exercise of power. Rather they amounted to the streamlining of these systems, to governing more with carrots than sticks, relying on what Marcuse called repressive tolerance in the Western context. Above all the critics believed that the ruling elites, whatever the degree of their ideological commitment, were determined to cling to their power and privilege, having convinced themselves-in some measure- of their legitimacy and historical mission.[5] Many of the pessimistic critics also believed that the authorities in these countries succeeded in indoctrinating their population to an extent that would prevent any overt expression of discontent, let alone organization of public opposition.

Those sympathetic toward these systems or at least "nonjudgemental" and disinterested in their moral qualities and vices, clung to a considerably wider range of misconceptions; they also evinced greater difficulties understanding and coming to terms with their recent transformations.

Generally speaking the sympathetic or nonjudgmental observers[6] were ill equipped to discern and fully grasp the profound weaknesses and moral failings of communist systems which proved consequential for their unraveling; preoccupied as they were with the corruptions and injustices of their own society they found it difficult to concede that any political system could be more flawed, onerous, unjust, or hypocritical than Western capitalist societies, especially the United States. The so-called revisionist historians even sought to revise (downward) the numbers of those killed under Stalin seeking to obscure the distinctive repressive qualities of the Soviet system even at its most totalitarian phase (for an exposition and critique of these views, see Kenez 1986).

A survey of the major misconceptions found among these commentators may begin with the idea that whatever was wrong with these systems was largely a result of unfortunate historical circumstances, underdevelopment, backwardness, lack of democratic tradition and often direct Western (or American) pressures (such as the arms race.) More generally this defense could be summed up in the maxim that "Socialism Would Have Turned Out To Be Much Better Had Capitalism Not Continued to Be Around To Corrupt It" (Fernandez-Morera 1991, p. 18). This idea was stunningly brought up to date by John Cole, an anthropologist, who suggested that

> the communist countries should have stayed on a road of purely socialist development instead of giving in to their citizens' demands for a more consumer-oriented economy. But because the West had the consumer goods, it was able in the 1980s to hoodwink the communist world into becoming trading partners which tied its economic well-being to the West's... 'The decline in the 1980s of world capitalism nailed Eastern Europe' Cole says, explaining the collapse of the East bloc (in Grossman 1991).

A crucial corollary of such beliefs was that nothing was seriously wrong with either the basic institutions of these countries or with the theory which inspired or legitimated these systems (Marxism or Marxism-Leninism); the difficulties lay only with the ways in which it was implemented. Some apologists seized the concept of Stalinism; not unlike Khrushchev, who in 1956 blamed all the ills and evils associated with Soviet rule on Stalin. For example Paul Robeson Jr. averred that the collapse of communist systems signified "the death of Stalinism and the birth of Marxism" (Baer 1990, p. 27). For the editors of *Nation* the exodus of East Germans into West Germany was proof that they did not abandon "the teachings of Karl Marx"; that would only have been the case had they chosen "Thatcher's Britain or après-Reagan America" ("Borderline Marxists" 1989, p. 1). Sam Bowles and Philip Green voiced the conviction that the collapse of these discredited regimes made Eastern Europe ripe for the establishment of authentic socialist systems "based on the writings of Karl Marx" (in Grabar 1989, p. 11). This conviction-that all was well with the theory-made it exceedingly difficult to grasp what went wrong with these systems, as it precluded an examination of the relationship between theory and practice as well as the recurring difficulty of applying the theory in the proper manner; and the reasons it lent itself invariably to distortions in the course of its attempted implementation.

Equally widely held was the notion that although not providing their people with "Western style" political freedoms, these systems met the major, basic needs of their populations perhaps at the expense of these bourgeois freedoms which, in any event, the people-raised in backward and antidemocratic societies-had no need or appreciation of. Even after the fall of these regimes, Harriet Gross, a professor of sociology, was not merely irritated with "all the self-righteous, sanctimonious celebration of the 'victory' of capitalism over Communism," but she also praised the accomplishments of these by now defunct systems: "These governments.., constructed massive social service delivery systems that eliminated illiteracy, petty street crime.., prostitution and a myriad of other social cancers.... Though disadvantaged in consumer gadgetry, their populations were well-educated and healthy" (1990). Her views echoed the tenacious, but erroneous and obsolete belief of Western sympathizers in the power of these systems to eliminate social problems such as noted above. In a similar spirit an editorial in the *Nation* summed up the victory of the opposition in the 1990 Nicaraguan elections as the accomplishment of "the freedom of the shopping mall" ("Spoils of War" 1990, pp. 367-368). What Gross and others sharing her beliefs were unaware of was that it was not merely the "consumer gadgetry" that these systems failed to provide in adequate quantity and quality but the basic necessities as well, such as food, housing, and medical care (on the deficiencies and decline of public health in the Soviet Union, see, for example, Eberstadt 1988, pp. 11-42).

Those more positively disposed toward communist systems also tended to believe that their leaders had a serious and abiding commitment to equality and in fact created egalitarian societies with modest income differentials. Thus, for instance, Sheldon Wolin wrote: "Even acknowledging gross distortions, Communist regimes have been the only ones that professed and to some degree achieved, a commitment to equality" (1990, p. 373). Apparently Wolin was among those nonjudgmental commentators who knew little about the nomenklatura and its vast, administratively allocated privileges which increased rather than diminished over time (see, for example, Matthews 1978; Voslensky 1984). In any event what mattered for him and others inclined to give these systems the benefit of doubt were their good intentions. As Richard Falk said about the Nicaraguan leaders: "(they) may be brutal, they may be imprudent in certain ways, but I think *they are basically trying* to create a much fairer social and economic order for their people. They have done wonderful things in education, extraordinary things" (1983, p. 9, emphasis added).

Perhaps the crucial, underlying misconception (flowing from the anticapitalist disposition of such authors) was that removing the means of production from private ownership was the key step toward a more humane, just, and caring society. Or, as Leszek Kolakowski put it, "once capitalists were done away with the whole world become a kind of Athenian agora: one had only to forbid private ownership of machines or land and, as if by magic, human beings would cease to be selfish and their interests would coincide in perfect harmony" (1981, p. *527).* These critics of capitalism also tended to believe that only under capitalism did social problems, such as crime, alcoholism, drug addiction, racial-ethnic discrimination, family instability, lack of work satisfaction, environmental destruction, and others flourish.

Interestingly enough, those favorably disposed toward communist systems often tended to confuse them with, or impute to them, the characteristics of traditional or partly traditional societies free of anomie, the excesses of individualism, social isolation, and spiritual malaise. It was widely believed that the communist states were successfully pioneering more humane forms of modernization which were compatible with the retention or reconstruction of sustaining communal ties. It was also widely held that these systems were possessed of a sense of purpose and in general better equipped to meet the spiritual needs of their people than Western societies.

Even if one had a more realistic view of these systems, fully aware of their repressiveness, inefficiency, illegitimacy, material and—spiritual poverty, endemic corruption, and mendacity it would still have been difficult to foresee their unraveling or postulate an approximate date when and how it would occur.

Why was this the case? What circumstances made it difficult to derive even from a correct grasp of the characteristics of these systems any prediction about their durability?

It would be futile to try to provide an answer that fits the case of each communist state that has undergone fundamental change in the last few years. In several (Hungary and Poland in particular) there was a period of a gradual erosion of the power of the party-state that preceded the dramatic changes of 1989. In the Soviet Union, although the changes did not go as far and so fast as in parts of Eastern Europe, the political relaxation was a lengthy and gradual process that began before Gorbachev and accelerated after his rise to power in 1985. If, as the conventional wisdom has it, the reforms were promoted by the perception on the part of the Soviet leadership of exceptionally grave economic difficulties, it must be asked, were these problems truly greater than those encountered earlier in Soviet history (which did not lead to liberalizing political responses), or was it *the attitude* of Soviet leaders which changed in confronting economic problems and popular discontent? It is my belief that the attitude of Soviet leaders had changed; that whatever the gravity of the more recent economic problems changes in these attitudes hold the key for understanding the transformations of the last few years.

What makes these shifts of attitude difficult to fathom is that the leaders displaying them were the product of a political culture (bequeathed by Lenin and institutionalized in the Party apparatus) in which holding on to power was the supreme value, overshadowing all other programs, policies, or principles. Nonetheless focusing on the Soviet political elite offers the best hope to unravel (or diminish) the mystery of the changes of the Gorbachev era and even the most recent developments, that is, the failed coup of August 1991, the ascendance of Boris Yeltsin, and the new measures introduced to transform Soviet political and economic life and what used to be the "union" itself.

Why these elites had lost their legitimacy (if they ever had it) is no great mystery. As Hans Zetterberg pointed out, "it is only the efficient elites- whether elected, appointed or self-chosen-that gain substantial support from those who are on the receiving end of their decrees, who buy their goods and services, who attend their sacred rites, who receive their knowledge" (1991, p. 21). They clearly were not efficient. These elites ceased to be what elites are supposed to be, "the strongest, the most energetic and most capable-for good as well as evil" (Pareto 1991, p. 36). Soviet political elites have become decreasingly efficient through the long Brezhnev era and were under Gorbachev incapable (or unwilling) to introduce the sought after reforms which would have addressed the needs of the economy and popular expectations. In fact, under Gorbachev shortages, inflation and inefficiency greatly increased. At the same time the determination of these elites to defend their power and prerogatives perceptibly diminished. As other declining elites, they became "softer, milder, more humane and less apt to defend... (their) own power" (Pareto 1991, p. 59). This even applies to the more conservative segments of this elite which in August 1991 sought to turn the clock back: Its coup attempt failed in part because it lacked the requisite ruthlessness and determination. The plotters failed to impose effective controls on the media (including foreign television reporters), they did not arrest at the very beginning (nor later) their political enemies and rivals such as Yeltsin, and did not use the troops at their disposal with the kind of cold-blooded determination the Chinese authorities had shown in June 1989 (or for that matter, which had been displayed by previous Soviet power holders confronting either domestic or foreign challenges to their power).

Why these attitude changes among the elite took place can only be a matter of speculation at the present time. The reasons are likely to include the generational factor and the delayed, lingering impact of Khrushchev's revelations and subsequent de-Stalinization.

In seeking better understanding of these matters further specific questions are to be asked. The answers hold the key to the broader question of why the attitudinal and institutional transformations occurred. Why did regular people (the nonelites) in the communist states, especially the Soviet Union, cease to be intimidated? More important, Why did the leadership, the decision-making political elite, lose the will to intimidate, and come to the conclusion that it was necessary to make sweeping political concessions in response to the economic difficulties? Why has the leadership lost its taste for coercive solutions and its capacity to control expectations? Why has it allowed more and more defiant forms of dissent to be voiced? Is it possible that the ruling groups themselves were also beginning to experience a crisis of belief, beginning to doubt their own legitimacy and historical mission? And if they did, was this merely the result of the discrediting of the Stalin period or other factors as well, and if so what were they? And if they too became disaffected did their doubts lead to indecisiveness and vacillation?

It is my belief that it is in the changing attitudes of the political elites of these states, and especially that of the Soviet Union, that we will find the answers to the mystery of the transformation of communist systems. As time goes by we will better understand the developments addressed above by gaining access to information about the evolution of the attitudes of the decision-making elites in the Soviet Union including their beliefs and moral conflicts during the past few years if not decades. Such information will also add to our knowledge of the behavior and psychology of political elites everywhere, even to our understanding of human nature, if such a notion can be entertained by a sociologist.

Notes

1. As in popular usage by "communist systems" I refer to those which were initially modeled after the Soviet Union (and of course the Soviet Union itself); more precisely, one-party police states which legitimate themselves by some variety of Marxism-Leninism and control the economy of the country.
2. The Brezhnev doctrine reserved the right to the Soviet Union to intervene militarily whenever any member of the "Socialist Commonwealth" was threatened by the possibility of being removed from this "commonwealth." It was formally announced in 1968 in justification of the invasion of Czechoslovakia. To be sure this was no change from earlier Soviet policy merely a more formal justification for it.
3. Just as I wrote these lines I saw on the news (on August 22, 1991) efforts of a crowd of young people in Moscow, including a special forces soldier, to pull down the statue of Dzerzhinski, founder of the Soviet political police, which stood in front of the headquarters of the KGB.
4. Attachment to the moral equivalence approach has been so strong that those who adopted it manage to find equivalents in the United States for each and every development in the Soviet Union and an occasion to mount criticism of the United

States. Thus even after the failed coup of August 1991 Tom Wicker wrote: "Some Americans have used that supposed (Soviet) threat to promote huge military expenditures or to thwart closer relations with Moscow; but their view- like the sour-faced men of the 'Emergency Committee'...has lost all credibility" (1991). Thus the occasion of this coup becomes a new opportunity to voice criticism of past American foreign and domestic policy and to equate the Americans who upheld these bad policies with the Soviet plotters, as both groups "lost all credibility."

5.   Gorbachev's reluctance, even after the failed coup attempt, to decisively renounce the Soviet Communist Party and the ideals this institution championed for so long, also illustrates the persistence of this commitment and the power of this sense of mission. It is all the more mysterious how other members of the same political elite, such as Yeltsin, and his many followers, could so decisively expunge these ideals and values from their outlook.

6.   Generalizations about these groups have to be qualified: for some decades now there has not been an undifferentiated group of left-wing sympathizers with all communist systems either in the United States or other western countries. In fact attitudes have varied considerably. What used to be called the New Left was disinclined to admire the Soviet Union and its East European dependencies while it was attracted at different points in time to various communist systems in the Third World, such as China, Cuba, Vietnam and most recently Nicaragua.

References

Baer, D. 1990. "Leftists in the Wilderness." *U.S. News and World Report* (March 19).

Barnet, R.J. 1977. *The Giants-Russia and America.* New York: Simon & Schuster.

"Borderline Marxists" (editorial). 1989. *Nation* (October 2).

Bunin, I.M. 1991. "Prospects for Democratization-A Roundtable on the Problems of Political Reform in the USSR." *Soviet Sociology* (March-April).

Cohen, S.F. 1985. *Rethinking the Soviet Experience.* New York: Oxford University Press.

Connor, W.R. 1991. "Why Were We Surprised?" *American Scholar* (Spring).

Conquest, R. 1990. "The End of Global Tick-Tack-Toe." *Washington Post* (April 2).

Demszky, G. 1991. "Building a Market Economy in Hungary." *Uncaptive Minds* (Summer).

Eberstadt, N. 1988. *The Poverty of Communism.* New Brunswick, NJ: Transaction.

Falk, R. 1983. Interview. *Prospect* (Princeton, NJ) (November).

Fernandez-Morera, D. 1991. "Materialist Discourse in Academia During the Age of Late Marxism." *Academic Questions* (Spring).

Friedrich, C.J., ed. 1954. *Totalitarianism.* Cambridge, MA: Harvard University Press.

Grabar, R. 1989. "Marxists in Area Predict Better Times for Socialism." *Daily Hampshire Gazette* (Northampton, MA) (February 8).

Gross, H.E. 1990. "Don't Count Communism Out Yet" (letter). *New York Times* (January 7).

Grossman, R. 1991. "The Marxist Brothers." *Chicago Tribune* (March 18).

Hollander, P. 1981. *Political Pilgrims: Travels of Western Intellectuals to the Soviet Union, China and Cuba 1928-1978.* New York: Oxford University Press.

_____ 1986. "Political Tourism in Cuba and Nicaragua." *Society* (May-June).

_____ 1987. "Socialist Prisons and Imprisoned Minds." *National Interest* (Winter).

Kenez, P. 1986. "Stalinism as Humdrum Politics." *Russian Review* (October).

Kolakowski, L. 1981. *Main Currents of Marxism* Vol. III, New York: Oxford University Press.

Kovacs, A. 1991. "Lattuk E, Hogy Jon?" (Have We Seen It Coming?) (symposium), *Buksz,* (Budapest), Spring.

Laki, M. 1991. Symposium, *Buksz* (Budapest), Spring.

Matthews, M. 1978. *Privilege in the Soviet Union-A Study of Elite Lifestyles Under Communism.* London: Allen & Unwin.

Morris, J. 1983. "Down, Down on America." *New York Times,* op-ed, November 13.

Pareto, V. 1991. *The Rise and Fall of Elites: An Application of Theoretical Sociology.* New Brunswick, NJ: Transaction Publishers.

Pipes, R. 1984. *Survival is Not Enough.* New York: Simon & Schuster.

Shenon, P. 1991. "Vietnam Party Vows to Maintain Absolute Power." *New York Times* (June 25).

"Spoils of War" (Editorial). 1990. *Nation* (March 19).

Tiryakian, E.A. 1991. "Modernisation: Exhumetur in Pace" (Rethinking Marcosocology in the 1991s). *International Sociology* (June).

Volslensky, M. 1984. *Nomenklatura-The Soviet Ruling Class.* Garden City, NY: Doubleday.

Wildavsky, A., and K. Dake. 1990. "Theories of Risk Perception: Who Fears What and Why?" *Daedalus* (Fall).

Wolin, S. 1990. "Beyond Marxism and Monetarism." *Nation* (March 19). Zetterberg, H.L. 1991. "Pareto's Theory of Elites: Introduction."

Zetterberg, H.L. 1991. "Pareto's THeory of Elites: Introduction."

15

Why Communism Collapsed in Eastern Europe

Most current problems in Eastern Europe fall into two broad categories. There are the structural, especially economic, problems following from the unprecedented historical move from a state socialist to a market-based or capitalist economic system undreamed of in the philosophy of Marx and his followers. The idea that a social system might move, that is, regress, from a supposedly superior, historically advanced socialist to a supposedly outmoded capitalist mode of production was inconceivable for Marxist theoreticians. Such possibilities were not even easy to entertain for non-Marxist, non-leftist critics. Re-privatizing on a national scale is a novel historical experience. The most concrete expression of the economic problems is found in declining living standards caused by rising prices, stagnant incomes, and the beginnings of unemployment.

The second category of problems may be called the morning after reactions. The communist dictatorship collapsed; the Soviet troops left; national independence has been regained; freedom of speech and association has been restored; political parties and other organizations have emerged in abundance; democratic elections were held; travel restrictions were lifted; streets were renamed; history is once more rewritten but in a more truthful manner. Still, not everybody is convinced that fundamental change has taken place. According to Imre Pozsgay, perhaps the best known "reform communist" in Hungary, what transpired was "a change of power of limited substance that involved merely an exchange of elites." Ottilia Solt, a parliament member representing the major opposition party and veteran opposition activist during the Kadar years, believes that Kadarism is being rebuilt by the new government. In her view the state domination of society persists. She is concerned about the centralizing intentions of the new government. A former Hungarian official in charge of cultural matters said: "We used to celebrate November 7th [the anniversary of the Russian Revolution] in the Opera House with long and boring speeches. Now we celebrate the anniversary of the 1956 Revolution in the Opera House with long and boring speeches."

Critics of the present Hungarian government also like to complain about the allegedly low quality of the current leadership. "Counter selection" was an expression often heard. The new authorities prefer loyalty over expertise, I was told. According to well-founded rumor, the pool from which the prime minister selected people for high positions was his graduating class at his Catholic high school. Perhaps it is not surprising that the initial euphoria has evaporated. One response to the vast changes, inconceivable for decades, is captured in the phrase and attitude: "So what? You cannot eat free expression or political pluralism." A taxi driver said: "Changing all the street names and the Hungarian coat of arms were not the most urgent tasks! These things cost a lot—including the new identity documents—while there is no money for children's hospitals and old pensioners have little to eat."

Many of the nagging major and minor problems of life undoubtedly persist. There is more crime in the streets than used to be during the decades of the discipline and fear of authority even a more moderate police state, such as Hungary, was capable of imposing. The police is said to be demoralized and badly paid hence not especially anxious to chase criminals. The housing shortages did not go away—indicated, among other things, by the fact that people still know exactly how many square meters their lodgings consist of. There is air and all other types of pollution. There are the basically meaningless and tiresome daily routines. The ends of life remain murky except for those participating in the religious revival. Life in an open, pluralistic society is in many ways less sheltered and more problematic than life under a regimented, authoritarian or totalitarian system. Vaclav Havel, the former president of Czechoslovakia, pointed this out when he said:

> Life under totalitarianism had certain advantages. These did not flow from its program, but rather from the fact that we were suffocated by the system. And that awakened certain potentials in people that would not be expressed to the same extent in a normally

functioning democracy. The crisis of values in advanced European civilization is a deep one. Because we have lacked much of what people have in free, prosperous countries, we have not succumbed to the crisis phenomena that come from a state of general prosperity...the Dutch prime minister told me that the main problem in his society was the loss of sense of the meaning of life. The young generation in particular is expressing frustration at the fact that they have everything.

Another aspect of the new problems and complications was noted by my interpreter in Prague, a young student of English and political science, herself a serious convert to Catholicism, locked in conflict with her atheistic parents: "Things were easier in the past when we were all united against the system and it was clear who we were for or against; now there are so many conflicts among the former critics of the system." Much remains to be learned about the discomfort associated with political and intellectual pluralism and the lack of certainty.

I spent November 1991 in Prague and Budapest to begin a study of the collapse of communist systems, a phenomenon I had trouble understanding despite the many theories and postmortems which have sprung up and despite my previous studies of these systems. Not only did I not imagine or anticipate the events of the last three years, and especially of August 1991 (as regards what used to be the Soviet Union) I also found it difficult to find satisfactory explanations in retrospect.

To understand one must be clear as to what it is that needs to be understood. Wherein lies the mystery or the puzzle of the collapse of communism, what exactly is there to explain? What remains to be explained is, most obviously, the enormity and speed of social-political change nobody had expected, the collapse, the total transformation of a political system centered in Moscow, the acquiescence or passivity of the political police forces, the fast unravelling of the Soviet Empire, and the corresponding political-social transformations in what used to be the communist states of Eastern Europe.

Also in need of explanation is why these changes occurred when they did, why they did so without external pressure (for example, war or the threat of war)? Why and how these systems managed to endure so long, given the depth and intensity of popular rejection that became apparent in the last few years? At last, why were these systems, and especially the Soviet Union thought to be so durable by those in the West? Why were the experts just as mistaken about these matters as the general public, the politicians and journalists? As historian Martin Malia wrote recently:

Mainline American Sovietologists have long misconstructed the Soviet system, making it appear much more of a success than it really was. They argued that the USSR developed into an 'institutional pluralism,' and was thus capable of a "transition" to some sort of social democracy. Their processing of flawed Soviet data through Western models for calculating GNP produced an economic success story that augured well for an evolution to democracy.... Thus we were presented with a maturing Soviet society quite prepared to make a wager of perestroika a success so such authorities as professors Jerry Hough and Stephen Cohen, for five years, regularly assured us. But the exit from communism, when it came, was not a transition or an evolution. It was a brusque collapse, a total implosion of a sort unheard of in history.

Did the leaders, who had committed their lives to the political culture and system that collapsed, realize that these systems were deeply flawed and did not work? Why did they give up power more or less peacefully? Or, as the commentator Melvin Lasky put it: "[Why did] the will of force [fail] and leaders who had been party-line dogmatists all their ideological lives started to stutter?" Finally, why and how did the people of these countries cease to be afraid of the authorities, a gradual and lengthy process that accelerated in these last few years?

I also sought answers, or some approximation of answers, to other more specific but no less challenging questions. What part did intellectuals play in these developments and especially in the complete delegitimation of these systems? How did members of the political elite perceive and explain the decline of these systems? What are the obstacles to further democratization and to privatization of the economies? What part did former elites play in the collapse of these systems? Did they too become disillusioned? How to explain the speed with which the systems collapsed and the apparent loss of political will of the leaders?

I began my efforts by interviewing two types of people: former dissenters, critics of the systems (many with prison experiences) and former functionaries, party intellectuals, officials some still in influential positions or retired. In Prague my informants included three members of the parliament, a professor of mathematics who used to be a highly placed university official, a retired professor of medicine, likewise a former party activist, a woman who was among the first to sign Charter 77 and had been imprisoned for years. Several other former dissidents politically active in various organizations plus Civic Forum people and a highly placed official in the foreign ministry, (former exile recently returned) were also among those interviewed. My interpreter was an additional and welcome source of information. She lived on the outskirts of Prague with her parents and brother, a young lawyer, with whom she had to share a room.

In Hungary I spoke to prominent writers, social scientists, journalists, former dissenters, former party functionaries in the cultural field. I also spoke to assorted friends, relatives, and many taxi drivers hence my information was not totally drawn from the intelligentsia. I also learned about results of recent opinion polls—one of the most interesting was the finding that a great majority in a national sample gave preference to material over spiritual or moral values.

Among the people I met and interviewed was a former colonel of the Hungarian KGB who spent much of his youth in what was the Soviet Union, assisted in the preparation of show trials, and now, decades after his involvement with the secret police, continues to agonize over his past. In the process he has become a competent historian of ideas and political scientist without classes to teach. There was a journalist who graduated from a Soviet university and still recalls the impact of Khrushchev's "secret" speech at the twentieth Party Congress on stunned Soviet party people. He was also among many who explained his own disillusionment by noting, "As we spoke of exemplary incorruptibility and purity in the ranks of the Party, I could observe daily my party boss who stole, embezzled, and cheated; he even ran over a pedestrian but got away with it..." He added: "What it all boiled down to [that is, the rationalizations and so on] was that we meant well." At the same time, he also averred, "I never met a highly placed functionary who was uncritical toward the system... [but] the moral conflicts these people had never took the form of being disturbed by their own misdeeds or abuses but always by those of others."

An aged former ambassador under Kadar, who had returned to Hungary after the Second World War from exile, told me: "Everybody with a brain was at the time (late 1940s) supporting the system. The spirit of the people was wonderful, they went to work singing... I believed the Rajk trial [the major Hungarian show trial] so did everyone else." A prominent Czech dissident and fellow defendant of Vaclav Havel in a 1979 political trial began her adult life as a communist. "Christianity led me to communism," she remarked. Her disillusionment (by contrast with some of the Hungarian functionaries) began with the Slansky trial—the major Czech show trial. She was struck by "the strange formulations" in the language of the confessions, which sounded so unlike people normally spoke. It took her some time to understand why they spoke the way they did. Eventually she came to the total rejection of the system and refused to cooperate in her job as a journalist. Subsequently she made a meagre living as a cleaning woman. During her long years in menial jobs, she had time to reflect on her previous involvement with the communist movement and realized that among the aspects she could not accept was the theory of class struggle. Although initially she was led to the communist movement through her religious values, subsequently it was her Catholicism that helped her to survive years of political persecution and material deprivation. She recalled that during her years as a dissident, the police placed microphones in her apartment through the roof which caused the roof leak so that when it rained she had to catch the water in buckets.

A prominent Hungarian writer, well-known opposition activist under Kadar and current member of the parliament, grew up in an orthodox communist family and only gradually realized, "what I and my parents regarded as the only natural way of looking at the world was in fact the ideology of a small minority." By 1968, after brief flirtations with Western-style New Leftism and even Maoism, he abandoned Marxism-Leninism of any variety.

A very different way of handling inner conflicts was sketched by another former Czech dissident, currently a member of the parliament. He said, "When people invest so much of their life in a political movement and belief, the only way out is to maintain some belief. . .you say to yourself 'there must have been some grain of truth in it...not everything was evil.' These are the people who became reform communists and moral relativists since it is their experience that in the past anybody with strong convictions [communist convictions] was ready to send people into jail or to the gallows."

Another life-long Czech critic of the system and currently highly placed official in the Ministry of Foreign Affairs was fully persuaded—unlike many Western intellectuals—that the system did have a lot to do with Marxism, which he called "a cruel, elitist, anti-human ideology." Said he, "The more Marx I read, the fewer humanist roots I could find in it."

A well-known Hungarian social scientist has suggested that the most profound shock, since the changes began in 1989, to the believers was that for the first time, and in total contradiction to Marx's most basic propositions, socialist systems were reverting to capitalism. This used to be unthinkable. The survival of Marxist categories of thinking was reflected in the explanation of the collapse of the system offered by a prominent former Hungarian Party intellectual. It was, he said, the growing contradiction between the modes of production—rigid, bureaucratic, overcentralized— and modern technology, communications, and information gathering. More generally he believed that modern technology and especially communications undermined the political system, which used to be inward looking, isolated, secretive. Even Ceauscescu's downfall was promoted by television which showed the unheard of negative audience reaction when he was addressing the carefully assembled crowds in Bucharest. He also believed that these systems could only function under warlike conditions, under stress, conflict, emergency—not during prolonged peace. Soviet leaders lost their messianic, millenarian aspirations. As soon as the system ceased to expand, it was doomed. As soon as the Party gave up its millenarian aspirations, it could not function any more. Soviet policies became reduced to old-style Russian militarism. He traced the process of collapse to the cynicism of the leaders, exemplified, among other things, in the joke Brezhnev told Willy Brandt (according to the German magazine *Der Stern)* during his visit to the Soviet Union. Brezhnev reportedly asked Brandt: "Do you know what Marx would say if he were alive today? Workers of the world, forgive me." The story made a deep impression on my Hungarian informant. It was, in his words, "as if the Pope made fun of immaculate conception. Surely that would be the end of the church as we have known it."

Unanticipated conversations were also informative. The first involved a member of the Czech working classes, a taxi driver, who drove me to the city from the airport and spoke some English. Although he drove what appeared to be a brand new Opel Kadet (made under license in South Korea), he was disgruntled and complained bitterly of the entrenched communist bureaucrats who resisted privatization through various bureaucratic obstacles. By contrast, the people I talked to later in Prague said that taxi drivers were among the new elites making an excellent living. Not so in Budapest which has 30,000 taxi drivers and only 10,000 are needed. Many of the unemployed drift into this occupation, I learned.

The problems faced by the new political systems, including privatization were aptly summed up in an article in the London *Spectator* by Gaspar Tamas, a former dissident and currently a member of the Hungarian parliament representing the major opposition party and also the head of the Institute of Philosophy of the Hungarian Academy of Sciences. He wrote:

> East European public opinion is impatient of elites. Like the proponents of the 'politically correct' (PC) adversary culture in America, my countrymen strongly object to anybody or anything being better than anybody or anything else. . .The communist state was rigidly elitist and authoritarian and now we are witnessing an unprecedented egalitarian backlash.. .The recognition that socialism did not work is coupled with an almost medieval rejection of business and trade ('usury')...in Eastern Europe 'capitalism' is still a dirty word...'business' means shady deals.

While this visit was only the beginning of my efforts to understand the collapse of communism—with special reference to matters social-psychological, rather than institutional or historical—it has altered my view of current conditions in Eastern Europe and brought to my attention matters unreported or neglected by the American media.

One of the first things I learned in both countries was that popular dissatisfaction is not limited to matters economic but also involves the political. Misgivings about the current government in both countries were abundant. Undoubtedly my "sample" was biased, consisting as it did mostly of intellectuals, former dissidents, members and supporters of the main opposition party in Hungary. It was the same in Prague except in one respect. I talked to few Jews in Prague and to many in Budapest.

In Czechoslovakia I heard concerns about reform (or other) communists surviving in various bureaucracies and possibly scheming to return to power, or else to pull the strings anonymously behind the scene. These apprehensions had much to do with the fact that the old Czech system remained solidly entrenched until the moment of its final collapse. No extended reform period existed comparable to that in Hungary, which softened the communist system while still in power. Hungary had decades of "reform communism" or soft communism—also called "goulash communism." It used to be called "the most cheerful barrack in the socialist camp."

Communist Party leaders in Hungary were influenced by liberal intellectuals. Opposition, dissent was more widespread, more legitimate, more readily tolerated. Janos Kadar said early in his rule that he who is not against us is with us. This was, of course, a reversal of the classical totalitarian principle and practice which demanded positive expressions of loyalty from all and denied the legitimacy of neutrality. In Czechoslovakia dissidents were a much smaller and more embattled group, far more harshly treated than in Hungary. These circumstances help to explain the greater intensity of anti-communist feeling among Czechs and Slovaks. The "Cleansing Law" (Lustracni Zakon) in Czechoslovakia was less controversial than similar measures in Hungary; some people complained that Havel's amendments watered it down. The law proposed that (as summarized by an English observer):

> ...a Commission...make a thorough check on the background of all those in top administrative positions—in the police, the armed forces, the judiciary, the schools and the universities—in order to discover those who were agents and collaborators of the former Secret Police. Senior Communist Party officials and members of the People's Militia (the armed wing of the Party) will be automatically banned for five years from holding office in the state administration, state media and state enterprises. The rank and file of the Communist Party will not suffer under this law. Neither will those middle ranking opportunists who joined the Party because it offered the only road to self-advancement.

In Hungary people complained more often about the material privileges (rather than the power) of former party officials, some of whom set up lucrative enterprises, while many continued to receive exceptionally high pensions determined by their earlier positions. But the opposite view could also be heard. The officials should not be purged since they were trained experts, badly needed for the economy.

Former Czech dissidents were apprehensive that the functionaries may seek a comeback. A member of the Czech parliament and former dissident thought that while some of the reform communists became moral relativists (overreacting to past commitments and their consequences), others retained belief in the role of the state and were resisting new policies designed to curtail it.

In Hungary there was considerable opposition among liberal intellectuals and the major opposition party leaders to the proposed "law of retribution" that sought to punish former communist officials guilty of crimes not prosecuted under the Kadar regime. George Konrad, the well-known writer, argued:

> a widespread disappointment and bad public mood predispose to search for scapegoats and enemies to be vengefully punished...[the new law] would introduce new criteria into the selection of personnel. Once more political criteria would become ascendant.

Expertise, professional qualifications would become secondary. . .Once more this could become a country where a literary genre—the literature of denunciation—would flourish as it often did at earlier times especially when political regimes changed...If we go down this road, then we will join ranks not with the first world but will sink to the level of the third.

Istvan Eorsi, another writer who had been jailed under Kadar, found the new law "disgustingly hypocritical" and feared that "the country would become the home to denunciations, a place where everybody would sniff around the dirty linen of his neighbor." He also wrote:

If we hang an eighty-three-year-old pensioner for his demagogic harangues delivered thirty-five years ago, that would of course satisfy the sense of justice of the Hungarian people. And how about those tends of thousands...who gave an ovation to the demagogue in question? Are they innocent? It is not only the demagogue who is responsible for the frenzied mob, but the mob too for the frenzied demagogue.

These impassioned comments can only be understood against the background of recent Hungarian history full of unhappy precedent. In 1944 when the Nazis came in and after 1945 when the Red Army occupied the country and the communist regime was established, the authorities were inundated with anonymous denunciations. The former Soviet Union faced similar problems as expressed by a high ranking KGB official:

We don't want civil war in our country...The problem of reporting, of mutual suspicion, fear, these are problems so deeply rooted in our soil and our genes, even if we open up certain things in many parts of our country, real vendettas will start. You had wives, children, informing. . .Most were not paid: they were forced into it.

There was mistrust of the current government in Hungary on other grounds as well. According to the critics, the government was seeking to control the media, especially television, and was reviving prewar nationalistic-conservative values and attitudes. Popular disappointment has also been shown in low voting participation and the small number of active party members—supposedly the total is 50,000 for all parties. But considering how meaningless political participation was made during the long decades of communist rule, it may not be surprising that people have come to mistrust politics and politicians with such intensity. Elemer Hankiss, a leading Hungarian sociologist, reported that a comparative study found that as of 1978 political participation—defined as the belief that the individual can exert some pressure to promote his interests—was the lowest in Hungary as compared not only with Western but also several third world countries.

The political process is also suspect because the tone of public debate is often acrimonious. Many people prefer dignity and decorum; the public is not used to rancorous debate, an aspect of political pluralism and democracy. Jews in particular are concerned with the revival of right-wing sentiment and anti-Semitism which was not allowed public expression under the communist regime. People in Hungary, and the rest of the former Soviet Empire, are not used to the idea that in a free society even repugnant views should be allowed free expression. Many people were horrified by a televised debate in the course of which members of the audience vocally demanded punishment for former communists. A journalist told me that threats were made against *Nepszava,* the daily newspaper of the former ruling party, now functioning as an independent paper.

Another characteristic controversy concerned the repatriation of the remains of Nicholas Horthy, who ruled Hungary from the early 1920s until he was arrested by the Nazis in 1944. He was a conservative nationalist, a soft authoritarian in the right-wing mold and quite popular. The current dispute was not about the repatriation of his remains as such (from Portugal) but whether or not the present government should in any way be involved with it. The resurgence of his popularity is one of several striking examples of the survival of past attitudes, values and preoccupations after forty years of communist rule. (Another example of these attitudes was the official and popular choice of the old royal Hungarian coat of arms, rather than a republican version, as the country's new emblem.)

While I was in Budapest a newspaper reported a reunion of former members of the titled nobility at the Hyatt Atrium hotel. I also learned that genealogical research is very popular and many people wish to discover or rediscover links to the nobility or the gentry. The revival of Hungarian nationalism may yet become the source of cultural anti-Americanism. For the moment, however, it is Americanization, superficial or not, that is prominent. It is, of course, difficult to separate it from Westernization which is reflected, among other things in the rising proportion of Western cars, and the new showrooms for Ford, Fiat, Volvo, various Japanese models, in computerization, advertising, familiar brand names, new office buildings. American popular music is prevalent on radio and television. American films, according to a Hungarian movie director, "are killing the Hungarian [movie] industry." No Hungarian film of the last two years, he says, has been able to stand the box-office test against Hollywood competition. Bookstores and vendors in the street sell American style self-help books on the usual topics—how to be loved, how to make friends, how to stay healthy.

There are also plenty of books on yoga and horoscopes (a research sociologist I know gave up her profession to become a full-time maker of horoscopes which provides her with an income several times what she made before). Both *Playboy* and *Readers' Digest* have (or are about to have) Hungarian editions. English words like shop, center, t-shirt, sneaker, discount, and more, have found their way into the Hungarian language. The pornography industry is gearing up. Video-stores are flourishing. Book publishing is in trouble. A publisher told me, "People who could afford will not buy serious books and those who would buy them cannot afford to." Even popular books, such as novels by the well-known author and popular public figure George Konrad, appear in much smaller editions than they used to.

An article in a Hungarian daily newspaper observed that whereas four decades of Soviet cultural invasion propagated with vast resources made no dent, American popular culture is eagerly embraced: "our countrymen are devouring everything American and it is to be feared that the unusual diet will cause indigestion...when the political system changed, the dam broke, we could gaze with childlike, innocent wonder at this new world and its offerings, almost the way the natives had looked at the conquistadors, America enters our lives like knife does butter."

The most serious and tangible problems are economic not cultural. Both Hungary and Czechoslovakia lost their Soviet and East European markets, everybody wants to trade with the West and prefers Western goods to their shoddy East European counterparts. People are hurting because prices are rising but not incomes, not for most people that is. But the villas of the newly rich have risen in the pleasant hilly neighborhoods of Buda (a development that predates the political changes of the last three years). Foreign businessmen or executives are paying thousands of dollars of rent per month in such buildings.

What did I learn about the sources of change, about the questions which took me to these countries? It goes without saying that Soviet reluctance (or inability) to intervene in Eastern Europe was a precondition for the transformation that took place. But that is not the whole story. Even so, to understand what happened in Eastern Europe one must first understand what happened in the Soviet Union.

As is often the case when major social transformations take place, several developments converge. There was a gradual generational change among the leaders in both the former Soviet Union and Eastern Europe. Gorbachev's generation was witness to de-Stalinization and the gradual subversion of the legitimacy of the Soviet system and Soviet history. They also witnessed, and were part of, the stagnation and corruption of the long Brezhnev era. Most important, economic malfunctioning intensified in the last twenty years. If the leaders harbored secret doubts about the system, there was much new evidence in the economic sphere to confirm them. One of the leaders of the former opposition movement in Hungary noted that an empire that was forced to buy its food from its supposedly mortal enemies was doomed. Interestingly enough a number of my informants in Prague as well as in Budapest took it for granted that the arms race, and especially its latest round associated with "Star Wars," bankrupted the Soviet empire.

Even the more restrained forms of liberalization planted the seeds of destruction—although this was far from apparent during the 1960s and 1970s. Pavel Bratinka, a member of the Czech parliament and former opposition activist, explained in the London *Times:*

> Although the regime was furious about Charter 77 [the first group of public critics] it was confident that it could contain it indefinitely. Here the regime made its first great mistake... The second error lay in the conceit of the regime that the Soviet Union would always provide support...remaining ever ready to send in tanks...the necessity of pretending to reform forced the regime to tolerate some debate about issues which had been taboo. Inevitably people began to lose their fear and to push the limits of the tolerated further and further out.

These systems allowed—in part to make a more favorable impression on countries whose financial and economic help they increasingly needed—a gradual build up of opposition which gathered force when economic difficulties became severe. Preserving the empire clashed with efforts to secure legitimacy—for example, via better food supplies and other imports. In several East European countries a critical mass of independent thinkers and critics developed during the 1970s and 1980s. Tocqueville's anticipation of the idea of "relative deprivation" applies:

> The evil suffered patiently as inevitable seems unendurable as soon as one conceives the idea of escaping from it. All of the abuses that have been removed seem only to delineate better those that remain and to make one's feelings more bitter. The evil, it is true, has become less, but one's sensibility is more acute.

The road to further delegitimation opened wider (under Kadar, Brezhnev, Huszak) when the authorities had declared individual consumption a legitimate goal, allowing that consumption was not a contemptible preoccupation. These processes were most advanced in countries—Poland, Hungary, East Germany—that had the largest Western debts. These preoccupations also found their expression in the "second economy." Thus for both political and non-political reasons, opposition to state interference in personal lives and economic activities grew.

Another theory of the collapse would rehabilitate the concept of totalitarianism, at least to some degree. While the totalitarian model never offered any hint as to how the systems might change—focused as it was on the determination of the leaders to stay in power—it nevertheless offers a clue to the speed with which they collapsed. Martin Malia suggests:

> It was a brusque collapse, a total implosion of a sort unheard of in history: a great state abolished itself utterly in a matter of weeks. The reason this happened is that the Soviet Union was in fact a total society, with all aspects of life linked in a 'mono-organization' whole. At its core was the Party to which all aspects of life were subordinated: the economy, government, culture, private life itself. This total society logically ended in a total collapse of all its interrelated parts at once.

Even without recourse to the notion of totalitarianism, it is plausible enough that a highly centralized system, such as that of the former Soviet Union, would unravel in the way described above. The reforms preceding the complete transformation of the system were most advanced in countries that had experienced popular, anti-totalitarian revolutions like Hungary and Poland. Whereas in Czechoslovakia in 1968 it was inside the Party where the "Prague Spring" reforms originated. The latter did not represent sweeping rejection of the system and ideology as was the case in Hungary and Poland.

Symptomatic of the far more retarded state of reform in Czechoslovakia, as recently as in 1988 (when I visited Slovakia), were the old-style political slogans and red stars still everywhere on buildings and loudspeakers blaring propaganda no longer in evidence in Hungary or Poland at the time. I was also held up on the Hungarian-Czech border for two hours while the border guards searched my car and luggage and carefully examined all printed matter in my possession.

Mihaly Bihari, a well-known Hungarian social philosopher and legal scholar, proposed three pathways toward the collapse. The first, the Hungarian, was the most unusual because of the long reform period. A quarter century of reform produced a reform intelligentsia of some quarter million strong. Many had studied in the West. Many were Party members of the nominal, opportunistic kind, a fact that nonetheless helps to explain why reformist trends also penetrated the Party. There were no such groups of comparable size in the other communist countries, including the Soviet Union.

But the limits of reform were reached by the end of the 1980s. The so-called "social contract" was breached—the government could no longer maintain, let alone improve, the living standard of the population in exchange for passive compliance. Bihari is among those who do not think that internal Soviet changes led to internal Hungarian changes. They only made them easier. He also recalled that in the fall of 1989 Cuba, East Germany, Czechoslovakia, and Romania briefly formed an anti-Hungarian and anti-Gorbachev alliance and issued a statement deploring Soviet and Hungarian reforms. Another unique feature of the Hungarian pattern of development is that several political parties appeared early in the transformation process.

The second path to change led through mass demonstrations in East Germany, Romania, Czechoslovakia. There was little prior reform. Then came the sudden collapse. The masses realized their strength. Ruling groups became paralyzed, panicked, and viewed the events with incomprehension. East German leader Erich Honecker for example, in a subsequent newspaper interview, expressed genuine surprise at his loss of power since he felt he presided over a benign system.

The third path was the Soviet one. It was not a real system change but a disintegration, growing anarchy. Until the August 1991 coup, Gorbachev appeared to believe that the system could be revived, reformed, streamlined. Developments in the Soviet Union signified not merely the end of socialism but also the end of empire and military superpower status.

One of the striking impressions is the apparent ease with which Soviet-type institutions were swept away in Hungary and Czechoslovakia and how little observable imprint—other than the economic chaos—these systems left behind. The past, history is reasserting itself not merely in the fervent desire to rejoin Western Europe, but also in the form of conflicts and attitudes which forty years of communist domination had suppressed. Still, ethnic conflicts in these two countries are not quite as deadly as in the former Soviet Union or in Bulgaria, Romania, or Yugoslavia. Hungary has no sizeable minorities, other than the Gypsies whose desire for autonomy is far from apparent, while the Slovak problem in Czechoslovakia is serious but had no violent expression so far.

Whatever the current dissatisfaction and uncertainty, no one can dispute that in Hungary and Czechoslovakia fundamental political transformations took place without violence. Freedom of expression is complete as is freedom of religion and movement. Nobody fears the police any longer and arbitrary arrests are unknown. The new legal foundations of social order are being established, free elections were held, numerous political parties emerged (to start with there were sixty-five in Hungary; twelve ran in the elections, and six gained parliamentary seats). In both countries, the parliaments are functioning institutions. Privatization has also been proceeding although its gains are still limited.

It would be unreasonable to expect that the societies of Eastern Europe, which were until recently under Soviet domination, would catch up with the West in one big leap, in either matters cultural, political, or economic. The accomplishments of the privileged countries of the West took centuries; yet they have become the yardstick and frame of reference for many people in Eastern Europe.

16

Moral Responses to the Great Mass Murders of Our Century

The American mass media greeted the discovery of Soviet mass graves of the past few years with remarkable equanimity. One alone, Kuropati, (near Minsk) was estimated by Russian sources to contain over a quarter million remains; Bykovnia (near Kiev) a similar number, killed during the 1930s. No Russian reporters or officials appeared on our television screens to comment on these discoveries and no American television correspondents reported breathlessly from the scene. We were also spared the reflections of academic specialists regarding the significance of these findings for a reassessment of the Soviet mass murders.

I

It has been customary in our times to make reference to the Holocaust whenever we wish to allude to some unrivalled evil. The Holocaust and its perpetrator, the Nazi regime became the undisputed and most readily available reference points to self evident evil, and for good reasons. By the same token words like "Nazi", "Auschwitz", "Storm troopers" or "Gestapo" are reflexively appended to political or social phenomena we wish to discredit conclusively.

It rarely happens that self evident evil is denoted by reference to the mass murders which were commited in the Soviet Union under Stalin. Words like "Soviet," "Soviet communist," "Kolyma" or "KGB" are rarely used to discredit political movements and practices. It is doubtful that one in a thousand Americans knows what Kolyma was, or would recognize the name of a single Soviet concentration camp. It is just as unlikely that one in a thousand Americans heard of the names of Beria, Serov, Yagoda, or Yezhov—people who used to be in charge of the Soviet mass murders. If somebody undertook a survey to find out how many Americans know about the mass murders committed in the former Soviet Union (and ask them to estimate the number about the victims) it would become clear that public information of such matters is virtually non-existent. The fact that no such survey has ever been made (as far as I know) is in itself significant. Although a recent (1993) poll showed that about one quarter of Americans were unaware of the Holocaust there can be little doubt that most Americans are far less ignorant about it than about corresponding mass murders in the former Soviet Union.

It is not the purpose of this article to call into question the uniqueness of the Holocaust. The question here raised is why,—in comparison to the abundance and intensity of the emotions and moral outrage released by the Holocaust—the Soviet mass murders have stimulated relatively little moral energy and outrage at any point in time?

It is this asymmetry in moral sentiment that calls for explanation especially at a time when the demise of the Soviet Union provides not only new opportunities for unobstructed information gathering but also for a historical postmortem of the Soviet system and its moral record.

II

It is the differences between the character and procedures of the Nazi and Soviet mass murders which most plausibly explain the different moral responses to these unparalleled slaughters of our century.

In Nazi Germany the state set up highly productive extermination plants (gas chambers, crematoria) with no less of a goal than the total elimination of the Jewish population of Europe, perhaps some day of the whole world. It was a carefully planned, meticulously organized operation that had spectacular results: the killing of 6 million Jews and lesser numbers of other groups in a few years. Never before had so many people been killed in such a short period of time so deliberately and efficiently.

These mass murders gave rise to the term of Holocaust and popularised the concept of genocide—so much so that since the 1960s they have been used with diminishing discriminanation. "Genocide" or "genocidal" have been applied to characterise situations far from murderous, such as the "cultural genocide" of some minority underrepresented in institutions of higher education, or birth control policies proposed to unwed mothers. Radical feminists called pornography "genocide" and a "holocaust"; for some "experts" of the so-called "recovery movement" childhood is a "holocaust"; the homosexual organization *Act Up* asserted that "Dinkin's policy is genocidal."

The Soviet mass murders were in significant ways different from the Nazi ones. There was no plan corresponding to the "final solution", (the killing of a group of people in order to purify the world of evil), no particular ethnic group was singled out for total elimination, the victims came from every social strata and ethnic group of Soviet society. There were no extermination camps using modern technology and machinery, such as gas chambers and crematoria. The victims were killed in relatively old fashioned and inefficient ways: either shot or allowed to die of starvation, cold and various diseases in what the Soviet authorities used to call "corrective labor camps". (It is of some interest that according to Mikhail Heller and Aleksandr Nekrich, two Russian emigree historians, "it was Lenin and Trotsky who were the first Europeans to use the term "concentration camp" as early as in 1918.)

On the other hand the total number of the Soviet victims was far greater than those of the Nazis, if we include all those who died in the camps and were victims of politically induced famine and deportations. According General Volkogonov, (head of the parliamentary commission on rehabilitation) "from 1929 to 1953... 21.5. million people were repressed. Of these a third were shot, the rest sentenced to imprisonment where many also died." These figures did not include famine victims and the deported ethnic groups.

A large portion of the Soviet victims, some might argue, were not actually killed, they just could not survive the harsh living conditions in the camps, including the bad weather not subject to human control. These living conditions, some might further contend, resulted less from ill will, or deliberate policy than from overall backwardness, sloppiness, and even the needs of the economy. After all, slave labor was badly needed to carry out the great projects of the early five year plans and if mortality rates were high, these regrettable sacrifices were exacted to accomplish worthy objectives.

III

It is another possibility that it was the *relative paucity* of information about the Soviet mass murders that explains the different moral responses. While in the post-Stalin era the quantitative dimensions of Soviet mass murders began to emerge, they remained an abstraction for the public at large, even for the well educated. As Arthur Koestler noted half century ago: "statistics dont bleed; it is the detail that counts." And when gradually the details were furnished by the survivors' accounts they were often denigrated (especially by the "revisionist" historians) for being too personalised and emotional to be treated as reliable data.

Until recently far more information was available about the Nazi death camps than their Soviet counterparts. The Nazi system was destroyed; cameramen freely entered the former camps; archives had been opened; many perpetrators of these crimes were studied, interrogated, and brought to justice. There was overwhelming visual evidence: a substantial portion of American and European populations were exposed to pictures of gas chambers, crematoria, heaps of corpses found upon the liberation of the camps, the emaciated survivors. Many of them settled in the United States and by their very presence might have contributed to the moral climate here discussed whereas far fewer survivors of the Soviet camps made it to these shores.

By contrast the Soviet system was a going concern for seventy years; Western reporters or social scientists could not investigate the former, or existing camps, gather information, reconstruct the past, interview former inmates or guards. Until Gorbachev came into power the Soviet system was highly secretive.

Lack of information as such about the Soviet mass murders (and the associated camp system) was not the decisive factor in the tepid moral reactions one seeks to understand. There was *some* information already in the 1930s, increasing after World War II (including the then definitive work of Dallin and Nicolaevsky published in 1948) and much more following the de-Stalinization campaign of Khrushchev after 1956. Since 1968 Robert Conquest's massive pioneering work, *The Great Terror* has been available. In 1978 he published *Kolyma: Arctic Death Camps*, a stunning study of the most murderous Soviet camps. There were even some comparative accounts (based on personal experience) of Nazi and Soviet concentrations camps such as *Under Two Dictators* by Margarete Buber and Gustav Herling's *World Apart*.

Whatever the nature and quantity of the information that was available (statistical or personal) it attracted little public attention and sparked little moral outrage; hence *it is the attitudes toward such information which invite further inquiry.*

The controversy that surrounded Victor Kravchenko and David Rousset is a case in point. The flower of the French intelligentsia vilified Kravchenko (a Soviet defector and author of two important books) in the late 1940s and ridiculed his allegations about Soviet camps. The attitude on the Left in the United States was no more charitable. The *Nation* reporter of the trial (Kravchenko sued a French publication for libel) sneered in 1949:

> The man (Kravchenko) is very cheap... What he lacks is distinction and culture... he is also a very poor propaganda agent. He commits mistakes by exposing his hand at points where the game demands that he hide it.

Frederick Schuman in a review of his book *I Chose Freedom* called him (in the *New Republic*) "A Soviet renegade" and a "socially myopic and politically unworthy careerist," the book full of "slanders."

At the time of his defection (in 1944) *Time Magazine* wrote: "Editorial comment (on him) was minimum and cautious. Most U.S. editors, mindful of the delicacy of U.S.-Soviet relations... and of the 26 year old difficulty in getting at truth in any item dealing with Russia, did not want to stick out their necks."

More recently Noam Chomsky expressed (also in the *Nation*) grave doubts about the credibilty of Cambodian refugees and their accounts of the massacres perpetrated by the Pol Pot regime.

In discussing refugees it must also be recalled that after World War II over two million Soviet refugees in Western Europe, (prisoners of war and slave laborers taken by the German troops) were forcibly repatriated (with the assistance of British and American troops)—an event which also failed to generate either publicity or moral outrage at the time.

The collapse of the Soviet Union created a new situation. It has now become possible to construct a visual (as well as historical-statistical) record of its dark deeds, to visit former camps, newly discovered mass graves, to interivew survivors and relatives of victims, the witnesses. While there have been a few reports, media interest has been limited, to say the least; American journalists have not been flocking to the sites and settings of Soviet mass murders; camera crews have not been recording the remains of the Gulag Archipelago; (rare exceptions include a 1989 *60 Minutes* segment about the "last political prioners" in the Perm 35 camp; in March 1990 the *National Geographic Magazine* had an article on the same camp entitled "Last Days of the Gulag?" and in March 1993 the *New York Times Magazine* had an article on the discovery of skeletons in Kolpashevo, Siberia). There have been no television documentaries of the Gulag—not on public television, CNN or the networks. If there are any oral history projects involving Soviet camp survivors supported by American foundations or universities they have not been publicised. Soviet (and post-Soviet, Russian) television programs about these mass murders have not been shown on American television.

No Hollywood movie has been made that used the Gulag as its background or attempted to show any aspect of Soviet repression and terror with the partial exception of *Dr. Zhivago.* (There was one English film based on Solzehnitsyn's *One Day in the Life of Ivan Denisovitch* and an American cable TV film shown in 1985 entitled "Gulag" that was more of a spy thriller).

There have been no conferences or symposia comparing the Nazi extermination camps and their personnel to the Gulag Archipelago; no inquiry into the applicability of the "obedience to authority" theory of mass murders (devised by Stanley Milgram to explain Nazi murderousness).

It is not unreasonable to believe that the same political predisposition which in recent times was expressed in ridiculing the idea that the Soviet Union was an evil empire played a part in the neglect of the topic of the Soviet mass murders and especially their comparative and historical moral implications.

IV

Those left-of-center on the political spectrum had the greatest difficulty expressing moral indignation about the Soviet atrocities even when their existence was no longer in doubt. If there ever was a book one would have expected to delve into the moral dimensions of the Soviet mass murders, or at least make some reference to them, it was *Sanctions for Evil: Sources of Social Destructiveness*, edited by Nevitt Sanford and Craig Comstock—a collection of 18 essays by American social scientists published in 1971. The first sentence on the dust jacket made clear that the moral concerns of the editors and contributors would not extend to the outrages perpetrated by the Soviet Union and other communist systems: "My Lai. Biafra. Detroit riots. Hiroshima. Dachau. Lynchings. Indian massacres. Salem witch hunts. Spanish Inquisition. Dynastic wars. The crusades. The inventory is endless."

The endless inventory had no room for the victims of the Soviet purges, labor camps and other outrages associated with communist systems. The only reference in the entire book to communism or communists could be found to them as victims of persecution in the United States! The fear of communism was a pathology of American society. There was also a vigorous defense of the exclusion of those on the left from the famous study of the authoritarian personality.

The volume captured the spirit of the 1960s. Not only was there no reference to any evil (or "social destructiveness") associated with communism, but the anti-anti-communist outlook (further discussed below) was fully displayed.

In 1969 Michael Parenti a political scientists and relentless critic of American society had this to say about Soviet camps:

> For many years anti-communist writers claimed that at any one time, anywhere from 15 to 25 million Soviet citizens were suffering the horrors of slave labor camps, with millions perishing over the years... By such statistics, the sum total of people incarcarated... over a 25 year period would have consisted of an astonishing proportion of the Soviet population; the support and supervison of labor camps would have been Russia's single largest enterprise. That the USSR could have maintained this kind of prison population, is to say the least, highly questionable.

Another illustration of the attitudes here discussed has been the fate of a remarkable document published in English in 1980, *The First Guidebook to Prisons and Concentration Camps of the Soviet Union*. It was put together by Avraham Shifrin a former inmate of these camps. This massive and meticulous work provided information about 2000 penal institution in every region of the Soviet Union, complete with maps, charts and even some photographs; it also included a list of 41 "death camps", "... where prisoners, forced to work under dangerous, unhealthy conditions for the Soviet warmachine, face virtually certain death." The book was barely noticed; its author did not appear on talks shows; he was not interviewed by mass circulation periodicals; the book received a total of two short reviews in the United States in publications few people read.

Another memorable example of the mindset associated with the moral asymmetries here examined was displayed in a public television program in 1987 entitled "The Faces of the Enemy" produced by Sam Keen, better known as author of *Fire in the Belly*, a popular male consciuosness level raising book. It was a program designed to explore the links between dehumanisation, political propaganda and extremism, yet made virtually no reference to such phenomena when manifested by communist movements or systems (I was moved to write to Mr Keen pointing out the one-sidedness of the program but got no reply). While the atrocities associated with Nazis, right-wingers, and U.S. policy in Vietnam were well covered there was no reference to the slaughters of huge proportions committed by the Soviet system; Stalin's name never came up, nor Mao, Pol Pot or the Chinese Cultural Revolution.

Mr Keen was well within the prevailing conventional wisdom. The highly differentiated approach to Nazi and Soviet horrors had its counterpart in the even more divergent treatment of right and left extremism which has endured to this day. Angela Davis, a former leader of the American Communist Party and durable supporter of the Soviet Union is professor (of all things in the "history of consciousness" program) at the University of California (Santa Cruz) showered with speaking invitiations on major campuses; David Aphteker, another former leader of the same organization and unwavering apologist of the Soviet Union under and after Stalin was honored at the University of Massachusetts at Amherst in the Fall of 1993. Johnetta Cole, formerly ardent supporter of Castro (president of Spellman College) almost made it into the Clinton cabinet and Bernardine Dohrn, former leader and underground activist of the Weathermen was recently the subject of a warm "human interest" article in the *New York Times* Home Section. Examples could be multiplied.

The historic amnesia and asymmetry here probed is also apparent in high school textbooks in social studies and contemporary history which rarely make reference to the Soviet (or other communist) mass murders alongside the Nazi ones. Teaching at a large public university for a quarter century I have yet to encounter a student who was aware of the Soviet mass murders before entering the university; the majority graduate without learning of such matters.

It should be noted that while social scientists in general paid little attention to the Soviet mass murders there were some important exceptions: Irving Louis Horowitz, author of *Taking Lives: Genocide and State Power* (1982) and Terence Des Pres, author of *The Survivor: An Anatomy of Life in the Death Camps* (1976). Both examined comparatively the Nazi and Soviet mass murders and concentration camps.

As the so-called revisonists (their common denominator a rejection of the totalitarian model and a far less critical view of the Soviet system) became more prominent in Soviet studies during the 1970s and 80s new attempts were made to reinterpret and minimise the Soviet mass murders. Best known for these efforts has been Professor J. Arch Getty who sought (in his 1985 book) to bring new perspectives to the Purges and the associated violence, treating them largely as an administrative procedure in the Party (whereby certain members are periodically expelled). He also sought to discredit the personal accounts of the surviving Soviet camp inmates. More recently Professor Getty in a journal article arrived at higher estimates of the victims.

In another publication of Professors Getty and Roberta Manning eds. (*Stalinist Terror: New Perspectives, 1993*) there is a continued effort to keep the numbers down. More interesting however, from the standpoint of the moral response to such matters, is the interpretation of the outrages acknowledged. The pursuit of detachment that emerges brings back a remark Czeslaw Milosz made in his *Captive Mind* forty years ago:

> From the moment we acknowledge historical necessity to be something in the nature of a plague, we shall stop shedding tears over the fate of the vitcims. A plague or an earthquake do not usually provoke indignation. One admits they are catastrophes, folds the morning paper and continues eating breakfast.

What one finds in the new analysis, if not exactly an evocation of "historical necessity", is certainly akin to a plague or earthquake. Getty and his colleagues are anxious to diminish both Stalin's personal responsibility *and* that of the political system he created; they consider it a mistake to seek "the origins of Stalinist terror in the person of the deranged dictator, the 'administrative system' of the time or the very nature of Leninism." What then are we left with?

We are left with a peculiarly diffuse explanation of these events which denude them of a moral focus or definition. Getty and William Chase wrote:

When the terror erupted in 1936-37, it quickly went out of control, chaotically reflecting personal hatreds (that is, at the local level—P.H.) and propelling itself with fear. Explanations of the terror ... should be supplemented by approaches that account for lack of coordination, local confusion and personal conflicts.

"Uncoordinated" terror reduces the responsiblity of the political system, as do the "local confusion" and "personal conflicts". Earlier in the same volume Getty and Manning also suggest (as they refer to the writing of Gabor Rittersporn, another revisonist) that

Stalin... Ezhov (chief of the NKVD) and highly placed NKVD operatives *sincerely believed* (my emphasis) that the nation was riddled with plots and conspiracies... He (Rittersporn) intimates that this response was rooted in traditional rural beliefs that the machinations of evil spirits accounted for commonplace misfortunes... Rittersporn's work suggests that the elements of pre-revolutionary rural culture helped fuel Stalinist persecutions, under the impact of... scarcity... and leaders who shared, politicized and used such traditional beliefs.

What Getty and his colleagues here suggest that conspiratorial fantasies help to explain the terror and possibly also its spontanous, uncoordinated aspects, as those imbued with them were gripped by these irrational impulses (rooted in traditional, pre-Soviet rural beliefs). It may be recalled the Nazis too sincerely believed in conspiracies, and especially the Jewish world conspiracy which in no way undermined their ability to devise efficient ways to get rid of the Jews, nor was the outside world inclined to diminish their responsibility for these mass killings on account of these delusions. The emphasis on non-Soviet or pre-Soviet factors such as the "pre-revolutionary rural culture" and "traditional rural beliefs" serve to further delute the responsibility of the Soviet system and its representatives for the mass murders.

Elsewhere in the volume Roberta Manning wrote:

In the late 1930s, reformist efforts gave way to terror under the impact of the desperate conditions of the times. Political, social and economic tensions, aggravated by the onset of German expansionism, the sudden escalation of ongoing border conflicts with the Japanese in Manchuria, the 1936 crop failure and national decisions to prosecute former members of defunct opposition movements created a tense political climate.

This "climate" led to the "exceedingly harsh measures" of the period "accorded many suspected offenders" Manning further explains, intent on showing that there was "considerable input from below" (i.e. at the local level) "as well as intervention from above".

When all is said and done "the new perspectives on Stalinist terror" proffer an exceedingly wide range of factors and explanations all of which appear independent of human political will. It is an approach that relieves the commentator from facing questions of moral responsibilty or experiencing a sense of outrage.

The moral sensibility here discussed has not not been limited to the American media, authors of social studies texts, left-of-center social critics or revisionist historians. A small empirical study of my own (reported in my book *Anti-Americanism*, 1992) revealed a similar pattern among a group of Canadian academics. When asked (in a mail questionnaire) to provide a listing of the most shocking historical events in this century, among those mentioned in the first instance 52% chose the Holocaust while nobody mentioned in statistically significant numbers any outrage associated with the Soviet system. Among the outrages mentioned in the second instance 15% made reference to the Stalin's purges. Further light was shed on these attitudes—when, in response to the question, whom they considered the least admirable political leaders in this century—Reagan was nominated in the first instance by 29% while Stalin by 8.5%

Another telling illustration of the attitudes here discussed has been the widespread ridicule President Reagan was subjected to (in the media and among academics) for refering (in 1983) to the Soviet Union as "the evil empire". So self evidently wrongheaded was this attribution that no one bothered to explain why exactly it was so absurd and laughable.

The unpopularity of Solzhenitsyn among American liberals and left-of-center intelligentsia is another reflection of the mindset under scrutiny. His unhesitating association of the Soviet system with evil, his fiery anti-communism and determination to give it a moral dimension did not go down well. It was admissible to express regret or sorrow over the Soviet mass murders but moral outrage was overdoing it, that seemed off limits. Solzhenitsyn also committed the unforgivable offense, (Tom Wolfe noted), of suggesting that not only Stalinism, and Leninism but Marxism and the pursuit of Marxist socialism led to the camps. Joseph Brodsky thought that Solzhenitsyn's unpopularity had to do with the "disturbing evidence" he presented which threatened the "mental fence that was constructed especially by the Western left..." around the topic of Soviet atrocities.

There is one notable similarity between responses to the Holocaust and the Soviet mass murders: in both instances there have been efforts to dispute the magnitude of the killings. However no reputable scholar or intellectual made such an attempt regarding the Holocaust victims (unless we include Noam Chomsky on account of his supportive introduction to the notorious volume by Robert Faurisson, a major Holocaust revisionist). Holocaust revisionists have been regarded as cranks and frauds. By contrast Professor Getty and his colleagues, although criticised by some, were hardly read out of the scholarly community. Purge revisionism has been far more acceptable than Holocaust revisonism.

V

At a time when at last the Soviet Union joined Nazi Germany among the great defunct tyrannies of modern history and perpetrators of mass murder unrivalled in scale, there is new relevance to the question why the revulsion occasioned by the outrages of the Soviet system has been far more muted than the corresponding sentiments stimulated by the Nazi misdeeds? Why *the* other great mass murders of modern times, and the political system that produced them, have not become the subject of similar, if not identical, moral revulsion, especially at a time when new evidence of every kind (from mass graves to archives) has become available?

Since public awareness of world events, including the great moral outrages of history, is largely the creation of the mass media it is important to reiterate that media coverage of Soviet mass murders was largely non-existent while they were committed and minimal in the subsequent years and decades. To the extent that the American public has become aware of the Holocaust it is because it has been given ample attention by the mass media and because the collapse of Nazi Germany allowed the creation and wide dissemination of visual images of the extermination camps.

By contrast even when the media has given some attention to the Soviet Union and its past, it was not, in most instances, to provide grounds for moral revelation and outrage. It may also be recalled here that spokesmen of and apologists for the Soviet system such as Vladimr Pozner and Georgi Arbatov regularly graced our television screens during the 1970s and 80s with their soothing tales of peaceful and humane Soviet foreign and domestic policies.

It should also be pointed out that not all Soviet mass murders were commited in the distant past. Spectacular mass murders of civilians were carried out by Soviet forces in Afghanistan under Brezhnev in the 1980s. These too received perfunctory coverage in the media.

If by now it has been established that atrocities of the Soviet system neither deeply penetrated popular and scholarly awareness (except that of a handful of specialists) nor stimulated moral responses comparable to those evoked by the Nazi ones, it remains to attempt to further explain this phenomenon.

One explanation, sofar not considered, may be found in the long standing, indeed chronic Western ignorance of and bizarre misperception of the Soviet (and similar) systems, products of attitudes ranging from affection to benefit of doubt. It is no longer in dispute that many Americans, and many highly distinguished ones among them, completely misread the nature of the Soviet system through much of its existence and especialy during its most murderous years and decades. What is less widely realised how long these confidently wrongheaded assessments persisted and how they might have influenced the moral responses, past and current, to the Soviet mass murders.

The roots of present day attitudes reach back to the 1930s. In those years when influential opinion-makers and intellectuals were most favorably impressed by the Soviet Union it was inconceivable that such an admirable system would commit mass murder; sometimes the atrocities were written off as the reasonable costs of the noble experiment.

Upton Sinclair wrote in 1938 about the victims of the famines and collectivisation:

> They drove rich peasants off the land and sent them to work in lumber camps and on railroads. May be it cost a million lives,—may be... five million—but you cannot think intelligently about it unless you ask yourself how many millions it might have cost if the changes had not been made.... There has never been in human history great social change without killing.

In the mid 1940s it appeared to Jerome Davis, (professor at Yale Divinity School) that during the purge period

> ... only a tiny percentage of the population was involved (in the Purges) and the same years which saw the treason trials saw some of the greatest triumphs of Soviet planning. While the screws tightened on a tiny minority the majority of Soviet people were enjoying greater prosperity.

In 1953 seeking to justify Soviet political violence associated with the Purges Leo Huberman and Paul Sweezy, two American academic Marxists asked:

> Is violence used to perpetuate a state of affairs in which violence is inevitable, or...(is) it used in the interests of creating a truly human society from which it will be possible at long last to banish violence altogether?

This was a rationalization the Nazis could also have gladly endorsed; after all, once they purified the world of Jews there was not going to be any further need for violence.

Thus to the extent that the Soviet mass murders and political violence were confronted by those on the Left, they were morally neutralised by the time honored device of viewing them as (regrettable) means to glorious ends. Legitimisers of Soviet violence were only interested in the ends and knew little of the means, nor were they anxious to learn about them. Sartre provided the most ambitious (and morally repellent) rationalisation for this position:

> Like it or not, the construction of socialism is privileged in that to understand it one must espouse its movement and adopt is goals; in a word, we judge what it does in the name of what it seeks and it means in the light of its ends...

Even more remarkable, in the 1930s the Soviet prison camps were often viewed as humane institutions of character reform rather than slow extermination. According to Anna Louis Strong, they were "remaking criminals." Professor Gillin, a leading authority on penology and former president of the American Sociological Society averred that "the system is devised to correct the offender and return him to society". Ella Winter was delighted to learn that criminals were not treated as outcasts. Harold Laski (the hundredth anniversary of his birth recently celebrated) had no doubt about the superiority of the Soviet penal system over its Western counterparts. He was also struck "by the excellent relations betwen the prisoners and the warders..." (reference to any such foolishness was missing from the article in the December 1993 *New Republic* entitled "Our Harold" written by his biographer.) The Webbs found the prisons "as free from physical cruelty as any prison in any country is ever likely to be." Maurice Hindus the veteran reporter on Soviet affairs concluded that "Vindictiveness, punishment, torture, severity, humiliation have no place in this system." Mr and Mrs. Corliss Lamont spoke to prisoners who informed them that they did not feel as if there were in prison and they had no difficulty believing this. And this was the 1930s. A decade later Henry Wallace and Owen Lattimore still found much to praise in the notorious prison camps of the Soviet Far East, thanks to the efforts of the camp administration and their own willingness to give every benefit of doubt to the Soviet system.

During World War II it was the wartime cameraderie and the illusions it generated that precluded discussions of, or inquiry into the moral outrages commited by the Soviet government. During the classic cold war years there was a greater readyness to criticise the Soviet system but the immediacy of the massive, well documented evil of the Holocaust helped to blot out concern with possible Soviet equivalents.

At the end of the 1940s McCarthyism arose and provided the most robust and enduring foundation for the attitudes here examined. Ironically, Senator McCarthy achieved exactly the opposite of what he had intended: he succeeded in discrediting, for decades to come, opposition to and criticism of communist movements and systems. To this day, any, but the most perfunctory critique of communism becomes labelled as a "witch hunt" or "red baiting".

In his book-length critique of anti-communism Parenti linked it to

> ... patriotic hooliganism, collective self-delusion, the propagation of political orthodoxy, the imprisonment of dissenters and the emergence of a gargantuan military establishment... Abroad anti-communism has brought us armaments races, nuclear terror, the strenghtening of oppressive autocracies... the death and maimimg of American boys and the slaughter of far-off unoffending peoples.... (it) brought us grief and shame.

After McCarthy a vocal anti-communist stand has become an embarrassment, an attitude in poor taste among self-respecting American liberal intellectuals, academics, journalists and even politicians.

From the 1960s until the rise of Gorbachev in 1985 it was the peace movement and the associated dread of nuclear war that exerted the major influence on the American (and Western) perceptions of the Soviet Union and the evaluation of its moral-political record. The peace movement successfully promoted the belief that a questioning the moral record of the Soviet system would undermine peace and that it was improper for other reasons as well (noted below) to criticise the Soviet Union.

Such was the fear of nuclear war that it was seen as imperative (on the part of peace activists and those under their influence) to abstain from questioning the legitimacy of the Soviet system, drawing attention to any of its wrongdoings at home or abroad, casting aspersions on the integrity of its leaders or to suggest that it was in any respect morally inferior to the United States. Instead we were urged to focus on matters which our two countries had in common, as for example the love of children and the basic goodness of ordinary people. Since trust was so ardently sought it was worse than impolite to dwell on, or seek to unearth Soviet policies of the past (and some of the present) which would have given a pause to those in pursuit of good relations. Critical views of the Soviet system were said to impede the cause of mutual understanding and goodwill; peace activists were also convinced that the tensions between the two countries had no foundation in reality (or if they had, they were caused by American conduct). The irrational, mutually reenforcing fears, suspicions, stereotypes and misunderstandings were to be dispelled by goodwill and friendly communication not judgmental attitudes.

An account of a 1983 meeting of Soviet and American women by a member of an American peace delegation to the Soviet Union was typical of these attitudes: "... what we lacked in knowledge we made up in enthusiasm and we shared a... faith that women of our two countries were probably more alike than different." It was further argued that "people who cultivate wheat cant possibly want war." Norman Mailer ably summed up these feelings: "We live with the scenario that Russia is an evil force. Now, the world is on the edge of destroying itself. Can we afford abhorrence any longer?" Two prominent peace activists, Drs. Chivian and Mack even found soothing explanations for Soviet concealment of the Chernobyl disaster in the laudable "tendency on the part of the Soviet leadership to downplay catastrophes and instead offer reassurance to the Soviet people so as to prevent emotional distress." They avered that such practices were beneficial for mental health.

Such attitudes were not limited to peace activists and intellectuals. A Yankelovitch survey in 1984 found that younger and better educated Americans were more willing to give the benefit of doubt to the Soviet Union and had more trusting attitudes; their majority believed that "we would be better off if we stopped treating the Soviets as enemies and tried to hammer out our differences in a live-and-let-live spirit."

Whatever the merit of these attitudes was for preventing nuclear war they were not apt to create an atmosphere in which Soviet mass murders of the past (or of the same period, i.e. those in Afghanistan) could be critically examined and evaluated, comparatively or otherwise.

The peace activists and their supporters were not only motivated by the fear of nuclear war. There was a cross fertilization between the peace movement and what came to called the adversary culture, spawned by the spirit and protest movements of the 1960s. Highly critical of American society, U.S. foreign policy and traditional American social-cultural values, these movements and their supporters were disinclined to be critical of any political system which was also critical of their own. Acutely aware of the ills of their own country, they were doubtful that any other system could be worse. Preoccupied with the ills of America they were unable to experience moral indignation about outrages commited by the Soviet system especially in distant locations such as Afghanistan.

It was under these conditions and in conjunction with the peace movement, that the concept of moral equivalence (between the United States and the Soviet Union) emerged and achieved a singular influence over the outlook of American elites, opinion makers and much of the general public. Sam Keen wrote,

> In the current USSR-US conflict, we require each other as group transference targets....We see the Soviets as making the individual a mere means to the goals of the state. They see us as sanctifying the greed of powerful individual at the cost of community, and allowing the profit of the few at the expense of the many. And so long as we trade insults, we are both saved from the embarassing task of looking at the serious faults and cruelties of our own systems.

Also characteristic of the mindset here recalled were the contentions of Richard Barnet in what I once called the definitive handbook on moral equivalence, *The Giants*, published in 1977. He suggested, among many other parallels, that "both societies were suffering a crisis of legitimacy", that "the madness of one bureuacracy sustains the other" and "each (country) is a prisoner of a sixty year old obsession." Marshall Shulman, the well known Sovietologist and former high ranking State Department adviser began a major article in *Foreign Affairs* in 1987 with what became a standard incantation:

> *Both the Soviet Union and the United States* (my emphasis) have been so constrained by parochial domestic interests and weighted down by outworn ideologies that they have been unable to summon up a competent and enlightened management of their affairs... proportionate to their respective and common problems.

The images of moral equivalence also deeply penetrated popular culture. Le Carré in his best selling spy stories portrayed the espionage establishments of the United States and the Soviet Union and their employees as equally corrupt, often the Americans markedly more so, "... idiots and/or fascistic puritans... objects of authorial loathing" as Walter Laqueur recently observed. James Bond movies made sure that the bad guys were rarely actual KGB agents but rather renegades of some kind, or merchants of death (power hungry capitalists) or deranged fanatics of no discernible political affiliation giving trouble to *both* Super Powers.

"The desire to see communist systems, even in their decay, as having the same problems as our own" was well and alive as late as 1990, Mark Almond writing in the *Spectator* pointed out.

There is no doubt that the deeply felt and entrenched belief in the moral (or immoral) equivalence between the United States and the Soviet Union was in large measure responsible for a climate of opinion in which it was not easy to publicly discuss, or evaluate the historic moral outrages the Soviet system had been responsible for.

Among the sources of the moral asymmetry here examined it should also be noted that until its actual collapse there was hope (in the West) that the Soviet system can be reformed. Unlike Nazi Germany the USSR survived much longer and that in itself seemed to prove something; as long as it survived it could be reformed. The reforms that followed the death of Stalin, and later Gorbachev's rise to power, provided something of an implicit retroactive justification for the horrors of the earlier era. Could the great sacrifices have been for nothing?

Gorbachev created high expectations of both reform and institutional continuity, so much so that Moshe Lewin, the historian could not entertain doubt (or apprehension) about the continued "political preemience of the party" and envisaged (in 1988) a rejuvenated Party and union of states:

> For the party is the main stabilizer of the political system and few groups would back measures likely to erode the integrity of the entire union or the centralised state. The party... is the only institution that can preside over the overhaul of the system without endangering the polity itself in the process.

There was new hope, among some American intellectuals that at long last under Gorbachev socialism with a human face might arise at the birthplace of the deformed system. Throughout the Gorbachev period and up to the present interest in the moral reassessment of Soviet atrocities has remained minimal.

VI

At the heart of the asymmetries and attitudes here examined two principal strands converge. There are on the one hand the remnants of an old pro-socialist idealism that cannot bring itself to believe the worst about a system which at one time was reputed to be the builder of socialism; it is galling for critics of capitalism to rank its arch enemy as a moral rival of Nazi Germany. Secondly and more importantly there is the hardy heritage of McCarthyism: its unintended discreditation of anti-communism that gave rise to anti-anti-communism, a mindset strenghtened by the rejection of Western values that emerged in the 1960s.

In the anti-anti-communist position two contradictory attitudes came together: on the one hand it was perfunctorily acknowledged that communist systems (or some of them) were bad, but this did not quite justify opposing them, or dwelling on their shortcomings; on the other hand the anti-communist attitudes were denounced as an obsession, a fantasy, a phobia, a pathology and a metaphor for everything that was wrong with American society.

From the anti-anti-communist point of view, any declaration of anti-communist belief amounted to an "obsession with communism". For the American liberal in good standing it was more important to make clear that he was disdainful of these "obsessions" than to articulate the moral condemnation of communist systems. Once the criticism of communism was deemed an aberration little room was left for freely expressing moral indignation over its misdeeds including the mass murders of Stalin.

Anti-anti-communism since the late 1960s has also increasingly merged with the revisionist view of the American communist movement as its supporters came to be portrayed as a much maligned group of idealists and true patriots, victimised by McCarthyism (as for example in Vivian Gornick's *The Romance of American Communism*).

As long as the attitudes here described persist—and especially the sentiment that the evils of American society outweigh all others and disqualify its members from passing judgement over the moral outrages committed by communist governments—there will be little incentive to confront and reasses the moral implications of the Soviet mass murders.

17

Digesting the Collapse of Communism: Responses of Western Intellectuals

"The main reason that communism has not been realized is that sufficient numbers of people do not *understand* why it is required and what it requires."—Peter Knapp and Alan J. Spector, *Crisis and Change: Basic Questions of Marxist Sociology*

The collapse of communist systems mattered most to two groups of people. One was those who had lived under such systems. The other comprised Western intellectuals who contemplated communism from afar, among them both its critics and those who continued to harbor affection towards its various incarnations and theories.

Why precisely the communist political systems, and the ideas which were used to legitimate them, were so important for Western intellectuals remains one of the most intriguing social-historical questions of our century. Examining the responses to the collapse ought to shed some light on it.

A large group of these intellectuals, mostly academics, is made up of people who wish to preserve their core left-of-centre beliefs through a variety of intellectual and psychological means. They include those who had hoped that Gorbachev's reforms would create a more acceptable socialist system with a "human face" and save the Soviet Union from collapsing. Even if they were not pro-Soviet, the observation made by Jorge Castaneda (in *Utopias Unarmed*, 1993) about the Latin American left seems to apply to them as well:

The self-destruction of the basic model signified the disappearance of the left's framework for conceiving of an alternative... The effects of the passing of the paradigm extended beyond those sectors of the left directly identified with the socialist experience... They helped discredit the central concept that was equally dear to every segment of the Latin American left: the role of the state in economic and social policy.

There are also those, conservatives and neo-conservatives, former "cold warriors" and outspoken anti-communists, who greeted the collapse with unalloyed pleasure. Their main intellectual problem has been to explain why they failed to foresee these developments, why they also assumed (like their fellow intellectuals on the left but for different reasons) that the Evil Empire was so durable.

The approach to legitimacy has been a major watershed separating these groups and their evaluation of communist systems and their collapse. Left-of-centre intellectuals, generally speaking, rarely questioned the legitimacy of communist states even when they were otherwise critical of them. On the other hand, the critics of communist systems who did not believe that they possessed legitimacy did not regard legitimacy as a key to their survival. They thought that, although dissatisfied, most people in these countries were powerless and resigned to live under a system of government they found reprehensible.

The reluctance to seriously question the legitimacy of communist states among left-leaning Western intellectuals was nurtured by a venerable source of the misapprehensions about communist systems, namely the fear of being "ethnocentric". Being critical of communist states was supposed to be ethnocentric because it implied attributing to their citizens the same needs and values that members of Western pluralistic societies cherished. Those anxious to avoid being ethnocentric professed that people could live in relative contentment under vastly different social-political arrangements, including those which ethnocentric Westerners found abhorrent.

The response of Western intellectuals of all persuasions was above all determined by the unexpectedness of the collapse. As Joseph Skvorecky, the émigré Czech writer, asked: "Has there ever been a case in history of a political system collapsing overnight, not as an aftermath of a lost war or bloody revolution but from its own inner rottenness?" Martin Malia, the Russian historian, observed that "the whole Leninist edifice imploded without any of its guardians offering serious resistance". Few in the West perceived what he called "a unique vulnerability at the very height of international power".

Neither the critics nor the latter-day sympathizers entertained the possibility of the rapid and complete disintegration of the Soviet Empire. As Strobe Talbott put it: "Most of us who tried to understand the USSR were profoundly wrong about it in one crucial aspect. We believed that bad as it was in so many ways, the system was good at one thing—its own preservation."

The critics of these systems attributed to them unusual powers of manipulation, social mobilization and an enhanced ability to intimidate their citizens. They believed that these governments succeeded in convincing their subjects that it would be costly and pointless to make any attempt to change the status quo. Some even thought of the Soviet Union in recent decades as coming to resemble a traditional society where major change was inconceivable, and a reflexive conformity was ingrained, at any rate among the vast majority.

Western intellectuals critical of established communist states tended to agree with Soviet dissidents such as Valentin Turchin, who observed in the early 1980s that: "The basis of the social order is considered by the citizens as absolutely immutable, given once and for-ever... They consider it as a given, as Newton's law. When you fall you don't blame gravity."

Thus belief in the durability of communist systems was not limited to specialists and intellectuals in the West.

Western critics saw the severe structural flaws and moral short-comings of communist systems yet were incapable of visualizing how and when they would change. The historical record did not suggest that political democracy and pluralism were irrepressible human needs.

Those who viewed communist systems with indulgence and re-garded them as relatively successful modernizing societies perceived their stability as resting on their capacity to satisfy the modest material needs of the population. After Gorbachev's rise to power the stability of these systems was further predicated (in these circles) on the policies of reform. Moshe Lewin, the historian, was among such optimists. He, among many others, could not envisage the disinte-gration of the Soviet Union, which resulted most directly from the very process of reform he applauded. In 1988 (in *The Gorbachev Phenomenon)* he confidently predicted that:

> Should the eventual turbulence produce some demands for a multi-party system, the leadership will cite national tradition and national interest to prevent an undue weaken-ing, let alone fragmentation of the party. This move would garner considerable public support. For the party is the main stabilizer of the political system, and few groups would back measures likely to erode the integrity of the entire union or the centralised state. The party, especially if it refurbishes its image, is the only institution that can preside over the overhaul of the system without endangering the polity itself in the process.

Then there were those like Abraham Brumberg—an increasingly impassioned American critic of conservative Sovietologists and the notion of "the Evil Empire" who insisted that since the Soviet system had unraveled so quickly this proved that it had never been as strong, aggressive or totalitarian as its critics used to believe.

The collapse of the Soviet "socialist commonwealth" also raises interesting questions about the survival of anti-anticommunism, a deeply ingrained attitude among left-of-centre intellectuals in the West. Anti-anticommunism was largely a product of the reaction against the obsessive and often irrational anticommunism associated with Senator Joseph McCarthy. In the wake of the collapse not many of the anti-anticommunist intellectuals have so far come to the conclusion that anticommunism was, after all, well founded, and neither irrational nor in bad taste.

II

Among the intellectuals responding to the collapse, those located at various points on the left-of-centre spectrum deserve the most attention here. They were people who followed with particular interest, sympathy or ambivalence the rise, evolution and decay of communist states (which always called themselves *socialist,* an appellation that was rarely challenged by outsiders, although sometimes it was modified by *state, existing, actually existing* or *bureaucratic.)*

The aftermath of the collapse of communist states provides a unique historical opportunity for reflection, especially for those who had high hopes for these systems. Many had visited the communist countries to express support and rejoice at close quarters in what they believed were morally ennobling experiments in the creation of social justice and material progress. Some of their responses to the fall of communism may be examined with, the help of the concepts Leon Festinger developed over three decades ago in his book *When Prophecy Fails.*

It was widely believed on the left that the Soviet Union, and the ancillary systems it spawned and controlled, would survive, perhaps with some modifications, and that these systems represented valid paths to modernity. The abrupt collapse of these systems constituted what Festinger calls "dissonance", given the belief in their durability. Such dissonance presumably was more strongly felt by those who not only believed these systems to be durable but also preferred them to capitalist ones. In contrast to such beliefs, the same intellectuals often anticipated and dwelt on the crisis and impending collapse of Western capitalism, which, however, failed to materialize. The ensuing situation could be examined with the help of the descriptions Festinger used, as for example: when "the convinced person has some investment in his belief" a "variety of ingenious defenses (spring up) with which people protect their convictions... to keep them unscathed." Festinger also said that "Dissonance produces discomfort and... there will arise pressures to reduce or eliminate dissonance."

Virtually all the forms of dissonance reduction Festinger specified came into play in the wake of the collapse. Two of these have been particularly prominent. One was redefinition of the situation—denial that the Soviet Union was socialist or Marxist, in which case the collapse did not matter and did not challenge belief in the durability of such systems, or undermine the belief that capitalist systems were more corrupt and doomed to earlier unraveling than socialist ones. The second popular strategy, in the words of Festinger, is "to forget or reduce the importance of those cognitions that are in a dissonant relationship." This meant simply ignoring the collapse, forgetting about communist systems and how their durability and legitimacy compared to those in the West, that is, to cease dwelling on matters which contradict established beliefs and preferences. This was a path chosen by many academic intellectuals who, rather than reflect on the collapse, immersed themselves with renewed vigor in other matters: multiculturalism, postmodernism, critical legal theory, revisions of American history, the many branches of feminism and so on.

Another reaction in line with Festinger's observations has been to predict improved opportunities for socialist movements in the West. (Festinger noted that true believers often respond to the failure of their prophecy by redoubling their activism.) Christopher Chase-Dunn, a professor of sociology at Johns Hopkins University, reassuringly concluded that "the revolutions in the Soviet Union and the People's Republic of China have increased our collective knowledge about how to build socialism despite their only partial successes." Geoff Eley, a historian at the University of Michigan, saw "a rich source of possibilities" in the socialist tradition for new organizational efforts on the left. Michael Walzer also sounded a hopeful note, observing that "the collapse of communism ought to open new opportunities for the democratic left, but its immediate effect has been to raise questions about many leftist (not only communist) orthodoxies."

Such and similar responses to the collapse gained strength from the substantial social support that has been available for them in the various subcultures of American society (especially the academic ones) where such beliefs and attitudes flourished, indeed had become institutionalized since the 1960s.

III

Erstwhile political pilgrims and tourists to the former lands of socialism constitute a group most predictably disposed to resist sweeping re-evaluation of the wreckage of the social systems they had been drawn to. There have been tens if not hundreds of thousands of such people in this century, most recently admirers of Sandinista Nicaragua.

Not many of the pilgrims who journeyed to the Soviet Union in the 1930's and 1940's survive, hence we shall miss their reassessments. Far more of the former admirers of China under Mao and Cuba under Castro are still with us. They could take the position (as some have) that the collapse of the corrupt Soviet empire need not have tarnished China, controlled by the determined old men who did not budge when confronted with the unruly young dissidents in June 1989. (On the other hand, the attractions of communist China diminished after Mao's death and in the wake of the compromises the system made with the spirit and practices of capitalism.)

Occasional bizarre exceptions remain and are worthy of note as examples of the uncommon persistence of belief in the face of overwhelming evidence. Mary Lou Greenberg, a former editor of *New China* magazine and a 1971 pilgrim to China wrote last year:

> In 1971 during the Cultural Revolution workers spoke to me with pride of their efforts to build a new... China. They were making prodigious economic gains... But even more important, new social relations were being forged...the Chinese I saw were characterized by dignity and optimism... It is no wonder that, in this centennial year of the birth of Mao Zedong, many in China, as well as around the world, are looking at the experience of the Maoist years not only with nostalgia but also for lessons for the future.

Cuba has remained less tainted by compromise, still led by its charismatic, revolutionary founder who continues to exude anti-

American rhetoric. As such it can still count on the sympathy of those on the left for its defiance of the United States and its unwillingness to follow its former allies along the path of political reform. Thus the conventional left-liberal wisdom, repeated on the evening television news, is still that the US economic blockade, and not the policies of Castro, is responsible for the difficulties of the Cuban economy. Even as recently as the summer of 1993 "seeing the bright side of Castro" (as the television critic for the *New York Times* put it) was a fair description of an American television documentary on Cuba. Cuba was also praised for "pioneering energy conservation" (as if it had a choice) and the friends of Castro vigorously campaigned across the nation to lift the economic blockade, motivated doubtless as much by the desire to save the system as by the impulse to diminish human suffering.

A remarkable example of durable affection for Cuba was provided by Carol Brightman, an editor of a 1971 volume entitled *Venceremos Brigade: Young Americans Sharing the Life and Work of Revolutionary Cuba*—a rapturous expression of abject admiration for Castro's Cuba still unsurpassed. On her 1994 visit Brightman was delighted by "Castro's efforts to devise a different kind of socialism" and boasted about getting Castro to autograph a baseball cap for her fourteen-year-old son.

Thus Cuba under Castro remains the only communist state that still elicits warmth among some Western intellectuals (although no longer quite so freely expressed as it used to be) in part because current economic hardships have reinvigorated its aura of the last uncompromising and victimized communist system.

Unhappily for many Western intellectuals positioned on the further reaches of the left, not only has the supply of appealing communist systems been largely exhausted, there is also a critical shortage of guerilla movements with suitable credentials. The Shining Path guerillas in Peru were described by Jorge Castaneda as:

The last movement to openly proclaim its allegiance to "Marxism-Leninism-Maoism", to unabashedly put forward the goal of communist revolution and to unhesitatingly reject any notion of electoral contention or dialogue with existing authorities or institutions.

As such the movement comes closest to having the proper credentials and appeals for some radical leftist intellectuals for example William Kunstler and John Gerassi, who in 1991 were among the supporters of the Berkeley-based "Committee to Support the Revolution in Peru," which sought to mobilize public opinion in favor of Guzman, the Shining Path leader who had been captured by the government). Sympathizers with these guerillas had to be capable of accepting large quantities of bloodshed in a revolutionary cause and to be impressed by the apparent unity of revolutionary intellectuals (such as Guzman) and authentic peasants displayed in inspiring mountain settings. The supporters in Berkeley were not alone, as James Brooke reported in the *New York Times:*

> From Berkeley to London to Stockholm, solidarity groups have formed to support a group that one human rights advocate, Juan E. Mendez of Americas Watch, recently called "the most brutal guerilla group that ever has appeared in the Western Hemisphere."

If any of the erstwhile pilgrims had second thoughts following the unraveling of communist states (not only in Eastern Europe and the Soviet Union, but also in Nicaragua, Angola, Ethiopia and Mozambique) they rarely made them public. There is reason to believe that silence will remain the dominant response. It is not easy to admit to political misjudgments and misperceptions the scale of which was extraordinary even at the time when nobody anticipated the collapse and final discrediting of these systems.

IV

It is hardly surprising that past assessments of communist systems conditioned the reaction to their collapse. Many Western intellectuals used to regard them (even in more recent times) with bemused tolerance while regretfully noting their occasional (or frequent, as the case may be) departure from the early ideals or the guiding theory. For the late I.F. Stone the Soviet Union represented (in 1983) a "distortion of socialism," nonetheless it was "still socialism." For him as for many other intellectuals on the left what mattered were the good intentions: even a deformed socialist system was preferable to an unreconstructed capitalist one; some day, actually existing socialist states might become more authentic incarnations of the ideal. In the meantime the Soviet bloc and the Soviet Union in particular were given credit for restraining American imperialism, aiding Third World liberation movements and propping up the supposedly more authentic socialist states such as Vietnam, Cuba and Nicaragua. Moreover, according to the authors of *Crisis and*

Change (a 1991 Marxist textbook in sociology), "The Soviets were trying something for the first time in history and it is hardly surprising that they made mistakes." These mistakes, the rather unusual argument ran, resulted from "the Soviets" using "old elitist managers and generals", in fact "capitalist managers, using capitalist principles."

The reflections on the collapse by leftist social critics have been pervaded above all by the concern that it might legitimate capitalism and actually existing Western democracies. Thus the continued hostility towards capitalism remains a major determinant of the responses to the collapse. Some even succeeded in blaming capitalism for the difficulties of the socialist states. Professor Cole of the Anthropology Department at the University of Massachusetts (Amherst) averred:

> The communist countries should have stayed on a road of purely socialist development instead of giving in to their citizens' demand for a more consumer-oriented economy. But because the West had the consumer goods, it was able in the 1980's to hoodwink the communist world into becoming trading partners, which tied its economic well-being to the West's... The decline in the 1980's of world capitalism nailed Eastern Europe.

According to Christopher Chase-Dunn:

> The communist states have been important experiments in the construction of socialist institutions, but they were perverted... by the necessities of survival... in the context of the capitalist world market... The communist states failed to institutionalize a self-reproducing socialist mode of production because of the strong threats and inducements emanating from the larger capitalist world system...

In short, in the words of a Cuban émigré scholar, Dario Fernandez-Morera, "Socialism would have turned out much better had capitalism not continued to be around to corrupt it."

Another recurring theme on the left has been that the collapse did not vindicate American foreign policies. Wade Huntley, a columnist in the *Chronicle of Higher Education,* spoke for many of his fellow academics on this matter:

> We set out to break the back of Soviet Communism but simply broke our own bank instead... But the cost of the cold war to the United States was perhaps even more spiritual than economic... The United States emerged from the cold war burdened by debt and poverty and carrying numerous scars from wounds to our cherished institutions—self-inflicted for the sake of superpower competition. In turning our nation into a hard-line cold-war combatant we undermined our "best traditions"... Considering what might have been, the United States was the loser in the cold war.

The Devil We Knew, by H.W. Brands, a volume devoted to the reassessment of the Cold War, argued that it served largely domestic political and psychological purposes for the United States, gratifying in particular the need to find enemies and "to affirm American identity and Americans' basic goodness":

> The Cold War had resulted largely from the efforts of the United States to export capitalism across the globe... The Soviet Union, far from being the aggressor, found itself on the defensive... the burden of responsibility for the Cold War rested on the United States.

As these suggestions so well illustrate, anti-anticommunism rested on the premise that there was no substance to the fears of, or the aversion to, communism (represented by the Soviet Union), domestically or globally. Similar views found expression in *The Fifties* by David Halberstam, who focused on the delusions driving US foreign policy during those years. E.L. Doctorow, the novelist and social critic, described American Cold War policies "as an act of national self-mutilation."

V

If the communist ideals have ceased to have even the most rudimentary embodiment in actually existing political systems (with the possible exception of Cuba) and if most of the systems which used to legitimate themselves by Marxism have ignominiously collapsed, for those who believed in those ideals it becomes all the more important to rescue and reaffirm them and to separate them from the disagreeable realities they were linked to. Such efforts have also been prompted by the disturbing, undreamed-of possibility that the Marxian developmental scheme is being reversed as socialist systems are being replaced by capitalist ones. Shlomo Avineri among many others maintained that: "The Soviet system was not and could not have been a socialist system... Marxism saw socialism as a stage that would follow capitalism and takes its place... (Soviet) society and socialism have nothing in common."

The authors of *Crisis and Change* wrote: "We do not believe that the failure is a failure of Marxism. Still less is it the final 'triumph of capitalism"'... Capitalism is still in crisis."

Stephen P. Dunn, a Soviet specialist, argued that:

> Marxism as a political movement ... had undergone a long series of setbacks since at least the 1930s. However, these political setbacks don't, in principle, reflect on Marxism's

viability as a social hypothesis—a means of explaining what happens—or as a vehicle for people's aspirations.

In Germany, Jutta Ditfurth of the Greens Party suggested that:

There simply is no need to re-examine the validity of socialism as a model... it was not socialism that was defeated in Eastern Europe and the Soviet Union because these systems were never socialist.

Stuart Hall wrote in *Marxism Today* that "we should not be alarmed by the collapse of 'actually existing socialism' since, as socialists, we have been waiting for it to happen for three decades". If such commentators had been anxiously awaiting the collapse of existing socialist systems for decades they succeeded in keeping it to themselves. Even during the Brezhnev era and well into the Gorbachev years, distinguished Western intellectuals including John Kenneth Galbraith, Paul Samuelson and Lester Thurow went on record crediting the Soviet system with sound and satisfactory economic policies.

Among those on the left it is now an article of faith that the ideas of Marxism and the now defunct political systems which legitimated themselves with these ideas had *nothing* in common. Marxism was often compared to Christianity, as a belief system that cannot be dismissed just because its precepts remain unrealized. Along these lines Pete Seeger, the venerable American leftist folksinger observed: "I still call myself a communist, because communism is no more what Russia made of it than Christianity is what the churches make of it."

VI

Some American intellectuals opted for ignoring the fall of communism altogether given their preoccupation with the impending, ongoing or approaching crisis of capitalism (or "late capitalism"); it is hardly surprising that they were inclined to miss the actual crisis of communism.

The multiplication of the causes which today energize and mobilize various adversarial groups in the United States is probably also related to the decline of the universalistic vision of Marxism to which communist systems paid lip service. Much of the adversarial energy which at earlier times led to the idealization of putative embodiments of socialism in various locations (most recently in Nicaragua) has found new outlets in the pursuit and advocacy of multiculturalism.

While interpretations of the concept vary, its essential core consists of intense anti-Western sentiments which include large doses of anti-capitalism and anti-intellectualism, as well as rejection of Western culture, tradition, rationality and social ideals.

Postmodernism, structuralism, deconstructionism, critical-legal theory and new varieties of feminism may be added to the ideological-intellectual trends and fashions which derived further sustenance from the eclipse of communist systems and ideals. They provide preoccupations and diversions for many intellectuals who might otherwise have had to ponder the lessons of the decay and collapse of existing socialism and its legitimating ideas.

VII

A discussion of the response of American intellectuals to the disintegration of the Soviet empire would be incomplete without at least briefly noting some of the concepts they had earlier used for characterizing communist systems. These concepts continue to color their interpretations of the collapse. Among them I will single out convergence, its successor, moral equivalence, and totalitarianism.

Central to the concept of moral equivalence was the insistence that nothing in American or Western social and political practices and institutions was morally superior to their communist equivalent. Those unable or unwilling to grasp the distinctive, and distinctively unappealing, characteristics of the Soviet and similar systems felt compelled either to see them as mirror images of the West (or the US) or in the process of converging with the West, or in any case, morally equivalent. This point of view seriously obscured moral as well as institutional differences between the United States and the Soviet Union and consequently made it difficult to discern the substantial, qualitative differences between the stability, legitimacy and durability of the two systems.

The convergence theory proposed that after certain levels of economic development are attained in the actually existing socialist states and they became more complex, a pluralistic superstructure would arise—in other words, civil society. It was a form of economic determinism that many Western intellectuals, located at different points of the political spectrum, found congenial.

It is also clear that the concept of totalitarianism embraced at earlier times by the conservative critics of communism provided little help in discerning the sources of change and the structural weaknesses of these systems and in anticipating their demise. The totalitarian model considered these systems durable, not because they met the needs of their people but because they found ways to stay in power *regardless* of those unmet needs. Anticommunist intellectuals (including this writer) overestimated both the coercive capabilities of communist states and the associated popular docility, as well as the determination of the communist political elites to hang on to power. Intellectuals rejecting the Soviet system on moral grounds considered it an evil empire that was durable and dangerous, because it is difficult to think of evil as transient and feeble, of an "evil empire" which would suddenly disintegrate.

VIII

The different perspectives of intellectuals regarding the sources of change in communist systems rested not only on political-ideological differences but also on different and usually unstated social-psychological assumptions. For those dubious about the capacity of these systems to reform themselves the theory-practice gap was important. By contrast, the notion that the moral revulsion of ordinary people, besides the material shortages, was a significant factor in the fall of these systems was not an idea readily embraced by left-of-centre intellectuals.

The belief that there was a cumulative and consequential popular awareness of the chasm between promise and reality suggests that people cannot be deceived indefinitely whatever their level of education and material circumstances. This point of view does not exclude the possibility that those aware of the official lies can nevertheless be compelled by force, or threat of force, to live for a long time under the system that disseminated the falsehoods.

How far in time the attitudes of estrangement reach back among the people who lived under these systems is indicated by the evidence of a little-known document, the diary of an old-line Hungarian communist, Ervin Sinko, who lived in exile in Moscow during 1935-37. In his diary he reports his astonishment when one morning in July 1935 he came upon an article in *Izvestia* reporting on the deplorable reading habits of young Soviet people. Not only did they read Western thrillers of the time such as Nick Carter and Pinkerton, but these dubious volumes "were passed from hand to hand as if they were treasures... They devour them feverishly." The article made use of a survey of the reading habits and tastes of the young undertaken by a Moscow public library in 1935. Virtually all of those surveyed agreed that the required school readings were boring; most preferred books on travel and adventure. The young readers repeatedly objected to the impersonal, didactic character of the heroes of socialist realist fiction, to the lack of mystery in these books. Of one character a reader wrote: "This Varia is a robot; mere executor of the will of the Party, unreal as a human being; I cannot conceive of a young girl only interested in matters social; this Varia has no personal life." Sinko concluded that the young readers displayed "a sense of deprivation contemporary Soviet literature could not assuage because it excludes the intimate, contradictory, painful and antibucolic longings of human beings."

If such were the long forgotten, indeed unknown attitudes of Soviet youth in the mid-1930s when terror was rampant and an oppressive docility seemed triumphant, one may conclude that the seeds of decay go back very far, and that many Western intellectuals, and especially those on the left, seriously underestimated the degree to which this system denied basic human needs, including those of imaginary gratification in fiction. These bits of forgotten information suggest that the collapse also had to do with matters more elusive but not necessarily less important than economic malfunctioning.

If so, a renewed attention to the less relativistic aspects of human nature and a greater emphasis on the part they play in politics may be among the welcome if unexpected consequences of the fall of communist systems.

18

Revisiting "The Banality of Evil": Political Violence in Communist Systems

The demise of Soviet Communism has opened up new possibilities for increasing our understanding of political violence in this century. We are now in a far better position to compare and in doing so narrow the gap between what we know about the two most murderous political systems in this century: Nazi Germany and the Soviet Union, especially under Stalin. Western and especially American levels of information and moral awareness of the political violence perpetrated by Nazi Germany are far greater than those of comparable activities of the Soviet Union and other Communist states. Correspondingly far more is known about the Nazi planners, organizers and executors of political violence and coercion than of their Communist counterparts. There are numerous studies of the major figures of Nazi political violence such as Adolf Eichman, Joseph Goebbels, Heinrich Himmler and Rudolf Hoess (the latter the commander of Auschwitz), of the elite troops and personnel assigned to these tasks (the SS and Gestapo), of the defendants of the Nuremberg Trials which established new standards for war crimes and politically motivated mass murders. Specific theories and concepts have been devised to conceptualize and understand Nazi murderousness and repression, such as "the banality of evil," "desk murderers," "authoritarian personality," and "obedience to authority." By any measure, corresponding information about the specialists in coercion and organizers of mass violence in Communist systems has been far more limited.

Even more striking that some Western visitors to Communist societies formed favorable impressions of their leading specialists in coercion and political violence, and of their penal institutions (based usually on conducted tours of model prisons) just as grotesquely misperceiving them as they did the political system as a whole. Romain Rolland referred to Genrikh Yagoda, who was in charge of the Soviet political police in the 1930s as "fine-featured, distinguished.... [and] ... impregnated with sweetness." Henry Wallace and Owen Lattimore on a conducted tour of Soviet concentration camps in Kolyma were most favorably impressed by camp commander Ivan Nikishov. More recently Tomas Borge, head of the Nicaraguan state security, charmed Gunter Grass as well as numerous American political tourists; an American professor of philosophy at my school thought Borge was a good poet and "ran a prison system known as one of the most progressive in the world." It was by no means an exceptional misjudgment of communist prison systems.

Political violence and its perpetrators in the now defunct Communist systems are also of interest because better information about them -increasingly available - sheds further light on the issue of the "banality of evil" (introduced by Hannah Arendt to account for the character and behavior of Nazi mass murderers) as opposed to other theories of causation. Much remains to be learned about the relationship between beliefs and behavior on those occasions when mass murders were designed and carried out.

The attitudes of those who worked for the KGB (and their equivalents in other Communist states) are also of special interest since, arguably, the collapse of Communist systems might be explained in part by their declining willingness to continue to suppress dissent or opposition. If indeed there was an erosion of political will and reflexive ruthlessness at the top of the political hierarchy, it presumably extended to the specialists in coercion as well, who were most directly responsible for maintaining the social-political order. (This erosion amounted to virtual paralysis, as became clear during the botched coup attempt against Gorbachev in 1991.) Markus Wolf, the former head of general and foreign intelligence of the East German Stasi suggested that "people didn't fight to keep it [the system] alive" because it "didn't correspond to our ideals." If indeed the perceived discrepancy between ideals and realities translated into the declining morale of the state security forces, it would be a most dramatic illustration of the impact of political disillusionment on the survival of the system.

We have limited knowledge of how the attitudes of the people directly involved with the coercive apparatus differed from those in other positions of power. Were they especially determined to resist threats to the integrity of their worldview? Did they fall back on different rationalizations for their activities? For how long did they succeed in convincing themselves that the very unpleasantness of the tasks they undertook was proof of their virtue and moral uprightness? Or were they simply cynics to begin with? It is hard to know what proportion of them were "idealists" and how many were attracted primarily by the elite status and the perks these positions guaranteed, or what mixture of motives were present. Presumably with the passage of time the number of corrupt careerists rose at the expense of the stern idealists.

There seem to be four models or archetypes of the specialists in coercion (and political violence) implicit in the existing literature, including that which deals with the Nazi case. In the first group are the ideologically driven, supposedly incorruptible, puritanical executioners (metaphorically speaking), exemplified in the Soviet case perhaps by Feliks Dzerzhinsky and Himmler in the Nazi one.

Resulting in part from the influence of Hannah Arendt the former type came to be eclipsed in popular as well as scholarly thinking by individuals of the second type such as Eichman personifying the "banality of evil." These were supposedly very ordinary human beings who found themselves in situations which imposed on them these unappealing roles; they followed orders without being driven by strong convictions. Money and privilege were sometimes factors, as in the former Soviet Union and communist Czecholovakia where even within the state security system there was distaste for domestic or internal surveillance. According to one former employee "'No one wanted to do this work—arresting and interrogating political people. So it paid well.'" As time went by the morale of the Czech state security declined: "By the end of the 1980s the StB didn't believe its own propaganda." Certainly in the lower echelons, convictions were not an essential occupational requirement, and underlings had better grounds for shifting blame to their superiors, as in the obedience-to-authority scenario. Among the latter a former colonel in the KGB argued, "The system made us develop hostility to each other ... Hostility, revenge, denunciations, spy mania, all that was encouraged—all stemming from the man himself, the man with the mustache. From top to bottom these base instincts were encouraged!" He did have a point: these attitudes were indeed encouraged but not everybody responded in the same way to such encouragement.

Not only former KGB officials, but even those who eagerly cooperated with the regime in the regimentation of the arts resorted to time honored excuses and rationalizations. One of them was Tikhon Khrennikov, a mediocre official composer and favorite of Stalin. He became infamous for the denunciation of Prokofiev and Shostakovich in 1948. More recently he asserted that he merely obeyed the order of the Central Committee, "he didn't write the speech that was thrust into his hands a few hours before he was due to speak." Moreover, "Nobody could say no to Stalin ... My conscience is clear.... You had to live in that atmosphere to understand what was going on."

Apparently the conscience of Vladimir Kryuchkov, the last head of the KGB (and leader of the 1991 putsch attempt against Gorbachev) was also clear. In a conversation with the American journalist and author David Remnick, he said:

> If there has to be repentance [for KGB activities], then let everyone repent. You should repent for what you've done to the Indians ... If you repent, we will too. My attitude toward Stalin is clear: I condemn the repressions. I condemn the totalitarian forms of rule that Stalin developed ... He became the head of the Soviet state when there was only a plow, and left it when the state had an atomic bomb . . . Believe me in twenty or thirty years Stalin will be referred to as a kind of genius.

Earlier in the conversation Kryuchkov also averred that he had "nothing to do with the struggle against dissent:' which led his interlocutor to conclude that he "seemed perfectly capable of lying with a serene sense of self-possession and righteousness,"—another apparent qualification for the position he had filled.

The third type of the specialists emerges from more recent references to the personnel of the KGB, portrayed as well-educated, often suave careerists who found satisfactory employment and mobility opportunities in this organization. Sometimes an adventurous disposition contributed to the attractions of such employment, as in the case of former General Oleg Kalugin who also claimed patriotic motives in joining the intelligence gathering branch of the KGB.

It is the fourth group—seemingly composed of individuals who gravitate toward the organizations of violence and coercion, and their repugnant activities—that has attracted the least social scientific interest. Victor Serge, an old Soviet revolutionary observed during the first years of the October Revolution the contrast between such individuals and the Dzerzhinsky types:

> The Party endeavoured to head it [the Cheka, that is, the first embodiment of the KGB] with incorruptible men like ... Dzerzhinsky, a sincere idealist, ruthless but chivalrous, with the emaciated profile of an Inquisitor ... But the Party had few men of this stamp and many Chekas: these gradually came to select their personnel by virtue of their psychological inclinations. The only temperaments that devoted themselves willingly and tenaciously to this task of 'internal defense' were those characterized by suspicion, embitterment, harshness and sadism. Long-standing social inferiority-complexes and memories of humiliations and suffering in the Tsars' jails rendered them intractable, and since professional degeneration has rapid effects, the Chekas inevitably consisted of perverted men tending to see conspiracy everywhere and to live in the midst of perpetual conspiracy themselves.

Similar tendencies were also observed in the Hungarian state security police (AVO or AVH). According to one former victim and analyst of the organization, the writer George Paloczi-Horvath:

> The SP [security police] was constantly purged by General Peter [that is, Gabor Peter, the head of it]. Many former SP officers were with us in jail. They were arrested for the slightest sign of elementary decency. With this method General Peter succeeded in finding in a few years that criminal and potentially sadistic five per cent which is there in any given population.

The idea that in every society there are groups of people who, for whatever reason, possess, or develop a personality congenial for the activities repressive police forces require has been noted by many authors. The Brazilian man of letters Antonio Candido observed that for these tasks "society needs thousands of individuals with appropriately deformed souls ... society draws from these people the brutality, the need, the frustration, the depravity, the defect—and gives them the repressive function." The Czech emigrè writer Josef Skvorecky, perceived the hardcore supporters of both Nazi and Communist systems as "people scarred by private hatreds, grounded in deeply negative personal experience ... [people] with physical or psychological malformations ... haunted by a feeling of insecurity... exploiting ideas and movements to achieve a feeling of self-worth and to devalue other people."

A connection between official policies and less than creditable human traits was also noted by Luba Brezhneva, the niece of Leonid Brezhnev:

> Continual official calls for crackdowns on the "enemies of the people" [in the 1930s, that is] had awakened the basest instincts, and searching out enemies evolved as part of

the national psychology ... Informers were praised and held up as role models for the youths; they were also given financial rewards and promotions ...

Doubtless, many intolerant, vindictive, resentful and authoritarian human beings found their way into the Communist political police forces—institutions that provided a sense of entitlement and philosophical legitimation for indulging their impulses and inclinations. Erich Mielke, a head of Stasi may qualify as such a prototype in whom a variety of unappealing personality traits and ideological convictions were mutually supportive, as David Pryce-Jones observed:

> He had risen from rigging show trials to run the Stasi in 1957 ... Thuggish and greedy, he was also vain. The list which he drew up of his 250 medals and orders covered eighteen pages ... in an echo of Herman Goering ... [in his office] ... is a portrait of Felix Dzerzhinsky, Lenin's policeman and killer-in-chief, [and] a death mask of Lenin ...

The arguments sketched above are in obvious and stark contrast to that popularized by Hannah Arendt and taken up with seeming relish by many Western intellectuals and the general public in the last few decades: the belief that mass murderers were ordinary, "normal" people, undistinguished by any moral stigma or deformity, who found themselves in situations which led to their brutal behavior, and that virtually anybody could become one under the appropriate circumstances. (The receptivity to this thesis points to strong social critical impulses: if all of us are so corruptible, it says something about the type of society that produced us; collective responsibility, "complicity" removes the moral distinctions between perpetrator and all those who were spared only by luck to be thrust in the same roles; attention is diverted from the individual to the social circumstances and pressures.) Stanley Milgram's ingenious experiments on obedience to authority have also been strongly supportive of this point of view.

It may of course also be argued that the four categories outlined cannot be easily separated, that they overlap especially when both material and ,'moral" incentives play a part. Thus, reportedly the Hungarian political police officers "were trained ... for devotion, blind discipline and were at the same time filled with a consciousness of mission and professional pride ... Their self-confidence was further inflated by the fact that they could fill their pockets with various allowances, bonuses and benefits ..."

If Nazi leaders engaged in the large-scale extermination of civilians could shift responsibility to higher authority and ultimately Hitler, their Communist counterparts had an even more helpful device at their disposal to accomplish similar ends: the myth of the infallibility of the Party. (They could also rely on beliefs deriving from Marxism-Leninism, especially the notion that they were on the right side of the historical process.) It was an article of faith among them that the Party was a unique, chosen instrument of history and historical justice. Whatever served the purposes and policies of this entity was beyond judgment. George Kennan's observation about Andrei Gromyko applies to many communist leaders: "... the Party became ... his mother, his father, his teacher, his conscience, and his master. He was never to question its ideals, its authority, its moral purity." The Party could be divorced from the errors of particular human beings who belonged to it, led it, and were mortal; it transcended the life-span of the individual. Kennan further observed:

> ... for anything undertaken in response to the will of the collectivity (in this instance the Party), no matter how distasteful, no matter how unattractive from the standpoint of individual morality, there could be no guilt, no questioning, no remorse. And if it turned out that what the Party required to be done ... involved apparent injustice or cruelty—well, one might regret that it was found necessary, one might wish that it could have been otherwise; but it was not one's own responsibility.

It was a part of Communist political culture—originating in the early Soviet political practices and traditions—that, as Nathan Leites put it

> ... it became ... forbidden to admit in public that any act of the Party was regrettable ... All acts of the Party are presented in public as entirely desirable .... [Moreover] the Party must be prepared to inflict any amount of deprivation on any number of human beings if this appears 'necessary' . . . The refusal to use necessary bad means appears to the Bolsehvik as an expression of stupidity ... or as imperfect dedication to the great goal; or as self-centeredness which keeps one more concerned with not touching dirt and not feeling guilt than with transforming the world ...

George Lukacs, himself not involved in the dirty business of keeping the system in power, had fully internalized this principle and expressed it with great clarity:

> The highest duty for Communist ethics is to accept the necessity of acting immorally. This is the greatest sacrifice that the revolution demands of us. The conviction of the true communist is that evil transforms itself into bliss through the dialectics of historical evolution.

Especially helpful was the idea (for the Communist revolutionaries and their successors) that there is and can be a radical discontinuity between the present and the future and that the latter will not be contaminated by the practices of the present; it was the denial (again as summed up by Leites) that

> ... the chance of attaining certain goals may be lessened by the ...protracted and large-scale use of means which are at extreme variance with them ... Bolshevik doctrine seems to imply that the actual or required state of affairs existing before the full realization of Communism will be reversed afterwards ... The use of means at sharp variance with the state of affairs under Communism itself will not interfere with its ultimate realization. The Party must accept as a matter of course any expedient degree of discrepancy between means and ends.

Such attachment to "ultimate realization," that is, a pervasive future orientation, derived from Marxism. Alexander Yakovlev, close associate of Gorbachev and one of the most important voices for reform perceptively observed:

> By making the illusory future more important than humanity, Marxism gave people carte blanche to use any means when it came to power ... thus placing them beyond good and evil. Positive values —kindness, conscience, love, cooperation, solidarity, justice, freedom, the rule of law - were unfit, useless. They weakened the class struggle.

Yakovlev, unlike those who absolve Marx of any responsibility for the outrages committed in his name, notes that Marxism grew into ". . . the conviction that everything that corresponded to the interests of revolution and Communism was moral. That is the morality with which hostages were executed, the peasantry was destroyed, concentration camps were built and entire peoples were forcibly relocated." Dedication to the best interests of abstractions such as "mankind" or "humanity" at the expense of real human beings played a similar role. Again, Yakovlev (among many others) was well aware of this fateful dichotomy: "Dostoyevky's Grand Inquisitor speaks of love for humanity. But complete contempt for an actual individual flows from this love."

Generations of Soviet Party functionaries, and before them revolutionaries, internalized the myth of the Party which allowed them to divest it of all responsibility for the errors and horrors commited on its behalf, in its name. By the same token, the myth of the Party also relieved of responsibilty those executing its presumed will. This included the early generation of highly-educated idealist revolutionaries, as for instance Lev Kamenev, who characteristically "shared the near mystical belief that the Party was the sole embodiment of correct thinking. And... [he shared] the desire to root out any thinking held to be incorrect." Eventually he too perished, a victim of one of the show trials. For them there was "no possibility of salvation outside the faith" as Adam Hochchild wrote, following an interpretation originally put forward by Arthur Koestler in *Darkness at Noon*. Even so it remains

> One of the great psychological puzzles... why so many intelligent, educated Communist Party members... looked into the abyss, saw the arrests, the midnight executions, the suppression of all dissent... recalled the reign of the guillotine that had followed the French revolution, vainly spoke out in protest - and then came back loyally to the Party fold.

Ideological convictions (or some primitive variant of them) were also helpful in later times, as the remarks of Dimitri Tokaryev, the commander of the murder squad at the Katyn Forest (where 15,000 Polish officers were killed on Stalin's orders), indicate. David Pryce-Jones related that Tokaryev justified his actions "on the grounds that these Poles were class enemies... 'I am proud of the work that I did in defense of our revolution!...'" Several decades later, "Judge Zubiets had sentenced the dissident Irena Ratushinskaya to prison for her poetry and religious faith. 'Times were different then [he said] I did my duty.'"

Of another generation of functionaries Pavel Sudoplatov, a former leading KGB official wrote in a similar spirit: "We must recall... the mentality of idealistic Communists in the later forties and early fifties... Party business was sacred..." Vladimir Farkas, who used to be a high-ranking officer in the Hungarian political police, recalled the part played by the idea of the Party in betrayals which would otherwise have been difficult to justify:

> I first observed in the case of my father [minister of defense and member of the "troika" of four running the country] and Janos Kadar [head of the Party for almost three decades] the capability of abandoning former comrades-in-arms, their mistreatment and the hideous point of view—which may be compared to that previaling during the Spanish Inquisition—that whatever they said was the word of the Party, and the truth of the Party, because the Party is never mistaken.

Loyalty to the Party or the Cause is less helpful for understanding the motives of the generation of post-Stalin, post-Khrushchev leaders and functionaries who were neither participants in a revolution nor highly idealistic pioneers of radical social change which followed it. It is more likely that what for the early generation of revolutionary leaders was legitimation by idealistic belief became for their successors a way of habitual thinking (or non-thinking), as far as the Party's power to legitimate expedient but amoral policies was concerned. Nonetheless it is probably safe to say that each generation of leaders and specialists (and their underlings) took it for granted that their goals were sublime enough to sanitize—from the long-range historical perspective—the means used to attain them; each subscribed to Lenin's belief that "our morality is completely subordinated to the interests of the class struggle of the proletariat" and that "everything that is done in the proletarian cause is honest ." There was of course a great latitude in deciding what were the interests of the proletariat and even in defining who precisely belonged to it. But there was no doubt that the Party and its leaders were the ultimate arbiters of these choices and decisions.

In the final analysis it is probably most fruitful to combine two approaches to account for the attitudes and behavior of the people whom I called the specialists in coercion. In the first, the emphasis is on idealistic commitment, in the second, on its seeming opposite: the love of power, the flaws of character, even human depravity. It is difficult to separate these two, since the lofty ideals were the most compelling justification for holding on to, or maximizing power by any means available, and for crushing mercilessly those who would challenge it.

In support of the first approach one may argue that the specialists were more deeply committed to the system and its values than those in other realms of the hierarchy whose tasks and roles required a lesser degree of ruthlessness. High-ranking officials in charge of the political police were directly confronted with the potential dilemma of ends and means; they had to use the most distasteful means; they needed particularly strong convictions and defenses to assure themselves that what they did was essential and justified by some higher purpose or morality. Even the Nazis were aware of this need and occasionally faced up to the task of explicitly justifying the mass murder of civilians, as in the notorious speech Himmler gave to SS leaders in which he acknowledged that the mass killing of civilians was not an easy task and required overcoming "human weakness."

The most satisfactory way to assuage incipient guilt or disgust was for the specialists to remind themselves of the long-range goals and benefits for which they were striving and the ideals enshrined in the theory which guided them. The struggle for the new world required painful sacrifices. Lenin warned that "there are no ... serious battles without field hospitals near the battlefields. It is altogether unforgivable to permit oneself to be frightened or unnerved by 'field hospital' scenes. If you are afraid of the wolves, don't go into the forest."

There was also the time-honored recourse to the claim of collective self-defense, as articulated by Molotov, who even in the 1980s insisted that the Purges were necessary, defensive and to the good of society. Soviet authorities always justified the various campaigns of coercion and political violence as strictly defensive measures, essential for the survival of the system under attack by internal and external enemies of exceptional cunning and evil. For instance, Vladimir Farkas recalled a high-ranking Soviet political police officer who illustrated the cunning of "the enemy" (the almost mythical entity and counterpoint to the Party) with a story about a group of unmasked anti-Communist spies who, when in front of the firing squad, cheered Stalin and the Soviet Union: "They did so ... in order to sow confusion even at the last moment of their lives, in the minds and hearts of the soldiers executing them, by suggesting that they were going to shoot loyal Communists."

More recently, vague references to "the times:' as in the case of Yegor Ligachev discussing particular mass murders of the NKVD in the 1930s, have served a similar purpose. Apparently during certain periods, seen as prolonged emergencies, a "temporary" suspension of ethical standards was acceptable. Anatoli Sudoplatov (who used to be in charge of assassinations abroad, among other things) also believed that the historical context provided absolution: ". . . I do not intend to justify what I did as a member of foreign intelligence service from the 1920s to the early 1950s. That was a different time, a different historical period." This was also the view of Ramon Mercader, the actual assassin of Trotsky who wielded the pickaxe (and whom Sudoplatov employed in this task). According to Sudoplatov, Mercader thought of himself as

... a professional revolutionary, proud of his role ... He told me: "If I were to relive the 1940s I would do the same thing, but not in the present day world [of 1969]".He did not repent his murder of Trotsky. He quoted the Russian saying "One does not choose the time to live and die" and said "I would add to that. One does not choose the time to live, die or kill ." It is clear to me now that present morals are incompatible with the cruelty of the revolution, civil war and power struggles that follow them.... There was no way for Stalin to treat Trotsky in exile as merely a writer of philosophical books; Trotsky was an active enemy who had to be destroyed.

Those involved in the planning and execution of political violence in Communist Hungary, and especially the notorious Hungarian show trial of Laszlo Rajk, clung to similar rationalizations. Mihaly Farkas, intimately involved in the Rajk case, said in 1957: "We acted in the best conviction that we fought the enemy." Mathias Rakosi, the head of the Hungarian Communist Party who used to be called, and with good reason, "the most outstanding Hungarian disciple of Comrade Stalin" in retrospect had this to say: "in the Rajk affair the Hungarian leadership too must bear responsibility. Nonetheless it must be taken into account that all that happened in 1949. The international situation must be considered; these matters have to be examined not from the perspective of abstract moral principles." At the time of Rajk's arrest Rakosi offered the Hungarian Politburo the following explanation:

"When there is trouble, it is always connected to the machinations of the enemy. We are not worried about suspecting everybody alive. The growth of suspiciousness that is going to occur, is all right. When you cut trees, the chips will fall." Rakosi also related that when he was in jail there was a man who had tuberculosis of the bone, his whole foot had to be amputated. He implored the doctors to cut only a small part. 'He was operated on four times, and four times the tuberculosis remained in the bones. His whole leg had to be amputated [in the end] but he died. Had he allowed to have his whole foot amputated early on, his life could have been saved."

It may be noted here that those advising, encouraging or ordering political violence often thrive on organic or surgical metaphors; the body politic is equated with the human body.

The second approach to understanding the actions and attitudes of the specialists relies more heavily on the attractions of power. In addition to ideologically inspired certainties and rationalizations, the likes of Beria, Yagoda, Yezhov, Sudoplatov, the Hungarian Gabor Peter and others were in all probability attracted to these positions and activities because of an overdeveloped need for power and a pleasure in its most obvious exercises. This is a disposition different from pure sadism, from the pleasure of inflicting pain. On the other hand, there is a continuity between the sense of power that comes from the ability to plan and order the imprisonment or extermination of large groups of people and the sense of power of the torturer-interrogator who can do whatever he wishes to a particular victim, short of killing him.

Many people who end up in positions of great, arbitrary power (but who do not have to dirty their hands) gravitate to these positions because they permit the ruthless exercise of power—the infliction of suffering and death from a distance, that can also be enjoyable. Andrei Gromyko recalled that Mikhail Kaganovich (a close associate of Stalin) wrote "'Hooray!' on the margin of the NKVD lists of names of those sentenced to death as 'enemies of the people.'"

On the other hand physical force can be justified as a necessity. Rakosi said in connection with the beating of the defendants in the Rajk case: "Beating is a necessary method of the AVH and it needs to be used." Gyula Princz, one of the officers who actually administered the beatings, said: "We beat them as long as they refused to confess." They were beaten because even during the investigation they continued their hostile activities, that is, they denied the charges. Some had to eat salt, others had to lick the toilet bowl or had water dripped on their head." Farkas instructed Princz to beat Rajk until he admitted being an agent of the imperialist powers. Gabor Peter, head of the AVH demanded that the interrogators show "unwavering hatred" to "the enemies of the Party:" that is, the accused in the Rajk case.

Eyewitness accounts of Soviet Party criticism and self-criticism meetings (where a certain amount of spontaneous audience participation was encouraged), the Cultural Revolution in China, and the Cambodian criticism-self-criticism sessions, among others suggest that these regimes were often also successful in tapping into the aggressive and scapegoating impulses of people not professionally involved with political violence and coercion. Actively responding to such inclinations and impulses, following official encouragement, is different from mere obedience to authority. At the same time we must remember that most of the political violence under communist systems (as under Nazism) was quite unspontaneous; it would be difficult to argue that the specialists of the KGB (and similar organizations in other communist states) were "carried away" either by their own impulses or spontaneous group encouragement. This still leaves us with the possibility, indeed probability, that many of those most intimately involved with ordering and inflicting violence found it a congenial rather than a painful exercise of duty.

19

Growing Up in Communist Hungary

The period 1948-56, while not life-threatening, was the most difficult and depriving in my entire life. Only in 1944 did I face greater danger, including the possibility of violent death. At the same time life under Communism, which coincided with my adolescence and young adulthood, was also full of challenges and colorful experiences which had no counterpart in my post-1956 life, tame and secure in the West. What challenges or risky adventures did I have to face in the West which would test my mettle? Hitchhiking across Western Europe and not knowing when I would get the next ride? Getting lost in a wilderness area in California at night? Taking a whitewater raft ride in British Columbia? Being turned down for a grant? Not only were the difficulties and dangers I encountered in the West far less serious, they were freely chosen risks, not deprivations imposed by hostile political powers.

In later years I often thought of those eight years, when I was between the ages of sixteen and twenty-four. They provided me with experiences which not only contrasted sharply with those of my life in the West but also greatly influenced my subsequent choice of a career as a sociologist. Those years have also given me points of reference and bases of comparison as I continued to confront the far more manageable challenges and difficulties as a graduate student and university professor in the United States.

I should emphasize at the outset that my difficulties in Hungary between 1948-56 had nothing or little to do with being Jewish. Hungarian Jews under the Communist system—about 100,000 had survived the Holocaust—were not persecuted on religious grounds. They were, however, overrepresented at both ends of the political spectrum: among those who occupied high positions in the government and the ruling Communist Party and also among those who came to be victimized by the system because of their socioeconomic background. Many Jews had, from the Communist regime's point of view, an undesirable socioeconomic background: they used to be capitalists, i.e., as businessmen, property owners, industrialists. Gradually the number of those in high position diminished and those victimized grew.

In 1948 a pro-Soviet, hard-line Communist government replaced the coalition government composed of several political parties, including the Communists, which came into power in 1945 as a result of free elections. The new government seized power through a mixture of force and fraud, assisted by the Soviet troops which were stationed in Hungary following World War II and stayed until 1992. Their assistance included the arrest of the head of the largest non-Communist political party in Hungary, whom they charged with conspiring against them. The new government set about energetically to remold society and create a political-economic replica of the Soviet Union under Stalin.

In the beginning, during 1945-47, I was attracted to the Communist Party because it was closely identified with the Soviet Union. In turn, I had warm feelings toward the Soviet Union because it was the Soviet Army which liberated Hungary from the Nazi troops and a pro-Nazi political system which engaged in rounding up and killing the Jews. My family and I were hiding in Budapest from late October 1944 until the arrival of the Soviet troops in mid-January 1945. We were supposed to be refugees from Transylvania, already occupied by the Soviet army. During those months the Hungarian Nazis or storm troopers (belonging to the so-called Arrow Cross movement) in power were diligently looking for hidden Jews who did not follow orders to move into the ghetto. Those discovered were shot on the street or on the edge of the Danube. The later the Soviet troops arrived the better chances there were for those outside the ghetto to be caught and executed. In those days I used to converse with my father about what it felt like to be shot since he had been wounded lightly in World War I.

My pro-Soviet, pro-Communist sentiments were reflected in my participation in the Communist youth movement (from 1945-48) in the high school (gymnasium). These activities included covering the blackboard in the classroom with Communist party stickers and slogans the teachers were reluctant to remove. (One of the stickers, I recall, demanded "Let's get rid of reactionary school teachers!")

I also took part in what I came to see (soon after it happened) as a misguided and shameful political incident. This is what happened. One of our teachers, a woman, often referred in class to the Soviet occupation troops as "the so-called liberators"—reflecting a sentiment widespread among the non-Jewish and non-Communist population, the vast majority—on account of the behavior of the Soviet troops. Upon arrival they engaged in an orgy of raping and looting (much of it I personally witnessed) whereas the German troops targeted only the Jews. These remarks of the teacher annoyed the Jewish students for whom the Soviet troops were genuine liberators for the reason noted earlier. Somebody mentioned these deprecating remarks to one of the older boys in the school who was already a member of the Hungarian Communist Party and some minor functionary as well. In turn he reported the matter to the Political Police.

Several of us, the Jews in the class, were summoned to testify about these remarks at the notorious Political Police headquarters (it had earlier been the headquarters of the Hungarian pro-Nazi, or Arrow Cross Party). This we did, though the details are fuzzy by now since these events took place in 1947 or 1948, close to half a century ago. Subsequently that teacher was arrested and sometime later tried in court. I do recall that virtually the whole class had to testify before a judge; the Jewish students recalled the remarks about the so-called liberators, the gentiles did not.

Why anybody should be arrested and punished for making such or any other remark was not an issue anybody would have considered raising. Free expression had few defenders in Hungary in those days, or for that matter at other times. The poor woman was convicted and sentenced to a year and a half in prison, which she served, for slandering our liberators. I do not remember how we, the Jews in the class who caused her downfall, reacted to the sentence, but I suspect —regretfully—that we were not displeased. It was not an episode I can look back on with pride or satisfaction. That miscarriage of justice was the result of a combination of the insecurity and vindictiveness of formerly persecuted children (or adolescents, we were about fourteen years old) and the policies of a government determined to establish a pervasive conformity and to silence and intimidate the population.

My pro-Communist attitudes and beliefs did not endure beyond 1948, the year in which the Communists seized power and imposed their repressive ways without any further restraint. The school curriculum changed, Western movies were no longer shown and few Western books were published. The compulsory public veneration of Stalin and his Hungarian disciple Mathias Rákosi reached new heights. Even more ominous were the political trials in which the accused were coerced into making fantastic self-incriminating confessions. Peasants were forced into collective farms. Huge and wasteful investments in heavy industry were made while the standard of living fell and consumer goods were increasingly hard to find or afford. More and more people were arrested and held in jail or detention camps.

I particularly disliked the all-pervasive official propaganda, shrill, self-righteous, bombastic. School children were obliged to attend official celebrations such as May Day, Liberation Day (April 4th) and the anniversary of the 1917 Soviet Revolution. I also recall that in school we were all expected to sign petitions demanding that whoever was being tried on some fabricated conspiracy charges (e.g. the Rajk group or Cardinal Mindszenty) be given the stiffest possible sentence. Anyone not signing these petitions put himself outside the pale of permissible behavior and undermined chances for admission to university later on. There was only one boy in my class who refused to sign the Mindszenty petition.

I must also point out that despite the difficulties and conflicts of the era created by the Communist authorities, my years in the high school had many pleasant aspects and not only in retrospect. I belonged to a group of friends, bookish boys, mostly Jewish, who enjoyed one another's company and activities appropriate to their age and some less so. Our class divided into the equivalent of jocks and aspiring mini-intellectuals. There were enough of us in the latter group not to feel harassed or ridiculed. Unlike in many American high schools there was no stigma attached to being bookish and a serious student though perhaps some saw such qualities as somewhat eccentric. The "mini-intellectuals" took pride in reading "heavy" books of world literature, literary history or philosophy before they were required in school, or even if they were not required.

A close friend of mine who sat next to me in class, George Konrád (who was to become an internationally known writer), used to put in earplugs so that he could read undisturbed by the teacher. The latter used to ask me, "Would you please ask George to take out his earplugs so that I could ask him some questions?"

Many school activities and subjects remained interesting and enjoyable despite the political indoctrination. We had several well-qualified and devoted teachers. I was most interested in literature and we were exposed not only to Soviet or Soviet-style Hungarian literature but also the classics of Western (and Hungarian) literature with the suitable ideological interpretation added. I was for some years an editor of a "wall newspaper," a Communist invention used for the cheap, localized dissemination of political propaganda. It was basically a glorified bulletin board with typed articles and announcements. This was not a problem as long as I was a sympathizer with the Party. When I ceased to be one, I also stopped being a wall newspaper editor.

I also belonged with five or six friends to a Jewish Boy Scout group until it was abolished in 1949. Our activities included several thoroughly enjoyable camping trips, by Lake Balaton and north of Budapest near the Danube. The pleasures of life during this period included various other outdoor activities: hiking and rowing with either friends or my uncle, who was a great outdoorsman. My family owned a scull-like rowboat (a type not used in this country), which was kept in a boathouse on the Danube north of Budapest. During the summer I regularly went on boating excursions of various length, sometime camping overnight. On the longest trip I took, with Konrád and an older boy, we went all the way from Budapest to Mohács near the Yugoslav border, a distance well over a hundred miles (downstream all the way). We returned by steamboat.

My problems, except those associated with adolescence, were entirely due to the social background of my maternal grandfather, who used to be a prosperous businessman before the Communist system was established in 1948. During the period of Nazi domination in 1944 he was a persecuted Jew. After he was twice arrested but miraculously released, he went into hiding with the rest of us. Although in 1948 his businesses were confiscated by the Communist government, he continued to be regarded by the authorities as a capitalist and a potential threat to the system. For good measure, in 1947, before his factory was "nationalized," he was jailed for a few months under the wholly unsubstantiated charge of "sabotaging the Three-Year Plan." (The Communist system introduced three- and later five-year economic plans specifying industrial developments and production targets.)

It was a characteristic of the Communist government to judge people not by their behavior or activities but by certain preconceived, broad sociopolitical criteria or characteristics such as occupation, social class or connections abroad. Having relatives in a Western, capitalist country was held against you. My grandfather was a self-made man, a capitalist who did not inherit his wealth but acquired it by being resourceful and hardworking. Presumably he was also lucky: moreover, he had only a grade school education. Since he, my parents and I lived together in the same apartment (after 1945) we were considered one family; and since he was considered a former capitalist, all of us were viewed as enemies of the new social order.

Thus it came about that one morning in June 1951 a policeman on a motorcycle came to our apartment building and handed my family an official paper informing us that within twenty-four hours we would be removed from our apartment (and Budapest) to a village about 120 miles to the east. It was designated as "a compulsory residence" *(kényszerlakhely)* which we were not allowed to leave beyond a four-mile radius measured from its center. There were also some restrictions (in weight) on how much of our belongings we could take. This was a form of exile but felt more like deportation since we were not allowed to go there on our own but were picked up during the night by a truck (which already had on it another family and their belongings). We were transported under police guard to a railroad station (normally used for freight trains only) on the outskirts of Budapest where a train was assembled carrying the deportees to various villages. I should point out here that we were not put into cattle cars as were the Jews headed to the extermination camps a few years earlier but in passenger cars with wooden seats. Each passenger was given a seat, but we were not allowed to open the windows or go to the platform of the railroad cars.

This was the beginning of a truly new and unpleasant chapter of my life. A lifelong resident of Budapest, at age nineteen in June 1951 I was sent with my family to a backward rural village. At that time in Hungary the gulf between city and countryside was profound; there was only one real city: Budapest. Small towns or cities (even those with populations over 100,000) were not city-like and not considered desirable places of residence by the more educated or better-off segments of the population. Villages were regarded, with good reason, as backward, uncivilized places, lacking basic amenities and services such as running water, paved roads, telephones, decent shops, libraries, movie theatres and other places of entertainment.

We were assigned to a small house (all of us in one room) thus imposed on a peasant family also regarded with disfavor by the authorities. They were classified as "kulaks"—the Russian word referring to more prosperous farmers who were reluctant to join collective farms and were harshly treated in the Soviet Union during the collectivization period of the early 1930s. I lived in the village for two years under police supervision. We were, for the most part, not obliged to work, because not much work was available. Occasionally I worked in the fields weeding various crops on the state farm or planting saplings for a future forest. These jobs were extremely badly paid even by contemporary Hungarian standards. We received pennies (or more likely, fractions of pennies) for each sapling planted. They were counted as we took them from where they were stored rather than after they were planted. As a result many of them did not get planted but buried. This procedure was far quicker and increased our wages. It was a destructive practice but none of us cared. Working for the state and being paid below subsistence wages led to such attitudes.

I also recall collecting scrap metal a few times with my father for the state collection agency. A couple of times we were forced to help with the grain harvest, an extremely unpleasant job. But for the most part I had little to do and was able to read a lot. Our livelihood was largely provided by relatives living abroad in Mexico and England who sent us packages, mostly secondhand clothing my mother was able to sell or exchange for food.

While it was a generally miserable existence, it had its bright side for me: during those years I had a torrid, secretive love affair with a fellow deportee, ten years older than I, whose husband for some bureaucratic reason was left behind in Budapest. He visited her on weekends. It is a matter of some social-historical (or perhaps anthropological) interest that our love life was conducted entirely outdoors regardless of the seasons, since private indoor accommodations were impossible to obtain or even contemplate.

After spending two years in the village, in the spring of 1953 I was drafted into the army, or rather a part of the army (the so-called construction battalions) in which the draftees were given no military training but had to perform manual labor on various construction projects. People placed into these units were regarded by the government as suffering from some socio-political stigma, untrustworthy to be given military training and access to weapons. Most of them were sons of "kulaks" mentioned above with a sprinkling of deportees from Budapest such as myself. I served a little over two years. If life in the village was awful compared to life in Budapest, life in the army was much worse than being a deportee in the village. The Hungarian army of the period incorporated some of the left-over, rigid and mindless military traditions of the Austro-Hungarian Monarchy as well as the regulations and the organizational principles of the Soviet armed forces as they evolved under Stalin.

There was much systematic harassment and no free time, especially in the first six months. Whatever we did had to be done in a hurry, under shouted, hostile commands. Our hair was totally shorn and not allowed to grow back for one year. During the first year there was no leave, though relatives were allowed to visit us after three months, if I remember correctly.

Our garments consisted of tattered, discarded pre-Communist army uniforms. Instead of socks we were provided with foot rags, thin pieces of cloth we were supposed to wrap around and somehow fasten on our feet. It took several months to learn to do this, especially since we were rarely given the regulation size; those in charge of distributing them simply cut off random pieces of cloth. If the rags were not properly wound around one's foot, blisters and other injuries resulted. Our boots were made in part of rubber, making them still more uncomfortable. Once every ten days we were provided with hot showers; on those occasions we also received clean underwear. Otherwise cold water was available for cleaning up and washing our clothing. Washing powder or liquid were not available but we were free to use the multipurpose crude bit of soap we were provided with. Standards of hygiene were not high.

In addition to the unpleasant conditions noted above, we were given little to eat and what we were given was of poor quality. The only thing we had enough of was bread. Breakfast consisted of some thin soup and coffee without milk or cream and some dark bread. The conscripts widely believed that some substance was put into the coffee to dampen our sex drives. Fresh vegetables, eggs, dairy products, fish or fruit were unheard of (except occasional rotten apples.) Only the most inferior and barely edible cuts of meat found their way to our plates and not very often at that. Actually we had no plates, but an all-purpose metal canteen and no silverware except a soup spoon.

Our sleep was often interrupted by "inspections" by the NCOs looking for specks of dust under the bunk beds or on our feet, which, for the reasons I described earlier, were not easy to keep sparkling clean. Another form of harassment was the inspection of beds after we got up (wake-up call was 5:00 A.M. in the summer, 5:30 A.M. in the winter). We were supposed to make the beds look like a brick or matchbox, sharp-edged, totally symmetrical. To achieve this ideal was difficult because the mattresses we slept on were stuffed with straw which sunk under our weight. Thus each morning we had to dive into the sack containing the straw and rearrange it to approach the matchbox ideal. These efforts were rarely found satisfactory by the NCOs who then demolished the whole bed construction (throwing off sheets and blankets) and ordering us to remake the bed several times until it attained the degree of perfection expected or until they got tired of it.

Although we were classified as political unreliables, or "class enemies" (of the working class), we had to attend political seminars just like the regular, supposedly uncorrupted draftees and most other citizens at their place of work. Evidently the authorities believed that our level of consciousness could be raised and our political disposition improved despite our unfortunate social background. To accomplish this and other objectives each unit had a so-called political officer or commissar, a Soviet invention, in charge of matters political-ideological, and everything else. The political officer was, needless to say, a member of the Communist Party and a genuine zealot, dedicated to the political system. In our case he was a man of peasant origins and little education who was now in a position to avoid working altogether. He was given a splendid uniform and power to coerce and browbeat some 150 reactionaries or their offspring. Evidently he had some difficulty performing his modest educational-indoctrinational tasks. So it came about that soon after induction and arrival at my first place of work (in Northern Hungary, where we were supposed to work on the construction of a tank training facility of the Hungarian army) I was summoned by our political officer. He handed me a pamphlet, a small training manual containing the lecture series for the political seminars. He ordered me to divide the material into bite size units, summaries or outlines for each lecture. The task fell to me since I was one of the handful of draftees in our unit who had completed high school and hence was reputed to be an educated or "literate" person. I welcomed the assignment because it offered relief from ditch-digging and similar activities. Typing lecture outlines (even of low-level propaganda) was greatly preferable to heavy manual labor. After work we had to march around and do various drills.

Earlier in my "military" career I made a doomed attempt to pass myself off as a skilled carpenter—an activity that promised more modest physical exertions than pouring foundations, moving bricks from a conveyer belt or shoveling earth on horse-drawn carts. My fraud was soon discovered when I delivered a grotesquely misshapen wooden lid for a vat—my first job. I was quickly returned to the ranks of the unskilled labor force.

At my second destination—the construction site of a nuclear research facility tucked in pleasant wooded hills near Budapest—I succeeded in attaining the position of warehouse keeper; I handed out tools and even building materials in return for receipts. Strangely enough, I, a politically unreliable draftee, was also in charge of receiving building materials delivered by huge Czechoslovakian-made Skoda trucks, often at night, by civilian truck drivers. Occasionally they offered me modest bribes for diverting entire truckloads, mostly of sand or pebbles for pouring concrete, and I cooperated. I did not do it for the money but to strike a symbolic blow against the system by such a gesture of sabotaging its construction projects. In retrospect, I am amazed that I was willing to take the risk; surely, if caught, I would have been jailed for years. That I and the truckers got away with such activities, doubtless multiplied manifold in the rest of the economy, helps to explain why these systems eventually collapsed.

About halfway through my military service the labor battalions were disbanded (this was a reflection of political change under Prime Minister Imre Nagy in the post-Stalin period). I was transferred to the infantry and given a rifle; I fired it on two occasions on the rifle range. Life under the new dispensation consisted mostly of guard duty at an ammunition dump and the rifle range of the garrison. They were located in a forest a few miles outside the agricultural town that housed the garrison. I recall one agreeable assignment: I was dispatched to the detachment guarding the rifle range, not for guard duty, but to paint warning signs (once more on account of my well-known, exceptional literacy) such as "Attention! Shooting with Live Ammunition in Progress! Keep Out!" I was supposed to paint five or ten such signs, which I could have done in a few days but I managed to stretch it out for a whole summer.

Life at the rifle range was peaceful; nobody bothered me, except the mice. (They lodged in the thatched roof of the peasant hut we stayed in.) The officer in charge of the small detachment (ten or fifteen infantrymen) at the time was in the midst of an intense correspondence with a woman he had fallen in love with. Evidently he had some trouble writing properly expressive and amorous letters and he regularly called upon me for assistance. The officer's requests helped to account for my prolonged stay at the rifle range after all the warning signs were completed.

I was discharged from the army in the spring of 1955. My parents (and all the deportees) in the meantime had been allowed to leave their places of exile but not return to Budapest and reclaim their homes. Consequently my parents rented a room in a distant northern suburb of Budapest and commuted by train to work. Since I badly wanted to live in the capital after four years in the countryside, I became a manual worker in the construction industry, which qualified one for a temporary residence permit.

I worked as an electrician's helper installing electricity in new apartment buildings. My boss was a moody highly skilled young man with a turbulent love life, as I learned over the long hours of work and its intervals. This time I was not asked to assist in writing love letters but merely to listen and offer occasional advice. The problem was a simple one: the woman he loved behaved in a sluttish way, and the electrician was tormented by jealousy. We must have spent half of the workday with these discussions weighing various possible courses of action. Since the alternative was to stand on a ladder hammering and chiseling holes and pathways for electrical wires and tubes into concrete walls and ceilings, I was a receptive listener and willing commentator on the problems of my boss.

By now the reader may be forming the impression that Hungarians under Communism led an exceptionally troubled and intense love life. In many instances the hardships of everyday life, the shortages and the political pressures and restrictions may have led to a heightened preoccupation with such matters. On the other hand, there certainly exists an abundance of venerable stereotypes about the romantic disposition of Hungarians and stereotypes usually have a grain of truth.

Six weeks prior to the revolution of 1956 I started a new job in a factory, as an apprentice of sorts, intending to become a skilled worker, a precision mechanic. (In retrospect, given my lamentable lack of manual dexterity and general practical ineptitude, it is questionable that I could ever have successfully completed the training program). While I was employed in this factory, the Revolution broke out. It had my wholehearted support, although I abstained from fighting. I did, however, take part in various marches and demonstrations, and I observed the pulling down of the huge statue of Stalin and saw many dead bodies on the streets, Russian as well as Hungarian. Hungarian political policemen were lynched, and hung by their feet from trees.

Only after the Revolution was put down by the new, huge influx of Soviet troops, in the first part of November, did I start thinking about leaving the country. I could have kicked myself for not doing it earlier, during late October and early November, when it was easier with the borders open. As it turned out, departing Budapest on November 17th was not too late; I did get through the border without much difficulty on the 19th. This major and most beneficial adventure of my life began as follows.

On November 16, 1956, I went to see my girlfriend in a distant suburb. Since there was no public transportation, I hitched a ride on a truck, a usual way of getting around at the time. I asked the driver if he or anyone he knew would be going to western Hungary (near the Austrian border, the escape route). He invited me to go to the garage and meet other drivers. One driver offered to take me the next morning for a sum of money I did not have. Returning home (I lived at the time with my cousin, her husband, mother and daughter), I told the story and my cousin's husband thought I should give it a try and gave me the money (it amounted to approximately one month's wage for an average worker).

Next morning I walked to the garage where I discovered that the driver who had offered to take me was no longer going. There was, however, another one, who asked for no money. But neither did he provide any assurance of safety. If I was taken off his truck at a roadblock, it was my problem; he was, in any case, transporting some legitimate goods from a plant to a border town. We drove to the plant to collect the goods, which turned out to be mostly people, including families with babies and small children, also intent on getting out of Hungary. There were some symbolic crates to be delivered. The members of the group also had documents alleging that they were going to repair machinery in western Hungary. (If I recall correctly, the firm they worked for specialized in repairing X-ray machines.) They kindly added my name to theirs on the documents as if I also worked there and off we went. There were indeed roadblocks manned by Hungarian troops but we made it. Near the border we spent the night in a hospital where somebody from the group had connections.

Next day we split into two groups to attempt the border crossing on two separate occasions. I was in the second group of about fifteen people (including children who had to be carried.) The truck drove us to a road that ran parallel to the border. There we got off and started walking in the direction we had been given: we had no guide, compass or map. We started around 11:00 P.M. After an hour or so the shadows of two border guards became visible in the field ahead of us. If we saw them they saw us too. We did not try to run away. They approached and said: "Hands up." We did as told and a strained silence followed for a minute or so.

At last one of the guards said: "Why are you trying to get across in such a big group?" This was not an unsympathetic remark and upon hearing it we surrounded them and pressed money in their hands even though they did not ask for it. We also told sad stories of the reasons for our desire to leave: family members killed, homes burned during the fighting and the like. The guards pointed us in the direction of Austria and we continued.

The sun slowly rose and even after considerable walking we still were in Hungary as a looming watchtower a few hundred yards from us made clear, for the Austrian border had no such towers. We did not know if there were sentries in the tower or not. At last we stumbled into the plowed strip, perhaps a hundred feet wide, which was supposed to show footprints; probably it used to be mined.

For eight years between 1948 and 1956 I had dreamed about getting out of Hungary and was convinced that it was a hopeless fantasy. Some of my close friends left for Israel in 1949 and I seriously considered joining them but did not on account of my mother's protest. With my escape on November 19, 1956, I realized an eight-year-old dream and the second most difficult period (1948-56) of my life was over. From then on I ceased to be buffeted by historical events and forces: in the West there were more choices to make and the problems to be faced were no longer political.

20

Thoughts on Travel in Russia

"Men who move because they are starved or frightened or oppressed expect to be safer, better fed and more free in the new place. Men who live in a secure, rich and decent society travel to escape boredom, to elude the familiar, and to discover the exotic." —Daniel Boorstin, *The Image*

"...of all methods of adorning the mind and forming the judgement, travelling is the most efficacious..."—Counte de Volney quoted in Boorstin

Never before in history have some many people moved from place to place for short periods of time for no more compelling reason than the pursuit of pleasure, relaxation or new experience. By contrast in the past large scale population movements were driven either by pressing material need or fear. At the present time tens of millions of people in North America, Europe and Japan not driven by poverty or fear of persecution remove themselves from their regular locations to visit other countries or less familiar parts of their own country in the hope of finding gratifications which elude them in the normal course of their lives, determined to make their lives temporarily more interesting or enjoyable.

While rapid mass transportation and the growth of discretionary incomes have been the preconditions of mass tourism, rising expectations and new human desires were no less important in these developments. The part played by travel in the recent, widespread efforts to make life more meaningful has been given little attention by either social historians or sociologists. Such neglect is likely to be a result of the belief that the motives for travel are self evident. If, as it is widely believed, recreational travel is highly desirable and pleasurable, its understanding need not require inquiry into the motives of the participants.

I believe that the motives to travel are more varied and not necessarily self evident and their better understanding may allow us to glimpse important characteristics of our times and the society we live in; these motives are less closely linked to the pursuit of pleasure than the pursuit of meaning.

Focusing on Western mass tourism does not imply that the migrations prompted by dire need no longer exist. Vast migrations of impoverished or persecuted people continue to take place, not necessarily because poverty or fear of persecution have globally increased but because more people in the impoverished parts of the world know about a better life in the West and are capable of reaching it. Western Europe and North America are the magnets drawing millions from the rest of the world. The motives of these migrants and would-be migrants hold little mystery given the frustrations and deprivations which prevail in their countries.

My recent (summer 1998) trip to Russia stimulated new reflections and questions about the gratifications and frustrations travel yields: What are the (non-economic) costs and contradictions of travel? Has the quality of the travel experience changed since it became transformed from an aristocratic-patrician passtime into a mass pursuit, an adjunct of mass culture? How do the diverse motives for travel—including both the simple wish to escape the routines of daily life *and* the grandiose quest for self realization—coexist? Why has travel, and especially the foreign variety, become a sensitive barometer of social status, a new way of displaying wealth, taste, education and refinement or the lack of them?

The phenomenon of travel and foreign travel in particular, although the shared experience of tens of millions is among the topics American social scientists generally fail to address. Migration and emigration have their sociological niche but short term recreational travel is largely ignored. There is especially little information as to what travel accomplishes for the participants as distinct from the balance of payments and national income it generates for the countries on the tourist circuit. Also overlooked are the disappointments travel generates when it falls short of the expectations which prompt it in the first place. One rarely hears about such disappointments except at the most trivial or practical level, i.e. in connection with lost luggage, articles stolen or being overcharged.

Much of contemporary travel may be seen as a metaphor for the incompatibility of human desires, the limited realizability of high expectations and the problem of unintended outcomes in personal lives.

Contemporary travel has many varieties. Its major form is recreational, either passive, relaxation oriented, or active, adventure-seeking. Recreational travel is undertaken individually or in organized groups. Group tours by themselves could be an intrigueing topic for the curious sociologist as they mirror society and its social-cultural differentiation. They are organized for the benefit of singles or families, people of less conventional sexual orientation, for the old or the young; they are ready to address a wide range of ethnic, cultural, academic or regional interests. In Japan and Taiwan special interest group tours include those organized for the purpose of visiting brothels in Thailand.

Travel associated with work or the exchange of ideas is another major contemporary variety in which the original purpose is often overshadowed by the unstated goal of "having fun" or having one's status confirmed by someone else paying for the trip. Attending conferences ranks high in this combination of work and pleasure; ostensibly not recreational, but in fact participants are motivated in part by the desire to be removed from their familiar routines and environment, to enjoy some minor luxuries, new opportunities for socializing and an enhanced belief in their own importance.

Another important and large group of travellers are the young, who between completing high school and college or between college and work (or graduate school) take prolonged trips abroad without a well defined destination. They embark, as they see it, on voyages of discovery and self discovery. I suspect that Americans are particularly susceptible to the belief that such voyages will be uplifting and spiritually enriching and will yield transforming experiences leading to personal growth.

Almost every type of foreign travel incorporates the usually unarticulated but strongly felt belief that there is something in other lands one's own fails to provide, that going abroad (or to some remote or exotic part of one's own country) will lead to insights which otherwise cannot be had.

Admittedly a large portion of travellers are not afflicted by such longings and curiosities; they are the people for whom travel has become what Daniel Boorstin has called a "pseudoevent." They seek the familiar and comfortable abroad, (or in the less familiar parts of their own country), they are eager to encounter replicas of the familiar, or small, packaged and manageable doses of the foreign and exotic that would justify the bother and expense of travel. Characteristically they seek to combine and reconcile what cannot realistically be expected to be combined. Boorstin wrote:

> We expect our two week vacation to be romantic, exotic, cheap and effortless. We expect a faraway atmosphere if we go to a nearby place; and we expect everything to be relaxing, sanitary and Americanized if we go to a faraway place... We expect the contrdictory and the impossible... Never have people been more the masters of their environment. Yet never has a people felt more deceived and disappointed. For never has a people expected so much more than the world could offer...
>
> Formerly travel required long planning, large expense, and great investments of time. It involved risks to health, or even to life. The traveler was active. Now he became passive. Instead of an athletic exercise, travel became a spectator sport. (*The Image*, 1964, p. 34, 84)

In short, travelers have become tourists. The difference between the two in Boorstin's view is that the traveller is active in pursuit of new experience, new people and adventure whereas the tourist is a passive pleasure seeker who goes "sight-seeing". Malcolm Bradbury thus distinguished between the two: "A traveller comes to see reality that is there already. A tourist comes only to see a reality invented for him..."(*Doctor Criminale*, 1992, p.236). Sight-seeing itself has become increasingly standardized, dictated by guidebooks, tour guides or snippets of the mass media: there are "must" sights the tourist is obligated to see (the Eiffel Tower, the Tower of London, St Peter's Basilica, the Parthenon and others of similar reknown). It is not for him to decide and discover what is worth seeing unless he belongs to another (much smaller) group of sophisticates who pride themselves in refusing to visit the prescribed itineraries and sites of mass tourism and make their own discoveries in anonymous villages and other places "off the beaten track."

While Boorstin correctly identified the links between mass culture and mass travel I believe that the high expectations shaping travel have another aspect and origin as well. For an increasing portion of American (and European) travellers the objective of travel is nothing less than the (temporary) escape of modernity, a flight into the past or an imaginary past and its presumed authenticity. (There were forerunners of this sensibility among Eighteenth and Nineteenth century romantics.) That is why so many modern travellers attempt to find "unspoiled" villages, small towns or islands, why the advertisements of the travel industry promise places without other tourists (no less!), "magic" places where life goes on "in time-honored traditional ways," where mass produced objects are still non-existent or scarce, where the distractions and taints of modernity, urban crowding, impersonality, timetables and standardising technology have yet to penetrate or be a massive presence.

What is so appealing about old villages and small towns, their architecture and artifacts? Why even Americans, generally mesmerized by the veneer of whatever is new, feel awe and respect when confronted with the physical evidence of the old and enduring?

The remnants of traditional settlements and their ways of life enchant us because we believe that they are, or used to be, free of the familiar problems and difficulties of modern urban and suburban life: crime, family instability, competitive status seeking, social isolation, the superficiality of human bonds, technological homogenization, poorly made material objects, planned obsolescence, anomie and meaninglessness. Many of us harbor the unspoken belief that the old ways were in some indefinable way, more authentic and superior to those modern life created.

The admiration of traditional ways of life, their physical settings and that of unspoilt nature are often connected; we tend to imagine that there used to be a more harmonious relationship between nature and human beings in traditional societies and communities than is the case in the modern world. (The eagerness of American Indian tribes to build huge casinos on their reservations illustrates the dubious nature of such beliefs.) Nature, unspoiled by human presence or activity, is the pinnacle of authenticity.

Travel and modernity are further linked in less obvious, more symbolic ways. Travel to new places is the most obvious attempt to amass new experience; those motivated by exploratory or adventerous impulses (as distinct from those who keep going to the same resort in search of tried comforts) rarely revisit the same place. If so each trip ends in permanent separation from a physical setting, an experience resembling the fleeting personal contacts and interactions which are part of modern life. The modern traveller, or a major type of him, relates to places as he relates to many people: encounters are brief, lacking in depth and continuity. Why to return to any particular place when there is so much to see?

In a different kind of tribute to modernity a large portion of tourists gravitate to cruise ships and huge resorts or "resort villages" where most decisions and arrangements are made for them, where they find themselves in a physical and social setting that often replicates (or improves upon) the comforts of the familiar, where everything is predictable and a frantic regimen of organized activities awaits them. In such places the focus of recreation is ample food and drink, physical comfort and the suspension of the work related and home-centered routines. Such recreational travel may include the promise of romance or the short-lived cameraderie of like-minded vacationers who rejoice in a shared, temporary freedom from responsibilities and immersion in pleasures denied in the familiar settings.

Modern travel also lends itself to status-seeking even though it ceased to be the prerogative of the rich. It is easy to incorporate status seeking into travel. The most obvious way is by spending huge amounts of money on luxurious accomodations and forms of transportation (the Concorde, private yachts, executive jets, first class, chartered boats, etc). For the status seeker it is also important to visit "in" places, at once fashionable and exclusive. The more adventerous traveller may seek status by finding new, hitherto unknown destinations of some distinction: cultural, geographic, natural or scenic. For millions of Americans going abroad for a vacation in itself has become a reassuring status symbol reflecting a gratifying standard of living and some meausure of cultural sophistication.

It is the ultimate paradox that modernity that has made mass travel possible has also created the conditions many travellers seek to escape.

My trip to Russia, apart from inspiring such reflections had some unusual aspects as it combined research, sightseeing and family reunion. It was my first visit to Russia (or the former Soviet Union) although in the course of my professional life I have written extensively on Soviet affairs and taught a course on Soviet society at two universities for almost thirty years. My failure to take the obligatory trip, or trips earlier had several explanations. For a long time I felt insecure, as a former Hungarian refugee of 1956 vintage to undertake such a visit; later on I felt that as a student of the Soviet system I ought to spend a substantial amount of time there yet I was reluctant to do so having considered the former Soviet Union an unfriendly as well as uncomfortable place for an extended visit. Of course I could have gone for a shorter visit as a tourist but if the goal was recreation or sightseeing I prefered going to Western Europe.

By the summer of 1998 several circumstances combined to make me embark on the trip. I was, needless to say, not getting younger; there was no more Soviet system to inspire (somewhat irrational) apprehensions; I got to know a Russian graduate student in history who was my part-time research assistant, a native of St Petersburg and son of a sociologist teaching at a civil service training academy in the same city. Father and son were going to find some people to interview for my next project, an examination of the responses of intellectuals in the West and East to the collapse of Soviet communism and of their current thinking about Marxism. I also had a book in press on the collapse of Soviet communism—a process I also hoped to discuss with some of the eyewitnesses.

More unusual, I have a first cousin in St Petersburg whom I was anxious to meet. I was curious to learn from her about my uncle (whose daughter she was) who perished in the purges in 1937. This uncle, Sandor Hollander, by training a military engineer served in the Austro-Hungarian army and was taken prisoner in Russia during World War I. He stayed, married a Russian woman, became (or perhaps was already) a communist, fought with the Bolsheviks in the civil war and subsequently came to occupy positions of some importance in the political-economic hierarchy (in the ministry of transportation among other places). He worked on some of the major construction projects of the first Five Year Plan such as the Moscow subway, the Kharkhov tractor factory and the Baku-Grozni oil pipeline. In 1937 he was dispatched to participate in the Spanish Civil War and in the early morning of the day of his would-be departure was arrested and eight month later executed as a spy. He shared the fate of many committed supporters of the Soviet system who were of foreign origin. As I learned during my visit he knew both Trotsky and Bukharin that undoubtedly increased his vulnerability to arrest.

I was also possessed of the normal tourist curiosity about Russia and its supposedly most attractive city. A research grant by the Earhart Foundation made it easier to undertake the trip.

It is a venerable requirement of travel writings based on short visits that sweeping generalizations about the social, cultural or political conditions prevailing in the country visited be preceded by ritualistic cautionary remarks about the tentativeness of the observations to follow. I was in a better position to learn about some facts of life than most short term visitors. Through my assistant I had connections with a small cross section or sample of the Russian intelligentsia. He himself is a serious, bright and very well educated young man, graduate of Herzen University of St Petersburg and currently graduate student in history at an Eastern state university in this country. He speaks English flawlessly taught as he was from an early age by his grandmother who still, in her seventies teaches English at the Russian Merchant Marine Academy in St Petersburg. He was in more than one way an interpreter of Russian life and especially that of the intelligentsia; his mother is a psychiatrist with an M.D., so is his grandfather (in his early eighties, still working as head of a department in a psychoneurological institute); his father is a research sociologist and author of many publications.

My other source of information was my Russian cousin and her daughter, a young woman who now lives in Hungary (married to a Hungarian) but by happy coincidence was visiting her mother when I was there. My Russian cousin teaches in an institute that trains adult education teachers. Her daughter although a resident of Hungary for a decade considers herself Russian and her children (born in Hungary) are bilingual.

There were also the people I interviewed who included academics, a former military intelligence officer, the head of a major library, a highly placed engineer and former head of a domestic airline as well as the grandfather of my interpreter, who in addition to being a head of an institute used to preside over a work-place party-committee.

Although I had not been to Russia before I had plenty of preconceptions based on extensive reading and conversations with friends who had been there for extended periods. I was eager to see to what degree "being on the spot" confirms or disconfirms these ideas. As the author of a book (*Political Pilgrims*) which documented how easy it is to misjudge countries on the basis of superficial impressions and a favorable prediposition I was by no means unaware of my own predispositions. I used to be an unembarrassed critic of the Soviet system but as far as post-communist Russia is concerned I have no axe to grind and am inclined to the benefit of doubt. I symathized with the effort, insofar as it has been undertaken, to build a pluralistic society with a free market economy. I was pleasantly surprised that the collapse of the Soviet system took place with little violence and bloodshed, that the well earned frustration of the masses did not lead, for example to the kind of looting and destruction that occurs from time to time in this country as a, by now, customary expression of the discontent of ethnic minorities in major urban areas.

I expected bleak material conditions and these expectations were largely met. The total neglect of maintenance was the most striking: whatever could rust was rusting, paint was invariably peeling or flaking, floor covers were curled up, walls cracked, objects which once fitted together were coming apart; screws would be missing or lose on whatever was once screwed together, things were literally falling apart that were poorly made or finished in the first place. In my bathroom (in the hotel belonging to Herzen University, an impressive early 19th century building) the water for the shower travelled from the faucet in the sink to the shower head in a makeshift plastic hose which was cracked and only allowed water to pass through if held upright while showering; the toilet tank would not refill unless one lifted off the top and put the valve cap back on a pipe after each flushing, otherwise the water would escape from the tank; the toilet itself was placed so close to the wall that the seat was difficult to lift up. These were all small inconveniences but they exemplify a certain carelessness, a neglect of the physical environment and its artifacts, an indifference toward small comforts, cleanliness or safety. In St Petersburg many drain pipes carrying rain water from the roof of buildings end a few feet above the ground spewing out water on the sidewalks.

Buses, trains, cars, elevators, etc. seem to be on the verge of breakdown yet somehow work. In a toilet of the National Library (used by the staff not the general public) bits of newspaper were provided instead of toilet paper—a usage that brought back memories of public toilets in Hungary during the 1940s and 1950s. Such phenomena reflect not merely neglect but scarcities as well; to keep things in a good state of repair costs money; toilet paper costs more than newspaper and it is an extra expenditure.

Poor maintenance reminded me of Mexico, the only third world country I know reasonably well. Another similarity between Mexico and Russia is the profusion of statues in streets and parks, symbols of national pride and reminders of the great figures of the past, usually staring ahead into a better future.

The decay of physical objects and poorly made consumer goods is, needless to say, not a matter of the "planned obsolescence" as it is allegedly the case in capitalist countries—Russian obsolescence has been entirely unplanned, the cumulative result of a (prior) government policy of stinting on consumer goods and private needs and of the deficient work ethic (conveyed by the old joke, "they pretend to pay us and we pretend to work").

The three apartments of Russian professional families I visited reenforced these impressions; in each there was a dismaying lack of space; rooms were tiny (I would estimate an average size 10x10 or 12x12 feet). Furniture was of poor quality, thin, feeble, rickety, badly made, of poor materials. Front doors in particular were in bad shape.

The roadways around one of the housing projects I visited were exceptionally potholed. My interpreters's father attempted to organize his fellow residents in a civic effort to repair it or pay for repairs (now that the housing is cooperatively owned) but his fellow residents were unwilling to invest time or money in this communal, quasi-public project,—an illustration of the proverbial gap between public and private concerns. This gap is all the more remarkable since for 70 years the Soviet system used all its resources to instill reverence for the public realm, to inculcate notions of collective interest—it was a discredited notion of public interest that never took root.

The most spectacular physical evidence of the difference between the Soviet era and the emerging capitalism, or between the public and private, can be found in the establishments of private commerce. Often one can see the ground floor of a building housing a private shop or office restored and repainted while the upper floors remain decrepit. A small supermarket near my hotel was not only well stocked with an impressive selection of imported and Russian goods, it accepted my Visa card and had a scanner for entering the price of each item like in American supermarkets. The private travel agency where I booked a boat trip on Lake Ladoga was also thoroughly up to date, well furnished, complete with smiling employees and computers (however the large number of papers relating to the trip were filled out by hand). A final material example of these contrasts were two luxury hotels (Astoria and Europe) I visited to change money, mail postcards and have ice-cream. As I learned upon my return the postcards bore Finish stamps, they were mailed in nearby Finland reflecting the scepticim of the hotel management about the Russian mail service.

The exception to these generalizations are the important public buildings and especially those of tourist interest which are in good condition or being repaired, including many churches and monasteries and the various palaces of czars and famous nobleman. The restoration of these buildings began under Stalin after World War II motivated undoubtedly by nationalistic considerations, they are reminders of a glorious past, the past power and splendor of Russia. St Petersburg (Leningrad at the time) was besieged by German forces for almost three years and the siege exacted an appaling toll in human suffering and destruction.

Despite the financial crisis already in high gear during my visit there was no discernible crisis atmosphere: on the streets people ate icecream, drunk sodas, children played, the young rollerbladed, couples were necking in public, shops were thronged. Such surface normalcy is, of course notoriously misleading and used to be a staple of past accounts of the happy lives of Soviet citizens even under Stalin. In those regimented days there were no beggars on the streets and now there are though not many and I did not see anybody readily identifiable as homeless, which does not mean that they dont exist.

Impressions of public safety are a further example of the difficulty the visitor has in pentrating beneath the surface. I never felt unsafe on the streets, subways or buses of St Petersburg; nobody seemed suspicious or threatening; nobody tried to pick my pockets, cheat me out of money, or sell me things I did not need. Due to the "white nights" streets were thronged at 11 p.m. and after. The existence of a Russian mafia was only vaguely suggested by occasional glimpses of bulky young men riding in or standing by expensive foreign cars and groups of them hanging around an expensive restauraunt in which customers had to go through metal detectors before being seated. (One of the luxury hotels too had metal detectors.) During my visit I read articles about unsolved assassinations of politicians and journalists and was cautioned by the natives about pickpockets.

Parking regulations are virtually non-existent and I saw no meters, parking lots or garages. In the case of moving violations, the offender is fined on the spot, (as it happened to the driver of a taxi I rode in) the traffic police give no tickets. It was not clear how much of these fines find their way to the public coffers.

Prices were strangely dissimilar, almost as if there was a two tier price system. My university affiliated hotel cost only $ 30 per night but it had certain liabilities (least of which were the shortcomings of the bathroom noted above). In this hotel, after considerable waiting, I could get breakfast for exactly 90 cents which, consisted of two uniformly dry pieces of bread with butter and a cup of tea. The most serious problem was the lack of screens or mosquito netting on the windows. I did not expect St Petersburg to be infested with mosquitos but it was. Many apartments have mosquite nets on the window. The hot and humid weather made matters worse; I had to choose between mosquitos or semi-suffocation without mosquitos, if I closed the windows.

The luxury hotels are islands of solid comfort and cleaniness built by Finish contractors. Prices began at $ 300 per day for a single room. Ice cream in these hotels cost $12-14, soft drinks $ 3-4 per small bottle. On the other hand the taxi to the airport (about one hour's ride with many traffic lights, there is no expressway) cost eight dollars; a subway ride 25 cents, surface transporation 20 cents per ride. Excellent sandwiches on the boat trip I took cost one dollar each. Meals in the new restaurants were expensive, main courses costing $ 20 or more, totally beyond the reach of the vast majority. My intepreter told me that his family or anyone he knew never go out to eat except perhaps to a fast food place.

In the museums, on trains and boats there are two sets of prices, one for foreigners, one for the natives. These differences could be substantial: in the Hermitage Museum admission cost about $ 10 for foreigners and $ 3 for the natives. While there is economic justification for such discrimination (foreigners can indeed afford the higher prices) I also felt that there was a nationalistic component, a "we" and "they" mentality added to the economic consideration.

The boat trip noted above (to Valaam island in Lake Ladoga famous for its natural beauty and the numerous monasteries and chapels) was another minor reminder of the new contrasts. As it turned out many of the passangers were on board to participate in a workshop on private pension funds; on the other hand, and reminiscent of Soviet times, before docking back in St. Peterburg passengers were informed on the public address system that they had to collect and hand over all used bed linen and towels in exchange for a receipt which would allow them to disembark.

The most remarkable contrast between the ever present neglect and poor maintenance was provided by the appearance of young women on the streets. I cannot recall when and in what city, European or North American, have I seen so many attractive, well groomed, well dressed young women as in St Petersburg. My Russian contacts informed me that Russian women have not embraced the version of puritanical Western feminism that disapproves of women dressing well if that means dressing in sexy, (male) attention-getting ways that includes short dresses and skirts, high heels and considerable exposure of flesh. I was told that Russian women, although most work, consider finding a man, a husband, an important project, central to their lives; they do not feel humiliated by providing visual delights to male eyes. Dressing in the manner described is probably also a reaction against the long years of Soviet era drabness and shortages when attractive and fashionable clothing was difficult to acquire and amounted to a display of Western orientation.

There are other more substantive indications of pro-Western ways and preferences and especially on the part of the intelligentsia. It was refreshing for an American academic normally surrounded by "celebrations of multiculturalism" (which generally translates into disdain for Western culture and ideas) to be among people who are unabashadly "Eurocentric." In the public library of St Petersburg (among the 10th largest in the world, I was told) I was reverentially shown the entire library of Voltaire, as well as the manuscript and rare book collections. I met librarians who on pitiful salaries retained their dedication to these relics of Western culture. I counted forty-one museums in my St Petersburg guidebook.

St. Petersburg and its public buildings and palaces are also manifestations of imperial political will and grandeur, bordering on megalomania; the city was built on unsuitable swampy land because of its Westernmost location and proximity to the sea. It is a planned city, full of massive public buildings (mostly designed by foreigners) and statues honoring not only czars, generals and statesmen but writers and artists as well.

St. Petersburg is a monument to the Western orientation in Russian history shared by czars, the nobility and intelligentsia—an orientation that always competed with reverence for indigenous tradition. The admiration for Western culture is manifest, among other things, in the design of the old buildings, the collections of museums, the thorough and serious information museum and palace guides provide, the curriculum of universities and the aspirations of the educated. As in Hungary and Czechoslovakia, I had the feeling that the former communist countries may yet become the most eager guardians of a Western culture, devalued and rejected by many Western academic intellectuals. This is not to say that there is no ambivalence toward the West and especially the United States.

Another impression that emerged from my interviews was similar to those yielded by the biographical and autobiographical sources I consulted for the study I mentioned earlier. The informants who held various official positions readily admitted that they used to harbor serious doubts about the system for years or even decades while performing their various official duties. To what extent this confession reflected a retroactive modification of earlier beliefs and attitudes in light of new realities is hard to know. As to their views of what was wrong with the old system, the responses were fairly uniform and predictable: it was inefficient, bureaucratic, over-centralized, it discouraged invididual initiative and innovation, subordinated the individual to the collective and was mendacious. No one disputed that glasnost was the most direct cause of the unravelling of the system by allowing widespread popular frustrations and discontent to find expression and coherence.

Unlike many American social scientists none of these people felt the slightest reluctance to refer to the Soviet system (and not just under Stalin) as "totalitarian". Some readers may recall that among American students of the Soviet system the issue of totalitarianism was the source of acrimonious debate for decades and it has been the spreading consensus since the early seventies that the Soviet Union should not be called and considered totalitarian.

Another common denominator of these conversations was the reported impact of Khrushchev's 20th Congress speech in 1956. While some of my informants were too young for first hand experience of it, they subsequently learned of its revelations and were stunned; several believed that it was the beginning of the end, a key point of departure in the loss of legitimacy that culminated in the late 1980s.

Several people I spoke to believed that the pace of change, especially in the economic realm, has been too fast, unsettling and conducive to widespread insecurity among the population. The newly created inequalities are symbolized, among other things, by the speeding luxury vehicles (mostly Mercedes, BMW, and Volvo) contrasting with most cars which are old, rusted and dilapidated Soviet models.

The former functionaries and members of the party-intelligentsia I spoke to shared a combination of criticism of the old system with regrets over its demise; there was little unambiguous rejoicing over the changes. Life used to be more predictable and secure, more risk-free in some ways. The government spent more on education, welfare, medical care, cultural institutions; prices were controlled, everybody had work.

By coincidence, during my visit James Billington, Librarian of Congress and historian of Russia, was also visiting. His observations echoed the views of my informants. He wrote: "...we have not understood the extent and depth of either the material transformation or the spiritual demoralization of the Russian people since the fall of communism. During a week of discussions with intellectual and political leaders I found an alarming degree of fatalistic expectation that Russia is heading in an authoritarian direction." (*International New York Herald Tribune*, June 18, 1998).

A more apolitical lesson of this trip belongs to the sociology of travel. I call it sightseeing fatigue. An individual, like myself who had done a fair amount of traveling and obligatory sightseeing in many countries sooner or later reaches a point of satiety when physical discomforts and the presence of fellow sightseers begin to weigh more heavily than the aesthtetic or spiritual appeals of great architecture and objects of art. There is something inherently demoralizing about mass tourism, of being immersed in crowds and sharing, willy-nilly, the obligation to see what one is supposed to see according to the authorities in art, architecture, history and travel literature. Moreover the dilemma is insoluble beacause in many instances what one is supposed to see is actually worth seeing: the Hermitage Museum in St Petersburg, the Louvre, the Prado, the British Museum, old Salzburg, the Rhine Valley, Venice and all the other familiar tourist destinations acquired their reknown with reason. But like the beauties of nature they cannot retain their attractions intact while masses of humans swarm over them.

I will conclude with an experience of a more personal nature that is indicative of the durability of apprehensions acquired early in life. I did not register with the St Peterburg police upon arrival because I had no idea that this was still required. I learned about this requirement when checking out of the hotel on the day of my departure, when the receptionist noted with consternation (examining my passport and visa) that I failed to register. I expected that this failure will be apparent to the border guards at the airport when they check my papers and might lead to some unpleasantness—a fine, delay, missing my plane. I felt, as in the old days, potentially at the mercy of the authorities. As it turned out the official at the passport controls paid no attention to the missing registration and I was neither fined nor detained. Thrills of political menace are no longer part of visiting Russia.

21

Western Views on Communism:
Judgments and Misjudgments

Trends and Patterns

The tenth anniversary of the removal of the Berlin Wall is a a welcome opportunity not only to examine the historical significance of the fall of Soviet communism but also to reflect on Western views of communist systems.[1] Sad to say, Western assessments of these systems were more often than not mistaken, both in their moral and factual aspects, sometimes grotesquely and spectacularly so. To be sure these systems were secretive, often inaccessible and far from welcoming inquiry into their character. Not only did they make it difficult for outside observers to learn about their institutions and the ways of life they created but invested huge resources in producing false or misleading impressions, facades of themselves. Yet, despite these efforts there was sufficient if incomplete information to apprehend the essential characteristics of these systems; limited access to data was a less critical impediment to their proper understanding than the predisposition of the obervers.

It has been my dubious privilege to harbor an almost life-long preoccupation with the Western views of communist systems and especially those among them I regarded as wrongheaded[2]. While this preoccupation crystallized during my professional life in the West, its roots are to be found in experiences in communist Hungary where I grew up. In the years and decades following my unathorized departure from Hungary (after the Revolution of 1956) I seized the opportunities to acquaint myself with Western views popular as well as scholarly of communist states.

My interest in the Western views of communism thus originated in the collision between widespread Western academic-intellectual perceptions of communist systems and my experiences in Hungary between 1945-1956. I found it deeply puzzling that some Western intellectuals admired communist states while many more took non-judgemental or benefit-of-doubt positions.

The discussion that follows will focus on the views and judgements of those who most readily made them known and available: prominent intellectuals, including academics, writers, influential journalists, opinion makers, some scientists and clergymen. The pervasiveness and influence of these views is suggested by the fact that entire professional associations, as for example the Latin American Studies Association in the United States have taken official positions over long periods of time in support of political systems such as Castro's Cuba and Sandinista Nicaragua. The professional association of American anthropologists too displayed similar sentiments on several occasions. In 1990 the Organization of American Historians defeated a motion (supported by one member!) that welcomed glasnost in Soviet historiography and expressed regret that the same organization "never protested the forced betrayal of the historians' responsibility to truth imposed upon Soviet and East European historians by their political leaders."[3] During the Vietnam war numerous other academic-professional organizations were on record supporting North Vietnam and the Vietcong. It would require another essay, preferably volume, to discuss in what manner these sentiments influenced American or Western policies toward communist states, or what their impact was on public opinion.

The views here examined have a moral-ethical as well as factual-historical dimension although the two are usually closely connected; people taking different positions on large moral-political questions usually manage to find facts to support them. It is also possible to agree about certain facts but offer conflicting interpretations of their meaning or significance.

There are numerous factual questions to which different answers and interpretations were given. Did the standard of living in communist societies improve or decline? Had the collectivization of agriculture increased or diminished productivity?, Did rates of crime, alcoholism, illiteracy, chronic illnesses and family disintegration go up or down? Were results of the one-party elections accurate? Did over 99% of the voters really chose the official candidates? It was often difficult to find reliable answers to such questions. It is also a factual question whether or not there was freedom to worship, travel abroad (or within the country), acquire and read publications not authorized by the government, etc.

In many instances the link between the factual and the moral-judgemental dimension is clear: if the standard of living declined, if more people were in detention (or killed) for political reasons than under the previous government, if life expectancy declined and rates of crime stayed high, etc., etc., a less favorable or downright negative moral judgement of these systems would be rendered. On the other hand curtailment of the freedom to worship might have elicited approval by some Western observers who regarded such activities an expression of false consciousness.

It is possible to acknowledge problematic facts (or some of them) without reaching generally unfavorable conclusions about the character of these systems if these facts are perceived and dismissed as temporary, epiphenomnal, or an acceptable price to be paid for other gains and benefits, and especially if the hoped for future realization of desirable goals is allowed into the moral equation. Questionable aspects of these systems may be acknowledged against the background of some greater good on the basis of what Arthur Koestler called "the doctrine of unshaken foundations." He wrote: "Weaknesses, failures, even crimes of the Soviet bureaucracy are admitted but claimed to be more surface symptoms which do not affect the fundamentally progressive nature of the Soviet Union, guaranteed by the nationalization of the means of productiom and the aboliton of the profit motive."[4] Upton Sinclair said about the collectivization of Soviet agriculture: "May be it cost a million lives—may be it cost five million ... There has never been in human history a great social change without killing."[5] Sartre explained his atittude "in reply to Albert Camus's criticism of Soviet labor camps... 'Like you I find these camps intolerable, but I find equally intolerable the use made of them... in the bourgeois press.'"[6] Here we had an early example of moral equivalence and the conviction that criticism of the communist systems however well founded must never be expressed in public since their enemies will exploit it. In the same spirit William Kunstler averred that he did not "believe in public attacks on socialist countries where violations of human rights may occur."[7]

Ignorance or denial of factual matters often combined with dismissing their moral-ethical importance. Few Westerners knew exactly how many people perished, for example, due to the forced collectivization of agriculture in the Soviet Union or during the so-called Cultural Revolution in China. The apologists generally opted for smaller numbers while simultaneously upholding the necessity of such sacrifices for the sake of long term benefits.

Sometimes social scientific ambitions shaped Western views of communist systems. It was thought by some that the pursuit of factual knowledge and objectivity required an abstention from "value judgements" or "moralizing" as far as communist systems were concerned. However the same considerations were not applied to Nazi Germany and other political systems or movements on the right of the political spectrum, nor did they inform research and analysis of Western democratic societies regularly denounced on moral grounds.

The erroneous views and misjudgements of communist systems encompassed explanations of their origin, key characteristics as well as the anticipations of their durability. This is not to say that such views completely dominated public or scholarly opinion; as will be shown below many Western observers were capable of insightful diagnosis and appropriate moral judgement of communist systems and their supporting ideologies; they also succeeded to provide solid factual bases for their moral judgements.

This essay while focusing on the specifics of the perceptions and judgements of communist systems will also seek to explain some of the patterns and trends in these perceptions—especially those which were grossly distorted. Paradoxically it is more difficult to explain what enabled some commentators to see these systems with greater clarity and reach conclusions which came to be vindicated by both historical events and authoritative voices in the communist societies themselves including former leaders, major functionaries and Party intellectuals.[8]

One may ask why does it matter—especially at a time when most of these systems are already defunct—what some people in the West had thought of them at various times? Why should we care who were right or wrong about their character? It is my belief that ideas, beliefs, moral and political judgements are not "ephiphenomenal," they matter especially when expressed by members of elite groups. Such judgements may influence the climate of opinion, as well as government and business policy; they may have an impact on the lives of human beings, sometimes millions of them. Moreover the ideas here spoken of entail important moral values, judgements and aspirations. As an American author argued recently: "If we cannot get straight the rights and wrongs of the struggle between Communism and anti-Communism, itself perhaps the greatest moral struggle of this century, then it is hard to see what other issues we will ever be able to address intelligently."[9]

The misjudgements and misperceptions also provide an opportunity to learn more about human nature, including human needs, goals and defining weaknesses. It is of further interest, constituting a mystifying puzzle, how distinguished, inquisitive and in some ways highly qualified individuals, often widely respected and influential, arrive at and hold over long periods of time with great confidence astonishingly wrongheaded judgements about political systems, movements and ideologies even when evidence challenging such views is available.

The perceptions of communist systems did undergo changes over time. During the early years of the Cold War and the Korean War there was an apparent anti-communist consensus stimulated in part by Senator McCarthy and his hearings. While politicians, journalists, many intellectuals and the general public were critical of the Soviet Union these attitudes failed to endure or lead to a nuanced understanding of communist systems. By the late 1960s attitudes began to change and the anti-communism of the earlier Cold War years came to be replaced by anti-anti-communism among many intellectuals and opinion makers—in part a delayed backlash against McCarthyism.

Anti-anti-communists believed that anti-communism had little foundation in reality, served nefarious domestic political purposes and amounted to a greater evil than communism[10], and that given the inequities of American and other Western societies their citizens had no moral basis for making critical judgements of the communist ones.

More than any other event it was the Vietnam war and its destructive, inconclusive nature that discredited critical assessments of communist systems and stimulated sympathy toward those in the Third World. As Francois Furet observed "what emerged from the protests, swept along by a theatrical compassion for Vietnam, was a resurgence of illusions about the Communist world."[11] This however was a new set of illusions as they concerned countries other than the Soviet Union.

The perceptions of the Soviet Union had changed earlier, after Stalin's death in 1953 and Khrushchev's revelations in 1956; there followed, on the left, a loss of interest and a measure of disillusionment with the Soviet system; the new and supposedly more authentic revolutionary regimes of Mao and Castro eclipsed the USSR. More moderate Soviet domestic policies under Khrushchev and Brezhnev also contributed to a decline of enthusiasm and interest. Adam Ulam observed that intellectuals who had earlier found "a certain morbid fascination in the puritanic and repressive aspects of the Soviet regime and also in its enormous outward self assursance..." found less to admire "when this facade of self-assurance began to collapse... after the revelations about Stalin in 1956..."[12]

Somewhat similar attitudes emerged toward China following its rapprochment with the United States under Nixon and its encouragment of private enterpize and consumption after the death of Mao. Interest in communist Vietnam too waned after it ceased to be engaged in war with the United States and also began to encourage private enterprize and foreign investment. Communist Cambodia's short lived attractions under Pol Pot vanished as soon as it became embroiled in war with another communist state, Vietnam and the mass murders of the regime were attested to by another communist government, that of victorious Vietnam. It is worth recalling that before its war with Vietnam reports of the mass murders of the Pol Pol regime were dismissed and ridiculed by Noam Chomsky and Edward Herman while Richard Dudman, a journalist highly regarded by Chomsky "did not find (in Cambodia) the grim picture painted by...refugees who couldnt take the new order."[13]

Despite the changes noted above there was a remarkable continuity and resilience in the basic perceptions of communist states over the better part of an entire century. Each new communist state came to be thought of as more authentic and virtuous than its predecessor and invested with the appealing qualities the more discredited ones were supposed to possess at earlier times.

It is noteworthy that the most favorable assessments of the Soviet Union prevailed during the early and mid 1930s, the period of the catastrophic collectivization, the famines, the Great Purge, the show trials, mass arrests and murders and the consolidation of the bizarre personality cult of Stalin. Western observers were either unfamiliar with these developments or dismissed their significance in light of the perceived accomplishments of the regime. In a somewhat corresponding manner Western intellectuals' admiration of communist China peaked during one of the most destructive and bloody chapters of its history: the Cultural Revolution of the late 1960s.

During World War II the USSR was romanticized as a valiant ally and the patriotism of Soviet people was confused with support for the political system. In the 1970s during the years of detente the United States government, the mass media and the peace movement discouraged criticism fearful of harming the cause of peace or what was earlier called "peaceful coexistence."[14]

Sandinista Nicaragua was the last communist system to be idealized as a foe and victim of American imperialism, the final incarnation of the hopes on the left to find a new geographical location for socialism with a human face.

Of all the communist systems, extinct and surviving, Cuba has retained to the greatest extent its earlier appeals because of the survival in power of its revolutionary leader unwilling to compromise or moderate his policies and abandon his anti-capitalist and anti-American attittude and rhetoric. This is not to say that the favorable views survived unscathed; the periodic exodus of refugees, the economic crises following the collapse of the Soviet bloc leading to the cessation of Soviet aid, the evidence of growing domestic social problems (crime, prostitution, black marketing etc.), the acceptance of the dollar as quasi official currency, have made a dent on the favorable perceptions. Nonetheless it is still ritualistically affirmed in much of the media and among academic intellectuals that communist Cuba has done all it could to improve the material existence, health and education of its citizens—a view the television critic Walter Goodman called "a portrait of Cuba without warts" reflected in a television program on Cuba. As of 1994 Dr Spock was among those who continued to give every benefit of doubt to communist Cuba[15]. The remaining sympathizers blamed Cuba's difficulties on the United States.

In both the 1930s, and later the 60s and 70s Westerners' predisposition and receptivity toward communist systems were shaped by conditions and problems in their own society. This was also reflected in the changing views of tradition and modernity in communist societies. In the Soviet Union of the 1930s industrialization and urbanization associated with material progress and the alleged attitudinal liberation of society from the shackles of the past made a deeply favorable impression on sympathetic Western observers. (Typically, Louis Fisher rhapsodized about "steel and iron... vanquishing Russia's wood civilization"[16]) countries like communist China, Cuba and Vietnam (and others in the Third World) were found appealing in part because they did not succumb to what was by then seen as the dehumanizing and depersonalizing processes associated with modernization. For example Harrison Salisbury was impressed in China by seeing "men and women (who) labored with their own hands, with a few animals, a few primitive implements—experiencing life so simple, so integrated with the land, the weather and the plants that its symmetry seemed almost magical."[17]

By the late 1960s many Western intellectuals and their followers were repulsed by many aspects of life linked to modernity: the decline of community, mass culture, urban crowding, bureaucracy, specialization, encroachments on nature, excessive consumption, the pervasiveness of the cash nexus, the loss of authenticity in personal relations and others. They were under the impression that the second generation of revolutionary communist societies and their simple, good people (representing a new version of the noble savage of the past) preserved some sort of a pre-industrial authenticity and innocence; they further believed that these systems would spare the physical environment from the ravages of industrialization and urbanization; these societies were not wasteful, they discouraged mindless consumption, they were not competitive and were led by kindly, caring leaders.

Another trend during the 1960s and 70s that influenced the perception of communist states and especially the USSR was the "convergence theory"—amounting to the belief that similar levels of industrial development will lead to similar political structures amd practices and hence a more developed Soviet Union (and other more industrialized communist countries) will become more Westernized, that is to say, affluent, democratic and tolerant.

A less benign version of the convergence theory, that of moral equivalence, emerged during the late 1960s stimulated by the Vietnam war and the alienation it inspired and reenforced. This was the conviction (and a mark of sophistication rapidly becoming conven-

conviction (and a mark of sophistication rapidly becoming conventional wisdom among much of the Western intelligentsia) that the United States was in no way superior or preferable to the Soviet Union, or capitalism to state socialism. The Soviet Union was no longer idealized but was still viewed with greater detachment and far less critically. The moral equivalence approach sought to discredit the United States by comparing and equating its flaws and inequities with those of the Soviet Union but at the same time judged the Soviet Union more leniently as no worse than the United States.

Another by product of the 1960s was the rise of the revisionist school of Soviet historiography which grew out at least in part of the anti-American animus the Vietnam war stimulated. It had three major thrusts. One was the insistence that the United States and the West had a greater share of responsibility for the Cold War and arms race than the USSR; the second was the denial that the Soviet Union was, or has ever been, a totalitarian society; thirdly the purge period and its repressions were reinterpreted, including the (downward) revision of the number of victims and the questioning Stalin's responsibility. On the one hand the revisionists reconceptualized the Purges and the associated mass killings as unfocused, localized, uncoordinated events and on the other as largely administrative proceedings providing new opportunities for social mobility. Not only were the number of the victims drastically reduced, survivor accounts were dismissed as unreliable.[18]

A final stage in the evolution of Western views of the Soviet Union occurred during the Gorbachev era. There was renewed hope among some intellectuals that the Soviet Union might yet realise the great expectations of the October Revolution, reclaim its founding ideals and become at last a democratic socialist society.[19]

One more interesting change in the assessments of these systems over time may be noted here. Before the Collapse the sympathizers were inclined to believe that these regimes rested on the insights and propositions of Marxism and this was a great source of their strength and attraction. Since their demise in 1989-91 many former sympathizers have come to argue—doubtless in order to salvage the theory from becoming historically compromised and discredited—that these systems had never been Marxist but distorted Marxism and fradulently claimed to be inspired by it.

Predictions of Durability

Few Western scholars, intellectuals, government officials or politicians predicted the collapse of Soviet communism. Riszard Kapuscinski, the Polish author observed that "just before the breakup of the USSR, the view of that country as a model of the most stable and durable system in the world had gained wide acceptance among Western Sovietologists... there was not one American political scientist who predicted the collapse of the USSR."[20]

Robert M. Gates, former head of the CIA confessed that "he was amazed by the breakdown of the USSR and rests his defense on the entirely fair observation that virtually no one in the defense or intelligence business predicted that the Soviet Union was bound for the dustbin of history until it hit bottom."[21] Walter Laqueur reminded us (following the collapse) that "...the general view in the West during most of the 1960s and 1970s was that the Soviet Union had no monopoly on serious economic problems, which seemed by no means incurable... With a few exceptions Western experts grossly overrated the Soviet GNP and thus underrated per capita arms spending and thus the defense burden for the population... According to a study published as late as 1988 by a well-known Western economist (E.A.Hewett) specializing in the Soviet Union, Soviet citizens enjoyed 'massive economic security.'"[22] Severyn Bialer, another well known specialist of Soviet affairs wrote in 1982 that "The Soviet economy... administered by intelligent and trained professionals will not go bankrupt... like the political system, it will not collapse."[23] Jerry Hough, the prominent Soviet specialist argued in 1991 that "economic reform in the Soviet Union was going ahead with amazing speed and that Soviet political problems had been grossly exaggerated..." He also wrote shortly before the historical events of the Summer and Fall of 1991: "The belief that the Soviet Union may disintegrate as a country contradicts all we know about revolution and national integration throughout the world..." and "Anyone who sees him (Gorbachev) as a tragic transitional figure has little sense of history."[24] Moshe Lewin, the historian saw in 1988 the Soviet Communist Party as "the main stabilizer of the political system" and could not conceive of conditions under which any group "would back measures likely to erode the integrity of the entire union or the centralised state. The party... is the only institution that can preside over the overhaul of the system..."[25]

It is clear in retrospect that both Western specialists and Western political elites were susceptible to impressions of strength and stability the regime projected often by means of coarse and primitive propaganda.[26] For many decades it succeeded to cover up or distract attention from its underlying weaknesses. Martin Malia wrote in 1990 that "... the world in fact was being hoodwinked by the assertion of efficacy and power in just one domain", i.e., heavy industry and military production[27]. John Lewis Gaddis noted that "nuclear weapons preserved the image of a formidable Soviet Union long after it had entered into its terminal decline."[28]

Senator Moynihan was among the handful who envisioned the eventual disintegration of the Soviet Union not merely on economic grounds but resulting from a profound malaise of the entire system. Robert Conquest wrote as early as in 1969 that "in the long run the system is not only inhuman but also unsuccessful, and crisis is not an accidental but necessary result." Richard Pipes was another observer who had few illusions about the long term stability of the Soviet system noting as of 1984 that it was in a "crisis" and "has outlived its usefulness and that the forces making for change are becoming well-nigh irresistible."[29]

Why was it so widely believed that the Soviet Union was virtually indestructible, or at any rate, stable and durable? Possibly, the reluctance to pay close attention to the attitudes and beliefs of particular human beings (in decision making positions) contributed to this state of affairs.[30]

Seymour Martin Lipset and Gyorgy Bence observed that the failure to anticipate the collapse was more common among scholars than journalists and politicians. By the 1970s and 80s (they wrote) "Most of the Sovietologists... were left-liberal in their politics, an orientation that undermined their capacity to accept the view that economic statism, planning, socialist incentives, would not work."[31]

Probably of all the reasons for the Western failure to anticipate the unravelling of the Soviet empire the belief in the superpower symmetry and moral equivalence were the most important. Several anciliary beliefs rested on the "the two superpowers" scenario. It was for instance widely held that global stability required an equilibrium between these powers. Critical views of the United States were also anchored in the seemingly objective equation of its shortcomings with those of the Soviet Union; the somewhat cynical, hence apparently impartial wisdom used to be that neither of the super-powers inspired much respect and each used the alleged threat from the other for various amoral purposes (including bloated defense budgets and unseemly domestic policies). Even when the domestic weaknesses of the Soviet Union were noted, its successes abroad seemed impressive, its superpower status resting on its spreading influence abroad and especially in the third world.[32]

Another important force contributing to the Western belief in the durability of the Soviet Union was the anti-nuclear/peace-movement. All those convinced of the imminence of nuclear holocaust who dedicated their lives, or at least their public lives to averting the di-saster,—and for whom the cause of peace and nuclear disarmament (unilateral, if necesary) became an important source of identity—had a vested interest in the persistence of the Soviet Union. The peace movement could not flourish without the Cold War. The former needed the latter as much, if not more, as the CIA and the KGB needed one another (another item in the inventory of "super power symmetry", part of the conventional wisdom of the period).

There were also those who were deeply (and hopefully) commit-ted to the idea that the "late capitalist" United States was in terminal decline, the most decadent society in existence; the Soviet Union could not overtake the U.S. in its rate of decline. In this view Ameri-can decadence was caused by, or associated with all the ills and evils of capitalism; a socialist (or even a semi or quasi-socialist) so-ciety such as the USSR was expected to have a greater staying power and a better chance to survive and solve its problems. Even as "ac-tually existing socialism" was in the process of collapsing in the Soviet Union and Eastern Europe some American intellectuals en-tertained hopes of its rebirth.[33]

There were also critics of the United States (at home and abroad) who believed that the Soviet Union was a crucial counterweight to the predatory imperialism of the Unite States and did not wish to contemplate a world without it. Such wishful thinking also contrib-uted to belief in the durability of the USSR.

With few exceptions (already noted) the critics of the Soviet em-pire were no more capable of predicting its collapse than those less averse to its prolonged existence. The "cold warriors" and unem-barrassed critics of the Soviet Union (among them this writer) had few illusions about the virtues and advantages of Soviet socialism over the alleged depravities of capitalism and were never tempted to consider the Soviet Union a successful modernising society. Their belief in the durability of the Soviet system did not derive from overlooking its moral, political or economic flaws; they were not under the impression that it had enjoyed a high degree of legitimacy in spite of its shortcomings (as many on the left believed); they did not believe that there was an implicit "social contract" between the rulers and the ruled. The anti-communist critics thought that it was a durable system because it seemed to them (wrongly, as it turned out) that the communist states had succeeded in building institutions of control which would keep them going regardless of their economic inefficiency and limited or minimal legitimacy, and because the USSR managed to offset domestic stagnation by expansion abroad and was capable of producing an abundance of modern weaponry enabling it to remain a formidable superpower.

In retrospect it is clear the anti-communist critics had overestimated the efficiency of the apparatus of control, the political cohesion of the Soviet ruling elite and its ability to manipulate the citizenry regardless of its growing discontents. The critics also underestimated the long term subversive impact of increased information about and contact with the West that began in the 1970s. Their views were influenced by the theories of totalitarianism which used to be helpful for grasping the character of the Soviet system but failed to stimulate anticipations of its end.

Fantasies and Projections

Regardless of the location, historical background or stage of development of the various communist states their misapprehensions had much in common because they had similar origins, mainly the desire to find alternatives to what many Westerners considered their own flawed and unjust social systems. More recently it was the deepening problems of secular modernity that created receptivity to societies which claimed to have found ways to deal with them effectively. The misperceptions grew out of the recurring desire of Westerners (at once highly individualistic *and* longing for a sense of purpose and community) to escape social isolation and lack of meaning. As Doris Lessing put it, these attitudes "... can only come out of some belief...that a promise of some kind had been made and betrayed. Perhaps it was the French Revolution? Or the American revolution which made the pursuit of happiness a right... Millions of people in our times behave as if they have been made a promise... that life must get... always better."[34] Of these millions only groups of intellectuals came to the conclusion that this better life was being or could be built in communist states.

The communist states were often envisioned by Western intellectuals as heirs to the goals and traditions of the Enlightenment, progress or a humane socialism, hence their symnpathies. As of 1967 Graham Greene wrote that "If I had to choose between life in the Soviet Union and life in the United States I would certainly choose the Soviet Union..."[35] (He was not compelled to make this choice). Georg Lukacs in 1971 said in the face of much disconfirming evidence he possessed: "I have always thought that the worst form of socialism is better to live in than the best form of capitalism."[36] During the Vietnam war Tom Hayden and Staughton Lynd wrote: "... we also discovered that we felt empathy for... spokesmen for the Communist world in Prague and Moscow, Peking and Hanoi. After all, we call ourselves in some sense revolutionaries. So do they. After all we identify with the poor and oppressed. So do they."[37]

The wishful misperceptions of communist systems peaked at times when Western societies faced serious internal problems: the economic crises of the late 1920s and early 1930s and the political-cultural ones of the 1960s and early 70s. In the former period only one communist system existed, the Soviet Union; in the latter there were several and their attractions eclipsed those of the USSR discredited to various degrees not only by Khrushchev's revelations in 1956 but also by the Soviet repression of the Hungarian Revolution of 1956 and of the Czech attempt in 1968 to humanize Soviet style socialism.

The Western misconceptions of communist systems were shaped by ignorance, wishful thinking, favorable predisposition and sometimes the manipulation of impressions and experiences (in the case of visitors to these countries taken on elaborate conducted tours). Ignorance was nurtured by a determination to overlook information that could have cast doubt on the favorable predisposition—the published recollections of former residents of communist states were in particular shunned, ignored or treated with suspicion as too subjective or biased.

Major facts of life in these countries thus remained unfamiliar and sometimes incomprehensible. They often included the standards of living of ordinary citizens, the wastefulness and inefficiency of the "planned" economy, the intimidation of the population, the treatment of political prisoners, the staging of political trials, the travel restrictions combined with the internal passport system, the privileges of the Party and government elite, the enormity of corruption, the mendaciousness of the official propaganda and the attitude of ordinary citizens toward their government.

Julian Huxley the British scientist sincerely believed, as of 1932, that in the Soviet Union the "level of physique and general health (was) rather above that to be seen in England."[38] George Bernard Shaw looking around an elegant restaurant in Moscow in 1931 dismissed the possibility of food shortages in the country at large while John Kenneth Galbraith on his tour of communist China—after shown the kitchen of a plant—concluded that "if there is any shortage of food it was not evident in the kitchen."[39] While Billy Graham found "no evidence of religious repression" in the Soviet Union he was also greatly impressed by the provisions he received noting that "the meals I had are among the best I have ever eaten... In the United States you have to be a millionaire to have caviar, but I had caviar with almost every meal."[40]

Spiritual nourishment was also highly rated. It was widely believed that there there was little alienation, that a sense of purpose and community permeated and animated communist societies and the conflict between the private and public, the personal and social was abolished or in the process of extinction. The Soviet system according to Malcolm Cowley "was capable of supplying the moral qualities that writers missed in bourgeois society: the comradeship in struggle, the self-imposed discipline, the ultimate purpose... the opportunity for heroism and human dignity."[41] Leon Feuchtwanger the German writer rejoiced in the "invigorating atmosphere" of the Soviet Union where he found "clarity and resolution."[42] John Dewey compared the ethos prevailing in the Soviet Union to "the moving spirit and force of primitive Christianity"[43] and Edmund Wilson confessed that "you feel in the Soviet Union that you are on the moral top of the world where the light never really goes out."[44] J.D. Bernal the British scientist found "sense of purpose and achievement" and was persuaded that "the cornerstone of the (Soviet) Marxist state was the utilization of human knowledge, science and technique, directly for human welfare."[45] Anna Louis Strong observed that the "remaking of criminals is only one specialized form of the process of remaking human beings which goes on... in the Soviet Union."[46] In Mao's China David Rockefeller found "a sense of national harmony... high morale and community of purpose... crime, drug addiction, prostitution and venereal diseases have been virtually eliminated. Doors are routinely left unlocked." Felix Greene, the British author reported that "China is today an intensely... 'moral' society."[47] John K. Fairbank, the widely respected Sinologist was convinced in 1972 that "The Maoist Revolution is... the best thing that happened to the Chinese people in centuries..."[48] Saul Landau claimed that Cuba under Castro "is the first purposeful society that we had in the Western hemisphere for many years... the first society where... men have a certain dignity, and where this is guaranteed to them."[49] C.Wright Mills the sociologist and merciless critic of American society also succumbed to the charms of Castro and revolutionary Cuba.[50] A publication of the National Council of Churches informed the reader that "permeating the Cuban educational practice is the concept that a new type of society will develop a new type of human being...(who) regards work as the creative center of life and is bound to others by solidarity, comradeship and love."[51] As for Vietnam, Susan Sontag obverved that "The phenomenon of existential agony, of alienation just dont appear among the Vietnamese", they are "'whole' human beings not 'split' as we are."[52] John Brentlinger, a professor of philosphy found Sandinista Nicaragua "a deeply spiritual country trying to... build a new version of socialism." The officials he met were "dedicated, intense... willing to admit mistakes... but insistent concerning their good intentions and the progress the revolution was making."[53] Gunter Grass, the famous German writer, escorted around Nicaragua by Tomas Borges, head of state security, reached the conclusion that in Sandinista Nicaragua "Christ's words are taken literally."[54] Harold Pinter the playright who compared Soviet intervention in Czechoslovakia in 1968 to American attempts to overthrow the government of Nicaragua was persuaded that the latter "set out to establish a stable and decent society." Noam Chomsky suggested that the many laudable social reforms of the Sandinistas could have had a subversive effect in Central America, "perhaps even the United States" which is why the United States sought to destroy the system.[55]

Plain or profound ignorance may also explain some of the Western responses to the Moscow Trials in the 1930s as well as those in Eastern Europe after World War II.[56] Joseph Davies, U.S. ambassador to the USSR and Walter Duranty, *New York Times* correspondent stationed in Moscow for many years did not have the slightest doubt about the authenticity of these proceedings. Davies believed that Bukharin's guilt was established "beyond reasonable doubt," that the purges "cleansed the country" and Vyshinsky, the vituperating prosecutor "conducted the case with admirable moderation."[57] Duranty averred that "it is unthinkable that Stalin... and the Court Martial could have sentenced their friends to death unless the proofs of their guilt were overwhelming."[58] Henri Barbusse, Bertolt Brecht and Upton Sinclair too considered these proceedings authentic and just.[59] Andre Malraux concluded with relief that "just as the Inquisition did not affect the fundamental dignity of Christianity, so the Moscow trials have not diminished the fundamental dignity of communism."[60] Julien Benda (who had earlier instructed intellectuals on how to avoid behavior incompatible with their lofty vocation) visited communist Hungary in 1949 in part to dispel French misconceptions about the possible innocence of Laszlo Rajk, the key defendant and victim of the Hungarian show trials after World War II.[61]

A combination of ignorance and wishful thinking might have prompted Sidney and Beatrice Webb to remark that Soviet prisons were "as free of physical cruelty as any prison in any country is ever likely to be."[62] Both G.B. Shaw and Anna Louise Strong inclined to the opinion that Soviet and Chinese prisons were so humane and comfortable that inmates were reluctant to leave them upon the completion of their sentences and sometimes people appealed for readmission to them.[63] Henry Wallace (accompanied by Owen Lattimore) on a conducted tour of Soviet labor camps in the Kolyma region (properly described by Robert Conquest as the "Arctic death camps") was most favorably impressed by what he saw (including Ivan Nikishov, the camp commander) perceiving these camps as a combination of the Hudson Bay Company and Tennessee Valley authority.[64] More recently Robert Thurston, an American historian allowed that the inmates of the gulag were not treated fairly by "Western standards of justice" but was comforted by the fact that in 1937 they had the opportunity to buy Soviet bonds—"...an indication that they were still regarded as participants in society to some degree." A reviewer of his book noted that "by this curious standard, sheep being led to slaughter are participants in agriculture."[65] Simone de Beauvoir was under the impression that "no administrative internment exist(ed) in Mao's China."[66] Basil Davidson an English author and journalist after visiting what undoubtedly were model prisons reached the conclusion that in China those sentenced for counter-revolutionary violence were better treated than violent criminals in Britain.[67] In a report of Cuban prisons published by the Institute for Policy Studies in Washington DC reference was made to the "strong sense of mission in most prison officials...(who) expressed great faith in their system and...seemed determined to work increasingly on their plan for reeducation and for incorporation of the penal population into work and free society... We heard no complaints about..torture... neither did we find any policy of extrajudicial executions or disappearances."[68] Salman Rushdie found Nicaragua's constitution "amounting to a Bill of Rights I couldnt have minded having on the statute book in Britain."[69]

Particular leaders and functionaries too were often monumentally misperceived, including Stalin, Mao, Castro, Che Guevara, Ho Chi Minh and the "commandantes" of Nicaragua. Sidney and Beatrice Webb considered Stalin "the duly elected representative of one of the Moscow constituencies to the Supreme Soviet... accountable to the representative assembly for all his activities..."[70] Anna Louis Strong (who later in life switched from the admiration of the Soviet Union under Stalin to that of China under Mao) was reminded by "Stalin's method of running a committee... of Jane Addams... or Lillian D. Wald... They had the same kind of democratically efficient technique, but they used more high pressure than Stalin did."[71] Ambassador Davis observed that Stalin's eyes were "exceedingly wise and gentle. A child would like to sit on his lap and a dog would sidle up to him."[72]

Franklin D. Roosevelt, no starry-eyed intellectual, "After his return from Yalta... described Stalin to his cabinet as having 'something else in his being besides this revolutionist, Bolshevik thing.'...(He) went on to tell his rapt audience (that) this might have something to do with Stalin's earlier training for the 'priesthood.'...'I think that something entered into his nature of the way in which a Christian gentleman should behave.'"[73] Hewlett Johnson the Dean of Canterbury (who had earlier distinguished himself as one of the most ardent admirers of the Soviet Union under Stalin and Stalin himself) discerned in Mao "an inexpressible look of kindness and sympathy, an obvious preoccupation with the needs of others..."[74] Sartre was overcome with admiration of Castro and Che Guevara perceiving them as heroic figures who could dispense with sleep and other routine activities of lesser humans, and "exercise(d) a veritable dictatorship over their own needs... (and) roll(ed) back the limits of the possible." Saul Landau saw Castro as "a man... steeped in democracy... a humble man."[75] A high ranking official of the Swedish Social Democratic party, Pierre Schori considered Castro a man of encyclopedic knowledge and possessing "the characteristics of a Renaissance Prince."[76] Che Gueavara reminded I.F. Stone of Jesus; "In Che, one felt a desire to heal and pity for suffering.... It was out of love, like the perfect knight of medieval romance, that he set out to combat with the powers of the world...he was like an early saint..."[77]

As of 1994 former president Carter on his goodwill visit to North Korea was favorably impressed by Kim Il Sung. According to a press report "Mr Carter heaped praise on Kim Il Sung... 'I found him to be vigorous, intelligent, well informed... and in charge of decisions about his country.'" The short visit also allowed Carter to note "the reverence with which they (the North Korean people) look upon their leader."[78]

The favorable assessments of communist systems were largely based on the projections of the hopes, ideals and fantasies of Westerners who became persuaded that their moral ideals and notions of a good society were being realized in these countries. Thus devout religious believers (among them ministers, priests and bishops) succeeded in persuading themselves that communist states respected religion and despite their atheistic rhetoric realized the essential precepts of Christianity (Hewlett Johnson considered Soviet policies "singularly Christian" and "Russia...the most moral land I know... During many months in Russsia... I never saw a sight I would screen from the eyes of a young girl."[79]).

The pacifists managed to overlook communist militarism, (later on, the unilateral disarmers the Soviet nuclear arsenal), environmentalists the destruction of the natural environment, populist anti-elitists the vast power and privilege of the leaders. Of this phenomenon Malcolm Muggeridge wrote:

There were earnest advocates of the humane killing of cattle who looked up at the massive headguarters of the OGPU (the political police) with tears of gratitude in their eyes, earnest advocates of proportional representation who eagerly assented when the necessity of the Dictatorship of the Proletariat was explained to them, earnest clergymen who walked reverently through anti-God museums... earnest pacifists who watched delightedly tanks rattle across Red Square... earnest town-planning specialists who stood outside overcrowded ramshackle tenements and muttered: 'If only we had something like this in England!'[80]

Eugene Lyons remarked that the Soviet tourist agency sold "the glories of mass production to... California back-to-nature, handloom fadists. Vegetarians... swooned in ecstasy of admiration of Soviet slaughterhouses."[81] Phenomena deplored under capitalism were reconceptualised and celebrated under communism. Beatrice and Sidney Webb were impressed by the higher purpose they associated with ordinary physical structures: "The marvel was not that there should be parks, hospitals, factories; after all these could be found in England as well. The marvel was that they should all, as the Webbs thought, be inspired by a collective ideal, a single moral purpose."[82] Koestler wrote of the same phenomenon: "For the addict of the Soviet myth the Dnieper Dam, the (Moscow) underground... polar expeditions, Soviet aviation and Soviet flame-throwers assumed the fetish-character of a lock from the hair of the beloved."[83] Waldo Frank, the American writer rhapsodized about a humane Russian locomotive.[84] Pablo Neruda found a visit to a Soviet hydroeletric plant unforgettable and described it as "the temple beside the lake."[85] Ronald Radosh reported that American feminists in a Cuban nightclub found nothing wrong "with a woman showing her body and moving it on stage."[86] Simone de Beauvoir decided that pedicabs in communist China—unlike under capitalism—were not degrading.[87] Jonathan Kozol, the American social critic was under the impression that Cubans didnt mind standing in lines: "The long lines... the ration cards and other forms of deprivaton do not seem to dampen the high spirits of most people."[88] Andre Gide too believed, before the drastic revision of his views about the Soviet system, that Russians had no objection to it either.[89] John Kenneth Galbraith came to the conclusion that the Chinese system under Mao "was remarkably efficient" in distributing consumer goods.[90] Jan Myrdal believed that China was held together by "discussions of Mao's thoughts".[91]

More recently—providing another remarkable demonstration of imaginative wishful projection—John Mack, (professor of psychiatry at Harvard medical school) found a benign interpretation for the withholding of information about the Chernobyl disaster as part of the "tendency on the part of Soviet authorities to downplay catastrophes and instead offer reassurance to the Soviet people so as to prevent emotional distress."[92] Perhaps not coincidentally, he was the same author who expressed firm belief (in a book devoted to the topic) in extraterrestrial visitors harassing American women.

The prestige of Marxism, supposedly guiding and legitimating the policies of communist systems also played a part in the positive assessments of academic intellectuals who believed that communist societies were shaped by this "science of society", by "scientific socialism". On closer inspection the attractions of Marxism appeared to be less than fully rational, more quasi-religious than scientific. As Leszek Kolakowski wrote:

> Marxism has been the greatest fantasy of our century. It was a dream offering the prospect of a society of perfect unity, in which all human aspirations would be fulfilled and all values reconciled.... The influence that Marxism achieved, far from being the result of its scientific character, is almost entirely due to its prophetic, fantastic and irrational elements.[93]

The favorable perceptions of these systems (including their official ideology, Marxism-Leninism) were more closely related to their stated objectives and intentions than their actual accomplishments although the latter were also highly praised and often vastly overrated. Even when sympahetic observers noted troubling matters, occasional discrepancies between ends and accomplishments, costs and benefits or ends and means, they succeeded in reassuring themselves by the grandeur of the goals and the historically unique vision the systems sought to realise.

E.J. Hobsbawm argued, in search of a more realistic basis for the attractions of communist systems, that "the Communist intellectual, in opting for the USSR and his (communist) party did so because on balance the good on his side seemed to outweigh the bad." For most of these intellectuals (including Hobsbawm himself) the overriding, axiomatic "badness" was capitalism and the evils associated with it: exploitation, the profit motive, the cash nexus, alienation, and inequality. Hobsbawm also wrote (rather self-servingly since he himself shared these attitudes as a lifelong sympathizer with communist movements and states) that "modern political choice is not a constant process of selecting men or measures, but a single or infrequent choice between packages, in which we buy the disagreeable

(!) part of the contents because there is not other way to be politically effective."[94]

There were additional misperceptions of communist systems associated with the attitudes noted above. It was widely believed that they brought about spectacular material progress while avoiding the pain, deprivation, injustice and alienation associated with modernization under capitalism. Peter Worsley, an English social scientist was impressed by "the Chinese attempt to transform human values and personal relaionships at the level of everyday life and to challenge assumptions that certain modes of behavior are naturally 'entailed' under conditions of industrial life... that some form of class systems is inevitable... (and) that the attractiveness of material gratifications must, in the end, reassert itself."[95]

It was one of the cardinal misconceptions—not limited to Mao's China—that social equality was energetically and successfully pursued in these societies and if there was any inequality left it was based on true merit. The privileges of the nomenklatura were unknown.

It was also widely believed that the standard of living of the masses hugely improved in each and every one of these countries resulting from the farsighted social and economic policies of their governments. Paul Samuelson the distinguished American economist reportedly believed, as of 1976, that that "it was 'a vulgar mistake to think that most people in Eastern Europe are miserable." Galbraith wrote in 1984 that the Soviet economy made "great material progress in recent years... one sees it in the appearance of solid wellbeing of the people on the streets..."[96]

A particular source of admiration was the belief that social problems plagueing Western, capitalist countries such as crime, alcoholism, drug addiction, unemployment, poverty, family disintegration, racial or sexual discrimination and ethnic strife were being substantially reduced and gradually eliminated in each and every communist state.

The one-party system of these countries far from suggesting lack of choice and alternatives was proof of the legitimacy of the government; few wondered about the plausiblity of 99 percent voter turnouts and similar pluralities the uncontested official candidates garnered.

Those who found virtue in the domestic political-social arrangements of communist systems also believed that their foreign policies were benign and basically peaceful, that aggression was alien to them and they became defensive or bellicose only when threatened by Western hostility. George Kennan who otherwise had no illusions about the nature of the Soviet system believed that its leaders were a group of quite ordinary men, to some extent victims... of the ideology on which they have been reared, but shaped far more importantly by the discipline of the responsibility they... have borne as rulers of a great country... men more seriously concerned to preserve the present limits of their political power...than to expand those limits... whose motivation is essentially defensive...[97]

Only a handful of those who harbored the misconceptions sampled above did subsequently admit their errors publicly.

Grasping Reality

Not all Western views of communist systems were permeated and shaped by ignorance, wishful thinking and misplaced sympathy. There were numerous well informed Western intellectuals, among them academic specialists, writers and journalists who suceeded in identifying the key characteristics of communist systems, had no illusions about their superiority over Western, pluralistic societies and were willing to make moral judgements of their defects without compromising their analytical faculties. It is hard to say what these observers had in common, what saved them from illusions, and why they were (or became) immune to identifying communist systems and movements with progress, humane modernization, the triumph of social justice and a new sense of community. Some of them were former supporters or sympathizers, or actually belonged to communist movements and parties who benefited from an inside view of the phenomenon they described and were transformed from admirers into critics. They include Rosa Luxemburg, Victor Serge, the contributors to volume *The God That Failed* (Louis Fisher, Andre Gide, Arthur Koestler, Ignazio Silone, Stephen Spender, and Richard Wright), Albert Camus, Milovan Djilas, Howard Fast, Eugene Genovese, Doris Lessing, Wolfgang Leonhard, Andre Malraux, and Bertram Wolfe.

Among academic specialists who made lasting contributions to the understanding of communist systems and especially the Soviet Union many were of East-Central European origin. They, or their families had personal experience of the systems they left behind.

Among them are Thomas Aczel, Zbigniev Brzezinski, Alexander Dallin, Alexander Gerschenkron, Jerzy Gliksman,[98] Peter Kenez, Leszek Kolakowski, Leo Labedz, Walter Laqueur, Tibor Meray, Czeslaw Milosz, Richard Pipes, Leonard Schapiro, Adam Ulam, and Ferenc Vali.

Equally illustrious contributions have been made by other scholars without such a background such as Raymond Aron, (among the first to expose the illusions of Western intellectuals about both the Soviet systems and Marxism)[99], Frederick Barghoorn, Raymond Bauer, Cyril Black, Abram Bergson, Walter Connor, Robert Conquest, Robert Daniels, Merle Fainsod, Lewis Feuer, Alex Inkeles, Nathan Leites,[100] Martin Malia, Barrington Moore, David Powell and Peter Reddeway.

Various aspects of Mao's China were revealed in the studies of Maria Chang, Michael Frolic, Merle Goldman, A. James Gregor, Simon Leys, Lucian Pye, Robert Scalapino, Ezra Vogel, Martin Whyte and Harry Wu (the last a former inmate of the Chinese gulag). Steven Mosher provided a revealing study of Western misconceptions of China.[101]

The understanding of communist Cuba was greatly advanced by the work of Alfred Cuzan, Jorge Dominguez, Jorge Edwards,[102] Mark Falcoff, Hugh Thomas, Irving Louis Horowitz,[103] William Ratliff and Jacobo Timmerman.[104] Shirley Christian, Robert Leiken and William Ratfliff were among the few who dispelled illusions about Sandinista Nicaragua. Per Ahlmark of Sweden has been engaged for decades in fighting the widespread and deeply rooted misconceptions about various contemporary communist systems prevailing among his fellow intellectuals in Scandinavia (his books have yet to appear in English). Anthony Daniels, also insufficiently known in this country, has brilliantly captured life in the communist states which survived after 1989, North Korea in particular.[105]

There has been far less public reassessment among former supporters of the second generation communist systems (mainly China, Cuba, Vietnam and Nicaragua) than among former devotees of the Soviet Union; those more recently disillusioned kept their revised judgements to themselves for the most part. There were some important exceptions such as Paul Berman, Maurice Halperin,[106] David Horowitz, Julius Lester, Ronald Radosh, Orville Schell, and Susan Sontag.

There were also numerous other distinguished Western intellectuals who understood communist systems without the benefit of either prior affiliation with or sympathy for communist movements or being born in one of the countries concerned. They include Malcolm Muggeridge, George Orwell, Jean-François Revel and Bertand Russell who early on took a good measure of Lenin and the system he was creating.[107]

There was at last the large number of former citizens of communist systems who left these countries—refugees, defectors and expellees whose accounts greatly enriched our knowledge of these countries but whose work would require separate and extensive treatment not possible here.[108]

The findings of those who understood communist systems converged in several respects. First and foremost they discovered the vast, delegitimising discrepancy between the official ideals, aspirations and promises and the actual character and performance of the social-political institutions and systems which were created. At the same time it is important to emphasize that despite the huge gap between theory and practice, ideals and realities, the ideas of Marxism and Leninism were not without responsibility for the political-institutional realities these systems created having provided initial inspiration and theoretical assurances for those who came to rule the communist countries.

Communist systems as diverse in their historical background, economic development and geographic location as Albania, Cambodia, Cuba, East Germany or North Korea shared several defining attributes and flaws. Most importantly they were all thoroughly repressive, often totalitarian. Secondly, most of them remained largely backward economically as far as popular welfare and consumption were concerned;[109] they were capable of producing long range missiles or tanks but not enough food, consumer goods or plumbing. Thirdly, they inflicted a huge amount of propaganda (some of it via formal education) on their people engaging in "a vast enterpize to deform language" that was designed to redefine the social realities their citizens experienced; these regimes tried (in vain) to "to defeat experience with words."[110]

Most of these systems for most of their existence were dominated by leaders surrounded by grotesque and compulsory cults.

These systems also had in common the failure to eradicate the problems and defects whose existence they deplored in capitalist societies: crime, family decay, urban problems, bureaucracy, environmental destruction as well as the kind of alienation associated with life in modern, urban, secular societies. As John Clark and Aaron Wildavski pointed out "every evil attributed to capitalism turn(ed) up under socialism"; these systems which were "to alter human relations from selfish isolation to altruistic communtarianism... created a caricature of capitalism in which everyone was forced to fend for themselves."[111]

The major insights into the nature of communist systems include the finding that the abolition of the market and private ownership of the means of production led to the loss of productivity, the decline of work ethic, endemic shortages and the chronic inability to meet consumer needs; central planning proved incapable of anticipating the needs of the economy and contributed to inefficiency, bureaucracy and corruption.[112]

Those who understood, through careful study or personal experienced life under these systems also learned that they were overwhelmed by the unintended consequences of their policies. The centralized economy did not lead to efficiency except in meeting the needs of the military; indoctrination did not produce loyalty or conformity in the long run; repression stifled initiative; demands of conformity interfered with learning about and rectifying a wide variety of institutional malfunctioning; allegedly public property did not inspire respect; scarcities under state socialism contributed to crimes against property as much as under capitalism; low wages and salaries undermined incentives for work; ethnic tensions and hostilities were not eliminated only temporarily suppressed. Last but not least every communist systems failed to achieve its proudest claim: the creation of a new, more ethical human being.

A major lesson, as Arthur Koestler formulated it a long time ago, has been that

> man is a reality, mankind an abstraction; that men cannot be treated as units in operations of political arithmetic... that the end justifies the means only within very narrow limits; that ethics is not a function of social utility and charity not a petit-bourgeois sentiment... every single of these trivial statements was incompatible with the Communist faith...[113]

*   *   *

Two major conclusions may be drawn from the Western misjudgements of communist systems. One is that disaffection from one's own society does not help to soberly evaluate and understand other social-political systems and can lead to their disastrous misapprehension. The second is that the attempt to judge the virtues and vices of any society must take into account the extent to which it accomodates or frustrates what seem to be basic human needs and dispositions. Much remains to be learned about the precise nature of these needs but the collapse of communism should stimulate their better understanding since arguably it occurred because of the determination to ignore them.

Notes

Not even a modestly systematic sampling of the huge literature on communist systems is feasible in an essay of this length. I listed the sources I quoted from or made specific reference to and a few of those I wished to draw attention to, important but neglected or forgotten works. The listing of the names of *some* who made important contributions to understanding (or misunderstanding) communist systems was similarly selective.

1. The communist systems to which reference is being made include the former Soviet Union and its "Socialist Commonwealth" in Eastern Europe; as well as Albania, Mao's China, Castro's Cuba, communist Vietnam, North Korea and Nicaragua under the Sandinistas. Communist states in Africa such as Angola, Mozambique and Ethiopia attracted lesser Western attention but they too were viewed with sympathy by many intellectuals as part of the "Third World" and victims of the West and capitalism.

2. The major product of these efforts was *Political Pilgrims: Travels of Western Intellectuals to the Soviet Union, China and Cuba*, New York, 1981 and 1983; Lanham MD 1990; New Brunswick NJ 1998.

3. See for example Alfred G. Cuzan: "The Latin American Studies Association vs. the U.S.", *Academic Questions*, Summer, 1994 and Wilcomb E. Washburn: "The Treason of Intellectuals," (pamphlet) *Young America's Foundation*, Herndon, Va., Spring 1991, p. 18.

4. "Soviet Myths and Reality" in *The Yogi and the Commissar*, New York, 1961, pp.123-124.

5. Sinclair in Upton Sinclair and Eugene Lyons: *Terror in Russia? Two Views*, New York 1938, pp. 11, 12.

6. Ferdinand Mount ed. *Communism*, Chicago, 1992, p. 166.

7. *Village Voice*, May 28, 1979 p. 25-26.

8. For a sampling of such views see Paul Hollander: *Political Will and Personal Belief: The Decline and Fall of Soviet Communism*, New Haven, 1999.

9. Joshua Muravchik: "Reds", *Commentary*, September 1999, p.43.

10. Ellen Schrecker for example believed that that "if communism was heterogeneous and creative, anti-Communism was... purely malignant. She argues that there was no good kind of anti-Communism..." (Jacob Weisberg: "Cold War Without End", *New York Times Magazine*, November 28, 1999, p.116)

11. *The Passing of an Illusion*, Chicago 1999, p.494.

12. "The 'Essential Love' of Simone de Beauvoir", *Problems of Communism*, March-April 1966, p. 63.

13. Noam Chomsky and Edward S. Herman: "Distortions at Fourth Hand," *Nation*, June 1977 pp. 789,791,792. See also by the same authors *After the Cataclysm: Postwar Indochina and the Reconstruction of Imperial Ideology*, Boston, 1978, esp. p. 290. Dudman was cited in Chomsky and Herman (1978) esp. pp. 147, 149.

14. Robert Conquest recalled that in the 1970s he came upon (in Westminster Library in London) "modern maps of northeastern Siberia showing camp settlements; they were labelled 'Secret: U.S. Air Force.' At that time a Washington proposal to publish a full layout of the camps was blocked by the State Department in the interest of detente." (*Hoover Institution Newsletter*, Spring 1999, p.5)

15. Walter Goodman, *New York Times*, April 6, 1991. See Dr Spock's letter in the *New York Times*, September 4, 1994. Carol Brightman another venerable admirer of Cuba and co-editor of the worshipful volume entitled *Venceremos Brigade* (New York, 1971) as of 1995 still considered critiques of Cuba "distortions." (Letter, *New York Times*, November 9, 1995)

16. *Men and Politics*, New York, 1941 p. 189.

17. *To Peking and Beyond*, New York 1973, pp. 73-74.

18. For major examples see J. Arch Getty: *Origns of the Great Purges*, New York, 1985; Getty and Roberta T. Manning eds.: *Stalinist Terror: New Perspectives*, New York 1993; Robert V. Thurston: *Life and Terror in Stalin's Russia 1934-1941*, New Haven CT, 1996. Revisionist (and non-judgemental) views of Stalin and Soviet history may also be founds in the work of Theodore von Laue.

19. Reflecting such hopes Stephen F. Cohen wrote: "The emergence of a Soviet leadership devoted to radical reform confounded most Western scholars... who had long believed that the Soviet communist system lacked any capacity for real change." Apparently Cohen believed otherwise. (Stephen P.Cohen and Katrina vanden Heuvel eds.: *Voices of Glasnost*, New York 1989 p. 14.

20. *Imperium*, New York, 1994, p.314.

21. Quoted in Thomas Powers: "Who Won the Cold War?" *New York Review of Books*, June 20, 1996, p. 20.

22. Walter Laqueur: *The Dream That Failed: Reflections on the Soviet Union*, New York 1994: 57, 59, 99.

23. Quoted in *Freedom Review*, 1992 July-August p.7.

24. Quoted in Laqueur 1994 *cited*, pp. 120, 211.

25. Moshe Lewin: *The Gorbachev Phenomenon*, Berkeley CA 1988, pp. 131, 133

26. David Pryce-Jones wrote: "The facade was completely false. An unbroken history of dissent, strikes, uprisings and armed rebellions was ruthlessly suppressed from the rest of the world in order to pretend to communist unity and solidarity." (*The Strange Death of the Soviet Empire*, New York, 1995 p. 36)

27. Quoted in William M.Brinton and Alan Rinzler eds.: *Without Force or Lies*, San Francisco, 1990, p.405.

28. John Lewis Gaddis: *We Now Know: Rethinking Cold War History*, Oxford, U.K., 1997, pp. 292, 222.

29. Moynihan in *Newsweek*, November 19, 1979 pp. 136, 141; Conquest in *New York Times Magazine*, August 18, 1969; Pipes in *Foreign Affairs*, Fall 1984 50, 60.

30. Richard Pipes suggested that "The fiasco of Sovietology... may well have had its root cause in the determination of political scientists to act like physicists or biologists... But... the study of mankind differs fundamentally from the study of nature... in part because unlike molecules and cells, human beings have values and objectives

that preclude their being analyzed in a value-free, unteleological manner." (*New Republic*, November 27, pp.160, 156)

31. "Anticipations of the Failure of Communism", *Theory and Society*, No. 23. 1994, p. 202.

32. See for example Alvin Z. Rubinstein: "Soviet Success Story: The Third World", *Orbis*, Fall 1988.

33. For example Bertell Ollman wrote: "Paradoxically enough, the objective conditions for socialism in the USSR are now largely present, but because of the unhappy experience with a regime that called itself 'socialist' the subjective conditions are absent... On the other hand...the Soviet Union might be saved by a socialist revolution in the West as our capitalist economy goes into a tailspin." (*PS: Political Science and Politics*, September 1991, p. 460)

34. *Under My Skin*, New York 1994, pp. 15-16.

35. Letter, *Times* (London) September 4, 1967.

36. Francois Furet: *The Passing of an Illusion*, Chicago, 1999 p. 117.

37. *The Other Side*, New York, 1966, pp. 17-18.

38. *A Scientist Among the Soviets*, London, 1932, p. 67.

39. Eugene Lyons: *Assignement in Utopia*, London 1938, p. 430; *China Passage*, Boston, 1973 p. 54.

40. "Graham Offers Positive Views of Religion in Soviet", *New York Times*, May 13, 1982; "Billy Graham Rebutts Criticism of Soviet Trip", *New York Times*, May 18, 1982; and "Billy Graham Back Home, Defends Remarks," *New York Times*, May 20, 1982.

41. *Dream of the Golden Mountains*, New York, 1980 p. 43.

42. *Moscow 1937*, New York 1937, pp. 149-150.

43. *John Dewey's Impressions of Soviet Russia and the Revolutionary World*, New York, 1929, p. 105.

44. *Travels in Two Democracies*, New York, 1936 p. 321.

45. Quoted in Gary Wersky: *The Visible College*, New York, 1979, pp. 148, 193.

46. *This Soviet World*, New York, 1936, p. 250.

47. "From a China Traveler" *New York Times*, August 10, 1973; Felix Green: *China*, New York, 1961 p. 157.

48. "The New China and the American Connection", *Foreign Affairs*, October 1972, pp. 31, 36.

49. "Cuba: The Present Reality", *New Left Review*, May-June, 1961, p.22.

50. *Listen Yankee*, New York, 196.0

51. Quoted in Joshua Muravchik: "Pliant Protestants", *New Republic*, June 13, 1983

52. *Trip to Hanoi*, New York, 1968 pp. 69, 77.

53. *The Best of What We Are: Reflections on the Nicaraguan Revolution*, Amherst MA, 1995 pp. 42, 36.

54. Quoted in Martin Diskin ed.: *Trouble in Our Backyard*, New York: 1983, p.247

55. *Contentions*, New York, September 1990, pp. 1-2; Noam Chomsky: *On Power and Ideology, Managua Lectures*, Boston, 1987, pp. 38-39.

56. On the French intellectuals' perception of the trials in Eastern Europe see Tony Judt: *Past Imperfect: French Intellectuals 1944-1956*, Berkeley, CA, 1992.

57. *Mission to Moscow*, New York, 1943 pp. 163, 168-169, 25.

58. *The Kremlin and the People*, New York, 1941, p.65.

59. Quoted in Paul Hollander: *Political Pilgrims*, New York 1981, pp.161-163.

60. Jean Lacouture: *Andre Malraux*, New York, 1975, p.230.

61. Gyorgy Faludi: *Pokolbeli Vig Napjaim* (My Happy Days in Hell), Budapest, 1989, pp. 313-315.

62. *Soviet Communism: A New Civilzation?* New York, 1936, p. 588.
63. *Rationalization of Russia*, Bloomington, Indiana, 1964, p.91; *This Soviet World*, New York 1936, p. 262.
64. Henry Wallace: *Soviet Asia Mission*, New York, 1946 pp. 33-35, 84, 217.
65. *New York Times Book Review,* May 1996, p. 14.
66. *The Long March*, Cleveland and New York, 1958 p.388.
67. *Daybreak in China*, London 1953 p. 183.
68. "Cuban Prisons: A Preliminary Report", IPS *Social Justice*, Summer, 1988, pp. 58, 59.
69. *The Jaguar Smile: A Nicaraguan Journey*, New York 1987, p. 32.
70. *The Truth About Russia*, London 1942, pp. 16, 18.
71. Quoted in Stephen J. Whitfield: *Scott Nearing: Apostle of American Radicalism*, New York, 1974 p. 185.
72. *Mission to Moscow*, New York 1943, p. 217.
73. Robert Nisbet: *The Failed Friendship*, Washington DC, 1988, pp. 11, 12.
74. *China's New Creative Age*, London 1953, p. 153.
75. *Sartre on Cuba* New York 1961, pp. 102-103; Saul Landau: "Cuba: The Present Reality," *New Left Review*, May-June 1961 p. 15.
76. Per Ahlmark: "Tyranny and the Left, A Summary", Stockholm, 1995 p. 28.
77. I.F. Stone: "The Legacy of Che Guevara," *Ramparts*, December 1967. pp. 20-21.
78. George Will: "Carter Misreads North Korea's Kim," *Daily Hampshire Gazette*, June 24, 1994.
79. *Soviet Power*, New York, 1940, p. 5; *Russia Since the War*, New York 1947, p. 89.
80. *Chronicles of Wasted Time*, New York, 1973, p. 244.
81. Lyons cited p. 329.
82. Gertrude Himmelfarb: "The Intellectual in Politics: The Case of the Webbs", *Journal of Contemporary History*, No.3., 1971, p.11.
83. Koestler cited p. 130.
84. *Dawn in Russia*, New York, 1932, pp. 121, 127.
85. *Memoirs*, New York, 1977, p. 243.
86. Ronald Radosh ed. *The New Cuba*, New York, 1976 pp. 64-65.
87. Beauvoir cited p. 49.
88. *Children of the Revolution: A Yankee Teacher in Cuban Schools*, New York, 1978, p. 102.
89. *Return from the USSR*, New York, 1964, p.17-18.
90. Galbraith cited pp. 104, 115.
91. *The Revolution Continued* ,New York, 1970 p. 191.
92. "Soviet Minds Sheltered from Catrastrophe", Letter, *New York Times*, May 15, 1986.
93. Leszek Kolakowski: *Main Currents of Marxism*, Vol.3., New York, 1978, pp. 523, 525. John Gray also noted that "The attraction of Marxism to the Western intelligentsia was... never that of an analytically superior theoretical system in social science. It was rather the appeal of a historical theodicy, in which Judeo-Christian moral hopes were to be realized without the need for a transcendental commitment which reason could not sanction." (Ferdinand Mount ed.: *Communism,* Chicago 1992, p.231)
94. E.J. Hobsbawm: "Intellectuals and Communism," in Mount cited, pp.116-117.
95. *Inside China*, London, 1975 p. 20.
96. Both of these observations were quoted in *Freedom Review*, July-Augst 1992, p. 6
97. Quoted in Paul Hollander: *The Survival of the Adversary Culture*, New Brunswick 1988, pp. 34-35.

98. *Tell the West*, (New York 1948), a particularly informative volume combines the sympathizer's perspective (including the experience of political tourism) with that of his later incarnation as inmate of the gulag.

99. *The Opium of Intellectuals*, London 1957.

100. In this section I am only citing works which have either been forgotten or never received the amount of attention they deserve. They include Nathan Leites: *A Study of Bolshevism*, Glenco, IL 1953.

101. Steven Mosher: *China Misperceived*, New York 1990. See also his *The Rural Chinese* (1983) and *Journey to the Forbidden China* (1985).

102. *Persona Non Grata*, New York 1977.

103. I.L. Horowitz edited the volume *Cuban Communism,* a major collection of scholarly studies of Castro's Cuba that had nine editions between 1970 and 1998.

104. Jacobo Timmerman: *Cuba: A Journey*, New York, 1990.

105. *Utopias Elsewhere*, New York, 1991.

106. See his *The Rise and Decline of Fidel Castro*, Berkeley, CA, 1972; *The Taming of Fidel Castro*, Berkeley, CA, 1981; and *Return to Havana*, Nashville, TN 1994.

107. Bertrand Russell: *Bolshevism: Practice and Theory*, New York, 1920.

108. For a discussion of some important accounts defectors provided see Ch. 2 in Paul Hollander: *Political Will and Personal Belief*, New Haven, 1999.

109. Czechoslovakia, Hungary and East Germany were more consumer oriented and developed economically; Hungary and Poland during the 70s and 80s were less repressive.

110. Dariusz Tolczyk: *See No Evil: Literary Cover-Ups and Discoveries of the Soviet Camp Experience*, New Haven, 1999, pp. 3, XXI.

111. *The Moral Collapse of Communism*, San Francisco, 1990, pp. 16-17, 311, 336.

112. A not widely known contribution to understanding the failure of planning and its political consequences is Ferenc Feher, Agnes Heller and Gyorgy Markus: *Dictatorship Over Needs*, New York 1983.

113. Koestler in Richard Crossman ed.: *The God That Failed*, New York, 1949, p.60.

22

Westernization and Anti-Americanism in Post-Communist Societies

In the middle of the twentieth century the United States emerged as a symbol of economic exploitativeness, social injustice and cultural corruption—a readily available, multipurpose scapegoat for a wide range of grievances: anti-Americanism became a widely shared disposition in many parts of the world. In retrospect it seems that the phenomenon had three major components: the Soviet-communist propaganda associated with the Cold War, the anti-Western sentiments in the newly created and struggling countries of the third world and last but not least the wave of intense and often embittered social criticism that was an integral part of the social movements of the 1960s in the United States and Western Europe.

It will be argued that despite the demise of Soviet communism anti-Americanism persists and that conditions in the former Soviet Bloc countries, and Russia in particular have been conducive to its revival in somewhat different forms: a more authentic, popular and ambivalent anti-Americanism largely replaced the official one.

It should also be noted that despite the suspicions and aversions noted above, in recent years as in the past, the United Startes has continued to attract millions of people from every corner of the world. Immensely popular with ordinary people of every race, color, nationality, ethnicity, and religious belief, it has mostly been groups of intellectuals or quasi-intellectuals who have specialised in the denigration of the United States.[1]

While anti-Americanism has a wide variety of sources and may sprout in many different corners of the world much of it is home grown. As Saul Bellow put it: "our own intellectuals have made the anti-American case worldwide... anti-Americanism is one of our principal exports." (Bellow 1995). It remains an empirical question how much awareness there is in different parts of the world of such indigenous critiques, including Eastern Europe and Russia. In any event to say that the anti-Americanism of (some) Americans has been among the stimulants or inspirations of corresponding sentiments abroad is not to suggest that other sources and stimulants were lacking.

Anti-Americanism is often an attitude of ambivalence rather than clear cut, unalloyed hostility. Once more Saul Bellow observed that the United States is "both the model and the menace" (Bellow 1992: 542) which is indeed the case in much of the world.

Before going further it may be useful to inform the reader what this author means by anti-Americanism:

> ... an attitude of distaste, aversion, or intense o hostility the roots of which may be found in matters unrelated to the particular qualities or attributes of American society or the foreign policies of the United States... anti-Americanism refers to a negative predisposition, a type of bias which is to varying degrees unfounded... an attitude similar to its far more thoroughly examined counterparts, hostile predispositions such as racism, sexism or antisemitism...
>
> ... What holds together the varieties of anti-Americanism is a sense of grievance and the compelling need to find some clear-cut and morally satisfying explanation for a wide range of unwelcome circumstances associated with either actual states, or feelings of backwardness, inferiority, weakness, diminished competitiveness, or a loss of coherence and stability in the life of a nation, group or individual. (Hollander 1995: LXXVII)

This definition encompasses several types of anti-Americanism some which is more likely to emerge in postcommunist countries than others. In addition to the domestic (American) and foreign varieties one may distinguish among cultural, political-nationalistic, and economic types as well as between spontaneous, or grass rooots, as opposed to institutionally orhcestrated and organized forms such as communist governments and movements used to produce. As to the latter, there were both theoretical-ideological and tactical-political reasons for these campaigns. The United States was attacked both as the most powerful embodiment of capitalist values and institutions and as the Superpower competing with the Soviet Union for global influence. From its earliest days the Soviet Union was in the forefront of these efforts partially suspended only during World War II; even in that period Soviet propaganda cast doubt on American goodwill by playing down American (and British) contributions to the war effort. These campaigns continued during the periods of "peaceful coexistence" and "detente" and persisted into the early years of perestroika and glasnost as exemplified by the worldwide campaign of disinformation that alleged that the AIDS virus was manufactured in military laboratories of the United States for the purpose of harming people in the third world (e.g., Schrieberg: 1990: 12).

The organized vilification of the United States by communist states and movements encompassed a wide range of themes to meet every local-regional need and susceptibility: American imperialism, neo-colonialism, predatory capitalism, cultural imperialism, the flaws of the American national character, ethnocentrism, white supremacy, racism, sexism, domestic repression—all came to be incorporated into these campaigns in varying quantities.

Of the remaining communist systems Cuba and North Korea continue to produce anti-American propaganda and of late China intensified efforts to guard its people against the "spiritual pollution" associated with the U.S. notwithstanding the growing economic ties with it.

Despite the substantial investment of resources by communist governments local (and often apolitical) susceptibilities and experiences in different parts of the world were probably more important in the creation and perpetuation of these attitudes. Foremost among them were nationalism and the difficulties of competing with the United States economically and in the realm of popular culture. The superpower status by itself—even while shared with the former Soviet Union—was conducive to antagonism the Soviet Union largely escaped: third world critics of "neocolonialism" as well as those associated with the peace movement in Western Europe and the U.S. tended to overlook Soviet imperialism and colonialism. In the third world the United States was identified with the "West" (and rightly so)—a concept and entity which in itself attracted hostility in these parts. Throughout the 1960s, 70s and early 80s third world anti-Americanism also found expression in the politics and rhetoric of the United Nations (see for example Moynihan 1978).

Most importantly and enduringly, anti-Americanism has been associated with the protest against modernity; as such it has been among the manifestations of the "counter-modernizing" impulse in the less developed countries. It was an impulse which at earlier times had created susceptibility to what Peter Berger called the "myth of socialism" that promised a path to modernity without its costs and contradictions (Berger 1977). In turn sizable groups of Western intellectuals have been unhappy with the experience of living in a modern (i.e. secular, consumerist, technologically advanced, communally weakened, politically pluralistic) society and vocally articulated such discontents.

Despite the large volume of the official propaganda it used to be hard to find genuine anti-American or anti-Western sentiments in the former Soviet Bloc countries. On the contrary the people, including the intellectuals, felt an affinity toward the United States and the West (even without knowing much about them), precisely because they were denounced by the authorities—the designated enemies of the rulers became the friends of the ruled. But there was more to these attitudes than reflexive sympathy with targets of official denigration: the United States and "the West" were fused into one entity; East-Central Europeans in particular had a historical longing for achieving the status of a "Western" nation, aspiring to be recognized as belonging to the heirs of European cultural traditions. The situation in the former Soviet Union was more complicated reflecting the historical ambivalence of Russians and Russian intellectuals toward the West. But even in the former Soviet Union a predominantly pro-American disposition prevailed, sometimes nurtured by particular historical experiences of the older generations such as the memories of the Lend and Lease program during World War II and personal encounters during wartime military service with American servicemen. The young admired American mass culture and fashions endowed as they were with the aura of forbidden fruit while dissenting intellectuals revered the institutions and practices of civil society found in the U.S. Even the communist elites were respectful of the economic, technological and scientific superiority of the United States.

Thus well before the collapse of Soviet communism attitudes toward and ideas about the United States played an important part in the thinking and imagination of people of Eastern Europe, Russia included. The U.S. was a counterpoint to their political system and everything their own society was not: rich, free, open, generous, exciting, colorful, a repository of opportunities and promises barely imaginable.

For the communist political elites the United States was both a model and counter-model: to be emulated for its scientific-technological and economic power and abhorred on ideological grounds as the embodiment of the moral corruptions of capitalism.

Virtually all the improvements sought by postcommunist societies may be subsumed under the term "Westernization" and its two major dimensions, the political and economic. The first amounts to the creation or stabilization of a civil society involving political democracy, pluralism, rule of law, institutionalization of tolerance and independent associations; the second component is a market economy based on private enterprize, yielding rising standards of productivity, living and consumption.

In the minds of many, probably the most people in postcommunist societies the United States has been the most potent symbol of the West and the country that was expected to help these countries to embark on Westernization and especially the rapid improvement of their economies. Modernization, Westernization and Americanization have been widely perceived as intertwined although some, and especially intellectuals differentiate between Americanization and Westernization especially in the context of cultural matters. "Western" may thus refer to Western European, or "true European" values and ideas which are contrasted to the vulgarities of American mass culture—the most tangible and undesirable form of Americanization.

How did the collapse of Soviet communism effect anti-Americanism worldwide and within the former Soviet Bloc?

There is little doubt that globally the collapse weakened and discredited anti-Americanism since anti-Americanism used to rest, at least in part, on a seemingly viable socialist alternative to American style capitalism, consumer society and political pluralism. The economic inefficiency and failure of state socialism dealt a strong blow to the anti-capitalist, anti-market sentiments which used to be closely associated with anti-Americanism in much of the world. Jorge Castenade wrote: "...the self destruction of the basic (i.e., the Soviet) model signified the disappearance of the left's framework for conceiving of an alternative.... The effects of the passing of the (Soviet) paradigm helped discredit the role of the state in economic and social policy" (Castenade 1993: 245).

More questionably it has also been argued that anti-Americanism has altogether disappeared, replaced in the post- communist era by a worldwide veneration of all things American. An influential German journalist wrote: "On the verge of the 21st century the United States isnt just the 'last remaining superpower.' It is a continent size 'demonstration effect'... the United States is No. 1. and soaring..." The writer also claimed that even those on the left have abandoned their erstwhile hostilities. He believes that the U.S. possess a "universal allure" because "America has the world's most open culture... America keeps drawing the world's best and brightest, allowing them to rise to the top within one generation. That makes for a universalist culture with a universal appeal" (Joffe 1997).

While these observations are not altogether groundless they overlook the ambivalence and large pockets of hostility that persist toward American society and culture even among those who enjoy their fruits. Joffe seems to conflate the power, wealth and creativity of the United States with its popularity. This latest "trend spotting" (the readyness to discover endlessly new trends of short duration, itself something very American) is also hard to reconcile with the reigning conventional wisdom of large groups of academic intellectuals in the United States who champion "multiculturalism" and "cultural diversity." The latter, while generally ill defined have one solid core: an unwavering anti-Western disposition which expresses itself in blaming the West and the United States in particular for virtually every existing social ill and affliction in the world, including poverty, racism, sexism, homophobia, environmental problems and inequalities and conflicts of every kind. In the "politically correct" subcultures which proliferate in American society (especially on college campuses and adjoining communities) reports of the alleged global popularity of the U.S. would be received with incomprehension, distaste and disbelief.

As to the postcommunist societies, it is essential to differentiate between attitudes toward the U.S. and the West in the more stable, developed or Westernized countries of the region (i.e., the Czech Republic, Hungary, Poland and the Baltic states) and all the others, and especially Russia (for a more refined scheme of differentiation see Tarifa 1998: 69). While admiration and ambivalence are increasingly linked everywhere it is safe to say that anti-Americanism in Russia greatly exceeds corresponding sentiments in much of Eastern Europe.

Further differentiation is to be made between the attitudes of intellectuals and ordinary people as well as between younger and older generations; attitudes about the past and present and toward things Western and American are often age-related. Survey data indicate, as will be shown below, that the young are far more Western oriented, pro-American and optimistic than the old, while the old are more bitter and gloomy about the difficulties of the post-communist era and for good reasons: those on pensions are for the most part impoverished. The younger age groups are better equipped with skills and enterpreneurial attitudes for the changing times.

Although it is premature to propose conclusive generalizations about anti-American or anti-Western sentiments in the postcommunist societies, it is possible to outline a constellation of conflicting factors which respectively predispose to, or counter the rise of anti-American attitudes.

Russian nationalism has been a major force conducive to anti-Americanism feeding on collective resentments and a "negative, envy-fuelled perception of the USA" (Shlapentokh 1998: 214). Russian nationalism in the recent past has been fuelled by the loss of Soviet superpower status and the subsequent perceived humilations (such as NATO expansion into East-Central Europe) providing strong incentives for linking nationalistic grievance with anti-American sentiments. The power, wealth and global dominance of the United States make it an inviting target of such sentiments: "Suddenly the West is the all purpose villain" (Specter 1994:32).

East European nationalism has also revived with the passing of communism. As Milovan Djilas wrote "Nationalism is the overriding fact of life in all the former Communist countries of Eastern Europe... In all post-Communist states nationalism is in the ascendancy." Under communist rule these sentiments were "hammered down only to bounce back with elemental forces..." (Djilas 1998: 318-320). To be sure there are significant differences between the virulence of such sentiments in the more and less advanced (or Westernized) countries of the region, as for example between the nationalism of Czechs as opposed to that of Serbs. There is also a greater appreciation of what civil society amounts to in the more Westernized of these countries, as exemplified by a recent Hungarian discussion of public life and morality in the United States vs. Hungary:

The two hundred year old United States could become in a century and half the most influentiual and richest nation of the world because its citizens have taken the notion of public good more seriously than those of all other countries...

After commenting on the financial disclosure statements of the Clintons and other presidents and public figures in the U.S. the article continues:

How would the Hungarian prime minister and our politicians who in similar disclosures give prominence to their ancient cars and miniscule, worthless real estate holdings, stand the test of genuine public scrutiny?...
    The important differences (between conditions in Hungary and the U.S., that is) must be sought not in the quality of our highways or the equipment of our hospitals but in the morality of the 'ruling class' that too has a considerable and not incidental bearing on the material welfare of a nation. While former president Jimmy Carter personally labors to build houses for the poor, our ministers... demand that the public pay for their fire places, formal gardens and villas... (Bruck 1998: 5)

In addition to the strong historical tradition of Russian nationalism that used to be intertwined with pride in the Soviet Superpower status, the very modest progress Russia has made (even in comparison with much of Eastern Europe) towards Westernization has been a major source of the intensification of recent anti-Americanism. Above all the economic stagnation has led to widespread frustration and resentment associated almost invariably with virulent nationalism. A Hungarian author noted that anti-Americanism is the strongest in the countries whose performance is the most obviously unmatched by their potential (Bruck 1998: 5).

It is then hardly surprising that in "a spiritually bankrupt society" (as Russia is described) where "moral malaise is widespread" and in which "widespread disorientation and confusion" prevail (as also revealed by public opinion research) (Kon and Star in Shalin ed. 1996: 185, 317) there are powerful incentives to seize upon some malignant entity upon which disorder and deprivation can be blamed. There is also a tradition of xenophobic mistrust of foreigners and things foreign hence it is not surprising that "A public that only three years ago viewed the West as the Land of Oz have come...to believe that foreigners have too much influence here..." (Specter 1994: 30). Igor Shafarevich a Soviet era dissenter, mathematician and well-known intellectual said:

It is natural to feel bitter about America because America is being shoved down our throat at all times... If you look at television today only American products are advertised there. Ice cream, gum, toothbrushes, whatever. All is American. If in an ad you need to portray something as attractive, they speak English. Air time on our Russian television is bought by Western preachers—Baptists for instance—while the Russian Orthodox Church doesnt have this opportunity. (Specter 1994: 30-31)

Historical antecedents and the legacies of the communist as well as the pre-communist times make the transition to a more Western-ized society difficult and fraught with frustration especially in Rus-sia and the less developed parts of Eastern Europe. Numerous at-tributes of both traditional Russian and Soviet society sharply con-flict with Western values and patterns of behavior. Already Dostoevski asked: "Is there not revealed something in the protesting Russian soul, to which European culture in its any manifestations has al-ways, ever since Peter, been hateful? I do think so" (Specter 1994:33) More recently Igor Kon, a Russian social scientist observed:

Soviet culture and personality were geared not to innovation and change but stability and stagnation... for ordinary people this stagnant lifestyle became the norm and when the winds of change finally began to sweep through society they caught the vast majority... totally unpreapered for the new challenges and opportunities... the Soviet system systematically discourged ... experimentation. Individuality was suppressed.... The primitive egalitarianism... the fear of competition.. stfile(ed) personal initiative (Shalin ed. 1996: 192-193).

There is moreover a widespread perception and experience of falling standards of living and an indisputable decline of public safety and order and proliferation of other social problems as well: "Con-ditioned by their Soviet upbringing, many of these hard-pressed Russians have linked the fast-living, decadent America portrayed in new, hard-sell advertisements to the explosion of crime and other social woes in post-Soviet Russia ("A New Chill in the Russian Air" 1993: 37). Yegor Gaidar, a young, staunchly pro-Western politician observed: "You have a stagnating economy. You have real poverty. You have enormous increases in inequality. You have rising expec-tations. You have a general sense of disorder and... shocking crime everyhwhere you look. I think this is an ideal platform for the en-emies of democracy" (Spector 1994: 33); an ideal platform for anti-American, anti-Western sentiments as well.

Besides the present conditions of disorder, frustration and scar-city which nurture the scape-goating impulse there is in Russia (more than in Eastern Europe), a long tradition of anguished ambivalence about the West and capitalism that persists to this day and finds ex-pression even in the writings of anti-communist intellectuals such as Solzhenitsyn (see for example Solzhenitsyn 1993) and even in state-

ments of Yeltsin who declared that "the country's continuing problems have been caused by the blind embrace of the Western-style
capitalist ideology and the disregard for traditional social values"
(Shlapentokh: 1998: 203). According to surveys of the All Russian
Center of Public Opinion "about 60% of Russians rejected the Western capitalist model for their country" (Shlapentokh 1998:209). Arguably such rejection had more to do with the widely experienced
failure of the economic reforms than a generalised, ideologically
based distaste for capitalism. More striking yet was the finding of a
1995 survey that "52% of Russians view the influence of Western
culture—as exemplified in commerce and advertising—as negative"
(Kondrashov 1995: 15).

Another national survey illustrates the splits in public opinion.
49% of those surveyed thought that "the goal of the West is to bring
Russia to a state of destitution and collapse" but these respondents
(mostly older, poorer and rural) were vigorously opposed by 36 percent predominatly younger, with higher income, engaged in private
enterprise and residents of Moscow and St Petersburg. 52 percent in
the same survey favored "a special Russian development path" and
54 percent the "spurn(ing of) Western aid"; 37 percent "insist(ed)
that relations between Russia and the West 'will always be built on
distrust.'"; 59 percent averred that "Russia stands alone and different from Europe."; 56 percent "are sure that 'the Western states, no
matter what they say, really want to turn Russia into a colony... a
source of raw materials and cheap manpower.'" On the other hand
60 percent of those surveyed "are convinced that relations between
Russia and the West can be truly friendly.'" The author of the article
quoting these figures rightly concluded that "people see the West as
a sworn enemy and ally... (and that) the publics attitude toward the
West is unsettled. There is more confusion and contradiction... than
there are well considered assessments" (Sazonov 1995: 14-15).

A content analysis of the Russian media in 1996-97 conducted
by Michigan University revealed that "the authors of 80% of the
articles evaluated the attitudes of the West toward Russia as 'hostile'" (Shlapentokh 1998: 207). The same study also found that about
two thirds of Russians "assume that the West is hostile toward their
country with 61% accpeting the proposition that "The U.S. is utiliz-
ing Russia's curent weakness to reduce it to a second rate power and
producer of raw materials" (Shlapentokh 1998: 209).

Again, it is important to bear in mind that these anti-Western, anti-American and anti-capitalist attitudes are concentrated among the older age groups and those with less education who benefited least from the political-economic transformations:

> Recent public opinion polls show a sharp contrast between older, less-educated rural population... and younger, better educated urban respondents... Of the respondents below twenty-five, 63% had positive attitude toward private property and the market economy, compared to 19% among those sixty years and older. (Kon in Shalin ed.: 201)

The same survey seeking to assess how people had evaluated perestroika (and by extension steps toward Westernization) found that the "younger, better educated...urban dwellers" were far more positive than the rest of the sample. "People from this category were more willing to take personal risk in economic competition and strenuously opposed egalitarianism" (ibid.). David Remnick too commented on these contrasts:

> While both the young and the economically nimble romanticize an America of 19th century capitalism and late 20th century hedonism, older people—mainly pensioners, nationalists and defeated Communists use this same America as a symbol of rot, ruthlessnes and foreign invasion. Where some see America as an economic model of efficiency, others see Russia being taken over by foreign prospectors... a vast resource pool that will enrich the foreigners but leave Russia even more of a ruin. For one side the United States is the symbol of ambition and hope; for the other, it is the basis for politics of resentment and revenge. (Remnick 1993: 38)

Remnick also observed: "For the older generation... America is the land of their defeat, a smug and garish landscape of success. But for the young, America is the romantic future. They are interested more in the ideal America than the one portrayed in Western newpapers, books and political discussions... Compared with the hole they are in the problems of the United States seem laughable" (Remnick 1993: 40-41).

It is important to point out that Russian anti-Americanism is not always or obviously associated with the experience of material deprivations and scarcities and the resulting bitterness. There is also an anti-Americanism among elite groups that is related to their loss of global power, prestige and influence. A Russian emigree sociologist wrote:

> ...while Russian politicians, business people and journalists rejoice in their new found wealth, they have lost the self-esteem and pride of representing a superpower, a great country... Today the Russian elites feel not dignity but national humiliation. With their

material needs fully satisfied, the members of the elite are particularly sensitive to the view that their country lost...its special standing in the world...the Russian elite, along with the majority of the population began to change their attitudes toward the West. The elite could not reconcile itself to the idea that Russia was doomed to be a backward country... Russian society needed an explanation why the country once again (i.e. since the fall of communism—P.H.) was unable to reach the promised, 'radiant future' of Western level economic prosperity. (Shlapentokh 1998: 206, 202)

If there is any single factor predisposing to anti-Americanism in the former Soviet Bloc countries it is the disappointment with the degree of material-economic improvements (or lack of thereof) and the modest Western and especially American economic assistance. Correspondingly popular expectations of the benefits of a free market and the consumer society have not been met and the distribution of these benefits has been uneven and limited. Large portions of the populations and especially those on fixed incomes lost the economic stability and modest security previous communist governments provided. A Russian social scientist wrote:

However arduous life was under the ancien regime, it accorded the individual a place in the social system and guaranteed employment, minimal standards of living, free health care... and a sense that one belonged to a great nation. When wild capitalism replaced cradle-to-grave security, many people were frightened... Blue and white collar workers now faced unemployment; intellectuals found their spiritual bonds threatened by inequality; artists lamented their lost subsidies; the once pampered millitary forces saw their prestige take a nose dive; collective farmers felt reluctant to strike out on their own as private producers... Everyone had to master the difficult art of private living with all its... uncertainties and opportunities.(Etkind in Shalin ed. 1996: 122)

There is finally the influx and popularity of American mass culture that is offensive to all who harbor nationalistic sentiment and pride in the traditional culture and forms of entertainment peculiar to various countries in the region. The concern over the massive penetration of American popular and especially youth culture is quite common in Russia where "It has now become fashionable to speak contemptuously about American culture." Moreover "The denunciations of the American style of life are similar to the articles prepared by hack Soviet propagandists before 1985. Once again the Russians read... that 'the Western style of life recognizes only one idol—money'" (Shlapentokh 1998: 207). The intelligentsia in particular is alarmed by the threat this culture and the associated forms of entertainment pose to high culture and cultural traditions and lament the susceptibility of the masses to its allure—an attitude they

share with Western European, Canadian and other intellectuals similarly critical of American or Americanized mass culture. Even ordinary people find aspects of this mass culture alien and threatening
of traditional values. Valentin Rasputin, Vasily Belov and Yuri
Bondarev, prominent nationalistic writers jointly warned: "Live rock
music has become the scourge and poison of our lives... Pop music... is kicking every new stream of youngsters into a spiritual void"
(Remnick 1993: 40).

As may be recalled under the communist system high culture, the
classics of literature and music provided escape from and an alternative to the didactic, politically saturated mass media and official
entertainments. Since the collapse there has been no need to look
for such alternatives to the agit-prop media: the new, thoroughly
Westernized mass media and their entertainments have become
readily available and eagerly consumed as "pirated Hollywood movies
and Hollywod style programming... jam Russian TV..." The Russian
critic of these developments also writes:

> Compared to the market-imposed uniformities the art produced during the Soviet era
> now appears to be complex, nuanced, pluralistic, daring and often inspired. It may be
> premature to talk about the decline of artistic culture in today's Russia, but we can attest
> to the precipitously declining public demand for art. When a book salesman can earn
> twenty times as much as a writer... the public turns away from art....
>
> Art lost its power to confer prestige on its practicioners and connoisseurs. Your
> place in the group hierarchy depends on your ability to tell the difference between a
> Toyota and Nissan more than on your ability to distinguish between Sartre and Camus....
> Now consumer culture has supplanted artistic culture, imported culture has pushed
> aside domestic culture, and mass culture has stamped out elite culture. (Dondurei in
> Shalin ed. 1996: 273-275)

These are classic themes of cultural anti-Americanism all over the
world where cultural elites contemplate with dismay the erosion of
traditional and high culture seemingly driven by the penetration and
popularity of Western and especially American mass entertainments.
The new capitalism also threatens Russian and East European intellectuals and artists in more tangible ways: the loss of state support is
keenly felt among writers, journalists, painters, movie makers—all
those who in the past found a measure of support or secure employment in government service as long as they displayed the minimum
required conformity to the official standards.

Among members of the Russian intelligentsia anti-American sentiment is also connected with the American support of the Yeltsin

government that has been judged far more unfavorably in Russia than in the West. Grigory Yavlinsky, a Russian economist and leader of a political party complained that "nothing seems to arouse American outrage on behalf of the Russian people... Russians feel abandoned by America. We cannot understand why, if we have followed all your advice we still face a profound economic decline" (Yavlinski 1997: 66). Feeling abandoned by the West has also been a familiar feeling all over Eastern Europe since World War II.

All these factors must be weighed against others including the generational one noted earlier: the younger, better educated, enterpreneurial strata in Russia and Eastern Europe have benefited from the changes and are neither anti-American nor anti-Western. Even among the strata of the population which are ambivalent about the West and the United States because of the new economic hardships there is an awareness that the political changes have been liberating and desirable and few would return to the political arrangements prevailing before 1991. The nationalistic resentments—and intense ideological commitments of any kind—are to some extent held in check by caution and the reaction against the discredited ideological commitments and political beliefs of the Soviet past, the system sought to inculcate.

Americanization, Westernization and modernization are becoming increasingly difficult to separate in the former Soviet Bloc as in the rest of the world. The United States has been in the forefront of the transformations associated with what has been called, for good historical reasons, "Westernization." Westernization has been the only successful form of modernization especially since the Soviet-communist, state supported attempt at modernization has proved to be a failure.

The deepest roots of the problems of modernization (and the associated anti-Western and anti-Americanisn attitudes) lie in the contradictory nature of the process which, while it satisfies many widely felt human needs and longings, simultaneously frustrates and undermines others. In the former Soviet Bloc as in much of the rest of the world people are simultaneously pursuing goals which are hard to reconcile with one another. The fruits of modernity—personal and group freedoms, social and geographic mobility, the availability of labor saving devices, the growth of leisure and consumption—are globally appreciated and in demand; people do not need cunning advertisers to persuade them of the benefit of mass produced consumer goods and the institutional arrangements which make them possible. But there is a price o be paid for these gratifications in the loss of traditional moral values, cultural standards, bonds of community, personal and social stability.

Increasingly anti-Americanism and the discontents of modernity are becoming fused all over the world as it becomes clear that American mass culture, fashions and styles of consumption have both wide appeal and unintended consequences. As a recent article in the *New York Times* observed in the Asian context:

> It used to be that when things started to unravel in almost any Asian country it was easy to finger the culprit: Americaniza- tion. Are families falling apart? Dig out the American divorce rates. Kids joining gangs? Talk about Los Angeles and American movies. ... The environment in ruins? Blame New York's air conditioners. AIDS? That's a Western disease....
>
> Now in cities and towns and satellite-dished villages across Asia—and in other parts of the world where rising incomes and greater access to goods and information are breeding consumerism and speeding modernization—it is getting much harder to hold the West particularly the United States, responsible for assaults on local cultures. (Crosette 1997)

It will take some time before these realizations spread to the postcommunist societies. In the meantime a precarious balance is likely to prevail between the forces which stimulate anti-Americanism and those who see the spread of the mass culture and consumerism as reasonable prices to pay for living in an open society.

Note

1.   Peter Berger noted the contrast between the attitudes of the ordinary people seeking entry (to the U.S.) and those of highly educated elite Americans: "...there are sizeable numbers of people coming into this country who have strong beliefs about...working hard and having strong families, and have not yet learned that every encounter between a man and a woman is an exercise in power politics... One should remember too that the balkanization of America...is driven not by immigrants...but by the graduates of the higher reaches of the American university system."(Berger 1995: 17)

References

Berger, Peter L. 1977. "The Myth of Socialism" in *Facing Up to Modernity*. Basic Books.
———————— 1995. "Immigration: The Solution is the Problems" *First Things*, February 1995.
Bellow, Saul. 1992. "Intellectuals and Social Change in Central and   Eastern Europe"

(symposium) *Partisan Review*, 1992.

———————— 1995. in Paul Hollander: *Anti-Americanism*, Transaction (back cover).

Bruck, Andras. 1988. "Csokok es Kezfogasok" (Kisses and Handshakes) *Elet es Irodalom*, (Budapest), December 11.

Castenade, Jorge. 1993. *Utopias Unarmed: The Latin American left After the Cold War*. Knopf.

Crosette, Barbara. 1997. "Un-American Ugly Americans" *New York Times, Week in Review*, May 11.

Djilas, Milovan. 1998. *Fall of the New Class*. Knopf.

Dondurei, Daniil, B. 1996. "Artistic Culture", in Shalin ed. (cited below)

Etkind, Alexander. 1996. "Psychological Culture" in Shalin ed. (cited below)

Hollander, Paul. 1995. *Anti-Americanism*. Transaction.

Joffe, Josef. 1997. "America the Inescapable" *New York Times Magazine*, June 8

Kon, Igor S. 1996. "Moral Culture" in D.Shalin ed. (cited below)

Kondrashov, Stanislav. 1995. "Who Are Russian Voters More Dissatisfied with: Clinton or Yeltsin?" *Current Digest of Post Soviet Press*, November 8.

Moynihan, Daniel Patrick. 1978. *A Dangerous Place*. Little, Brown.

"A New Chill in the Russian Air" 1993. *U.S. News & World Report* September 13.

Remnick, David. 1993. "America: Love It Or Loath It" *New York Times Magazine*, June 6.

Sazonov, Vadim. 1995. "The West: Friend of Foe?" *Current Digest of Post Soviet Press*, January, 4.

Schrieberg, David. 1990. "Dead Babies", *New Republic*, December 24.

Shlapentokh, Vladimir 1998. "'Old', 'New', and 'Post' Liberal Attitudes Toward the West: From Love to Hate" *Communist and Post-Communist Studies*, September.

Shalin, Dmitri N. (ed.) 1996. *Russian Culture at the Crossroads*. Westview.

Solzhenitsyn, Alexander. 1993. "To Tame Savage Capitalism" *New York Times* (op-ed) November 28.

Specter, Michael. 1994. "'The Great Russia Will Live Again'" *New York Times Magazine*, June 19.

Starr, Frederick. 1996. "Conclusion" in Shalin ed. (cited above)

Tarifa, Fatos. 1998. "East European Puzzles: Old and New," *Sociological Analysis*, June.

Yavlinski, Grigory. 1997. "Shortsighted", *New York Times Magazine*, June 8.

23

The Cult of Personality in
Communist States[1]

Virtually every communist system, extinct or surviving, at one point or another, had a supreme leader who was both extraordinarily powerful and surrounded by a bizarre cult, indeed worship. In the past (or in more traditional contemporary societies) such cults were reserved for deities and associated with conventional religious behavior and institutions. These cults although apparently an intrinsic part of communist dictatorships (at any rate at a stage in their evolution) are largely forgotten today.

The term was born of an attempt of Nikita Khrushchev to explain away (in a highly un-Marxist manner) the deformation and defects of the Soviet system under Stalin. Khrushchev introduced it at the 20th Party Congress in 1956 to describe and define Stalin's misrule and notorious abuse of power. The officially enforced cult of him was one aspect of his misrule. As Khrushchev saw it, or wished his audience to see it, Stalin's personality—including his desire to be an object of a cult—was responsible for everything that went wrong with the Soviet system.

Stalin, Mao, Castro, Ho Chi Minh, Kim Il Sung, Enver Hoxha, Rakosi, Ceascescu, Dimitrov, Ulbricht, Gottwald, Tito and others—all were the object of such cults. The prototypical cult was that of Stalin which was duplicated elsewhere with minor variations. Arguably some other cults and the intensity of the worship they entailed—notably those of Mao, Kim Il Sung and Hoxha—exceeded Stalin's.

It is a surprising aspect of the study of communist systems—and especially its comparative variety—that this cult has been of little scholarly interest and hardly ever identified as one of their shared, institutionalised characterisic. Why has it received so little attention is in itself an interesting question. Perhaps because of an all too ready acceptance of the claims of these systems as highly rational under-takings (which would be incompatible with such a cult), or with the difficulty of reconciling their official Marxist ideology with a phe-nomenon such as the cult; possibly this lack of attention may also be connected with Western attitudes which sought to differentiate com-munist from other totalitarian systems which too had such cults.

While cults of leaders were also often characteristic of non-com-munist dictatorships, right-wing cult figures and dictators tended to be more often than not genuinely charismatic figures (at least ini-tially) such as Hitler, Mussolini, Franco, Peron, Chlang Kai Shek and others. Moreover it seems that their cult was somewhat more circumscribed, they were not presented to their people quite as god-like, omnipotent and omniscient as the communist leaders, although this proposition needs to be further verified.

It would be of further interest to learn how the cults in communist systems resembled or differed from the cults of traditional rulers especially in theocratic societies and in more recent times those in the third world which too had its share of dictators who were not satisfied by power alone but wished to become cult figures as well.[2] Many of these third world figures also espoused some version of Marxism-Leninism and in that respect resembled the leaders of the communist states.

Even if the phenomenon is not entirely limited to communist states the puzzling questions remains how it could have emerged and pre-vail in political systems claiming Marxist theoretical-ideological foundations and credentials which emphatically reject the impor-tance of the individual in the historical-political process?

Communist systems never acknowledged the contradiction be-tween the cults and their official Marxist belief system, or for that matter that such cults existed at all. On the contrary the objects of the cult were invariably characterized as uncommonly modest indi-viduals, and, adding to their qualifications, as the most authoritative disciples and interpreters of the ideas of Marx, Engels and Lenin. They were also frequently portrayed as exercising power in con-junction with or on behalf of the Party and embodying its best quali-ties.

What circumstances gave rise to these cults, what were their shared characteristics and what functions have they performed? How did it happen that political systems committed in some manner to the principles of Marxism ended up as being shaped, led and dominated by single individuals of enormous concentrated and unchallenged power? Why did these systems encourage and demand the worship of such leaders making them the major repository of authority and legitimacy? To what extent were these cults spontaneous reflections of the popular recognition of the compelling qualities of these leaders? Were they truly charismatic or were the cults fabricated by the agit-prop apparatuses of these states?

If not charismatic, what was it in their personality that predisposed them to erect a cult around themselves? Were these cults an essential, and sofar largely overlooked part of the so-called totalitarian syndrome (one-party rule, control over the economy and the mass media, planned economy, official ideology, terroristic political police)[3] or not? Each totalitarian state had such a leader at some stage in its history but such cults may also be found in autocratic systems which fell short of the totalitarian designation.

Let us turn to explanations. There is the possibility of self selection: people who end up as objects of these cults may have an insatiable need not merely for power but also adulation. The yearning for such politically induced public adulation may be a form of personal pathology. But while there may be many people with such needs and desires only a handful have been able to realize them. They must have power first to create the cult. Castro's case (among others) suggests that a combination of belief in one's sense of mission and an extraordinary need for personal power are among the preconditions of the development and institutionalization of such cults.[4] The same is also true of Mao whose extaordinary lust for power was similarly intertwined with a grotesquely bloated self conception.[5] But special circumstances and powerful institutions are required for such personal needs to find durable and widespread public expression.

It is the need of new, revolutionary political systems for legitimation and for filling the gap left behind by the destruction of prerevolutionary institutions and values, (especially religious ones) that probably best explains the phenomenon. Arguably such cults represent a form of continuity between authority relations in traditional and communist societies. The need to rely on such figures for legitimation and social cohesion and using them as substitutes for conventional deities (such systems sought to dethrone) may be the most persuasive explanation.

Before further proceeding with possible explanations and a discussion of conditions which facilitate the rise of the cults it is necessary to sketch their character since they have remained largely unfamiliar to Western publics and even scholars and intellectuals. What then were their attributes and how did they differ from other, more familiar forms of admiration for political leaders, from familiar forms of hero worship?

Two features of these cults stand out. One was *pervasiveness:* the images of and accolades to the cult figures were omnipresent and inescapable; not only was the official mass media the major vehicle of these cults but the arts as well: the leaders' images were reproduced endlessly in paintings, scpltures, movies and posters; writers and poets extolled their character, accomplishments and service to the nation and mankind; sometimes composers composed music honoring them; the system of education disseminated the same images from kindergarten to university. In North Korea all citizens were expected to wear a Kim Il Sung button.[6] In China the citizens were expected to reflexively refer to the ideas and benevolence of Mao in the most astonishing variety of situations (as will be shown below); in the former Soviet Union in schools, factories, offices, army barracks there were "red corners" reserved for the worship of Stalin. While he was still alive an enormous marble structure was erected over the humble peasant dwelling where he was born. Upon their death several of these leaders were embalmed and their remains displayed to the masses, as the remains of saints used to be.

Secondly these leaders were portrayed not merely brave, shrewed, determined, heroic, popular and wise but *godlike*; they were deified and worshipped like gods used to be in traditional religious practices. They were portrayed as the singular force determining the lives of millions amd hundreds of millions of people, the fate of countries, omniscient and omnipotent—altogether different from ordinary human beings. They were portrayed as universal geniuses capable of solving the most intractable problems of their society, (or human existence), grand tacticians in war, masters of politics, unequalled judges of the arts and literature, profoundly knowledgeable of science—no sphere of human activity was foreign to them. Stalin read the manuscripts of important writers before they could be published and participated in a debate on linguistic; Khrushchev (although himself a major critic of Stalin's cult) overrode experts in deciding what should be grown and where and decided what paintings were to be allowed to be exhibited; Castro fancied himself an expert an agriculture, animal husbandry and virtually everything else. Mao's expertise and abilities ranged from matters of state, millitary affairs, ideology, poetry, and the arts, to how to grow bigger water melons, play better table tennis, remove cancerous tumors and make the mute regain their speech. (An article proclaimed: "Mao Tse Tung's thought (is)—key to success in rare abdominal operation").[7]

All these leaders were singularly and puritanically devoted to their historical role and social-political tasks and had virtually no private lives and enjoyments—or so they were presented in the official media. In a Soviet film Stalin was shown during World War II as hardly ever sleeping and not allowing himself even to smoke a pipe until the report of a major victory reached him. Admittedly Mao enjoyed swimming (and his swimming across the mighty Yangtse river was made into a legend) but this served as a model for the rest of the population and was not merely a matter of personal fun.

While they were often shown in the company of and admired by children (who usually handed them flowers and embraced them) the official media hardly ever made any reference to *their* children, wives or mistresses.

A sampling of the cult as reported in various contemporary sources is essential for understanding the phenomenon.

According to a Soviet author writing in the early 1950s about "the figure of Stalin in Soviet fiction" portraying Stalin involved "an incredibly huge responsibility" (no irony intended!). He further noted that

> no work of art has been created (on Stalin) the artistic merits of which measure up to the magnificence of the topic... The folksingers/bards frequently complain about the insufficiency of their vocabulary, about their inability to find appropriate artistic means to bring to life the features of the great man... (the same applies to) every poet, writer or playright who attempts to portray Stalin.... "The folk songs compare him most frquently to the sun; to him does the whole world owe life and light."[8]

In spite of the difficulties alluded to above many writers volunteered to undertake the task. Their writings more often than not conjure up images of divinity, including the Christian idea of sacrifice for mankind.

A Soviet writer's effusions at the 1935 Soviet writers' conference further captures the spirit of the cult:

> Thank you Stalin. Thank you because I am joyful. Thank you because I am well... Every time I have found myself in his presence I have been subjugated by his strength, his charm, his grandeur. I have experienced a great desire to sing, cry out, to shout with joy and happiness... I shall be eternally happy and joyous, all thanks to thee, chief of our great country. And when the woman I love presents me with a child the first word it shall utter will be: Stalin.[9]

The religious imagery is also present in a portrait by Ilya Ehrenburg (the once-famous Soviet writer): "I often think of this man, his courage and grandeur who took upon himself an enormous burden. The wind will always blow, people carry on with their daily activities...nurse children...sleep peacefully and He stands at the helm."[10] These outpourings were all the more remarkable since Ehrenburg was among the elite of the regime who could have had few illusions about the true nature of Stalin.

A Hungarian writer visiting the Soviet Union after asking repeatedly where he could see Stalin was told: "All over the country. Everywhere where people are working there is a part of him."[11]

The image of the helpless people protected by Stalin also appears in a poem included in the volume celebrating his seventieth birthday:

> You brought up and protected the orphan of Lenin, the people ...The Teacher of great rivers, feeder of the hungry sea whom the mountains serve... who made an alliance with, and whose companions are the elements... The people you brought up... are alive...[12]

Elsewhere the power and benevolence of Stalin was contrasted (once more) with the helplessness of the people he took care of: "The nation scatters if there is no one to watch over her. You name their struggle... you plant the sword in their (the workers') hands, courage in their hearts..." [13]

Tibor Dery the famous Hungarian writer (who became a dissident and was jailed after the Hungarian Revolution of 1956) had this to say in 1953 of Stalin: "We celebrate a man who destroys with one hand and builds with the other... who makes the perishable perish, who destroys the decadent.... We celebrate the man who built himself so that he could later build the world."[14]

Anastas Mikoyan one of the durable members of Stalin's inner circle observed that "He knows no fear... and is unshakeable, circumspect and calm, he doesnt tolerate around him those who waver, complain and find fault with everything. After a victory ...he restraints the hotheads."[15]

The quasi-divine tributes lavished on the Hungarian supreme leader, Mathias Rakosi bear striking resemblance to those accorded Stalin. Again in the words of a poet: "He holds a lovely stalk of wheat: the radiant fate of the nation. He knows no fear... He takes to his heart the troubles of millions." To further illustrate the point: "Today Rakosi speaks on the radio... The wind subsides and the heart of the country is throbbing in the palm of his hand..." [16] Another writer thus reported meeting him: "Miraculously I managed to talk to him as calmly as I did with my father. He exuded tranquility. I was tired and gained strength."[17] A Hungarian worker writes of him: "What a man he is... his every word, every casual remark compel you to think things over! As if he were ready to answer all my questions, even those I have not even asked but were smouldering inside."[18]

As in the case of Stalin the very name of Rakosi was subject of special reverence, an inspiration to moral uplift: his name was pronounced by ordinary people "... as if it stood for an uncommon human purity, meaning, firmness and goodness." [19]

Mao's cult was perhaps even more extreme and bizarre than those of Stalin and the lesser leaders in Eastern Europe; it had the most in common with traditional religious worship. Presumably China being a far more traditional society (even after the vehement communist efforts to eradicate traditions) had something to do with the character of this cult. The following quote from the Chinese press of the times offers a glimpse of the spirit of this cult:

> ... A thunderous ovation resounded through the Great Hall of the People. Excited faces turned to Chairman Mao like sunflowers to the sun. With overflowing enthusiasm and happiness, the revolutionary fighters waved their copies of the *Quotations from Chairman Mao Tse-tung* and with great feeling, continuously shouted: "Long live Chairman Mao!"... "Long live the great thought of Chairman Mao..."
>
> (afterwards)... the revolutionary fighters joyfuly sang: "The heavens are great, the earth is great but they cant compare with the greatness of what the Party has done for the people. Dear as are father and mother, Chairman Mao is dearer...
>
> Many wrote on the flyleaf of their treasured red books: "At 7.30 P.M. 14 November 1967 I met Chairman Mao, the red sun that shines most brighly in our hearts..."[20]

According to the newspaper of the Chinese armed forces:

... Chairman Mao is the most outstanding, greatest genius of the world... his thought is the unbreakable truth. In implementing Chairman Mao's directives, we must completely disregard the fact whether we understand them or not... we should implement resolutely Chairman Maos' directives which we understand as well as those which we temporarily do not understand.[21]

Farm workers carried his pictures to the fields and they "reported" to them, as if praying. His famous book of quotes was treated precisely as the Bible used to be: it was the repository of unquestionable authority applying to every situation, problem or dispute; on every occasion there was an appropriate quote (usually a ringing, vacuous generality or platitude) mouthed with utmost reverence.[22]

Virtual miracles were also attributed to him and the dying comforted themselves with his words. For example,

...Mai-Hsien-teh was unconscious or semi-conscious for a quite a long time after being admitted to the hospital. People anxiously awaited his regaining consciousness, the nurse tested his reactions by showing him a pictorial magazine. As she turned over the pages she noticed his lips quivering. His eyes were concentrated on a picture of chairman Mao. With great effort he managed to raise his left hand, which had remained useless since his admission to the hospital and with trembling fingers he touched the picture...

He suddenly exclaimed "Chairman Mao!" It was the first time since he had been in the hospital that he had spoken so clearly.

The image of the great chairman Mao and his brilliant thought roused Mai Hsien-teh from his stupor. He became fully conscious and was able to think clearly.[23]

There was also the incident involving a fatally injured miner who asked for photogpraphs of chairman Mao ever since he was a boy; he liked to look at the photographs of the leader and murmur:

'Chairman Mao', 'Chairman Mao'. When his pain became very acute... he opened his eyes and gazed at the portrait of Chairman Mao repeating this quotation from Chairman Mao over and over again: 'Be resolute, fear no sacrifice and surmount every difficulty to win victory.'

Another worker who lay dying with burns over 90% over his body was reported to have "mustered his last strength to say, in a voice barely audible: 'Act in accordance with chairman Mao's teaching.' Uttering these words this most loyal fighter of Chairman Mao's... breathed his last' The (Chinese News) Agency Reported."[24]

On another occasion

A provincial radio station disclosed that trapped passangers closely packed in a violently derailed railway coach which was in imminent danger of falling into a river were rescued after they had shouted 'Long Live Chairman Mao!' instead of 'Help!.' And in Canton a woman is reported to have declared that she could bear the amputation of a cancerous breast without an anaesthetic because someone stood beside the operating table reciting from the Chairman's works.[25]

A Chinese table tennis champion disclosed that he was decisively helped by the ideas of the Chairman (in addition to thinking of the pingpong ball "as though it were the head of Chiang Kaisek)" that made his strokes more forceful.[26]

In the case of Mao, more than in those of other cult figures, there was an unusually great emphasis on his physical prowess and much was written about his swimming talents. For example,

> The happy news about Chairman Mao's latest swim...spread through Wuhan. The whole of this...city was overjoyed...Everybody was saying 'Our respected and beloved leader Chairmam Mao is in wonderful health. This is the greatest happiness for the entire Chinese people and for the revolutionary people throughout the world.' The great event in which Chairman Mao once again swam with ease some 15 km-s in the deep chasm of the Yangtze, stirred the hearts of all people. The cheering 'Long live Chairman Mao' on both banks of the river lasted well over four hours. This moving scene was expressive of the infinite love and respect of the Chinese people for their great leader... Under the guidance of the brilliant thought of Chairman Mao Tse-tung...the Chinese pople train their eyes on the future and are riding the wind and breaking their waves in their forward advance.[27]

These examples were far from atypical. There was an endless supply of such stories, reports and accolades especially during the years of the so-called Cultural Revolution when the worship of Mao reached new and singularly grotesque extremes.

One more example of the cult, that of Kim Il Sung of North Korea, another durable leader who held power for over four decades.

Like the places of birth of Stalin and Mao, Kim Il Sung's too has been "the holiest of all shrines in North Korea... only one of a growing number of political shrines erected to the glory of Kim and even to members of his family..." In addition,

> every town, village, factory and army barrack in North Korea has an elaborate 'study hall' where young and old alike, men and women gather to discuss... the guidance offered by the 'beloved leader' ... a well arranged day should consist of 8 hours sleep, 8 of work and 8 of studying Kim's works. In fact everyone is required to devote 2 hours to Kim study daily and 4 hours on Saturday. In primary school I find children chanting a chapter from a 480-page book the lst volume of *Lets Study the Great Revolutionary Idea of marshall Kim Il Sung...* There are 5 volumes and the students are required to commit them all to memory...
>
> At 14 He is said to have lectured his schoolmates for independence. At 15... (he was) 'convinced that only Marxism-Leninism was the true revolutionary faith...' at 19 'he advanced the true revolutionary line at various meetings...'

At a museum the hunting rifle and stuffed dog of "the beloved leader" are preserved. "At a factory at Hungnam there is an enormous table model of the plant on which in incandescent lights, is traced the path Premier Kim Il Sung followed on a factory tour. Also carefully preserved in a special museum are the several chairs were he sat, the table on which he leaned his elbows, the wheelbarrow he 'personally touched.'"

As to the official view of all this, according to a spokesman of the North Korean government "Foreigners who have visited here and looked into the matter found there is no such cult—only an undying affection for our respected and beloved leader."[28]

Not surprisingly the 70th bithday of the beloved leader included "a nationwide refurbishing and polishing of some 30,000 statues and monumenal busts of President Kim... Many of the celebrations which will include gymnastics, mass singing of 'hymns' and praise of the 2 leaders (his son was included in 1982), will be held in newly constructed structures... one of which cost more than \$50 million."[29]

From these and other expresions of adulation the Supreme Leader emerges as an infallible, and fearless universal genius endowed with a sense of justice, kindness, and concern for all and mercilessness toward the enemies of his great Project, a person of exceptional physical and mental prowess, puritanical simplicity, capable of self-denial and superhuman sacrifice.

Some further explanations of this amazing phenenomenon may be attempted. The immense concentration of power is an obvious precondition; the more power the more intense worship and more obedience can be extracted; on the other hand, once deified the leader can more plausibly claim unconditional obedience. An extraordinary human being can demand extraordinary power and people are more willing to grant it if convinced of his extraordinary attributes.

The totalitarian character of these systems also supports this suggestion. As the late Bertram Wolfe (an early American supporter of Stalin who later became a vocal critic) wrote: "... the whole dynamics of dictatorship cries out for a dictator, autocracy for an autocrat, militarized command... for a supreme commander, infallible government for infallible leader, for a Duce, Fuhrer, Vozdh."[30]

These propositions do not fully explain the nature of the cult and especially its religious undertones. It is the problem of legitimation and the anti-religious disposition of these systems which offer the best explanation of the religious aspects of the cult.

Communist systems were (and remain) poorly legitimated; they usually emerged through a violent seizure of power by a militant minority, or were exported by the force of arms (as in Eastern Europe after World War II). They never held meaningful elections as distinct from one-party elections in which the official candidates usually gained over 99 percent of the vote. At the same time these systems made great demands on the population with regard to work, public participation, and the overall subordination of the private to (alleged) public interest. Policies of rapid industrialization (combined with chronic and substantial mismanagement) and disproportionate resources devoted to militarization led to endless scarcities. In short these systems continuously demanded defered gratification. Under these conditions it was helpful to persuade (or attempt to persuade) the population that their country was led by an exceptional human being possessing wisdom, forsight and profound knowledge of virtually everything, whose judgement was beyond questioning, a quasi-deity leading his people to a better future.

Secondly, it may be argued that the cult of personality was a counterpart of, or complement to the atheistic policies of the same regimes. The latter came to power, for the most part in traditional societies where religion was a vital force and key institution. It is not difficult to come to the conclusion that the Cult was intended to become a substitute religion and the Leader an incarnation of qualities earlier ascribed to God. It has also been argued that totalitarian systems were based on secular-religious beliefs. If so, secular religions need, just as the traditional ones, a personified essence of their values and aspirations. If a religion is to provide action-oriented belief (not that all of them must do so) it has to offer something "tangible" and personal instead of abstractions. A crowning divine image is useful to validate and increase the persuasiveness of such beliefs. The image of the divine and supreme provider and protector offers a sense of hope and optimism since (as an American student of religion pointed out) "Religion is an attempt to bring the relative, the temporary, the diasppointing, the painful things in life into relation with what is conceived to be permanent, absolute and cosmically optimistic."[31]

Whether or not and to what extent these leaders were actually perceived by their subjects in the manner sketched above remains an open questions and increasingly difficult to answer with the passage of time. Although the cult was manufactured by the propaganda apparatuses of the Party-States involved it is possible that at times it struck a responsive cord in the citizens or some portion of them. It has been for example widely reported than large numbers of Soviet citizens broke into tears when the death of Stalin was announced and hundreds were trampled to death in the course of the funeral ceremonies in Moscow. Many felt that they lost a supremely powerful protector even as he presided over (or was the cause of) the hard times they experienced. Nor was there ever a shortage of people lined up at the mausoleum of Lenin to gaze at his embalmed body, though again it is not quite clear what conclusion one can draw from such behavior. (Lenin's cult was more genuine as well as less absurd in its claims than Stalin's). Likewise the fervor of the Red Guards towards Mao during the Cultural Revolution appeared authentic, if shortlived.

As the cliche has it, further research is needed to better understand the phenomenon; it should involve both the people who were instrumental in creating and maintaining the cults—functionaries, journalists, assorted propagandists and those who were exposed them, their consumers, or, if you will, their defrauded victims. Finally the personality of the leaders and their apparent need to be worshipped needs further study as well.

It remains to be conclusively established to what degree these figures were "leader(s) who by (their) personal qualities aroused the loyalty and following of revolutionary masses... or (individuals) about whom the air of charisma was deliberately created for the sake of holding together an established state and preventing revolution from occuring."[32] Last but not least it would also be of great interest to compare the actual personality and abilities of these leaders to the images the cults disseminated. The differences were in all probability profound and may offer the best illustration of the great discrepancies between ideals and realities, or theory and practice communist systems perpetuated.

Notes

1   Paper presented at the *Annual World History Association Conference in* Boston, June 25, 2000.

2.   An interesting third world case was Jean-Bedel Bokassa of the Central African Empire who in 1977 became "the world's newest emperor." He was crowned in the sports stadium in the capital and received "a crown encrusted with 2000" diamonds.

450 pounds of (French) rose petals were tossed under his feet and "35...horses especially trained in France to pull...the 8 ton, gold-lined coronation carriage" were also flown in from France. ("Extravaganza Set to Unfold for Bokassa I," *New York Times*, December 4, 1977.)

3. See Carl Friedrich ed.: *Totalitarianism*, Cambridge: Harvard Unicersit Press, 1954.

4. The case of Castro is particularly interesting as it combines genuine charisma with the official policy of enshrining the adulation of the leader. In his case personality has played an unusually large part. According to a Cuban psycbhiatrist (living in Cuba) who studied his personality over the years "He has a psychopathic syndrome that is characterised by a strong narcissism with paranoid tendencies, such as fear of disloyalty and betrayal... It is power that drives Fidel... Everything in his life, including other people is at the service of this power. He does not love anyone else truly. How can he loves himself so?" Accoding to a Catholic cleric (also living in Cuba) "He truly believes he is the savior of Cuba. First he saved us from North American imperialism, then he defended the Fatherland against Yankee intervention, and now he is the savior of the remnants of socialism." (John Lee Anderson: "The Old Man and the Boy," *New Yorker*, February 21 & 28, 2000, pp. 226, 235)

5. For a recent discussion of such attributes see Ian Buruma: "Divine Killer," *New York Review of Books*, February 24, 2000.

6. See e.g. Anthony Daniels: *Utopias Elsewhere: Journeys in a Vanishing World*, New York; Crown, 1991, p.44.

7. "At Fire in Peking, Thoughts of Mao", *New Tork Times*, Oct 17, 1969, p. 7.

8. G.S. Cheriomin: *The figure of Stalin in Soviet fiction* (in Hungarian) Budapest, 1951, pp.5, 48, 47-48.

9. A.O. Avdienko quoted in T.H. Rigby ed.: *Stalin*, Englewood Cliffs NJ: Prentice Hall, 1966 p. 11.

10. I.Ehrenburg: "Great Feelings" (in Hungarian) *Szabad Nep*, (Budapest) December 20, 1949.

11. Gyula Illyes in *Hungarian Poets Saluting Stalin On His 70th Birthday* (in Hungarian) Budapest, 1949

12. T. Aczel in *Hungarian Poets Salute Stalin on his 70th Birthday*, cited, pp.53-54

13. Ibid. pp. 53-54, 26-27.

14. Tibor Dery: "Celebration" (in Hungarian) *Csillag*, January 1953.

15. Quoted by M. Rakosi in "The 70 year old Stalin" (in Hungarian) *Szabad Nep*, 1949, December 21.

16. From *Hungarian Writers on Mathias Rakosi* (in Hungarian), Budapest 1952, pp. 255, 52.

17. Ibid. p. 266.

18. Ibid. p. 275.

19. Ibid. p. 311.

20. George Urban ed.: *The Miracles of Chairman Mao - A Compendium of Devotional Literature 1966-1970*, Los Angeles: Nash Publishers 1971, p. 138.

21. Ibid. pp. 153-154.

22. I am not suggesting that the Bible is a compendium of such platitudes only that the two sources have been used and abused in a similar manner.

23. Urban Cited, p. 144.

24. "Words of Mao Held a Comfort to Dying", *New York Times*, November 6, 1966.

25. Dennis Bloodworth: "China Today" *The Observer* (London) August 18, 1968.

26. Seymouir Topping: "Mao Theory Aids Ping Pong Victors" *New York Times*, April 25, 1965.

27. *New York Times*, July 31, 1966.

28. Mark Gayn: "The Cult of Kim", *New York Times Magazine*, October 1, 1972, pp. 24-25.
29. Henry Scott Stokes: "North Korea Leader Plans Huge Fete for Son," *New York Times*, March 17, 1982.
30. Bertram Wolfe: *Communist Totalitarianism—Keys to the Soviet System*, Boston: Beacon Press, 1956, p. 23.
31. J. Milton Yinger: *Religion in the Struggle for Power*, 1946, p.5
32. Raymond Bauer: "Thre Pseudo-Charismatic Leader in Soviet Society," *Problems of Communism*, No.3-4, 1953.

24

The Crimes of Communism

Why was this book written and published in France and not the United States? Surely there are greater academic resources available here than in France including documentary materials, research facilities, funding and scholars capable of conducting such research and a far greater (potential) number of readers.

How then has it been possible, that (as Martin Malia observes in his excellent inroduction), social processes which resulted in such a vast number of victims "never aroused a scholarly curiosity proportionate to the magnitude of the disaster." Or, as one of the authors of the volume asks, "Why such a deafening silence from the academic world regarding the Communist catastrophe which touched the lives of about one third of humanity...?" In the following I will suggest some answers.

It is difficult to discuss the crimes of communism without morally rejecting communism and this is where the problem begins. Anti-communism in the United States had been discredited (among intellectuals and other elite groups) first by Senator McCarthy and later by the Vietnam war perceived probably by the great majority of academic intellectuals as a particularly destructive and irrational outcome of anti-communism. In the wake of Vietnam it has become the enduring conventional wisdom that the Cold War, the arms race and the (alleged) failure of American society to pay proper attention to its social problems and injustices can be blamed on anti-communism that provided an excuse to ignore them.

The idea of super power equivalence, or moral equivalence—popular between the late 1960s and the collapse of the Soviet Union—provided further disincentives to looking closely at the crimes of communism. Fear of nuclear war too had its share in silencing criticism of the Soviet Union: the peace movement (anxious to combat attitudes conducive to conflict) prefered to dwell on the similarities not differences between the super powers.

The rise of the third world revolutionary societies—China, Cuba, Vietnam and later Nicaragua—promised to restore the good name of communism (or socialism,) compromised to some degree by the Soviet Union even in the eyes of those on the left.

Most importantly the 1960s bequeathed a greatly enlarged awareness of the defects,—for many, the crimes of the United States or American society associated with capitalism, the white race, white males, and the Western world as a whole. Many of those left-of-center increasingly preoccupied with the evils of the United States represented and its alleged responsibility for a wide variety of global problems deemed it morally unqualified to criticise communist states. The communist systems and their spokesmen offered critiques of the United States (and the Western world as a whole) which were congenial to the native critics. If President Reagan's reference to the Soviet Union as "evil empire" inspired widespread and enduring derision among liberal intellectuals (which is most intellectuals) so would the idea of "the crimes of communism".

In the field of Soviet studies the so-called revisonists held the United States responsible for the Cold War, dismissed the concept of totalitarianism (or at any rate its applicability to communist systems) and sought tenaciously to redefine the "crimes of communism" (without of course using such terminology) as far as the victims of Stalin's regime were concerned. Those of other communist states were almost totally ignored except Cambodia. These scholars were also anxious to dismiss any connection between Marxism-Leninism and the practices of communist states. They prefered to attribute their repression to chaos, bungling, accident, local feuds, unintended consquences,—anything that was not a major, defining attribute of these political systems and their leaders.

Discussions of the crimes of communism have also been scarce because the topic almost inevitably leads to totalitarianism. Few of those who reflected on these crimes could fail to see that they, or the worst of them, were connected to the totalitarian charateristics of these states. Stalin's Soviet Union, Mao's China, Pol Pot's Cambodia, Cuba under Castro (for much of his rule), North Korea under (and after) Kim Il Sung were totalitarian. But so was Nazi Germany and for that very reason the term came to be avoided as it drew attention to the similarities between political systems wholly and unequivocally discredited (Nazism, fascism) and those—the communist ones—many sought to save from total disrepute on account of their putative, early idealism (good intentions) and association with the ideas of Marxism. The latter were also viewed, by these intellectuals, with greater indulgence because they were seen as counterweight to the power of the United States, NATO, or the West. Moreover in the United States but apparently not in France, the far better known and documented evils of Nazism also diverted attention from the evils of communism.

Further reasons for the evolution of these attitudes include the prestige of the Soviet Union, as ally of the United States and Britain during World War II and awareness of the sufferings of its people in those years.

Also important that until very recently there was virtually no photographic documentation of the crimes of communism, (unlike those of Nazism). Such visual images may be necessary to arouse moral indignation that translates into sustained inquiry into the causes of the horrors portrayed.

At last it may be that the kind of conformity detected in America by Tocqueville survives and helps to account for these attitudes even among supposedly iconoclastic academic intellectuals. Once certain conventions and beliefs become established and upheld by a vocal minority few apparently have the stomach to challenge them and become unpopular in the circles they move. As the public expression of anti-communist sentiments became both morally reprehensible and a matter of poor taste (in liberal circles) American intellectuals were not going to probe the crimes of communism.

Even after the collapse of Soviet communism it remains difficult for a large segment of the academic-intellectual community to come to terms with the fact that Soviet communism was not merely inefficient but morally wrong and that its original ideals and goals (derived from Marxism) were unrealizable and conducive to the "excesses" and misjudgements which culminated in the crimes.

Why social and cultural conditions in France were different making it possible to produce such a volume is not easy to answer. It appears that disenchantment with communism and Marxism among French intellectuals was more powerful and widespread than in the

United States especially after the publication of *The Gulag Archipelago*. Perhaps because in France Marxists and communists were for a long time a legitimate and dominant cultural and political force, an establishment of its own (embodied among other things in the huge French communist party), their beliefs and loyalties inspired a stronger reaction. By contrast in the United States communists and their supporters were a far more marginal and sometimes persecuted minority, (especially in the post-war period) until the Vietnam war and the questioning of anti-communism it inspired restored them to a quasi-heroic status within parts of the intellectual community.

It would be hard to discuss this volume without adressing two questions: what was communism and what were its crimes? Although these are no great mysteries here there remains much obfuscation when "crimes" and "communism" are linked. Some authors are likely to argue that we cannot talk about such crimes because there was no unitary political system called "communist", that the whole concept is fuzzy, perhaps a form of conceptual "red baiting."

But there were "communist systems" and they do not defy definition and understanding, or no more than other concepts refering to complex social-political realities like capitalism, socialism, feudalism, democracy, etc. To start with, it was more than a meaningless gesture that these systems called themselves and the movements which gave rise to them "communist" whether in Vietnam or Bulgaria, Albania or Cuba. Secondly, every one of them legitimated itself with the ideas associated with Marx, Engels and Lenin and attempted to realise or apply some of them. For instance they shared an ideologically generated and institutionalised intolerance of private property (of the means of production) and believed that its abolition will usher in abundance and social solidarity; they abhored and repressed religion; they held peasants in contempt and forced them into collective farms. Thirdly, all of them were governed by a ruling and putatively infallible party (quite different from ordinary political parties) often in combination with an infallible and deified leader. Fourthly, they all relied heavily on propaganda to complement coercion. Fifth, they all interfered with the free movement of their peoples, especially across borders with non-communist states. Sixth, they all developed powerful and highly differentiated political police forces. These shared characteristics do not mean that they were identical systems throughout their existence.

What of the crimes of communism? Here again some would argue that the crimes were the responsibility of individual leaders, their personal pathologies, and abuse of power (as Khrushchev argued blaming Stalin for all the evils of the system) or resulted from bureaucratic "excesses," the flaws of human nature and other "non-systemic" matters.

What then were the crimes documented in this volume? First and foremost mass murder on a spectacular scale; imprisonment and the institutionalization of forced labor on a similarly grand scale; the deprivation of people of a wide range of political, personal or group freedoms or rights; the adoption of policies resulting in widespread material deprivations (sometimes famines) in the service of rapid industrialization and militarization. Official lying on a grand scale and the encouragement of the citizens to spy on one another that contaminated public discourse and undermined trust and any sense of civil responsibility.

Even a volume close to 900 pages cannot do justice to this long overdue stocktaking. The mere cataloging of these crimes is a vast undertaking and the amount of available documentary information is uneven. The book devotes the most space to the Soviet Union (268 pages) whose crimes are the best known and documented while the lesser known crimes of communism get short shrift. 93 pages are given to the whole of South-Eastern Europe (of which Poland gets 31), 83 pages to China, (that leads in the absolute number of victims), 58 to Cambodia, (that leads in the number of victims as a ratio of the total population), 35 pages to communism in Latin America (mostly Cuba but including Nicaragua and the Shining Path guerillas of Peru).

Surely China and Cambodia would have deserved far more space, Cuba a chapter of its own, Afghanistan more than twenty pages, Laos and Vietnam more than eleven pages, Ethiopia, Angola and Mozambique combined more than twenty-one. These are derisory amounts of space although better than nothing. There are three other chapters (not well integrated into the volume though valuable in themselves) on the "The Comintern in Action," "The NKVD in Spain" and "Communism and Terror" as well as concluding and introductory sections to *some* of the five parts of the book.

The book is divided into Part I. The Soviet Union; II. "World Revolution, Civil War Terror;" III. Eastern Europe; IV. Asia; and Part V. The Third World. The reader is not informed how the somewhat haphazard organization of the book was arrived at or how the contributors were chosen. Nine of them are French (or reside in France) one Czech and one Polish.

What did the authors hope to accomplish? Two major goals were to right the historic imbalance between information about the crimes of Nazism and those of communism (or, to present "a balance sheet of... Communism's human costs") and second to provide a "memorial" to the victims of communism.   Both goals have been accomplished to some degree however incompletely and unevenly. But it is an accomplishment in itself that a volume reexamining the crimes of communist states and their commonalities was put together. It is also commendable that the authors did not feel compelled to abstain from moral judgment—unlike many scholars writing about communist systems.

The Black Book reaffirms the magnitude of the crimes, a total of approximately 100 million people killed and hundreds of millions brutalised in other ways. The toll breaks down as follows: USSR: 20 million, (a rather conservative estimate), China 65 million, Cambodia 2 million, North Korea 2 million, Afganistan 1.5 million, Eastern Europe 1 million, Latin America 150.000.

The book makes clear that, in the words of Malia, "there never was a benign, initial phase of Communism before some mythical 'wrong turn' threw it off the track. Moreover the Soviet Red terror "cannot be explained as the prolongation of prerevolutionary political cultures" —a proposition that will not endear the book to a substantial portion of our left-liberal intelligentsia.

Most important is the reaffirmation of the common link between communist political violence and the official ideology and especially the doctrine of class struggle curiously missing from many recent Western discussions of the connection between theory and practice. The original and major source of communist political violence was the Marxist belief in class struggle as the "violent midwife of history" even if it had other stimulants as well, such as intra-party struggles for power, personal pathologies, bureaucratic overzealousness, and the commitment to create a huge and permanent slave labor force. As the chapter on Cambodia points out the "intention was to create an egalitarian society in which justice, fraternity and altrusim would be the key values, yet like other Communist regimes it produced a tidal wave of selfishness, inequality and irrationality."

Rather than attempting to summarise the diverse chapters a small sampling of the lesser known facts and aspects of the crimes of various communist states will be illuminating.

As already noted above it did not all begin with Stalin. For instance,

> ...the Kholmogory camp, on the great river Dvina, was sadly famous for the swift manner in which it dispatched a great number of its prisoners. They were often loaded into barges, stones were tied around their necks, their arms and legs were tied, and they were thrown overboard into the river. Mikhail Kerov one of the main leaders of the Cheka, had started these massive drownings in June 1920 ... a large number of mutineers from Kronstadt, together with Cossacks and peasants from Tambov province... were drowned in this fashion in 1922.

As far as Tambov was concerned Order No. 171 stipulated that in that area "any citizens who refuse to give their names" should be shot on sight and "whereever arms are found execute immediately the eldest son in the family."

Another monumental crime was the Soviet famine of the early 1930s the occurence of which may be familiar to a handful of educated Americans but few are likely to know that it was not due to natural causes but human-political design. Thus "In all regions affected by the famine, the sale of railway tickets was immediately suspended, and special barricades were set up by the GPU to prevent peasants from leaving their district" to make sure they would not escape the famine. In 1933 when millions were dying of hunger the Soviet government continued to export grain.

Reminiscent of the Nazi compulsion to divert badly needed railway carriages and manpower from the war effort in order to complete the extermination of the Jews—"At a time when the Red Army was retreating on all fronts and losing tens of thousands every day... Beria diverted more than 14,000 men from the NKVD for..." the deportation of the Volga Germans to Kazakhstan and Siberia.

In national communist Yugoslavia on the penal colony of the island of Goli Otok

> Torture was the daily bread of the internees. Among the methods was one known simply as 'the bucket,' which forced a prioner's head into a receptacle filled with

excrement... The most widespred method used by reeducators—reminiscent of works done in Nazi camps—was stone-breaking...To complete the humiliation, the stones were thrown back into the sea at the end of the day.

China provided "denunciation boxes" resembling mail boxes, complete with forms, on the streets of cities. Widespread denunciation leading to the mistreatment of vast numbers of people was also a major practice, most zealously encouraged and institutionalised in the Soviet Union, East Germany and Cuba as well.

China excelled in the public exhibition and humilation of "the enemies" especially during the so-called Cultural Revolution. They had "notices stuck on their backs, were dressed up in ridiculous clothes and hats... and forced into grotesque and painful positions. Their faces were smeared with ink, they were forced to bark like dogs on all fours... In August 1967 the Beijing press declared that anti-Maoists were 'rats that ran through the streets' and should all be killed." Tortures included forcing people to eat "nightsoil", electric shocks, "being forced to kneel on broken glass" and "being hanged 'like an airplane' by the arms and legs ... " In Tibet people were "not only shot, but were also beaten to death, crucified, burned alive, drawn, quartered and beheaded."

In North Korea at last forty seven crimes are punisheable by death. Refugees have attested to the routine execution of civilians for crimes such as prostitution, treason, murder, rape and sedition. The crowd is invited to participate and sentencing is accompanied by cries of hatred, insults and stone-throwing. Sometimes the prisoner is kicked and beaten to death while the crowd chants slogans.

As in Stalin's Soviet Union "entire families have been sent to camp because one member has received sentence...this form of punishment was often extended to include three generations... Sometimes the executions were turned into a game with prisoners being shot as though they were targets in a shooting competition..." North Korea has also been distinguished by the mistreatment of the handicapped, (not allowed to live in the capital). Dwarves were sent to camps and prevented from having children. Kim Jong Il said that "the race of dwarves must disappear."

The crimes of the Cambodian regime are better known thanks largely to its conflict with another, more respectable communist state, Vietnam, which after its victory authenticated the massacres. The Cambodian communist regime came perhaps came closest to approximating the ideal type of a totalitarian system and its control of the individual. Aside from its well known massacres and tortures a

> ...strict dress code was imposed: people had to wear black, long sleeved shirts buttoned up top the neck. There were also strict codes of behavior: all public displays of affection were banned... People were forced to attend interminable meetings and while there to look alert... People with handicapps were simply treated as shirkers and executed... People were killed for losing cattle and tortued to death for having struck a cow... Any sexual relations outside marriage were... punished with death...
> ... 53% of the victimd died from blows to the head.

In Cuba too a broad range of tortures were inflicted on political prisoners:

> Prisoners were forced climb a staircase wearing shoed filled with lead and were then thrown back down the stairs... The guards also used attack dogs and mock executions; disciplinary cells had neither water nor electricity... troublemakers were forced to cut grass with their teeth or sit in latrine trenches for hours... The G-2 Center in Santiago de Cuba... possesses cells with extreme temperatures (both high and low). Prisoners are awakened every 20 or 30 minutes... Kept naked and totally cut off from the outside world... Iron cages are still used in some prisons...

Cuban homosexuals were put into special forced labor units. Beatings and bayoneting by the guards were common. Public executions "took place in a carnival-like atmosphere."

A few major, shared characteristics of communist political violence (central to the crimes of communism) may now noted. Above all people were victimised, for the most part, not for specific actions but for belonging to certain categories, or for harboring (or being suspected of harboring) certain ideas, attitudes or opinions.

The intense desire to reshape social institutions, practices and human beings themselves is the key to communist political violence and coercion. It leads to an extraordinarily polarized view of the world and human beings and to the dehumanisation of all those designated as the enemy. From Lenin's description of the enemy as "harmful insects," "lice," "scorpions," or "bloodsuckers" to Vyshinky's calling the defendants in the Moscow Trials "rabid dogs" (among many other things) to the Chinese communist designation of the political enemy as "devils" to Castro's preference for "worms" for his enemies—such terminology is a precondition of the brutalization and extermination of large numbers of people.

Communist regimes also claimed that their official values and theoretical guidelines were "scientific", that their goals were rational and the outcomes of their policies predictable, arrived at by the careful deliberation of enlightened leaders guided by an invincible theory. Relying on it guaranteed that nothing in human beings or the social world would be unknowable; the leaders firmly grasped the laws of history, politics and sociology; the idea of unintended consequences was foreign to "scientific socialism" and its most qualified interpreters. It was a disposition which vastly increased the self-assurance of the leaders and regimes in question and removed hesitation when suffering had to be inflicted in the service of the great, scientifically determined goals.

Admittedly the crimes of communism could not have been commited and the heights of brutality could not have been scaled by human beings obeying the commands of these systems (nor could policies been devised which could only be implemented with brutality and ruthlessness) without the human potential for evil, an old fashioned idea to be sure. These systems excelled, historically and comparatively speaking, in mobilising and harnessing to their goals the darker sides of human nature because it was done in the (alleged) interests of huge, idealistic projects of social, economic and political transformation.

If anything can be learned from these crimes it is that they are most lilkely to be commited when prompted and justified by ideas which promise ultimate and total liberation from all the known burdens and deprivations of mankind, an end to injustices of every description, and to all scarcities, including those of solidarity and empathy. The magnitude of the crimes was proportional to the political-ideological aspirations and their unattainability. Only when good intentions are single mindedly pursued by human beings who seized uncommon amounts of power will crimes be institutionalised on the scale we have witnessed in communist states.

25

Andre Gide and the Soviet Union: Infatuation and Disaffection

"... what leads me to Communism is not Marx, it is the Gospel.
It is the Gospel that formed me..."—*Journals* 564

"... there is something tragic about my Soviet experience. I had come as an enthusiast, as a convinced supporter, to admire the new world and to win my affections I was offered all the prerogatives I abominated in the old one."—*Afterthoughts* 62

I

The political peregrinations of Andre Gide are emblematic of the pursuit of meaning through politics many Western intellectuals engaged in during this century and especially during the 1930s and 1960s. As one of his biographers suggests, he was "representative of the modern intellectuals's contradictory longing for individualist freedom and comforting submission to authority..." as well as of "the isolation... the sense of guilt, the schizoid anxiety of the modern intellectual—and his alternating impulses toward order and anarchy" (Guerard VIII,13), to which one may add elitism and egalitarianism.

An understanding of Gide's politics helps to understand the period and the writer, although of course the political attitudes do not illuminate his non-political writings, nor do they distract from his literary contributions.

Like many of his contemporaries and the intellectuals of the generation of the 1960s, Gide too hoped that radical political transformations might decisively alter the human condition, that all the corruption, irrationality and evil he saw around him could yield to new, bold schemes of social engineering and the focused political will undergirding them. It is much easier to explain why Gide was attracted to the Soviet Union at the time when he was than his abrupt disaffection following his visit.

The politics of Gide, and especially his admiration for the Soviet Union under Stalin will strike many contemporary readers as not only implausibly dated and wrongheaded but defying belief and common sense. How could a writer of his talents and moral sensibility revere a monstrously repressive political system? To perceive its intimidated and deprived citizens as joyful and liberated? To say that he was by no means alone in doing so does not fully answer the question but helps to understand these perceptions and the attitude underlying them. In the 1930s many of the most distinguished Western intellectuals and artists admired Stalin's Russia and revered Stalin; Gide's attitudes were part of a widespread phenomenon, of the *Zeitgeist*. But if Gide's veneration of the Soviet Union under Stalin was wrongheaded and grotesque, his subsequent revision of these views remains a valid and durable critique of the moral flaws of all communist systems.

Recalling and reflecting on the political beliefs of Gide also helps to remind ourselves that being an intellectual, and even a highly distinguished one does not provide protection against fundamentally wrongheaded political judgements, against the urge to submit to unworthy political impulses, against confusing what is with what one would like to be. This reminder is of particular relevance at the present time when once more many Western and especially American academic intellectuals are beholden to a variety of dubious beliefs and commitments ranging from multiculturalism, deconstructionism and radical feminism to postmodernism, all linked together by an intense aversion to Western culture and ideas. If these present day intellectuals do not go on pilgrimages similar to those of Gide and his contemporaries it is only for want of appropriate sites in the postcommunist world—their rejection of their society and culture matches those of their estranged predecessors of the 1930s and 1960s. The currently fashionable beliefs and allegiances demonstrate (once more) that intellectuals are capable of suspending their critical faculties, and do so with ease and relish when propelled by what they consider a good cause, or lofty ideals.

There is finally the question, always intrigueing, of the connections between biography and work, the relationship between Gide's life and personality and his political beliefs. According to his biographers it was an unusually close one.[2]

Andre Gide and the Soviet Union   403

Gide like most prominent intellectuals of his time was drawn to the "Soviet experiment" because he found it a promising alternative to the Western capitalist societies of the period, a wholly new and inspiring departure in the ways of organizing society and improving human beings. As early as in 1932 Gide wrote that "I admire nothing so much in the USSR as the organization of leisure, of education, of culture" (*Journals* 547). This was part of his vision of creating the New Man of higher moral and cultural sensibilities. He believed that the Soviet Union and what it stood for represented a cause the socially and morally engaged writer, or intellectual was bound to support; he believed that intellectuals were obligated to take political-moral stands.

An important factor in his his support for the Soviet Union, as was the case with many of his contemporaries, was his revulsion from Italian Fascism and Nazi Germany and his perception of the USSR as the major counter-weight to Nazism; he was, correspondingly also impressed by the Soviet support to the loyalists in the Spanish civil war.

In 1931 Gide wrote: "...Fascism strikes me as a return to the past, whereas that of the Soviets seems a tremendous effort toward the future. That costly experience interests humanity... and may liberate it from a frighful weight. The mere idea that it might be... forced to fail is insufferable to me..." (*Journals* 524).

In one crucial respect Gide differed from most of his contemporaries similarly disposed in political matters, as well as from the later generations of intellectuals who were admirers of the new, third world communist political systems: unlike most of them he was capable of radically and *publicly* changing his mind about the Soviet system. While Gide was by no means the only well known Western intellectual to reassess his enthusiasm toward the Soviet system over time, he stands out as quite possibly the only one who had done so suddenly and dramatically and under the impact of his experiences as a pampered visitor to the Soviet Union in 1936.[3] While for most Western travellers the visit to the USSR reenforced favorable predispositons, for Gide it had the opposite effect, it compelled him to rise to intense moral indignation—to become disenchanted in spite of the immense flattery lavished upon him, inspite of everything his handlers had done.

The distinctiveness and significance of this change of attitude cannot be overestimated. The vast majority of Western intellectuals who were attracted to the Soviet Union (and later to China, Cuba and other third world communist systems) had great difficulties admitting and expressing their disenchantment with these systems, if and when it set in.[4] There were many ways to rationalize such reticence but they had in common two principal motives: one was the determination not to give comfort to the enemies of the Soviet Union (or other communist systems) who were also enemies of the Western supporters of the Soviet cause; the other reason was the great personal anguish and embarrassment intellectuals seem to experience whenever compelled to admit to flawed judgement about matters of political or moral importance. Intellectuals are people who take their own opinions very seriously and believe that others should too. For them to admit that they were wrong, or even worse, deceived and self-deceived is almost intolerably hard.

Thus George Lukacs said that "...even the worst socialism is better than capitalism." (Tokes 469) Presumably motivated by similar sentiments William Kunstler, the American radical lawyer refused to "believe in public attacks on socialist countries where violations of human rights may occur"(Quoted in Hentoff 25-26). Numerous authors who finally did make public their disillusionment with the Soviet system (as for instance those in the volume *The God That Failed*) dwelled on their prolonged agony in doing so in view of the comfort their revelation would give to the enemies of the Soviet Union.

Gide himself recalled later in life (in 1945) the ways in which his critics rationalized the refusal to make any critical comment about the Soviet system:

> ....those who became angry over my criticism of the USSR were the very ones who had applauded when the same criticisms were directed against the by-products of 'capitalism'. There they admired my perspicacity... my courage in denouncing. In Russia, they suddenly said, I had been incapable of understanding anything... And if some admitted the justice of my observations... they considered them untimely. At most a few imperfections were admitted among comrades, but the time had not yet come to speak of them. One had to realize the overall sucess and close one's eyes to the temporary, inevitable deficiencies... (*Journals* 733)

He also noted in *Afterthoughts*: "You, intelligent communist you agree to recognize this evil, but you consider it better to hide it from others less intelligent than yourself, others who might be made indignant by it." (69) But just about a year earlier he himself wrote that "It is in great part, the stupidity and dishonesty of the attacks against the USSR that today make us defend her with a certain obstinacy." (*Journals* 593)

Most ertswhile admirers of the Soviet Union slowly faded away, sunk into silence or oblivion, while others took the position, much later, (many only after its collapse) that they were always aware of the flaws of the Soviet experiment. Many of them came to criticise it in public at least perfunctorily. But for few was the travel experience itself decisive, a source of attitude change; rarely was it recognized or publicly admitted that the trips were conducted tours, that the hosts made use of favorable predispositions in devising the techniques of hospitality that was to mislead the visitors in specific, highly calculated ways. The tours were successful precisely because the visitors' critical faculties were suspended, overwhelmed by seeing what they had wished to see. Especially painful and embrassing would have been to admit that once they stepped on the soil of the USSR (and later, on that of China, Cuba, North Vietnam, or Nicaragua) they ceased to be critical intellectuals, ready to discern and expose sham, the gulf between appearance and reality, facade and substance.

Although Gide learned a great deal from his experiences in the USSR—and these experiences and impressions apparently became the major determinant of his drastic change of attitude—that is not to say that *Return from the USSR* is an unambiguous document of disenchantment. Rather, it is one that still reflects a struggle between new insights and prior dispositions; nonetheless the book was a watershead, not only in Gide's life but in the emerging debate among Western intellectuals about the nature of the Soviet system.

The discussion that follows will focus on three topics. One is the specifics of the appeals the Soviet system held for Gide; the second will be the sources and process of disillusionment with the "Soviet experiment" and finally an attempt will be made to understand Gide's politics in the context of his personal life and his non-political attributes.

II

Gide's *Return,* the first major document of his disillusionment still reflects the appeals of the Soviet system and the intensity of the inner conflict the expression of his critiques created. The preface itself is apologetic:

It is precisely because of my admiration for the Soviet Union and for the wonders it has already performed that I am going to criticize, because of what we had expected from it...

... were not my convictions still firm and unshaken that, on the one hand the Soviet Union will end by triumphing over the serious errors I point out, on the other, and this is more important, that the particular errors of one country cannot suffice to compromise a cause which is international and universal. (*Return* xiv, xvi)

In the same preface he refers to the USSR as "an unprecdented experiment" of which he used to think as "linked to the future of culture itself," "more than a chosen land—an example, a guide... A land... where Utopia was in process of becoming reality.... (where) Whole regions have already taken on the smiling aspect of happiness" (*Return*).

For Gide, like for many like-minded political tourists, what mattered most in the new society was the transformation of the human beings, (who seemed to radiate a new found authenticity), and the beneficial ways in which the political realm intersected with the personal.[5] It seemed that the Soviet system changed people for the better. This was apparent to him even even as he was observing the crowds in the parks and "palaces of culture" who were uniformly good natured behaving with "propriety and decency" and "pervaded with a kind of joyous ardor." He described in detail their wholesome recreational activities adding "All this... without the smallest vulgarity; these immense crowds behave with perfect propriety and are manifestly inspired with good feeling, dignity and decorum... without any effort and as a matter of course"—a peculiar observation in light of what we know from other sources about the public behavior of Russians especially when inebriated, a common enough part of their recreation. The Festival of Youth in Moscow at the Red Square with its vast numbers of seemingly joyous participants marching past was further proof of the creation of better human beings, and "a magnificent sight" (*Return* 5, 6-7, 9). It didnt occur to Gide that similar marches of similarly radiant young people in perfect formations were also performed in those years in Nazi Germany and that highly regimented political systems could put on such shows at will as they also had done in China, Cuba etc. in later years.

The sense of community and warmth of human relations were overwhelming and implicitly contrasted to the calculating nature of personal relations in capitalist societies. Gide wrote:

Nowhere indeed, is contact with any and everyone so easily established, and so immediately, so deeply, so warmly as in the USSR... nowhere is the feeling of common humanity so profoundly, so strongly felt as in the USSR... I had never anywhere felt myself so fully a comrade, a brother. (*Return* 13)

In retrospect one may of course wonder how Gide had reached these conclusions and in what measure these feelings were based on actual experiences as distinct from projections of what Gide hoped and wished to experience? To what extent could he communicate spontaneously and unsupervised (and without an interpreter) with Soviet people and how were those he met selected? One must also wonder how realistic his observation had been regarding "the extraordinary prolongation of youth" (*Return* 13) he claimed to have noticed.

Children in the pioneer camps he visited were especially "radiant with health and happiness... their eyes are frank and trustful; their laughter has nothing spiteful or malicious in it..." (*Return* 4-5). Again the reader may wonder if children in France laughed maliciously or if many of them appeared to the casual observer as unhealthy and unhappy? As the practices of political hospitality were relatively new when Gide visited the USSR he had no reason to reflect on the use of children as devices of political legitimation. Hitler's Germany too excelled in producing multitudes of exuberantly happy children for purposes of propaganda, as did the communist regimes of the third world in the 1960s and 70s.

There is more in *Return* about the simple, authentic, spontaneous humanity Gide found in the Soviet Union and the streets of Moscow: "into this crowd I plunge; I take a bath of humanity." On the same streets he also found "everyone...like everyone else. In no other place is the result of social levelling so obvious... a classless society of which every member seems to have the same needs as every other." Even standing in line, he thought, was an activity Soviet citizens enjoyed! (*Return* 17, 16, 18)—a particularly good illustration of how far removed he was of Soviet reality and of the intellectual's capacity to project his own fantasies on an unfamiliar social setting. Probably Gide felt that standing in line was also some sort of an agreeable communal activity, a delightful social bond that afforded further opportunity for face to face contact and lively exchanges of ideas.

It is of further interest and indication of Gide's unresolved inner conflict (regarding his attitude toward the USSR) that at the end of

Return (in one of the appendices) he had reprinted the speech he gave in Moscow at Gorki's funeral. In it he still avowed that "The fate of culture is bound up in our minds with the destiny of the Soviet Union. We will defend it." He also pointed out that Soviet intellectuals were no longer compelled to play an adversarial role as intellectuals elsewhere, did but (miraculously enough) "while remaining a revolutionary, the writer is no longer a rebel." In a hastily added footnote he wrote: "This was where I fooled myself; I was obliged, alas, soon to admit it." In the same section of the book he also reprinted a speech he gave on the same trip "to the students of Moscow". In it he averred that "on the future of the USSR depend the destinities of the rest of the world" (*Return* 67, 68, 73).

The appendix also containts an account of his visit to Bolshevo, the model penal colony that was routinely shown to distinguished Western visitors[6]. Gide as many other visitors was convinced that what he had seen was genuine, a triumph of the Soviet penal system, that the enligthened treatment of the inmates he witnessed was typical and produced character reform: "Bolshevo is one of the most remarkable successes on which the new Soviet State can plume itself" (*Return* 90).

Why did he feel compelled to reprint these speeches and, more generally speaking, to publish a book that mixed praise and criticism? It is possible that at the time Gide still wished to remind the readers (and himself) of his pro-Soviet credentials; mixing praise and blame showed that his attitudes were not lightly taken, that he came to criticise in sorrow not relish.

III

Let us turn now to the critiques. Gide's second book on his Soviet experiences makes clear that he was more gullilble in the beginning of his journey, when, for example he "still believed... that it was possible to speak seriously of culture in the USSR and to discuss things sincerely" (*Afterthoughts* 20). As Gide's narrative proceeds one has the impression of the narrator awakening; he begins to see things the way they are: for example the low quality of goods for sale, the tasteless displays in the shop windows in Moscow, the scarcities, the phoney production records of Stakhanovities, (the shock workers producing miraculous amounts)[7], the untroubled enjoyment of material privilege by the new elite, the stage-managed aspects of his entire tour, and in general the vast distance separating appearances from reality.

The visit to a "highly prosperous kolkhoz" (collective farm) produced a "queer and depressing impression," in particular the homes of the workers redolent with "complete depersonalization". In Sochi, the Black Sea resort, he discovered that housing for the workers of the model sovhoz (state farm) that provided produce for the luxurious hotel (where he stayed) consisted of "a row of hovels" (*Afterthoughts* 25, 37).

Poverty was not just a matter of backwardness, or deprivations equally distributed and shouldered by all, as sympathetic political tourists often believed. Gide came to realize (well before Djilas, though not before Trotsky or Victor Serge) that new, politically based inequalities were emerging and growing, and that the poverty of the masses was in stark contrast with the luxuries of the privileged; "bourgeois instincts" were flattered and a new aristocracy appeared ("the aristocracy of respectability and conformism"). Gide recognized a most repellent feature of social inequality:"...the contempt, or at any rate the indifference, which those who are...'on the right side' show to 'inferiors', to servants, to unskilled workmen... to 'the poor'." (*Return* 39, 40) He wrote later:

> The new bourgeoisie ...has all the defects of ours... it despises the poor. Greedy of all the satisfactions it was so long deprived of... 'Are these really the men who made the Revolution?' I asked in my *Back from the USSR*. And answered: 'No ; they are the men who profit by it.' They may be members of the Party—there is nothing communist in their hearts. (*Afterthoughts* 64)

Gide was also troubled by the law against abortion and homosexuality ("non-conformism is hunted down even in sexual matters".) All these developments made clear that the Soviet Union ceased to be a revolutionary society: "the feelings which animated the first revolutionaries began to get in the way... the revolutionary spirit (or even simply the critical spirit) is no longer the correct thing... What is wanted now is compliance, conformism." (*Return* 38, 41-42)

Equally fundamental and penetrating were his discoveries of the lack of intellectual and political freedom. He wrote: "In the USSR everybody knows beforehand...that on any and every subject there can be only one opinion... Every morning the *Pravda* teaches them just what they should know and think and belive." Soviet people are

"In an extraordinary state of ignorance concerning foreign countries" and for that reason suffer of a "superiority complex" believing for example that France offers no playgrounds to children comparable to those found in the USSR, and actually doubt that public transportation and esp. subways exist in France" (*Return* 27, 30, 31).

Even while he continued to sympathize with the goals the Soviet system supposedly pursued, he realized that they were compromised by the means. Sadly he came to the conclusion that "the USSR is not what we had hoped it would be, what it promised to be, what it still strives to appear. It has betrayed all our hopes" (*Return* 48, *Afterthoughts* 71).

Gide does not tell much to the reader *how* the process of disillusionment got under way: were there any specific or dramatic revelations, experiences which led to new insights and conclusions? Was it a matter of slowly accumulating experiences and impressions which led to definitive conclusions? We do not know and it is not a topic he deals with in his *Journals* either. It is however likely that revelations on the part of Soviet citizens were significant and had a huge impact. Among them was the case of the painter who in the hall of a hotel in Sochi sought to convince him in a loud voice that Marxism—besides its other benefits—will also produce great works of art and that Gide's defense of the autonomy of the artist was misguided. A few moments after this conversation the painter came to his room and said "Of course you are perfectly right... but there were people listening...and I have an exhibition opening very soon" (*Return* 54).

In another incident one of his Russian speaking travelling companions asked a workman to buy him a packet of better quality cigarettes costing five rubles a packet; the price was "a day's salary" the worker informed him with a laugh. Another, in some ways more sinister experience concerned the efforts of Bukharin to speak to Gide in private. On the first occasion this was frustrated by the unexpected and unannounced arrival of "a so-called journalist" who pushed his way into Gide's hotel suite and whose appearance prompted Bukharin to leave. Three days later Gide met Bukharin at Gorki's funeral and Bukharin asked him once more if he could visit him in his room at the Metropole Hotel; Gide eagerly agreed but shortly after Koltsov (an official who looked after Gide) "took him (Bukharin) aside" and Bukharin made no further attempts to talk to Gide (*Afterthoughts* 99-100, 76-78). Such and similar experiences impressed on Gide that Soviet society was hardly a breeding ground of spontaneity and authenticity. By the time he wrote *Afterthoughts* he didnt flinch from concluding that "spying is one of the civic virtues" and friends expected to betray one another to prove their loyalty to the system (*Afterthoughts* 32-33).

Despite the furious attacks *Return* provoked it was a document of ambivalence. It was in *Afterthoughts*, a second short book devoted to the same topic, that Gide's critiques and rejection of the Soviet system found full and unconstrained expression. It was also a book in which he confronted some of his critics and reproduced some of the correspondence *Return* occasioned. In writing *Afterthoughts* he benefited from the advice and work of others who did not look at the USSR through rose colored lenses.

Once the favorable predisposition was shattered hardly any aspect of Soviet society remained immune from his criticism. He learned for instance from the book of Walter Citrine that the vaunted child care system could accomodate only one in every eight children, that the real wages of workers stagnated or actually declined, elections were meaningless and "the proletariat no longer posses(sed) the possibility of electing a representative to defend its injured interests... all connection between the people and those who are supposed to represent it...(was) severed" (*Afterthoughts* 17, 41-42, 46, 51).

Above all Gide argued, unlike his critics, that what went wrong in the USSR and what he reported, were not minor, atypical or temporary lapses. He also came to realize—and this is an observation of continued relevance—that it is possible to industrialize a country in a way that leads to few benefits for the population at large, that the endemic shortages in the Soviet Union were directly related to the attempt to "outdo capitalism by building gigantic factories" which had little to do with "the welfare of the workers". Another example of the hugely wasteful misuse of resources Gide cited was the plan to build a gigantic "Palace of the Soviets" topped by a 200-foot plus high statue of Lenin—a project the costs of which Gide contrasted with the undernourished workers. (The palace was never built, as it turned out.) Generally speaking Gide was most disturbed by the condition of the workers made all the more shocking because the regime's insistence that it was "enviable" (*Afterthoughts* 19, 54-55, 29).

In the *Afterthoughts* Gide also comments on the influence of the handlers on the visitor's capacity to observe and register aspects of the social landscape, an observation he originally made on his trip in Africa: "... as long as I travelled in French Equatorial Africa accompanied by officials, everything seemed... little short of marvellous. I began to see things clearly when I left the Governor's car and decided to travel on foot and alone, so as to...get into direct contact with the natives." It needs to be pointed out here that he could not have taken such liberties in the Soviet Union, that is, to travel by himself and have direct, unsupervised contact with the natives.

In the *Afterthoughts* there is no longer any doubt that all the factories, school, clubs, parks and palaces of culture he was shown were exceptional specimen carefully chosen for the delectation of the visitor (*Afterthoughts* 11-12). There is more information in *Afterthoughts* about the specific experiences which had a negative effect than in *Return* and especially about the aspects of lavish hospitality which backfired. Gide wrote:

> When after escaping with great difficulty from official receptions and official supervision, I managed to get into contact with laborers whose wages were only four or five rubles a day, what could I think of the banquet in my honor...? An almost daily banquet at which the abundance of the hors'd'ouvre alone was such that one had already eaten three times too much before beginnig the actual meal; a feast of six courses which used to last two hours... The expense! Never having seen the bill I cannot exactly estimate it but one of my companions who was well up in the prices of things calculates that each banquet, with wines and liqueurs must have come to more than three hundred rubles a head. (*Afterthoughts* 60-61)

Few other Western visitors entertained similar misgivings as they were feasted and toasted by their hosts; few felt unease at the contrast between their material comforts and they way the the ordinary natives lived. Gide also observed:

> I had never before travelled in such sumptous style. In special railways carriages or the best cars, always the best rooms in the best hotels, the most abundant and choicest food. And what welcome! What solicitude! Everywhere acclaimed, flattered... feasted. Nothing seeemed too good, too exquisite to offer me... But these favors constantly brought to mind privileges, differences where I had hoped to find equality. (*Afterthoughts* 60)

What disturbed him most "was not so much to find imperfections, as to meet once again with the advantages I had wanted to escape from, the privileges I had hoped were abolished... I did not go to the USSR to meet with privileges again."[8] Unlike Gide most of the distinguished Western intellectuals had no difficulty to accept and enjoy this kind of treatment; presumably they regarded themselves as deserving it or just a manifestation of the natural hospitality of a socialist society; it is possible that some of them were unaware of the vast difference between their comforts and the way of life ofordinary citizens.

Gide's rejection of the Soviet system was further stimulated by his belief that writers and artists must be "essentially non-conformist... (who) make(s) head against the current" (*Return* 51); most importantly his "basic mistrust of all orthodoxies" (Fowlie 101-102) conflicted with and cut short any durable veneration of the Soviet system.

IV

It is not difficult to find in Gide's life and personality factors predisposing to the political stands he took and abandoned. His political (as well as non-political) attitudes prior to his visit to the Soviet Union help to understand why he undertook that trip and why it had such a shattering impact. In 1932 he wrote that "Emotionally, temperamentally, intellectually I have always been a communist. But I was afraid of my own thought and in my writings, strove more to hide than to express it" (*Journals* 539). But if Gide fancied himself a communist he was the kind whose political and religious beliefs were profoundly intertwined and was led by religious impulses to political convictions. The latter were intensely moralistic and tinged with religiosity associated with his Catholicism. As Thomas Mann observed: "There beckoned... two ports and comforting shelters that have served as an escape to many a contemporary: Communism and the Catholic Church. Gide, whose nature needed commitment as much as freedom from it experimented with Communism out of sheer rebellious spirit..." (Guerard xxvi-xxvii). Gide was among many Westerners (priests and ministers included) who believed at some stage in their lives that while the religious institutions of their own societies abandoned true Christianity, in the Soviet Union, despite the official atheism, the true values of Christianity (and especially its concern for the poor and a non-materialistic way of life) were being realised. As one of Gide's biographers wrote, "...he had no trouble visualizing a communism which would reconcile itself with the essential teachings of Christ. The very destruction of family and orthodox church would prepare the way for a truer Christianity." (Guerard 27) In turn Gide wrote in his *Journals*:

> ...'mysticism' today is on the side of those who profess atheism and irreligion. It is as a religion that the Communist doctrine exalts and feeds the enthusiasm of the young today... they transfer their ideals from heaven to earth, as I do with them...
> The mere idea of... having to defend Christ against Communist comrades strikes me as profoundly absurd. It is against the Russian popes, the priests etc. that I want to defend him and to restore him... It is against religion that I am protesting, against the Church, dogmas, faith etc. (566, 564)

But in the same breath Gide also admitted that "Communist religion involves...too a dogma, an orthodoxy, texts to which reference is made, an abdication of criticism..." (*Journals* 566). Moreover Gide unlike so many of his fellow intellectuals had not been enamoured with Marxism:

> In Marx's writings I stifle. There is something lacking, some ozone or other that is essential to keep my mind breathing. Yet I have read four volumes of *Das Kapital*, patiently, assiduously, studiously; plus... the volume of extracts...chosen by Paul Nizan... I have read all this with more constancy and care than I brought to any other study... with no other desire than to let myself be convinced... And each time I came away aching all over, my intelligence bruised as by instruments of torture...
> I think that a great deal of Marx's prestige comes from the fact that it is difficult of access... When one doesnt understand one bows down... (*Journals* 618)

Gide's reservations about Marxism are congruent with a conclusion he reached after his visit to the Soviet Union and one which had been a centerpiece of the corresponding political disillusionment of all those who broke with the Soviet system and the communist movements supporting it. Gide wrote: "Let us be aware of those who want... at whatever cost, to plough straight furrows on a curving field,[9] of those who prefer to each man the idea they have formed of humanity" (*Journals* 619).

There are a number of personality traits and circumstances which help to account for Gide's political attitudes and beliefs. If a strongly felt outsider status is the crucial point of departure for the development of moralistic social-critical impulses Gide certainly had reasons for such feelings. A sickly child who lost his father at age eleven he had a troubled childhood:

> He suffered from nervous tension, from timidity, from a sense of being unattactive, from unnamed fears and nightmares ...from loneliness, from a feeling of inferiority with schoolmates who made his life so miserable that he invented symptoms of illness sufficient to keep him away from school... Despite the many advantages of his social

position and wealth, despite the attentivenss and affection of parents and relatives, Gide had... an unhappy childhood... (Fowlie 13-14)

He also had a father who was Protestant in a Catholic country and suffered ridicule and worse for his Protestant background while in school.[10] He was a homosexual at a time when being one was a source of shame not pride—these are aspects of the personal background that help to understand (though of course not to predict) Gide's later attitudes and worldview.

Thomas Mann credited his homosexual dispostion with being "the root and font of his moral dynamism of his revolutionary disavowal of everything respectable-traditional..."(Guerard xxv). To such a trait predisposing to the questioning of the social-moral order one may add his privileged conditions of life which were free of material problems, filled with leisure, allowing for reflection. Gide—like so many other Western intellectuals of comfortable means in more recent times—was apparently in the grip of guilt feelings:

Perhaps the strongest emotional force at work was class-guilt: the intolerable feeling that he was one of the favored. Only privilege had made possible his voyages, his quiet and civilized plesaures, and the prolonged self-examination which nourished his books.... This sense of unmerited privilege and of surrounding distress together with the old faith in progress, pushed Gide toward communism... (Guerard 26)

Gide himself wrote: "What brought me to Communism... was the fact of the privileged position which I personally enjoy—that seemed to me preposterous and intolerable... I cannot accept a place in a lifeboat in which only a limited number of people are saved" (Crossman 153).

But, as was noted more recently "Along with guilt and compassion for the wretched poor, vanity beguiled him. Doubting as he often did whether his ouvre justified his fame, he was reluctant to forego the vehement praise of young Communists everywhere. No more could he resist the opportunity to humble a society in which, despite the laurels it heaped on him, he still felt himself to be reprobate."[11]

Thus Gide's attraction to Soviet communism, like the corresponding quests of the more recent generation of Western intellectuals, began with an unease with his own society prompting a search for alternatives. This unease was, in large measure, nurtured by an idealistic-moralistic disposition conventional religion did not satisfy. Although highly successful and respected Gide's social status was rendered vulnerable by his sexuality, unconventional and deviant for his times. While there is no obvious or logical connection between sexual and political preferences, when a particular sexual disposition is ostracized it often becomes the emotional basis of a more diffuse and deeper estrangement from the social order that can take political forms. At the present time homosexual activists are intensely critical of American society converting their sexual preferences into political activism and social criticism.[12]

A pursuit of the unusual and exotic, an escape from his own constraining society was also reflected in Gide's numerous trips to Africa preceding his journey to the Soviet Union. His visit to the Congo in 1926 in particular became a source of revelation and indignation regarding the social injustices in colonial Africa. According to Enid Starkie the trip to the Congo was pivotal in the development of his social concerns: "He now became the champion of victims and underdogs—criminal offenders for whom he demanded more sympathetic treatment; women for whom he asked equality... colonial natives whose causes he pleaded in the two travel books..." (Crossman 148.) Gide himself was well aware of certain parallels between this trip to the Congo and to the USSR. He also shared with contemporary Western and especially American intellectuals a sympathetic interest in common criminals: "His entire nature would incline him to taking the side of the outlaw..." (Fowlie 99).

While at the present time Gide's attraction to and rejection of Soviet communism may be of historical interest only, the larger circumstances giving rise to these beliefs and attitudes appear remarkably contemporary. As one of his biographers wrote of Gide's times:

> The early years of the century were characterised by a fairly widespread lack of faith in rationalism...
>
> The major supports of man which had provided him with a sense of security in the world: religion, science, a coherent psychological life, nationalism—were all being questioned and invalidated...
>
> The universe again became incomprehensible...
>
> The adolescence and young manhood of Gide coincided with a period of European civilization when the conventions that had protected and reassured men's peace of mind began to collapse. During the last decade of the nineteenth century, and well into the twentieth, individual man found himself much more alone than in earlier periods because moral and social values were being questioned more... the personal crisis which Gide went through in his twenties... was to be raised to a level of universal meaning... (Fowlie 4, 6, 4)

These are conditions and problems all too familiar to contemporary intellectuals and those who may read Gide at the present time.

Gide's inner struggles and his short lived attempt to find solution for personal and moral problems in the political realm will be especially meaningful to those of our contemporaries who lived through the 1960s and emerged from it with a new understanding that the political is not, and should not be the personal and that the deepest problems of human and social existence cannot be resolved by the embracing movements or ideologies promising radical collective solutions.

Notes

1. Reprinted from Tom Conner ed.: *Andre Gide's Politics: Rebellion and Ambivalence*, New York: St Martin's Press, 2001
2. See for example Guerard cited pp. 3-4
3. Perhaps the case of Malcom Muggeridge was somewhat similar; he was certainly deeply effected by what he had seen especially in the countryside and he described these experiences unhesitatingly; on the other hand he was less of an admirer of the system to begin with.
4. To this day it is not clear how many had in fact become disenchanted and for what reason given the prevailing silence on the subject. As I noted elsewhere there was far more public admission, delayed or not, on the part of the pro-Soviet intellectuals of the 1930s than on the part of intellectuals of the 1960s supportive of third world communist states. I believe this can in part be explained by the massive subcultural support the latter beliefs enjoyed in what I called enclaves of adversary culture usually in or around academic settings. Anti-Western or anti-American social criticism (providing the basis for the idealization of distant revolutionary societies) was far more widespread in the 1960s than in the 1930s.
5. The theme of an inevitable and ironclad linkage of the personal and the political was revived enthusiastically and approvingly by American radical feminists in the 1960s and has remained a cornerstone of their beliefs.
6. See Paul Hollander 1981, pp. 154-156
7. A group of visiting French miners "asked to relieve a shift of Soviet miners and then and there, without puttig themselves out in the least, and without even being aware of it, turned out to be Stakhanovites." (Return 23)
8. Ibid. pp. 57-58:
9. A figure of speech reminiscent of "the crooked timber of humanity" Isaiah Berlin used as a title of one of his books (New York: Knopf, 1991) originating in an observation of Kant.
10. "His...school-fellows persecuted him for his Protestant Heresy... Every day he was chased home by a howling mob, and he reached his horrified mother covered with mud and bleeding at the nose." (George D. Painter: Andre Gide: A Critical Biography, London: Weidenfeld & & Nicholson, 1968, pp.5-6)
11. Frederick Brown: "The Oracle," *New Republic*, May 17, 1999, p. 40
12. For example Larry Kramer a prominent and vocal homosexual activist and spokesman used the AIDS epidemic to indict Amerian society as a whole: "... the AIDS pandemic is the fault of the white middle class, male majority. AIDS is here because the straight world would not grant equal rights to gay people... AIDS is our holocaust and Regan our Hitler. New York City is our Auschwitz... we are witnessing...the systematic, planned annihilation of some by others with the avowed purpose of

eradicating an undesirable portion of the population." (Larry Kramer: *Reports from the Holocaust: The Making of an AIDS Activist*, New York: St Martins, 1989, pp. 178, 173, 263)

Another example of a likely connection between intense political estrangement and unconventional sexual preference is Gore Vidal, relentless critic of American society who chose to live in Italy.

References

Brown, Frederick. "The Oracle." *New Republic*, May 17, 1999: 40.

Crossman, Richard, ed. *The God That Failed*. New York: Harper, 1949.

Fowlie, Wallace. *André Gide: His Life and Art*. New York: Macmillan, 1965.

Gide André. *Afterthoughts: A Sequel to Back from U.S.S.R.* Trans. Dorothy Bussy. London: Secker & Warburg, n.d.

_____. *Journal* 1926-1950. Ed. Martine Sagaert Paris: Gallimard, Bibliothèque de la Pléiade, 1997.

_____. *Journals*, 1889-1949. Ed. and trans. Justin O'Brien. Harmondsworth, U.K.: Penguin, 1967.

_____. *Retouches à mon Retour de l'U.R.S.S.* Paris: Gallimard, 1937.

_____. *Retour de l'U.R.S.S.* Paris: Gallimard, 1937.

_____. *Return from the U.S.S.R.* Trans. Dorothy Bussy. New York: McGraw Hill, 1964.

Guerard, Albert J. *André Gide*. Cambridge: Harvard University Press, 1969.

Hentoff, Nat. "Joan Baez's 'Cruel and Wanton Act.'" *Villiage Voice*, May 28, 1979: 25-26.

Hollander, Paul. *Political Pilgrims: Travels of Western Intellectuals to the Soviet Union, China, and Cuba, 1928-1978*. New York: Oxford Univeristy Press, 1981.

Kramer, Larry. *Reports from the Holocaust: The Making of an AIDS Activist*. New York: St. Martin's, 1989.

Painter, George D. *André Gide: A Critical Biography*. London: Weidenfeld & Nicolson, 1968.

Tokes, Rudolf. *Hungary's Negotiated Revolution*. Cambridge University Press, 1996.

Name Index

Subject Index